Charlie Brooker's *Screen Burn*

Charlie Brooker has worked as a writer, journalist, cartoonist and broadcaster. His TV writing credits include *Nathan Barley*, BAFTA-nominated satirical horror *Dead Set* and the Rose d'Or-winning sci-fi festival-of-cheeriness *Black Mirror*. He also writes and presents the RTS-winning '*Wipe*' series of BBC shows, Channel 4's *Ten O'Clock Live*, and Radio 4's *So Wrong It's Right*. He is also well-known for his weekly columns in the *Guardian* newspaper. But so what? One day, he will die.

'Charlie Brooker doesn't so much "go for the jugular" as decapitate his targets altogether.' Jim Shelley, *Daily Mirror*

'He watches these things so we don't have to. Bless him for that.' Graham 'Father Ted' Linehan

'This belongs on everyone's bookshelf. With a big spotlight pointing at it.' Julie Burchill

'The funniest newspaper columnist in the world.' *Racing Post*

Charlie Brooker's *Screen Burn*

ff
faber and faber
guardianbooks

First published in 2005
by Faber and Faber Ltd
Bloomsbury House
74–77 Great Russell Street
London WC1B 3DA
on behalf of Guardian Books
Guardian Books is an imprint of Guardian Newspapers Ltd
This paperback edition first published in 2012

Typeset by Faber and Faber Limited
Printed in England by CPI Group (UK) Ltd, Croydon, CR0 4YY

A CIP record for this book
is available from the British Library

ISBN 978–0–571–29763–4

FSC
www.fsc.org
MIX
Paper from
responsible sources
FSC® C101712

10 9 8 7 6 5 4 3 2 1

Contents

For Liz, with love

Foreword *by Graham Linehan*

Imagine watching television for a living.

You wake up, you're at work. Your boss (you) has no problems with his sole employee (also you) sitting in a cornflake-spattered T-shirt and undies while trying to focus on *Trisha*. You don't feel guilty watching *Trisha* because it is your job to watch *Trisha*. If you weren't watching *Trisha*, you wouldn't be doing your job! A dream ticket! The perfect crime!

But there's something shifting and swirling in the pit of your stomach. You were up late last night, watching a page-3 girl eating a maggot (it was your job to watch that too). That was followed by a programme in which people described catching rare genital diseases while on holiday. And then there was that show in which an elderly woman demonstrated her blowjob technique on a brightly-coloured dildo while a studio audience went into spasms of delight and her son (her son!) shook his head, laughed and pretended to enjoy himself?

Your breakfast, you now realise, hasn't gone anywhere.

An explanation. During the time that Charlie Brooker was writing these pieces for the *Guardian*, British television underwent a reverse evolution. Early pioneers on shows like *Eurotrash* and *The Word* showed that there was an audience for pure, 100 per cent, evil, ugly, drunken cak, and others took that ball and ran with it, and so here we are. Television has a curved spine, a jutting lower jaw and its knuckles are red and raw from being dragged along the ground. It's as if someone, somewhere said, 'Why isn't British television more like Italian television?' and was promoted rather than slapped across the face.

Good, attention-grabbing television is achieved in one of two ways. The first is quite complicated and involves a certain amount of expertise behind and in front of the camera. A memorable production might involve a strong cast, a timely subject and a director who knows how to tell a story. Or it could require years spent waiting with a movement-sensitive camera for a crab to crawl onto a beach at exactly the right time and impregnate a turtle.

The second way is simpler and currently very much in vogue. Basically, you get a few *Big Brother* contestants, dress them up in school uniforms, give them enough booze to make a table stagger, and hope that security steps in before someone gets raped or killed.

Disasterporn, funography . . . Call it what you will, to be a TV critic at this point is to be subjected to the sort of imagery that previously only film censors of the seventies and eighties had to endure. You need the sort of reckless disregard for your own sanity shared by war photographers and people who have to work with Elton John. You need a very special sort of person, someone who has the ability to stare into the abyss and, when it stares back, make it look away in shame. If this were a trailer for a big US film, this would be the moment when the President looks just to the right of the camera and says 'Get me Brooker.'

Imagine Charlie's surprise when television started mirroring his entirely made-up 'TV Go Home' satirical website. Imagine how that felt – conceiving an imaginary TV show so appalling that it bends your brain like a Gellerspoon and then turning on the TV to find that programme is on after the news. That's why only he has the undercarriage to do this job; anything television throws at Charlie, Charlie throws right back. How he has maintained his sense of humour is beyond me, but somehow he has managed it. It is now at such a keen pitch, in fact, that the mere idea of Charlie reviewing certain shows is enough to make me laugh. Anyone who calls Tiff Needall Tiff "Quick Turn Over" Needall needs no lessons from the Chuckle Brothers on how to provoke a laugh. Anyone who points out that Ross Kemp could stare out a man with two glass eyes doesn't need an introduction from the likes of me. (As I write, my wife is reading through Charlie's columns nearby. She's laughing like a drain . . . a fleeting happiness soon to be violently cut short by my asking her to review this foreword.)

Charlie is the funniest TV writer around, and the only person who truly understands British telly as it is in these final years before the world ends. This is not something to be envied. Spare a thought for him now, because as you read this, he is probably watching a programme in which a party of celebrities need to eat each other's eyes in order to win a dildo.

He watches these things so we don't have to. Bless him for that.

Introduction

Apart from a stint behind the counter at Music and Video Exchange in Notting Hill Gate, every job I've ever had has come about by accident. Writing 'Screen Burn' was no exception.

It was the year 2000, and I was writing a website called 'TV Go Home', which consisted of nothing but spoof TV listings. These were the kind of hoary old whimsy you used to find in *Not the Nine O'Clock News* spin-off books several decades ago, but because it was on the Internet and was jam-packed with foul language, it was considered shocking and cutting-edge. This was just before the dot.com bubble burst, naturally – a feverish time when even a cross-eyed farmhand could be valued at billions if he put on a foil hat and claimed to be a pixel.

Furthermore, because 'TV Go Home' often laid into people in the media, people in the media *really* enjoyed it, because every single one of them secretly hates themself and wants to die, or should do.

Thanks to all of the above, I was now so cool and underground and bleeding-edge, the *Guardian* invited me to pen a few articles about television for their G2 section. Shortly afterwards, when the *Guide*'s Jim Shelley decided to stop writing his excellent 'Tapehead' column, they tried me out in the same slot. And I've clung on, like a desiccated tagnut ever since.

Still, I may have become a TV critic unintentionally, but I picked an interesting time to fall into it. The first series of *Big Brother* was broadcast in the summer of 2000, marking the start of the reality TV boom, and, in a roundabout way, the beginning of an era during which TV finally jettisoned any pretence at being an important, socially beneficial medium and simply concentrated on sticking its bum in our face and giggling.

Or did it? In fact, alongside the attention-grabbing luridness, there were arguably more high-quality shows on our screens during the 2000–2004 period than ever before (the majority of them, admittedly, were American). But you won't find much praise in this book, largely because good shows are far duller to read or write about than the rubbish, the stupid, the grotesque or the gaudy.

You don't need me to tell you how good *The Sopranos* is. In fact, you don't need me to tell you anything, and I'd have to be a pompous little tugwad to think otherwise. The bits that matter are the jokes, the stupid asides and the odd bit of savagery.

Speaking of which, looking back through these columns, I finally understand why the editor keeps complaining about the amount of violent scatology that creeps in: I can't even review, say, a simple cookery programme without veering off at a tangent about someone getting a spoon rammed down their pisshole, or up their bum, or down their pisshole *and* up their bum. I counted ten separate and entirely needless references to people shitting pine cones, most of which I've now removed in a desperate bid to appear less bumfixated. There are other recurring obsessions too – Peter Sissons, petri dishes, made-up videogames, bizarre acts of violence . . .
But I'll shut up now and let you stumble across them for yourself. Enjoy the book.

Prelude: Pre-Screen

Before landing the 'Screen Burn' column, I wrote a few pieces on television for the Guardian*'s G2 section. This was the first one, covering Ricky Butcher's exit from* EastEnders.

Ricky's Luck   [20 April 2000]

It's bye-bye to TV's Mr Boo Hoo. After twelve years of unrelenting gloom, Ricky Butcher, Walford's human raincloud, has finally had enough.

'There's nothing left for me here,' he keeps muttering, intermittently performing that funny swallowing, gulping, staring-from-side-to-side thing he does whenever he wants us to know he's really upset. He's leaving Albert Square the only way he could: in unfettered misery.

Ricky stumbled onto our screens in 1988, and fate has pissed mercilessly into his eyes ever since. It's been nothing but disappointment, heartbreak, humiliation and plodding, battleship-grey drudgery. And while he may not have suffered with dignity (there's nothing dignified about him) he has at least avoided pulling an 'Arthur Fowler' and plunging into full-blown mental unhingery. Until now.

Previously, Ricky coped with life's bleaker interludes by slumping morosely on the special 'crisis' bench in Albert Square gardens, peering into the depths of an abyss he's simply too dim to understand.

Now, with pro-am cuckolder Dan contesting ownership of his dad's pub, and estranged wife Bianca happily settled in Manchester with baby Liam, Ricky's finally overdosing on despair.

Tuesday night's episode in particular contained scenes of harrowing indignity on a par with the infamous male rape scene from

1

the film *Scum*: Ricky on his hands and knees cleaning a pub toilet; Ricky watching his own sister flirt with Dan; Ricky having his IQ compared to that of a mop by the notoriously half-witted Barry Evans, while the entire population of the Square stood laughing in his face. All that was missing was a sequence in which he found himself unpleasantly surprised by an empty toilet-roll dispenser and forced to frog-hop around the Vic in search of a crumpled beer mat to wipe himself with.

In tonight's episode, Ricky finally breaks down and confesses to feeling suicidal. And what precisely does he have to live for anyway? Not love. There are backward farmhands with more successful private lives.

It's hard to see why. Despite having all the charm of a bit of old flannel hanging off a bush, Ricky is at least blessed with intriguing looks.

Constant failure has battered his face into an amalgam of glum dejection and astonished distress. Despite the bruiser's physique, the sour mouth, the flattened nose, there's something childlike about his permanent state of upset: Ricky has the sorrowful eyes of a small boy watching a clown die in a grotesque circus accident. He also does a very good line in tireless devotion. Compared to, say, Phil, he's quite a catch.

Nevertheless, he always lucks out. First he fell for Sam Mitchell (Daniella Westbrook), younger sister to Phil and Grant, who soon twigged she'd got herself hitched to the human equivalent of a Little Chef gammon steak, eventually deserting him on the grounds that he was simply too dull to actually matter. Then he met Bianca (Patsy Palmer). She spent years tirelessly henpecking him into teary-eyed bewilderment, before launching into a pointless and doomed affair with her mother's surly boyfriend.

Finally, in the most glamorous moment of Ricky's life, their marriage came to a tearful halt on a grimy Euston concourse.

Leaving Walford is clearly a good move, even if he has to do it in a box.

You'll have to tune in this evening to find out what happens, but here's an alternative ending, which, while admittedly outlandish, is at least in keeping with Ricky's luck thus far. But be warned: the following paragraph contains scenes not suitable for viewers of a nervous disposition . . .

So, then. Seeking a new life, Ricky Butcher boards a coach bound for Amsterdam, carrying all his worldly possessions with him, three sets of overalls and an old teaspoon. But 20 miles out of London, a baby lamb runs into the road and the vehicle overturns. The other passengers die horribly, but Ricky miraculously survives. Dazed and bleeding, yet largely unharmed, he is slowly counting his lucky stars on the fingers of one hand when the wreckage catches fire. Trapped in his seat, he gapes in horror as the flames rage towards him. Unable to face the prospect of a fiery death, he grabs the teaspoon from his knapsack and rams it into his eye in a desperate attempt to pierce his brain and finish himself off. But alas! Seconds later a rescue team arrives to douse the blaze. Surgeons at the nearby hospital are unable to remove the spoon, leaving Ricky to walk around with the handle jutting from his head like a miniature diving board.

Monumentally depressed, he returns to Walford to continue his job as a mechanic, with the protruding spoon repeatedly pranging the underside of every vehicle he tries to fix. Finally, after five months of unbearable clattering, Ricky dies of a violent headache. OK, so that's absurdly grim and unfair. But, hey, it's also very Ricky Butcher.

Sid Owen had left the soap to pursue a recording career, kicking off with a cover of Sugar Minott's 'Good Thing Going'. Two years after this article appeared, Ricky Butcher returned to Albert Square, and hung around pointlessly while the scriptwriters failed to come up with anything for him to do. He left for a second time soon afterwards.

Contentious? Moi? [7 July 2000]

Tonight sees the start of the thirteenth series of *Eurotrash*. Yes, the thirteenth. Channel 4's high-camp helping of sleaze, sex and undulating silicone returns once more, providing queasy chuckles for an audience of boggle-eyed stoners, simultaneously saving the nation's most desperate bachelors the bother of having to use their own imaginations (although the show is an onanist's minefield – one minute the screen's full of trampolining supermodels, the next there's a Scandinavian Chuckle Brother lookalike unblocking a sink in the nude).

For tonight's curtain-raiser, it's a case of same old, same old: there's a look at the world of erotic lingerie, an artist who paints with his own semen, a magician placing his penis in a guillotine and a lengthy report on a female wrestler whose breasts are covered with oil. As ever, it's linked – at considerable length – by the ever-likeable Antoine De Caunes (minus the late Lolo Ferrari), and enlivened with appealingly garish graphics and sarcastic voice-overs.

But there's a problem. *Eurotrash* simply doesn't outrage any more, and not just because it has reached season 13. No. The trouble is that in the years since the programme first spurted onto our screens, everything else on television has steadily degenerated into a slew of dead-eyed, opportunistic, utterly heartless quasi-porn, which leaves *Eurotrash*'s recipe of cheerful, cheesy smut looking positively archaic. On any commercial station you care to mention, unashamedly lecherous programming piles up in the schedule like sour-smelling refuse sacks in a midnight alleyway. ITV brings us documentaries on sex, swinging and strippers (well, they look like strippers – and since they were renamed 'lap dancers', it's apparently OK to show them on TV every 67 seconds). Channel 4 parades *Caribbean Uncovered*, *Something for the Weekend*, and *Naked Elvis*. The whole of Channel Five feels like nothing but a single nightmarish, drawn-out edition of *Euro-trash*, complete with unconvincing voices (*Sunset Beach*), harrowing male nudity (Keith Chegwin's *Naked Jungle*) and profoundly dispiriting 'erotica' (courtesy of about a zillion assorted pornographic schedule-pluggers with titles like 'Nude Saxophone Cops' and 'When Checkout Girls Bend Over'). Digital and cable viewers, meanwhile, can wallow in the nightly shock-orama of *Bravo* or the joyless *Granada Men and Motors* (demographic: underachieving loners interested in motoring, glamour photography and self-abuse).

These days, watching television is like sitting in Travis Bickle's taxicab, staring through the window at a world of relentless, churning shod. Some day a real rain's going to come and wash the scum off the screens. Until then, sit back and gawp in slack-jawed indifference as television slowly disappears up a lap dancer's bottom. In close-up. To the echoing strains of 'Roll With It'.

The upshot is we've become hopelessly desensitised – but it's not just the box that's to blame. Consider the impact of technology. The past five years have seen a dramatic increase in the number of people with Internet connections in the workplace, enabling office-bound tragi-bores to access and distribute stomach-churning muck with tiresome ease and gusto. Once you've got accustomed to having your attention regularly drawn to the kind of extreme imagery previously reserved for the racier shop windows of Amsterdam, all pornography rapidly becomes a crashing bore, no matter how bizarre. Hey, look – an MPEG clip of a circus clown sodomising a wolf on the deck of a Mississippi steamboat. Yawwwwn. Seen it before. Seen it twice. Rather watch a bit more Microsoft Excel, thanks.

So, faced with competition from a bottomless technological smutweb on one hand, and a range of post-ironic pornorific TV programming on the other, what chance does *Eurotrash* have? Not much. To compete in the current climate it needs to grow harsher, less affectionate, more ruthless. Scrap the 'Euro' prefix; have the show re-christened just 'Trash'. Ditch the wacky German fetish bars and Dutch pot-smoking contests; shoot each edition in the seediest quarter of Bangkok. Throw out the irony and humour; exchange it for eerie, misplaced fascination. Replace Antoine with a naked amputee who sits on a barbed-wire toilet seat repeatedly threatening to murder members of the audience, reading their addresses out on air and nonchalantly toying with a bloodied switchblade. Broadcast the entire show in 3D, pumping each and every image directly into the viewer's cerebellum via a length of magic spacewire connected to the Internet. Sorry, Rapido, but that's it. That's the only way to restore the outrage.

That's how low we've all sunk. It's either that or you have to kill the whole thing off. Who'd have thought it? Sleazy, scampish little *Eurotrash* – slowly rendered far too innocent to survive. These are dark days, readers. Dark days.

Now wash your hands.

Live and Dangerous [20 July 2000]

Heard of screen burn? It used to affect computer monitors. If you used a particular program a lot, some of its prevailing visual features – the menu bar, for instance – would, over time, become permanently etched onto the screen, remaining faintly visible for evermore. Screensavers were invented to prevent this kind of damage, hence their name.

Fascinating stuff. The point is this: if a similar phenomenon afflicted regular TV screens, you could be forgiven for expecting to find your set indelibly stained with Carol Vorderman. Not that you'd notice the change: it feels like she's permanently onscreen anyway. But she isn't the worst offender. In fact, in a list of the most-seen presenters on television in the latest edition of industry magazine *Broadcast*, Vorderman finishes fourth. You're far more likely to wind up with Richard Madeley's face burnt across your Trinitron, like some nightmarish twenty-first-century Turin Shroud: he and wife Judy Finnegan squat proudly at the top of the league. The charts were calculated according to 'exposure factor': the time in minutes they are seen by an 'average' viewer in one week. Richard and Judy win with 14.06 minutes for *This Morning*.

The rest of the list contains several surprises, such as the news that the *Antiques Roadshow*'s Hugh Scully (number 19 on the overall list) enjoys more exposure than Johnny Vaughan and Lisa Tarbuck (languishing at number 24, thanks largely to the state of *The Big Breakfast*'s ratings, currently at art-house cinema levels). There's also the non-appearance of Jamie Theakston or Dale Winton in the top 25, and the shocking revelation that Gloria Hunniford is still working – although only on Channel Five, which means she might as well be reading Ladybird books to a bunch of worms in a skip. Oh, and one truly terrifying fact: the average viewer watches Jim Davidson for a full 6.49 minutes every week. Coincidentally, this is also the precise amount of time it takes to grind your own teeth to powder in an impotent rage.

But the list also shatters several key TV presentation myths – such as the assumption that to enjoy success you have to be young and attractive. This simply isn't true.

Take the 'attractive' bit. Consider Michael Parkinson (number 25), a man with a face like a corpse's shoe – or the downright Tolkeinesque Alan Titchmarsh, who could wander through a forest scaring knotholes from the trees simply by smiling at them. Think: did you really splash out on that top-of-the-range brushed-aluminium Panasonic set just so you could experience Titchmarsh's inadvertent gurning in digital widescreen? So you could hear your kids screaming about the scary man with his face pressed against the glass? Well? Maybe it's just me, but whenever Titchmarsh turns to camera I always imagine he's about to lean out of the screen and try to lick my neck. It's frightening. But there he is regardless, sitting unpretty at number 9. Then there's Davidson, Whiteley, Scully . . . all of them about as easy on the eye as a handful of shattered monkey-nut husks unexpectedly flung in your face by a passing drunk.

Still, it's unfair to judge people on appearance. There's age to consider as well. And the nation's top telly faces are old, man. The average age of the top five BBC1 presenters is 47.8, while their ITV equivalents are even older, at an average of 50.8 years of age. Even the painfully hip Channel 4, which arrives at work riding a pavement scooter and clutching a punnet of takeaway sushi, can only manage 45.6. The unseen, ghostlike Channel Five has by far the perkiest presenters – their top five come in at around 38.3 years old, despite the handicap of a sixty-year-old Hunniford dragging their average age coffinward.

So if duff looks and senility aren't handicaps, what will hold you back? The answer, it would appear, is a personality, since the majority of names on the list are about as inspiring as a scratch on a Formica desktop. Lineker (2), Lynam (3), Aspel (20), Kilroy (23) . . . they may be professional, but they sure as heck ain't interesting. Perhaps the blandest of the lot is Steve Rider, described as 'TV's Mister Charisma' for the first and only time in his life in this very sentence, straight in at number 14, thanks to his *Grandstand* appearances (doing a regular sports gig is a good way of gatecrashing the list, which explains the appearance of David Vine, six places ahead of Carol Smillie at number 10).

There are bright spots. Ant and Dec (6) are chirpy and likeable, and even if you can't bear Barrymore (18), or Tarrant (5), they're at least vaguely anarchic in spirit. Otherwise, it seems we like our TV presenters to encompass everything we wouldn't look for in a potential sexual partner: aged, ugly, and utterly personality-free. And considering the amount of time we're going to end up spending with them, that's downright sick.

No Pain, No Gain   [22 November 2000]

Last week, *Coronation Street* was accused of sadism. Not because of that aggravating theme tune (the aural equivalent of having half-chewed, week-old Battenberg cake dribbled into your ear canal by a senile grandparent), but because of the bothersome antics of Weatherfield's number one bad guy, Jez Quigley – a seriously unpleasant cross between John 'Cold Feet' Thomson and the head Blue Meanie from *Yellow Submarine*. The majority of complaints were provoked by a scene in which Quigley attempted to smother *Street* wideboy Steve McDonald as he lay injured in hospital. Having been confronted with some genuine menace for once, as opposed to the *Street*'s usual pantomime whimsy, a bunch of easily rattled simpletons phoned the ITC in protest. The regulator agreed that, yes, it was all a bit unpleasant, wasn't it? Foul Mr Quigley had appeared to 'enjoy' inflicting pain, and that simply wouldn't do. Well, look, he was hurting Steve McDonald for God's sake – an oily, opportunistic skunk so astoundingly unsympathetic that an arthritic priest would can-can for joy at the news of his violent death. The main thrust of the ITC's condemnation was that Quigley's lurid display of sadistic nastiness might have upset the show's younger viewers – presumably they'll go on to declare that in future, all fictional drug-dealing villains should be played by one of the Chuckle Brothers, in order to lessen any potential trauma.

Still, out of many millions of viewers, only four actually complained, while the rest gawped on in pleasure, drowsily spooning mouthfuls of congealing Bolognese into their glistening chops while Quigley eventually sputtered his last, courtesy of a broken rib poking through his lung. With any luck the success of this unusually bleak *Street* story line will encourage Granada to crank up the show's violence quota considerably, turning it into something akin to an Alan Bennett adaptation of *Fight Club*.

Even the sponsorship stings could join in the fray: whose heart could fail to be lightened by a sequence in which one of those cheery Cadbury's chocolate proles unexpectedly plunges a short-bread screwdriver into a co-worker's forehead, then jigs with delight as the caramel brains ooze out and slap messily against the marshmallow cobblestones? Well?

If the *Street* fails to capitalise on its gore-spattered lead, the remaining soaps should seize the initiative and usher back in a golden age of needless violence. Remember *Dynasty*'s machine-gun massacre? *Brookside*'s Jordache stabbing? We deserve to see their like again.

EastEnders should try harder. For starters, they can forget about supposed arch-baddie Nick Cotton. The man simply isn't menacing; he's half as terrifying as an Argos catalogue. Whereas Jez Quigley looked as though he'd enjoy riding an onyx stallion through a field full of groaning, recently impaled victims before galloping home to bathe in the blood of the fallen, Nick Cotton merely looks like he might, at a push, dispute the price of a dented tin of custard with a supermarket checkout girl while you wait behind him, wondering when he last washed his hair.

Here's what they should do: with a nod to the recent box-office success of *Gladiator*, they should dig up that drab little garden in the centre of Albert Square and replace it with an immense coliseum in which Walford residents settle their differences. Phil Mitchell is no Russell Crowe, but what a thrill it would be to watch him mercilessly pursuing Sonia around a sand-filled arena, frantically twirling a mace. They could take bets on the BBC website, and donate the proceeds to Children In Need: I'll have a tenner on Barry Evans (trident, net) versus Beppe (twin daggers, shield). And Roy could make an excellent thumbs-up/thumbs-down Caesar figure, although you'd have to shield your eyes if he turned round suddenly and his toga rode up.

Speaking of togas, our soaps could do with more naked flesh too.

Sex-crazed *Hollyoaks* (aka 'S Club 7 Street') is currently the market leader – it's like watching a group of aroused, anatomically correct Chapman Brothers dummies jostling in a tube carriage. It recently featured an entirely implausible naturist swimming club, and now both *Brookside* and *EastEnders* are to follow, showcasing special 'nudity' subplots. Albert Square is set to be rocked by plans for a nude calendar shoot of Queen Vic regulars. If you're reading this while eating, you'll be delighted to learn the April page features a blistering close-up of a full-frontal Ian Beale sprawling open-legged on a leather sofa.

Not really. Still, thank your lucky stars Ethel's dead, or they might have crowned her Miss July. Then again, they still might.

PART ONE 2000

In which Casualty *is slated, Sadowitz is praised, and a man called Craig wins the first* Big Brother.

The Very Worst Careers Imaginable [12 August]

Hate your job? Weep yourself awake each Monday morning? Spend the working day toying with your desktop icons while nonchalantly contemplating suicide? Ever considered doing something – any-thing – else? Then whatever you do, don't look to the coming week's television for inspiration. Tucked away in the schedules are four glaring examples of the very worst careers imaginable this side of 'oil-rig bitch'.

First up servile pandering, or 'being a butler', as it's commonly known. *Country House* (BBC2) charts life at Woburn Abbey. We watch as newbie butler Grant, a fresh-faced cross between Tintin and Rick Astley, is inaugurated into the laugh-a-decade world of the stately-home servant.

He receives a lesson in pointlessly polishing silverware from a man who's spent 30 years pointlessly polishing silverware himself, and doesn't care who knows it. Grant learns it takes over half an hour to 'do' a single tiny lid, scrubbing away while the great smell of ammonia slowly chews his face off. Later, he has to polish the entire contents of an immense cabinet full of ornate heirlooms. Presumably his predecessor bashed his own brains out with a pewter kettle during some kind of despair-fuelled epiphany.

Crap job number two: the drudge-a-rific life of the secretary. Not that *The Lipstick Years: Sec's Appeal* (BBC2) could give two hoots about anything as mundane as that. Instead Lowri Turner, adopt-ing the presentational style of an actor in a DFS commercial, takes a scattergun look at wildly unrepresentative examples of the 'per-sonal assistant'. We're treated to soundbites from current and for-mer aides of Mohamed Al Fayed, Max Clifford, Ian Fleming and Andy Peters, coupled with worthless observations from Samantha Bond (Miss Moneypenny) and Anneka Rice (on the grounds that she used to be a secretary), punctuated by clips from old films and comedy shows. The few interesting revelations are so hopelessly lost behind the mass of knuckleheaded showbiz static that by the end you'll have formed absolutely no opinions at all, except one: Lowri Turner is extremely annoying.

Job number three is easily the worst: sitting in a laboratory with a hood over your head while a scientist pumps the stench of rotten meat and shit up your nose until your stomach starts convulsing.

This takes place in the wonderful *Anatomy of Disgust* (C4), a new series pondering the 'forgotten emotion'. Even when offered financial incentives, we're told no one can withstand the hooded nasal ordeal for more than five minutes. The idea is to come up with a 'stink bomb' alternative to tear gas that can aid crowd dispersal. 'We prefer to end the experiment before the subjects actually vomit into the hood,' chuckles the maniac responsible.

The programme is packed with interesting theories (apparently we find excrement disgusting because it's an 'ambiguous substance' – not because it stinks, then) and several truly arresting sights. Professor Paul Rozin of the University of Pennsylvania attempts to cajole children into taking bites from a dog turd sculpted from chocolate (toddlers will, eight-year-olds won't). Later, in a truly bizarre demonstration of our capacity for disgust, he taps a nasty-looking Ritz cracker on a Nazi officer's cap, and then offers it to a woman, who suddenly decides she'd rather not eat it, thanks. (Attention, Brit Art wannabes: tape the show, isolate and slow down this sequence, loop it, dub 'You Win Again' by Hot Chocolate over the top, and bingo: a video art installation.)

Job number four is similarly strange: quantifying the beliefs of the woefully mistaken.

In *Jackpot* (BBC2) William Hill employee Graham Sharpe calculates the odds for unusual bets, a task which involves dealing with countless UFO / Loch Ness Monster buffs, and people like Peter Boniface.

In 1994 Boniface put £25 on each of his three children having a number one hit single by the age of 21, even though they sound like a dog getting its scrotum caught between the spokes of a passing motorcycle.

'I don't believe people are born with talent . . . a passion for what you're doing, that's what makes a champion,' he announces cheerfully, sitting in front of a bookshelf closely resembling the self-improvement section of Waterstones (you know: titles like

'Conquering Reality: Enjoy Imaginary Success Through the Miracle of Delusion').

Charitably, Sharpe gave odds of 250 to 1. Boniface gets £27,500 if his children succeed; enough to keep him in upbeat go-getter manuals until the apocalypse. Magic.

I Wuv Monkey-Wunkies   [19 August]

Is Dr Charlotte Uhlenbroek real? A faultless cross between David Attenborough and a Stepford wife, she makes it through the whole of *Cousins – The Monkeys* (BBC1) without once losing her saccharine poise, even when clambering up a tree or wading knee-deep through a murky river in search of a camera-friendly primate to fawn over. She seems to have been programmed to address the camera with a non-threatening smile every 15 seconds, and to be honest, it's a little bit frightening.

Maybe she isn't actually there at all. Maybe she's some kind of sinister virtual avatar, digitally inserted into every scene by a fat Californian in an air-conditioned Santa Monican FX lab, silently licking Dorito salt from his lips as he subtly adjusts the camber of her left eyebrow. This pixel-perfect grace, combined with her movie-star looks and jolly-hockey-sticks-up-the-jungle attire, makes her practically identical to 'Tomb Raider' heroine Lara Croft – although, unlike Croft, whenever Uhlenbroek encounters a wild animal she doesn't blast it repeatedly in the face with a shotgun while performing random somersaults through the air.

Pity – a spot of acrobatic violence would improve things immensely. The overall tone is so unrelentingly, chokingly benign they may as well have ditched the title *Cousins* and called it 'I Wuv Monkey-Wunkies' instead. We see almost as much of Smiling Uhlenbroek as we do of the simians themselves, and in each shot she's beaming like a Persil mum, gooning and cooing over the wretched things until you feel like snatching one from her hands and kicking it into the sky. Kids will love it, but kids are fundamentally stupid, really, aren't they?

Fundamental stupidity of a different kind abounds in *I Dare You*

(C5), a gaudy look at the world of daredevils. This week, a Roberto Benigni lookalike calling himself 'Super Joe Reed' performs a bungee jump from a helicopter hovering 200 feet above the whirling blades of a second helicopter situated on the ground.

If helicopter number one dips too low, or the elastic rope snaps, Super Joe will be instantly carved into a thousand gruesome slices – so it's nice to know his wife and two young children are on the ground, recording Dad's potential death plunge on the family camcorder.

'I do get concerned sometimes, but Joe is very safety-conscious,' says wife Jennifer, as her husband prepares to yo-yo above a twirling razor-sharp rotor for the sake of low-brow entertainment.

'I'm going to come what they call "dangerously close" to those blades,' announces the man himself, authoritatively.

Before the leap, we're treated to a soft-focus flip through Joe's biography. A Fed Ex deliveryman during the week, his obsessive drive to indulge in derring-do grew from a need to impress his Vietnam vet father. 'I was trying to get Dad's attention every time I jumped off a ramp on a motorcycle,' he confesses, over moving slo-mo footage of himself sustaining a serious injury. He seems genuinely unfazed by the potential dangers of the helicopter-bungee stunt. 'If I'm going to go out, I'm going to go out in a blaze of glory,' he says – although 'in a hideous accident' would surely be more accurate.

Disappointingly, come the jump itself, he doesn't lose so much as a fingertip – and despite the presence of cameras on the ground, we're only shown the crucial moments from an overhead angle, making it impossible to judge how close Super Joe actually came to the blades.

Still, watching him dangle above the churning rotor prompts an intriguing question: if the stunt went wrong, what kind of exotic, disjointed thoughts would pulse through Super Joe's fevered consciousness at the precise moment the top of his head was lopped off and his brain got sliced into a tumbling flock of slippery grey mind-steaks?

I have absolutely no idea, but the accompanying visions probably wouldn't be a million miles away from the luridly hallucino-genic look of *The Powerpuff Girls* (Cartoon Network), a demented Hanna-Barbera cartoon series that plays like a cross between Japanese anime, Roger Ramjet, and the sort of thing you might see while suffering an unexpected blow to the back of the head.

Endlessly inventive, subversive and surreal – in a sane world this would be broadcast each night in place of the news. One of the recurring characters is a monkey: Dr Charlotte Uhlenbroek could tune in especially to smile at him. For ages.

Untertainment at its finest [26 August]

They may be plastic, they may be dull, they may even be managed by Pete Waterman, but ho ho ho, we all love Steps really, don't we?

No. And nor will you if you're reckless enough to watch *Steps into Summer* (BBC1), a Bank Holiday extravaganza which is less fun than falling over and breaking your jaw on a door frame.

The show maintains an air of market-town mundanity from beginning to end, and contains several scenes some viewers may find distressing, such as an excruciating montage in which Michael Buerk, John Craven, Handy Andy, Titchmarsh, Dimmock, and countless other dignity-phobic nano-celebs are seen capering about awkwardly in time to Steps' cover of 'Tragedy'. Does anyone else find these 'amusingly' edited musical interludes almost impossible to withstand? Earlier this year, the obscene sight of Anthony Worrall Thompson miming to 'Ooh La La' by the Wiseguys in a *Food and Drink* trailer made me want to sew my eyes shut with fishing wire; this new Steps poptrocity makes me want to saw my own head open and scrape the memories out with a spoon.

The group's sterile song-and-dance numbers are punctuated by a series of mesmerisingly lame sketches, each revolving around an awkward cameo from a celebrity guest. The stars in question include Les Dennis, Melinda Messenger and Noddy Holder – pre-sumably more popular and up-to-date acts would have appeared, but Louise Woodward and Kelly Monteith weren't available.

The single amusing moment occurs during the dance routine for

'Summer of Love', when all five Steps briefly replicate the frantic double-handed tugging motion of a hardcore porn actress attempting to bring two symmetrically positioned penises to climax on either side of her face, but this probably isn't intentional and therefore doesn't count.

On this evidence, it is no longer 'OK' to like Steps, even in a flimsily ironic sense. They're not harmless fun, they're slapdash trash. 'H' is not a loveable scamp: he's a blank-eyed glove puppet with half the charisma of a discarded ping-pong bat rotating slowly in a pool of pig-trough rainwater. *Steps into Summer* represents untertainment at its finest and will be warmly welcomed by anyone who regularly sits in front of the box with a loaded shotgun in their mouth, trying to pluck up the courage.

Your time would be more gainfully employed watching Terry Jones host a stealthily informative documentary called *Gladiators – The Brutal Truth* (BBC2) instead. This is proper family entertainment: enough grisly detail to shake the younger viewers up a little, dispensed with intelligence and wit. Better still, they're showing *Spartacus* directly afterwards.

Further decadence looms in *One Night Stands* (C5), home to a parade of odious braggarts eager to share their casual misogyny and knuckleheaded worldview with thousands of viewers, most of whom will doubtless have switched on Channel Five in the hope of encountering some casual late-night nudity to masturbate to.

Tough luck to the porn-miners, since the programme features no naked women whatsoever. It does, however, include countless gruesome shots of alco-sodden halfwits baring their buttocks, waggling their tongues, and flashing their flaccid dicks for the camera. It's about as arousing as a fart in a birdcage and will make you want to cry for hours.

Much of the action centres around a duo named Simon and Lawton, both of whom claim to have enjoyed literally hundreds of one-night stands, apparently with girls too drunk to find the prospect of being violated by a gurgling imbecile in any way troubling.

As a team, they appear unevenly matched. Simon resembles a

cross between Jean-Claude Van Damme and the lead singer from the Stereophonics, whereas Lawton has a face like a freeze-frame snap of a frog's head exploding. The moment they open their mouths, however, all disparities vanish: each is as boring, stupid, and hopelessly self-centred as the other. 'I always wear a condom, usually,' drones Ugly Lawton, while Please-Hate-Me Simon brags of bedding *Daily Sport* models and reveals his preferred method of dumping his one-night girlfriends: mobile-phone text message.

We follow them on a night out, which involves wandering around a gaudy nightclub leering at cadavers. This would be depressing enough, but it's also interspersed with explicit talking-head testimony from other one-night aficionados, mainly ugly grinning men with appalling views on pretty much every facet of anything you care to think of.

The programme would be massively improved by the insertion of a protracted final sequence in which each participant is glued to a deckchair and kicked down a stairwell. Forty-seven million times.

The Justice League of America   [2 September]

Christopher Timothy misses the good old days when he stood in damp fields with half his arm up a cow beneath the gaze of millions, according to *Starstruck: Holding On* (C4), which examines how celebrities cope once their star has faded.

The former *All Creatures Great and Small* star is shown visiting a fête to plant a tree in front of a desultory gathering of locals, many of them kids who clearly don't know who he is and would have been far more impressed by an appearance from any one of the following: 1) Jeremy Spake; 2) the angry money-throwing man from the Direct Line home insurance commercial; 3) a bit of old inner tube dangling off a stick; 4) a hen; 5) nothing and no one.

Timothy's lot looks sad and humiliating, but at least he hasn't been reduced to earning a crust as a QVC stallholder or comically manipulating his scrotal sac for small coins inside a dockside bunco booth. Still, there's hope.

He says he misses his television appearances, and yearns to

return and play a villain: not just a minor baddie, but a major bastard, 'a real piece of work'. He should write to the producers of *Manhunter* (Sky One) a true-crime reconstruction show that's unpalatably wrong in every respect – and therefore totally mesmerising.

A sort of 'Best of . . .' companion show to *America's Most Wanted*, *Manhunter* is hosted by a terrifying thing apparently called Jaaaahrn Walsh. Jaaaahrn's delivery lurks halfway between John Wayne and an animatronic theme-park dummy employed to entertain queuefuls of impatient visitors by wailing outside the ghost train. He shouts, overemphasises every other word, and punctuates his speech with so many ridiculous hand gestures he'll have his own eye out if he's not careful. He also has a plastic head, hair like a futuristic combat helmet and was probably spawned in a microwaveable Petri dish by the Justice League of America.

The title sequence forms perhaps the most jaw-dropping introduction to any programme ever. To the toe-snappin' sound of howling power rock, Jaaaaarrhn bellows that we're about to see case histories involving 'fugitives without compassion' over reconstructed footage of a wild-eyed madman blowing up a car. Then we see a flicker-book cascade of real-life mugshots. And then . . .

And then, suddenly, a photographic montage of a young, smiling boy fills the screen. Jaaaarrrhn explains there's a personal link.

'In 1981 my six-year-old son Adam was abducted and murdered,' he booms, and your brain does a backflip before you realise that, yes, you really are watching the host of a ruthlessly downmarket crime-tertainment oglefest reduce the death of his own son to a schlocky title sequence interlude. Whoever told him that this was a good idea deserves to be sealed inside a packing crate full of jackals and razor wire and rolled down a hill.

Next we cut to Jaaaaarrhn striding through a darkened alley billowing with dry ice. 'I was shattered,' he yells, almost cracking the lens with a hand flourish. 'I was mad at the whole world. I was bitter, angry. I didn't want justice, I wanted revenge.' And he got it by reinventing himself as a histrionic TV arsehole.

The show itself opens with Jaaaaaaaaaahrn hollering that 'drugs are the poison of American society, and its highways are the veins through which that poison is spread' – a clumsy metaphor that sets the scene for a reconstruction so offensively one-sided it's like watching a crime take place in the imagination of a particularly idiotic fascist.

Two painfully young Mexicans caught smuggling marijuana get pulled by a rookie highway patrolman and find themselves facing a needlessly harsh 25-year sentence. Understandably aggrieved by this, and egged on by a minor felon sharing their police-station cell, they make a desperate bid for freedom using a bit of glass as a makeshift knife. Any sane viewer will be rooting for them.

The story of their ill-fated escape is told with soullessly slick camerawork, wailing rock guitar and numerable close-ups of them sweatily rolling their eyes around in the manner of a schizophrenic mime artist glaring at a boxful of snakes. One of the escapees evaded capture for months until his case was featured on *America's Most Wanted* – at which point he foolishly turned himself in, receiving 48 years in prison for his trouble.

Sexual Swearwords [30 September]

You and I did nothing. The police, the government, the army and the navy all failed to intervene. No one lifted a finger, so now that Simon Bates is back we have no one else to blame.

Yes, frogchops himself is fronting a TV incarnation of his legendary radio sob-story-and-song spot *Our Tune* (Sky One). It is, of course, entirely hypnotic.

Confronted with Bates addressing the camera directly, it's hard to shake the memory of his legendary video-certification announcements, which used to appear at the start of rented movies and generally proved far more disturbing than anything in the film itself, thanks to the palpable crackle of excitement as he mentioned 'sexual swearwords'.

Our Tune doesn't last much longer than those videotaped cautions: it's a few minutes long, and is sprinkled throughout the Sky One daytime schedule like tragic croutons in a bowl of poo soup, bobbing to the surface on the hour throughout much of the day.

The format is identical to the radio strand: Bates relates a real-life tale of misfortune sent in by a member of the public with all the sympathetic compassion of an automated voicemail assistant, then plays a tear-jerking request; invariably a gooey ballad rather than anything with a genuinely appropriate lyric, like 'So Fucking What?' by the Anti-Nowhere League.

This being television, the stories benefit from the illustrative pictures: mainly vague visuals, such as a shot of a calendar with an 'aged film' filter laid over the top, or if you're really lucky, snapshots of the luckless subjects themselves.

The music videos are interrupted every 30 seconds by a large yellow strap informing viewers what they're watching. Presumably this is an attempt to catch the attention of channel-hoppers who might otherwise assume they'd stumbled across a VH-1 Michael Ball retrospective, but it also detracts from any sentimental value the song might have – it's like watching sobbing relatives burying a loved one in a coffin with a corporate logo stamped down the side.

Now, imagine you're a bored, lonely, loveless male, slumped in front of your television flipping aimlessly through the showshaker tinseldrift of station after station when suddenly you chance upon *G-String Divas* (C5), a tawdry little fleshburst lurking out there in the schedule, waiting to seize listless channel-hoppers just like you and mesmerise them into corroding their own self-esteem via a sorry act of desultory armchair onanism. Here's what you'll see.

First, Cashmere, a lap-dancer. Then Brett, a pony-tailed yee-haw who pays for regular private sessions in which Cashmere bends down and grinds her hips while he glowers at her silently, like a circus bear staring at a cat on a meathook. Brett is a tragedy in Bud-streaked denim: currently enmeshed in a bitter divorce, he talks of his plans for a 'long-term relationship' with Cashmere, despite the fact that a) he's a drawling overweight truck-hick who looks like the sort of goon you see getting a pool cue smashed across their skull in an especially bad Chuck Norris film, b) she's engaged and c) he has to keep shoving banknotes into her hand so she'll talk to him.

Anyway, that's the back story. The rest of the programme consists of repetitive close-ups of Cashmere circling her buttocks into the lens as if inviting us to check whether she's wiped properly. It's a sorry example of that curious new TV hybrid, the masturmentary: a programme which exists solely to assist masturbation (to the point where it may as well be introduced by a stern-faced drill instructor who blows a whistle and commands everyone watching to commence jerking off immediately) yet is forced to adopt a flimsy documentary guise in order to appease the broadcast authorities – the modern-day equivalent of 1950s nudie flicks sidestepping the censor by masquerading as earnest examinations of naturism.

The result satisfies no one: self-abusers have their mental-visual playground spoiled by the constant intrusion of fiercely anti-erotic talking-head soundbites from loserboy Brett, while anyone wanting to watch an actual documentary will have seen through the ruse by the third lingering buttock-shot.

Perhaps C5 should employ Simon Bates to issue a generic warning at the start of shows like this. Something along the lines of: 'The following shitcast contains no viable content whatsoever.' Then again, they'd wear the tape out in a fortnight.

Craig Something   [21 October]

Question: what's worse than a bland, toothless BBC holiday programme featuring Trude *Vets in Practice* Mostue? Answer: a bland, toothless BBC holiday programme also featuring Jeremy Spake, which is precisely what you'll see if for some mad reason you decide to squander half an hour of the only life you'll ever have on *Holiday Insider's Guide* (BBC1).

It's presented by a walking vacuum of a man who looks like he's wandered straight off the set of a Gillette commercial to fill in for a couple of hours before his next assignment: appearing as a semi-naked fireman in a vaguely homoerotic Athena poster. Not sure what his name is: Craig something, and that's about as much attention as he deserves.

Yeah, yeah: in real life he's undoubtedly a really super guy, but on screen he demonstrates all the personality of Microsoft Excel, simpering around delivering trite links with his nice hair and his nice non-threatening blarney-lite patter, so screw him. Why don't they go the whole hog and hire a doily to front the show instead? They could tie it to a bit of string and dangle it in front of picturesque locations, accompanied by captions and a nice bit of Julian Bream on the soundtrack. Far cheaper, less insulting.

Anyway. This new incarnation of *Holiday* purports to offer a true 'insider's guide' to its featured destinations, thanks to the genius ruse of sending a bunch of nano-celebrity no-marks out to cover locations they're already familiar with, through having lived or worked in them at some point in their lives. Hosting boy Craig Wotsit opens the show with an uninspiring gawp round his home town of Dublin (being an expert on the city, the first thing he does is wander into a tourist information centre).

Then we get Marie Helvin lording around Hawaii, in perhaps the single least informative travel report ever shot. All we really learn is a) that Marie Helvin likes the landscape, b) that Marie Helvin likes hula dancing, c) that Marie Helvin likes everything else about Hawaii as well. The one decent piece of advice she dishes out is this: bring a riding hat with you if you're considering an afternoon's pony trekking. Hands up everyone affected by that piece of essential guidance. Considering the towering wisdom of these experts, it's surprising none of them manage to pack more information into their reports – there's little you couldn't discover by scan-reading two paragraphs of an average travel guide.

To prove the point, before you can scream 'This programme is rubbish', dull blonde vet Trude Mostue bounds onto the screen, to tell us the shops in Oslo are good but expensive, quickly followed by Sean Maguire in the Algarve (who reckons the beaches are nice), and finally, spoiling your view of St Petersburg, woo-hoo! it's Jeremy Spake – the only man in existence who can sound overly enthusiastic and embarrassingly wooden at the same time.

During Spake's piece, repeated cutaways to apparently bemused Russian onlookers watching him camp it up are used in an attempt to underline his loveable quirkiness – instead they appear to be thinking, correctly, that he's a bothersome prick.

Really, what's the point of this infuriating half-hour wrongcast? While these gurning chimps swan around the world on behalf of your licence fee, you're sitting at home in front of a box, a motionless black plastic box with a huge glass screen, pissing this sanitised marionette's pageant into your bloated little eyeballs, while you pork out on Jaffa Cakes, wishing you were dead or at the very least too wounded to see.

Still, if you binge on too many biscuits, tune in to the disturbing *Witness: Living on Light* (C4), which examines the idiotic charms of Jamuheen, a deluded Australian woman (a sort of evil, blonde Sian Lloyd) who claims to have mastered the art of existence without food.

Three people have died trying to follow her '21-day process', which consists of a merciless starvation regime, at the end of which you're supposedly able to take leave of food for good. The documentary crew visits a group of would-be fasters: the sight of them lying on the floor, barely able to move after four days without food or drink, smiling weakly even as their kidneys start to fail is handsdown the most upsetting image of the week.

Oh, all right, apart from Jeremy Spake.

All the Fun of a Slow-Motion Hanging   [28 October]

Confessions: several years ago, I had a brief spell as a TV news 'expert'; specifically, I was a high-tech pundit, occasionally called upon to pass comment on computer-related current affairs even though my qualifications were shaky, to say the least. I was billed as a 'technology journalist', an astoundingly highfalutin way of saying I reviewed video games for a living (which in most people's eyes is the lowest a man can sink short of playing the role of 'anguished receiving-end farmhand' in a bestial-porn movie).

I was appearing on BBC News 24 at around midnight so hardly anyone was watching – fortunate, considering most of the time I didn't know what the hell I was going on about. Computer games were simple enough, but the moment I was asked to comment on anything else we entered extremely shaky ground. Knowing my pearls of ignorance were being spilt on live television exacerbated the situation: I still get the sweats when I recall the moment the host turned to ask whether I'd seen any evidence the Internet was having a thawing effect on Chinese society, and I responded by making a long, strangulated, non-committal 'Mmmmmnnnnnuu-uurrrmmm' – the sound of my brain drying, live on air.

Still, I came away having learned two valuable lessons: 1) never believe anything any 'expert' says; and 2) whatever the appearance may be, any televised conversation is going to be about as unforced and natural as a chat between Lieutenant Columbo and a man with a blood-encrusted shovel in his toolshed.

It's surprising, then, that talk shows don't go abysmally wrong more often. Just about every instance over the last twenty years in which they have done is covered in *It Shouldn't Happen to a Chat Show Host* (ITV), a compilation of car-crash television which manages to entertain from beginning to end despite the presence of Gloria Hunniford (an achievement on a par with successfully climbing a spiral staircase with a dead horse strapped to your back).

Ignore the regulation-dull talking-head soundbites; the archive footage is great. Watching talk shows derail themselves completely is immeasurably more interesting than sitting through successful ones, which tend to be as diverting as an automated platform announcement.

Michael Aspel, so bland he probably poos boiled eggs, features heavily: for a man with a reputation as a steady albeit uninteresting hand, he's been responsible for a surprising number of calamities. First, there's the infamous appearance by an impossibly drunk Oliver Reed in which the bearded alco-sponge reeled around the set looking like he was about to start vomiting eels. Aspel describes it as 'a great TV moment', although 'an unplanned and monumental embarrassment' is nearer the mark.

Still, were this a humiliation contest, his subsequent encounter with Willis, Stallone and Schwarzenegger would surely take first prize. Desperate to bag this all-star triumvirate, the producers agreed to their every demand. Unfortunately the three were hell-bent on turning the entire show into an extended commercial for Planet Hollywood, their newly founded chain of mediocre dunce-troughs.

The result was mesmerising for all the wrong reasons: a trio of world-famous waxworks plastered head to toe in Planet Hollywood logos (Willis even had one painted on his chest) smirking openly while Aspel asked meaningless questions about burgers and cookery, at one point reduced to reading the menu out loud. He'd have retained more dignity if he'd dropped to his knees and fellated the lot of them, clapping his hands like a circus seal and playing the kazoo with his backside.

Other highlights include Anne Bancroft drying completely for a 10-minute trial-by-awkwardness during a live edition of *Wogan* (all the fun of a slow-motion hanging), and the jaw-dropping moment Keith Chegwin unexpectedly confessed to alcoholism in the middle of a chirpy Richard and Judy chinwag. Anyone sheeplike enough to doubt Chegwin's credentials as a genuine TV hero should be forced to watch this – he's one of the most honest, couldn't-give-a-monkey's people on television.

Concrete and Piss   [4 November]

If you like your drama gritty, uncompromising and guaranteed to depress, then boy oh boy are you in for a treat, because this week on Channel 4 there's a major new series called 'Concrete and Piss', in which an unemployed alcoholic stands in a tower block stairwell on the Thatcher's Legacy estate, mindlessly thrashing a mouldy old mattress with the ulcerated leg of his dead junkie son, pausing every three minutes to scream, swear, and receive violent blows to the face and neck from a hunchbacked loan shark.

OK. Not really. But you have to admit it's a brilliant title. Instead, there's a new mini-series called *Never, Never* (C4), which fulfils pretty much every other criterion of 'gritty, uncompromising' drama you could think of. Let's run through the recipe and check off the ingredients.

First, and most important, do we have a bleak contemporary setting? Check: the action takes place on a grim London council estate that looks as though it was designed by a misanthropic concrete fetishist with a massive grudge and an even bigger migraine; a sprawling campus of despair that sucks all the hope out of everyone inside, then pisses it down the walls of the malfunctioning elevators. This is not *The Vicar Of Dibley*.

How about some social comment? Check: the series centres on a cold-blooded salesman (John Simm) who makes his living coercing downtrodden inmates of said estate into buying expensive brand-name goods from a sinister company charging absurd rates of interest. Thanks to their undesirable postcode, the customers can't get credit anywhere else – but their kids are demanding Phat Nikes and Pokemon play sets, and won't stop screaming till they get them. The hapless parents sink into a mire of debt while the salesman cackles himself sick.

Next: Casual violence? Check: a major character endures a vicious baseball bat attack within the first 25 minutes.

Additional unpleasant, hand-wringing, gracious-me-isn't-modern-society-going-tits-up touches? Check: immediately after the beating, the comatose victim is robbed of his shoes by a pair of opportunistic schoolkids (who could have scored bonus points for weeing in his face and laughing, but didn't).

Rasping cockneys? Check: you know that unbelievably raspy and weather-beaten young cockney bloke who played a scrawny nihilistic smackhead with a spider's web tattooed all over his apocalyptic chops in *Nil By Mouth*? The one who could never, in a million billion years, land the head role in a Noel Coward biopic but could convincingly play all four members of the Sex Pistols at once? He's in this, playing a scrawny nihilistic cockney in a stained vest.

Perhaps I'm alone on this, but I've always found him incredibly watchable: he should have his own series, playing an unconventional inner-city detective who chases suspected criminals down alleyways, wielding a bit of scaffolding with a razorblade taped to the end, signing off each episode by squatting in a phonebox pumping smack into his eye. Come on, ITV: you could do with gritty new Morse for the twenty-first century.

Speaking of heroin, does *Never, Never* also feature substance abuse? Check: toilet-bound coke-snorting, an old man plied with whisky, and an unconscious junkie flopping to the pavement. There's also a bit where John Simm spoons custard into his mouth as though it's a tub of liquid crack, but that doesn't really count.

Gratuitous bad language? Big bold check: this is possibly the most swearsome broadcast of the year. Someone says 'fuck' every couple of seconds. It's like product placement for the Fuck Corporation. Even the walls and ceilings appear to be saying it at times. All your other slang favourites put in an appearance too, with the exception of the c-word, although I think at one point a trail of saliva dribbling from the mouth of a collapsed drug addict is trying to spell it out, and gets as far as the letter 'n' before someone else says 'fuck' and the spittle sighs and gives up and it cuts to a different scene.

Of course I might be making that bit up, and am.

Anyway, overall *Never, Never* fulfils its quota admirably. Oh, and it's also a reasonably good piece of television drama, despite a lot of padding in the form of pointless slow-motion sequences of John Simm wandering around the squalor pit while a long piano chord chimes mournfully in the distance.

They can be let off for that. What can't be forgiven is not having the guts to call it 'Concrete and Piss'. Cowards.

A Momentary Adrenaline Rush   [11 November]

I'm a coward. I'm scared of everything. Last night I got up to fetch myself a drink of water and, while filling a glass in the darkened kitchen, briefly glimpsed a scrumpled-up carrier bag that looked a bit like a grinning skull. Terrified, I leapt on the sideboard and screamed for the neighbours to call the police, but instead they just hammered a shoe against the wall for 28 minutes before venturing outside to hurl rocks at my window – which failed to scare the bag away.

In fact I'm still up on the sideboard now, tapping away on a laptop, with a tea towel draped over one side of my head as a kind of makeshift sightscreen that prevents both me from seeing the skull-bag, and the skullbag from sensing my fear.

Whimsy aside, cowardice is one of my driving characteristics, which is why I've always regarded anyone engaged in 'extreme sports' as inherently alien and untrustworthy. Skateboard, snow-board and BMX aficionados all seem to lack the fear of a snapped ankle or shattered pelvis, while anyone prepared to climb rock faces or take part in a street-luge event is clearly just insane. (For the uninitiated, a street luge is a kind of gigantic skateboard for maniacs to lie down on and race through steep city streets in the most precarious and vulnerable manner possible. It's a sport that raises questions, namely: 1) How do you casually 'get into' it? 2) Where do you practise? And most baffling of all, 3) where do you actually buy a street luge? Halfords?)

All of the above explains why I found this week's *Cutting Edge: Seconds To Impact* (C4) so terrifying. It takes a hideously involved look at the world of BASE jumping – a pastime in which eerily calm men and women climb high objects, leap off, plummet toward the ground and release a tiny parachute at the very last possible second. Unsurprisingly, it's illegal in the UK. As sports go, this is as perilous and extreme as it gets, short of wolf-raping.

The programme follows three jumpers called Rob, Jon and Greg, as they spend the summer hopping off a variety of vertigo-magnets, including the Cheddar Gorge, the Park Lane Hilton, various Norwegian mountains, and in one especially shiversome sequence shot with tiny helmet-mounted digicams, an impossibly tall and exposed chimney stack slap bang in the middle of nowhere.

For a bunch of fearless lunatics, the trio are pleasant and normal enough, although I wouldn't invite them round for dinner on the grounds that anyone prepared to leap off the Cheddar Gorge for kicks is probably equally prepared to unexpectedly lunge forward and poke a fork through your eye for the sake of a momentary adrenaline rush.

Few viewers will doubt the macho credentials of anyone about to hurl themselves from the top of the Park Lane Hilton, yet during the preparations for just such an event, Rob is curiously at pains to inform us just how heterosexual he is.

He squints accusingly at the camera: 'Normally I'd never cuddle a bloke in a million years,' he grunts, going on to explain, almost apologetically, that he and his fellow jumpers occasionally share a vaguely tender slap on the back and a few kind words in the moments before a jump – restrained behaviour under the circumstances, yet Rob appears genuinely more troubled by the thought of viewers at home laughing and 'calling us faggots or whatever' than by the immediate prospect of the potential death plunge.

In the event, Rob and Jon survive to cuddle in an entirely non-sexual context another day. But not all BASE jumps go according to plan, and just as you've become accustomed to the sight of these likeable daredevils hurling themselves off ledges and somehow escaping unscathed, death makes an appearance and the programme takes an altogether darker turn, and the carefree blokey thrill-seekers suddenly start to look more like self-destructive junkies, pornographically videotaping each new conquest then gathering to watch the recording later, endlessly driven to jump and jump again, hooked on life affirmation through the repeated defiance of monumental risk.

Still, their collated footage makes for genuinely exciting television, so who cares, eh?

Next week in the same time slot: a man with a camcorder glued to his forehead feeding himself face-first into a threshing machine. If we're lucky.

Casualty Is Rubbish [18 November]

Casualty (BBC1) is rubbish – sick, thick, knee-jerk, leery, cynical rubbish; so unrealistic it might as well revolve around an imaginary hospital in the centre of a glass pig's eye.

Above all, it's a mess – a local-pantomime-standard blend of patronising hand-wringing and reactionary finger-wagging, slung together into a single, predictable awkward soap (the dull inter-staff feuds and romances are so calculated and forced, they may as well be conducted at gunpoint) and stuffed to bursting point with as much needless gore as possible.

This is (and always has been) rubberneckers' television, appealing to the sort of closet ghouls who, on spotting the remains of a car smash, gently slow down the Rover for a good slow-motion porno-peer at the limp arm dangling over the side of a stretcher.

If the BBC went mad and broadcast *Zombie Flesh Eaters* in the same mid-evening slot, *Casualty* viewers would be the first to complain – even though *Zombie Flesh Eaters* is a) only 4 per cent more gruesome, b) 44 per cent more exciting and believable, and c) 2006 per cent less likely to feature yet another variation on the scene in which a pretty nurse delivers a stinging put-down to a man impatiently banging his fist on the reception desk.

Incidentally, hands up everyone who couldn't give a pliant duck about the ongoing child-custody subplot involving Charlie Fairhead. He's a smug, soft-spoken, holier-than-thou dishcloth of a man, who deserves as much misfortune as scriptwriters can throw at him. And he's got tiny eyes. He looks like a cross between a drama teacher and a dormouse: his son's better off without him.

Charlie's method of dealing with anyone runs as follows: calmly talk them down in the manner of a pre-school children's TV presenter demonstrating how a quiet, steady voice can hypnotise livestock, while simultaneously exuding the faintest whiff of malevolent sarcasm that suggests he doesn't actually give two shits about the trowel they've got lodged in their forehead. For a man who's supposed to represent trust and dependability, he's strangely incapable of maintaining a fixed gaze on the person he's talking to. Instead, whenever delivering one of his regular appeasement monologues, his pixel-thick eyes continually wander left or right, or stare into the middle distance, while the rest of him shuffles from toe to toe like a man reluctantly sharing half-hearted conversation as he waits for the in-flight toilet to free itself up. I wouldn't trust him to fix a cup of Lemsip.

Tonight's episode contains all your other *Casualty* favourites: vomit, blood, a visit from the police, glassy-eyed extras, an unsympathetic patient who relentlessly complains, staff friction of metronomic predictability, and a lonely-but-noble old woman gasping her last on a starched white hospital bed. In true *Casualty* tradition, this last character is played by an 'ooh-what-have-I-seen-them-in-before?' celebrity (Lou Beale from *EastEnders*).

Best of all, there's a textbook example of that most knuckleheaded *Casualty* cliché, the Case of the Injured Tearaway. According to the rules of this overfamiliar subplot, all gangs of teenage ruffians are led by a painfully soft-looking, middle-class actor struggling to project an air of gritty urban malice by means of an unconvincing display of shrugs, slouches, and half-hearted scowls, generally accompanied by an indisputably terrible stab at a working-class accent. Furthermore said gang leader is a one-dimensional coward at heart, who will lamely bully his cohorts into participating in a major criminal misadventure during which the most innocent teenager in the group will suffer nightmarish injuries.

Tonight's example doesn't disappoint – a cheerfully naïve Pogo Patterson lookalike rips his face open trying to vault a barbed-wire fence during a bungled robbery. Then there's the additional bonus of a deep-rooted dysfunctional family dynamic of poster-colour improbability that gets completely straightened out within 28 minutes of his parents' arrival at the hospital. Plus we get to see him bleed and scream a few more times.

A few hours later, further porn in *Amsterdam: City Of Sin* (C4), which gawps at the sex industry. We see everything from a woman squatting over a live webcam to a man cheerfully browsing through a range of forearm-sized dildos racked up on a wall like weapons from some hideous future sex war.

And what do we learn? Nothing, bar this: these days you're shown naked breasts every 18 seconds on Channel 4: it's nothing more than Live! TV with a WAP phone in its pocket and a punnet full of sushi on its lap.

Sadowitz [25 November]

Quick, name a likeable magician. Three . . . two . . . one. Time's up.

Think of any? Course not: they're bastards. For all their supposed skills at achieving the impossible – sawing women in half, making doves fly out of their faces, tying tigers in knots in a box full of fire – they're useless at making themselves seem even vaguely human.

Paul Daniels? A seething, dry-lipped pepperpot. Siegfried and Roy? Upholstered aliens with too much gold and a big-cat fetish. David Copperfield? Look into his eyes for six seconds and shudder as the yawning abyss within swirls out to engulf you.

Then there's Jerry Sadowitz; best known as a nihilistic comic, also a gifted magician. Sadowitz doesn't use dry ice and strobe lighting to mask the fact he's a shit: he performs spartan close-up card tricks and wears his unpleasantness on his sleeve – nailed to his forehead, in fact – and for this he deserves our support.

His new C5 vehicle *The Jerry Atrick Show* is an endearingly shambolic attempt to showcase his talents.

An uneasy mix of card tricks, gleefully puerile sketches, and stonefaced four-letter misanthropy, it's like an edition of the *Paul Daniels Magic Show* fronted by Howard Beale, the suicidal newsreader from the movie *Network*.

And it doesn't quite work: confused direction renders many of the card tricks hard to follow, while the sketches, taken from his live show *Bib and Bob* (an exercise in escalating puerility that would make any sane person laugh till their eyes pissed acid), suffer in isolation from the motiveless, enthusiastically infantile whole. But amongst the misfires and disappointing VTs lurk some tantalising moments unlike anything else on TV, and while the tricks need to be seen live to be appreciated, they represent a rare opportunity to watch someone doing something they genuinely, passionately adore.

For proof of why the presence of wrecked-but-authentic performers like Sadowitz in the schedules is more necessary than ever before, stare no further than *Making the Band* (C4) a reality show chronicling the genesis of a manufactured American boy band.

Perfectly scheduled between *Hollyoaks*, *Futurama* and a whirlwind of adverts for garage compilations, pay-as-you-go mobiles and spot cream, *Making the Band* is essential viewing for anyone who suspects the world might be fucked and secretly hopes it is. It's mesmerising.

The idea is simple: 25,000 hopefuls slowly whittled down to five band members while the camera looks on. If you're tuning in tomorrow, I'm afraid you missed the final pruning, in which two wannabes got the chop in a hilariously cruel and drawn-out firing session. But don't worry: tomorrow, as the chosen ones enter the recording studio, there's still time to appreciate the show's core appeal: the hateful insincerity of everyone involved.

The five remaining 'performers' are a bunch of hissing Styrofoam meerkats desperately clawing over each other, craning their necks to suckle from the withered tit of fame; whining, mewling, preening, bitching – they couldn't be more dislikeable if they strode around in Nazi regalia firing nailguns at ponies. (Note to anyone working on a British version of *Making the Band*: stop what you're doing right now. Just put your hands down and walk away. Please. Or there'll be an uprising, and we're talking heads-on-poles.)

The music is nondescript, the band is called O-Town – the 'O' apparently stands for Orlando although it may well represent the ice-cold hollow zero lodged in the heart of this absolute shit.

They should, of course, have used one of the following names instead: a) Puppet Squad, b) Edifice, c) Apocalypse Yo!, d) Attack of the Omen Five, e) Grinning Despair, f) Your Dreams Lie Crushed Beneath Us, or g) The Petri-dish Kids.

One minute banging on about 'living their dreams' and 'realising their destiny', the next moaning about their workload, this is a tale of five repugnant egos. Every time they speak, every time their bleating little mouths pop open, you'll feel like standing on your chair to hurl shoes at the screen. Artless gimps like this shouldn't be on television or in the charts at all: they deserve to be locked in a cupboard with a gigantic genetically engineered mantis that'll shift and itch and scratch its spiny little legs against their weeping faces, for a period of no less than sixteen thousand years.

Still, don't just take my word for it: tune in and learn to hate them yourself.

Cynical Scoffing at Saddos   [2 December]

Here's what watching TV will be like in the year 2006: you stroke a nubbin on the tip of a matchbook-sized mobile phone, and with a satisfying 'schhhhick' sound a gigantic plasma screen unfurls, covering the wall like a tapestry. Next, a huge holographic head rotates slowly in the centre of your living room, reading a list of your favourite programmes, while behind it in the screen it lists 19,000 stations catering for all conceivable interests, from the James Belushi Movie Channel ('*Curly Sue* to *Red Heat* and back again, 24-7') to the Santa Goose Hedge Pointer's Network ('*all* people leaning over hedges to point at a goose dressed as Santa, *all* the time').

Having made your choice, the programme begins – except it isn't a normal programme at all. No: thanks to 'convergence', it's a magical cross between TV, the Internet and the most sophisticated arcade game you've ever seen. If you're watching *Ground Force* 2006, for example, you'll be able to push a button to digitally graft Alan Titchmarsh's head onto the body of a dancing cat, and take potshots at it with a light gun, earning Amazon tokens for each paw you blow off.

LSD users can do that already, of course, but until 2006 arrives the rest of us have to make do with the likes of BBC Choice's E-Mail Weekend – a selection of programmes that 'gives viewers a chance to browse through the ups and downs of online life' and – oops – a few myths into the bargain.

Alongside documentaries on cyber-talking, a simplistic and self-conscious comedy-drama 'about communication, or rather mis-communication' called *Talk to Me* (BBC Choice) and the unflinchingly realistic movie *Weird Science* (BBC Choice), lurks a series of 10-minute shorts called *Looking 4 Love* (BBC Choice), in which goonish presenter Dan Rowland visits people using the Internet to further their love lives, expecting us to gaze in astonishment as though he'd uncovered a race of talking unicorns. Since the banal reality of a typical online romance (two parties aimlessly exchanging flirtatious e-mails) isn't significantly salacious or peculiar, the show largely focuses on the predictable extremes – an unpleasant ageing Stringfellow type using the net to woo women, a lanky oddball with a cybersex addiction, and a fat man from Barnsley who married an American he met online, only to have her scarper back to the States a short while later.

Trouble is, not one of the assembled interfreaks is half as strange as Rowland himself, who perpetually gurns and mugs like a man sitting on his hands trying to stop a bee crawling up his nose, and has an incredibly annoying habit of facing the camera to raise an eyebrow whenever someone says something even vaguely risqué, which they manage to do approximately every six seconds.

His final visit brings him to a fetishwear convention with an incredibly tenuous online link (it's advertised on the web – just like say, the Ideal Home Exhibition, which wouldn't have made prurient viewing). By now utterly uninterested in talking about the Internet at all, he simply walks around pulling 'oo-er' faces at leatherwear and strap-ons until you feel like crawling into the screen to slap him back to normality.

As with the majority of programmes about hobbyists, the underlying attitude is one of cynical scoffing at saddos – but who's the more tragic: the person using the Internet to communicate with a living, breathing person, or the bloated sofa-bound dunderhead who spent hundreds on a digital box, just to watch Dan Rowland jig around like a sneering marionette?

Westlife and Rain   [23 December]

This year's been a swindle. As a child the mere mention of 'the year 2000' conjured up images of people with purple hair piloting miniature bacofoil hovercraft round and round inside a gigantic doughnut-shaped space station. Yaay! Exciting! And what did we get? Westlife and rain. Thanks a bundle, history.

This year's television has been particularly disappointing since the last few months of nigh-on uninterrupted drizzle have meant we've had little to do except sit indoors watching the box (or if you're in a flooding hotspot, watching the box bob up and down).

And by God we must be bitter: this year's most talked-about programmes all revolved around cynical voyeurism and mean-spirited in-fighting. The inescapable *Big Brother* flummoxed everyone by being both appealing and mesmerising at the same time, drawing a huge audience as it slowly whittled down ten cackling boredom-droids to one goon-eyed dum-dum. Craig's elevation to hero status was always going to be short-lived the moment he stepped outside that rickety little house; hopelessly inarticulate, he'd have trouble explaining the price of a chisel in a B&Q commercial let alone wowing the crowd on a chat show – and besides, he doesn't really do anything annoying, unless 'having large biceps' counts as a bona fide gimmick these days.

Still, at least he had the decency to donate his winnings to a worthy cause – the others would have blown the lot on jet-skis and fun. Next year they're reportedly raising the stakes by dragging the contestants away from the isolation of the diary cupboard to vote one another out in a bad-tempered, face-to-face Judas session in the main living room. And come series three you'll be able to go on the Internet and click a button to make the ceiling rain piss, while the ejection process will consist of effigy-burning and lethal injection.

The Weakest Link was a huge success, thanks to the simple device of letting Anne Robinson tell the contestants they were rubbish and stupid. Trouble is, they weren't rubbish and stupid – the questions were often genuinely tricky. What we really want is a quiz show in which authentic dimwits have their efforts mercilessly pilloried – a version of *Family Fortunes* in which millions of viewers can phone a special number to collectively heckle the idiocy of everyone participating, with the resulting cacophonic abuse relayed live in the studio. Or maybe just an edition of *Wheel of Fortune* where John Leslie finally snaps and cracks a simpleton in the face with a broom.

After months of smirking foreplay, life-wrecking pub quiz *Who Wants to Be a Millionaire?* finally achieved climax, awarding its maximum payout to an upper-class woman who everyone agreed didn't really deserve it (she's already spent the proceeds on a mechanised android horse that fires chillum-seeking missiles at hunt saboteurs and a pair of solid-gold wellies for the next Countryside

March). Of course, now the magic figure's actually been handed over, the stakes no longer seem so unattainably impressive. Don't be surprised if it transforms into 'Who Wants to Win Two Million Pounds and Some Shoes and a Kite?'

And now, a quick break for a word about adverts, and in particular the Year's Most Baffling Commercial: the AA insurance ad, in which a woman who has organised a policy via the AA website bickers with her petty, sulking husband. There's no punchline and no love-you-really resolution; either I'm missing something, or it's actively intended to make you associate AA insurance with loveless, sniping relationships. Still, at least neither of them tries to scare the viewer into obeying, unlike the terrifying angry money-throwing man in the Direct Line Home Insurance commercials, who'll make an excellent alternative Bond villain one day.

Irritating phenomenon of the year was, of course, the Budweiser 'whassup' ads; the initial, mildly amusing lo-fi opening 'episode' soon turned out to be merely the opening salvo in a cynical pre-mapped campaign designed to bully its catchphrase into the mouths and minds of imbeciles nationwide.

If you – yes, *you* – greeted a friend with 'whassup' just once – yes, *once* – then congratulations: you're an inexcusable dunce. Please make the most of the festive season by drinking yourself to death (but don't pick Budweiser; it'll make you fat and take far too long).

Welcome back to part two. Now, if there's a particular genre that really took off during 2000, it's the iconic retrospective clip show. All year long the schedules heaved beneath the collective weight of thousands of tiny footage blips jostling for position alongside patronising soundbites from Paul Ross (shtick: blokey enthusiasm), Stuart Maconie (shtick: sarcastic nit-picker), Phil Jupitus (shtick: scripted one-liners) and if you were really unlucky, 'entertainment journalist' Rick Sky (shtick: looking like he'd been shaken awake in a shop doorway and ordered to enter a Malcolm McLaren lookalike competition).

What with *I Love the Seventies* (BBC2), *100 Greatest Moments from TV Hell* (C4), *It Shouldn't Happen to a Chat Show Host* (ITV), *The TV Years* (Sky One), *Top Ten* (C4), the completely useless *Smash*

(ITV) and countless theme-night 'celebrations' of everything from David Frost to Morphy Richards (probably), trying to watch a single channel felt more like flicking through 600 variations on UK Gold in a green room full of sneering B-list celebrities, rendered even more depressing by the knowledge that in 20 years' time you'll be tuning into watch Ant and Dec's sniggering offspring introduce archive footage of Paul Ross discussing archive footage of *fingerbobs*.

So was there anything worth watching? Of course there was, notable examples being *Black Books*, *The Sopranos*, *Jam*, *Louis Theroux's Weird Weekends* and, of course, *Renegade*, the abysmal 80s throwback action series which looks like a cross between a Patrick Swayze movie and a Jon Bon Jovi video and goes out on ITV at about 3 a.m. or whenever you're least expecting it.

Now, let's wave goodbye to grumpy old 2000 and welcome the arrival of a sunny, smiling 2001. We could all do with a laugh, so look forward to Simon Munnery's *Attention, Scum* (BBC2) and with any luck, a big-budget Jerry Sadowitz Channel Five vehicle that'll make up for *The Jerry Atrick Show* being shot on tuppence.

That's it. Now run along and enjoy yourselves. Oh, and if you only picked this up to watch while digesting your Christmas lunch, then tough: they're showing *Octopussy* (ITV).

PART TWO   2001

In which Simon Cowell makes his debut, Jim Davidson's Generation Game *makes a poor impression, and* Touch the Truck *heralds a new golden age of television.*

Roly-Poly Piddlebox Paul   [6 January]

Got Sky digital? Or an ON Digital box? Yes? Great! Quick! Turn to
Discovery Wings – the exciting digital channel dedicated solely to
aviation documentaries – you might just get there in time to catch
Flight Deck: DC9-41.

And hoo-boy, it shurrr does sound like a treat: according to the
listings it's an in-depth look at the flight deck of the DC-9 and the
MD-80 aircraft. For a whole half-hour! Here's hoping they show us
which button makes the thingy flap do that flappy thing.

Naturally, there's stiff competition from the other digital stations:
why, at any moment you could tickle the remote and watch Yvette
Fielding doling out DIY tips in *Simply DIY* (Granada Breeze), Alan
Coxon preparing aubergine fritters in *Coxon's Kitchen College* (Carl-
ton Food Network), or Paul Coia sitting in a trough full of urine,
rolling marbles down the inside of a scaffolding pole in 'Roly-Poly
Piddlebox Paul' (Distraction Network).

Of course that Paul Coia vehicle was a figment of my imagination. But you knew that anyway – it was the only one that sounded
remotely interesting. Question is, who's watching the other programmes? Answer: everyone with a digibox – but only for a
nanosecond, as they flutter from station to station, grazing acres of
vacuum television in search of a watchable programme that somehow never arrives.

Where are they, these elusive nuggets of must-see TV? Somehow
they're never around when you need them. And even when they
are, you just can't latch on. Take tonight's schedules; at 6.30 p.m.
there's the first-ever episode of *Rising Damp* on Granada Plus.
Should be interesting, but I'll watch for five minutes before my
trigger finger twitches – 6.30 in the evening is too early to settle
down to a single channel for a whole half-hour, and besides, aren't
they showing that Bill Murray comedy which doesn't sound very
good, but you might want to watch anyway, on one of the movie
channels at the same time? (Yes: *The Man Who Knew Too Little*, Sky
MovieMax.)

Of course, that's no solution. Lingering at the back of my mind is the knowledge that said film will be rebroadcast ad nauseam, so I'm under no obligation to watch it right now: one hour in, and during an inevitable slow patch I'm likely to bring up the channel menu and idly browse for an alternative. Ooh: at 7 p.m., Eminem's choosing two hours of video programming on MTV (EMTV). That'll stave off the boredom for a moment. I'll get back to the movie later . . .

Hundreds of channels in crystal-clear digivision, and I can only procrastinate about the stuff I want to see, even while I'm seeing it. The one thing I would stay put for is a welcome repeat of *It's Garry Shandlings's Show* on the Paramount Comedy Channel – but that's on at 3 a.m., and I'm not that carefree nocturnal scamp I used to be. I need pre-midnight dazzlement.

So I slump there, static, staring, prodding, fritzing one image onto the next. An MTV video ends and an advert begins: a soft-metal compilation with a leather-clad catwoman pirouetting through a warehouse of fire and chains. At one minute long, it's too much to bear. Fetch the remote and enter freefall. There goes *Knots Landing*. There's a man grilling tuna. She's pretty. Don't want to buy one of those. That is Keith Barron. Not *Fargo* again. Phonebox vandalism is a sport? Couldn't eat a whole Poirot. Didn't he used to be Kelly Monteith?

And so on and so on, until the programmes I contemplated have ended unseen, and I feel so empty inside you could screw a handle to my back and use me as a cupboard.

How long before my remote has a 'random play' feature that automatically carousels its way through every channel at a rate I can barely withstand? Or, if it's truly attempting to mimic my viewing habits, repeatedly fiddles with the widescreen settings in an obsessive bid to fill as much of the screen as possible without rendering everything hopelessly horizontally elongated (am I the only person in the country who can't watch 14:9 ratio broadcasts on a 16:9 screen without feeling drunk or irritable?).

Fuck progress. There's too much choice and I'm sick of it. Take the extra channels away. Just leave me the regulation five.

And smash that remote while you're at it. Let me stand up and prod when I want to flip sides. My muscles are turning to limp strips of tripe and according to the Health Channel I must work out or die.

Multiplex Livestock   [13 January]

Fame! They want to live for ever!

Who? Why, the glory-chasing wannabes of *Popstars* (ITV), of course – ITV's prime-time approximation of *Making the Band*, 'the boy band genesis' documentary Channel 4 used to air on Sunday lunchtime; the show about which I said the following back in November: 'Note to anyone working on a British version of *Making the Band*: stop what you're doing right now. Just put your hands down and walk away. Please. Or there'll be an uprising, and we're talking heads-on-poles.'

And did they listen? No. The arrogance!

Still it's here now, so we might as well get used to the idea, which is this: a trio of talent scouts tour the country auditioning an end-less procession of potential teenage pop icons, slowly whittling them down from 16 billion amateur shriekers to five polished automatons, while we sit on the sofa enjoying the inevitable humil-iation that occurs en route.

Two initial impressions. First: tragically, this is nowhere as hideous as *Making the Band*. Yet.

MTB centred exclusively on a dizzyingly hateful boy band full of preening Yank jockboys with names like Eric and Brett and Shunt and Testosterone Zitpop Jr. *Popstars* is packed with UK multiplex livestock rather than US mallrat scum. Plus it's got girls in it. The final line-up is likely to consist of fresh-faced interchangeables called Sarah, Sandra, Lorraine, Simon and Tom, and it's going to be far harder to get wound up by them, in the same way that getting annoyed by S Club 7 is a bit like waving your fist at a Lakeland Plas-tics catalogue.

Second, and more worryingly, some of the participants show signs of being genuinely likeable – such as Claire, the uncompro-mising chunky Scot with the powerful voice. In order to enjoy *Pop-stars*, the viewer should ignore any glimmer of congeniality emanating from a contestant at all costs. Concentrate on Darius, the slick-haired beanpole who manages to combine inarguably strong vocals with a nauseating overconfidence that makes you want to tattoo an indelible 'kick me' sign on his back, so that one day, years from now, a disaffected orderly in an old folks' home will spot it during bath time and plant their foot so far up his arse it'll get jammed between his vertebrae.

Still, at least he can sing, unlike the 18 zillion no-hopers rejected last week by Nigel Lythgoe, talent scout extraordinaire.

Ahh, Nigel. Glamour with its shirt tucked in. He looks like a man ordering gammon steak in a motorway service station. He looks like Eric Idle watching a dog drown. He's got faintly sad eyes, the world's least fashionable hair, and the complexion of a man who's held his hair out the window of a speeding car for the past two days. Standing before the tide of wannabes, he exudes deflated insincerity with every glance, each gentle dismissal of a shivering tune-dodger followed up with a deadpan backstage barb regarding their overall worthlessness.

And he's right: most are rubbish. Of the instant losers, the boys in particular all appeared identical – each resembling an anxious Dixons trainee moving limply in for the kill on a damp Saturday afternoon. The girls at least displayed emotion by bursting into tears and shouting bleepwords at the moment of jettison.

(How come winners and losers alike deem it necessary to adopt the same hideous homogenised transatlantic 'singing voice' when they perform? You know the one – Robbie Williams uses it permanently, and it knocks all the soul from a tune with the brutal efficiency of a carpet-beater.)

Yes, *Popstars* is pretty mindless; yes, it's yet another programme that insists on treating the canon of Ronan Keating/Robbie Williams/Celine Dion with wholly undeserved respect, and yes it's exploitative, but hoo, boy – can't you feel the SADISM?

Despise the aforementioned megastars? Then tune in to this week's instalment, as several hundred fame-chasers have their dreams bent, shattered, cracked and pissed on by Nigel and co. – then televised for the whole world to see? Yuk yuk!

And when the final five are in place, we can settle down to some agony and in-fighting. Then slag off their records together.

Right there's where they start paying. In sweat.

Out in the Digital Neverwhere [20 January]

Anyone who enjoys watching sport on television is an imbecile; a dangle-mouthed, cud-chewing, salivating ding-dong with a brain full of dim piss, blobbing out in front of a box watching a grunting thicko knock a ball round a field while their own sad carcass gently coagulates into a wobbling mass of beer and fat and thick white heart-attack gravy.

That's my opinion anyway, which is why I wasn't the slightest bit annoyed when Sky began gulping up all the major sporting events, whisking them away from the terrestrial networks to be sealed inside a trio of peek-a-boo pay channels I'd be perfectly happy to hurl at the moon. The less sport on mainstream TV the better – it leaves more room for truly entertaining stuff, like comedy.

Except it doesn't. To the terrestrial audience, comedy's turned invisible. Oh, it's still being made all right, but it's lurking off the corner of your screen, out in the digital neverwhere with the sport and the pop and the documentaries about skirting boards. New comedy is getting banished to the wilderness of cable and satellite, where it's forced to fight over scraps until it's considered mighty and strong enough to be allowed back inside Terrestrial Kingdom.

This is the age of the 'feed channel' – digital offshoots of major networks that nurture and develop new shows until they're ready to be broadcast by the mothership. BBC Choice, ITV2 and the freshly minted E4 all function as feeders to some extent. A good idea? Well, yes and no.

Case in point: *Attention, Scum* on BBC Choice; perhaps the finest title for any television programme ever, and a potentially brilliant show clearly handicapped by a restrictive budget. It stars Simon Munnery (as the League Against Tedium), using a relentless multimedia lecture to remorselessly bully laughs from your mouth in the manner of a SWAT team tossing tear gas through a window to force a suspect into the line of fire.

And at first, it's thrilling – stark captions declare the viewer to be a teeny speck of awful nothing, while Munnery loudly demands that you 'pay attention'. Cut to Munnery atop a transit van, bemusing passers-by with salvo after salvo of smart aphorisms and cheap jokes, bellowed like the commands of a terrifying robot god. Cut to a weird sketch with Kevin Eldon. Cut to some rude opera. Cut to a piece of wilfully crude quasi-animation, accompanied by another bellowed lecture. Cut back to the transit van. And so on and so on. After half an hour of relentless shouting, you've just about had enough: it's all too one-note, like being cornered on a stairwell by an entertaining madman while a Styrofoam cup of coffee burns the palm of your hand.

But invention and ability aren't the problem: time and money are. Sketch shows are phenomenally expensive, which is one reason why running gags using a single character and location feature so heavily: you can shoot loads of them at once, thereby freeing up time and money to lavish on your one-off set pieces.

Attention, Scum seems to have a budget capable of sustaining a small collection of lo-fi running gags and little else: as a result there's too much enforced repetition – leaving each half-hour edition feeling more like three 10-minute broadcasts crammed together.

It doubtless cost twenty times as much as Munnery's previous digital shows – *FuturTV* and *Either/Or*, both created for music and comedy channel PlayUK for about 16 pence. The cheaper the show, the harder everyone connected with it has to work: Munnery must be knackered. Someone give him the money to do it properly before the poor bugger keels over.

In other news, *Popstars* (ITV) continues to amuse and appal, despite last week's edition being practically identical to the first. From here on in it starts to get nasty. And there's also the prospect of the finished band being named by a public vote – the Australians went for the dull-sounding Bardot when the series ran down-under, so we owe it to ourselves to pick a more suitable, memorable moniker.

Your suggestions will be gratefully received – e-mail them in, and I'll announce the finest. To get you started, my initial suggestions are as follows: 1) Synchronised Yelping Head Multiplex, 2) Songy-Wongy, 3) Funtrocity, 4) Sweatshop Jailbait, and 5) Misery Distraction Patrol. But you can do better. Get scribbling.

Spiritual Liposuction [27 January]

Kids today, eh? They've had all the innocence sucked out of them, like they've undergone some kind of spiritual liposuction operation. You know it's true. You've heard them at the back of the bus, swapping *Fight Club* stories and the kind of filthy anecdotes that could get you thrown off an oil rig. You've seen them knocking each other insensible in the playgrounds, gleefully twirling nunchakas, biting and kicking like uniformed participants in a special dwarves edition of 'Tekken'. They're scary.

As a 10-year-old, the mere mention of the word 'fart' was enough to make me giggle until milk came out of my nose, even when I wasn't drinking any; a modern 10-year-old wouldn't laugh unless they were carving it into a pensioner's forehead with the lid of an old tin can. I was once so frightened by a midnight showing of *King Kong* on BBC2, I spent a largely sleepless night with my head tucked under the duvet, half-expecting to be attacked by an animated gorilla. These days the average primary-school child can sit through thirteen consecutive hours of 3D bestial porn on a WAP-enabled Internet bong without so much as blinking.

Blame television. Go on. Never before have kids been presented with such an endless stream of glamorous images they don't have a hope of living up to. When you realise, age nine, that you're far too ugly and normal to be in S Club 7, you figure you might as well spend the rest of your life flicking snot at the walls, shouting 'Bollocks to everything' every six seconds. And who can blame you?

Here is hope. *Grange Hill* (BBC1) is still going. And it's just as good as it used to be. Better, in fact. Of course, it's changed a bit. Don't worry, they haven't replaced the famous 'hurled-sausage-on-a-fork' from the opening titles with a severed penis impaled on a syringe, although the iconic 'comic strip' sequence and twangy signature tune are long gone – replaced by a nondescript visual collage and a theme tune which, unless I'm mistaken, is a weedy plinky-plonk cover version of the theme from *Cagney and Lacey*.

To these weary eyes, most of the kids look identical to one another but that's probably got more to do with my age than their faces, which seem to blur into one creaseless, eyebag-free wash of young flesh after 10 minutes. Nevertheless, a few stand out, traditional *Grange Hill* archetypes: the evil one (who's selling cigarettes to the little kids), the pair of scheming loveable chancers (this week trying their hand at busking), the 'weird' kid (apparently autistic), the male and female heart-throbs (you never get over your first *Grange Hill* crush), and the kids with the problems at home (a boy with a dad in prison, and two girls whose parents are splitting up).

Some other traditions hold firm: the teachers are just quirky enough to appear eccentric without being sinister, and the sixth-form teens remain the most crashingly tedious, self-righteous shop-window dummies on earth.

The changes, then – starting with the pace, which has been upped considerably (lots of short, snappy scenes), and the camera-work, which is more stylised and energetic than ever before. Almost every sequence seems to end with a visual punchline: a sudden jump to an overhead shot, or an arrangement of pupils so symmetrical you could be forgiven for thinking you'd stumbled across an unreleased Peter Greenaway film (albeit one far less tedious and with at least 86 per cent less Philip Glass).

It works. It draws you in and keeps you entertained. It's nowhere near as patronising as, say, *Casualty*, and it treats its audience with 16 million times more respect than any ITV drama starring Ross Kemp (a man who always looks like he's trying to win a staring competition with a couple of knotholes). Best of all, it simply doesn't have time for any of the self-obsessed, navel-gazing designer angst of 'youth' favourites such as *Dawson's Creek*. Long may it reign.

Last week's request for names for the final *Popstars* band drew an encouraging response. So far, printable highlights include: 1) Enterpainment, 2) Dry Dream, 3) Vacant Lot, 4) Orchestrated Plebian Wonder Machine, 5) Stairs, 6) The Flipchart Demographics, and my favorite to date: 7) Nigel.

Faceless Dolls   [2 February]

Shipwrecked 2 (C4) marks a turning point for reality television: the point where outright boredom smothers any voyeuristic appeal.

Here's the premise: take seventeen youngsters, maroon them on a desert island for ten weeks, then stand well back and see what they do.

And here's what happens: they flirt and argue.

The viewer is expected to find this mesmerising. Why? What's the big deal? Strand seventeen youngsters at a bus stop for ten minutes and they'll flirt and argue just as much. Why bother zipping them halfway round the world – especially when they're essentially as bland as a bunch of bathmats?

Answer: because it's a good excuse to film them frolicking about in swimwear. Most of the castaways appear to have been chosen on the strength of their looks, giving the entire exercise the feel of a strange feral edition of *Hollyoaks*, albeit one with fewer sympathetic characters – on the whole the boys are the most irksome: a blend of bratty I'm-the-leader public-school types, and unapologetic lads whose idea of a civilised afternoon probably revolves around scrawling comedy dicks in the margins of 'Bum Hair Monthly'.

Still, they're young; they're allowed to be dumb. Perhaps it's just a phase they're going through. *Shipwrecked* may be irritating, but it isn't their fault.

So what's the problem? Isn't it interesting to see how they cope with the harsh realities of survivalism? Somehow, no. Well, surely you godda admit it's kinda fascinating seeing the group dynamic crumble as island life gets tougher, right? Once again, the answer is no: they just come across as a group of bickering idiots – and the programme's to blame. It's deliberately structured like an argument factory – a situation contrived to provoke irritation and confrontation. You could achieve similar results by locking the castaways in a warehouse in Bristol, making them wear hessian sacks and flicking rice in their ears. It might kill off the flirting, but by God there'd be some cracking rows. Plus it would be funnier than watching someone in a grass skirt munching a coconut.

So why did they make *Shipwrecked 2* at all? Because too many people believe anything vaguely confrontational immediately equals 'good television'. Yes, as any twinkle-eyed pop-culture spoonbrain will attest, it's 'good television' to strand a bunch of wannabe loudmouths in the middle of nowhere and watch them squabble and bicker until your ears ring to bursting point with their bleatings. It doesn't have to make you think, it doesn't have to lift your spirits – it only has to keep you staring at the box in the corner of the room. Any old antagonistic crap will do, provided it's nicely packaged and slung at your eyeballs.

Thing is, it is entirely possible to make a youth-oriented reality show that entertains more than it infuriates, as proven by ongoing smash *Popstars* (ITV), which benefits heavily from skilful editing and a sprinkling of sympathetic participants, although ever since Darius got the shove any incentive to tune in has plummeted.

Yes, Darius. Stop your protests: his fame is entirely deserved. He'd be the finest comic creation for ages, if it weren't for the fact that he's real. Last week's interview in which he described his plan to dive headlong into the shallow world of fame and materialism 'to see if I can change it (slow blink, loaded pause) and if I can't . . . at least I'll know I tried' is unlikely to be topped as the laugh-out-loud-moment of the year.

It's a crying shame he's gone, but hooray: your suggestions for band names continue to flood in. Top ten from the mailbag this week: 10) Queens of the Stone Deaf, 9) Cliché and the Sunshine Brand, 8) Processed Cheese, 7) Ploy Division, 6) . . . And You Will Find Us In the Bargain Bin, 5) Boxfresh Gibbon Kidz, 4) Freebase Aspartame, 3) Dad Erector – but sitting pretty at the top of the pops, two suggestions culled from a genuine press release regarding official *Popstars* merchandise, which arrived alongside your fictional entries: ' . . . Amongst the companies keen to exploit the band's inevitable popularity is Character Options, who have been appointed exclusive distributors of the *Popstars* dolls. Faceless dolls will be unveiled at the largest toy trade show of the year . . . the dolls will appear in their official outfits but remain faceless until the final band line-up is revealed.'

Can't argue with that: so at number 2) it's Character Options, and at number 1) – in with a bullet! – Faceless Dolls.

Pick a favourite: vote now.

'You're watching *Breakfast*'   [10 February]

Never trust a morning person. Anyone who leaps out of bed with a smile on their face and a spring in their step is deranged. And breakfast television is aimed at these lunatics. It must be: who the hell else has time to watch TV in the morning? Most of us are still in bed, pawing blearily at the snooze button until it's too late to procrastinate further and we have to head bogwards for the first and darkest piddle of the day.

Here's the ideal breakfast TV show, one that would work brilliantly on that 14-inch portable at the base of your bed: an abstract collage of soothing shapes and colours undulating in time to some muffled ambient throb, suddenly interrupted half an hour later by a maniac with a foghorn shrieking 'LATE FOR WORK!' at the top of his voice.

But that isn't on, so what are your options? Well, BBC1 has a rolling new programme called *Breakfast*. Not 'Breakfast News', or 'Breakfast Report', or 'Breakfast Briefing': just *Breakfast* – which means the presenters sometimes say, 'Good morning, you're watching *Breakfast*.' Weird.

It gets weirder: *Breakfast* is described as a 'relaxed' current-affairs show – which means you're confronted with newsreaders sitting on a sofa. Newsreaders who smile and want to be your friend. They grin a parental grin as you stumble into the room, still dazed from dreamland, blinking, yawning, and scratching at your hair. Look! They've poured you a mug of coffee and fanned the day's papers across the table. They're watching you with the serene patience of cult members.

'Hello. Hope you slept OK. You did? Hey, that's great!'

You notice the breezy colour scheme and the onscreen clock in the corner. The one that tells the time in *that* typeface, that impersonal font the brand-conscious Beeb use for everything these days. Your hosts pause and emit a loud cough.

'Um. Now, look – we don't want to worry you, but there was a bit of Armageddon while you were slumbering.'

Armageddon? ARMAGEDDON?

Reassuring smile.

'Yes! Isn't it exciting?'

No – God, no! Don't let this happen. We don't want laid-back newsreaders flopping about on sofas, cutting us knobbly slices of rustic bread. It isn't right. We want stern-faced Peter Sissons types sitting bolt upright and staring straight through our skulls, booming information like a 500-foot Tannoy of the Apocalypse. Unless there's a major news event billowing, you'd have to be crazy to watch *Breakfast* voluntarily. It's just too bloody creepy.

On ITV, *GMTV* decants its standard blend of celebutainment, human-interest stories and garish background fauna; just behind the sofa, peeping o'er the presenters' shoulders, lurk the sort of floral arrangements usually depicted on canisters of Shake 'n' Vac. Fitting, since if *GMTV* had a smell, it would be lavender – the antiseptic, chemical lavender that wafts from cheap plastic air-fresheners and vaguely reminds you of hospitals and death. Good morning, Britain!

In the absence of scent-broadcast technology, they have to make do with undemanding interviews with celebrity guests, who generally look about as comfortable as someone trying to rectally ingest an entire garden rake. And who can blame them: woken at the crack of dawn, perched on the edge of a sofa in a brightly lit set apparently modelled on a Travelodge lobby, answering questions too bland to pass muster in a *Marketing Now* readership survey, half the interviewees seem too oddballed out to know what's happening. It's useless until Lorraine Kelly comes on, useless.

Then there's Channel 4 and the revamped *Big Breakfast*, whose set now resembles a cross between a Hanna-Barbera space station and one of those trendy London bars that looks more like a diagram than a watering hole.

New frontman Paul Tonkinson is good, being both funny and reassuringly ugly. His face is at rest most of the time, but every so often it springs into 'gurn' mode and looks as though it's about to leap off his head and go beat up some daffodils; in full grimace he starts to resemble one of the melting Nazis from the end of the *Raiders of the Lost Ark*.

One glaring problem: the programme is rendered nigh-on unwatchable by the relentless offscreen bellowing of the crew, who accompany every utterance with gibbonoid barking and laughs so forced they've probably been dislodged with a broom. Shut up: you sound like witless old drunks at a megaphone convention on the Planet of the Apes, and some of us are trying to listen.

There you have it: breakfast television. I vote for oversleeping every time. Prise off that snooze button: you may wind up unemployed, but you'll never see Eamon Holmes again.

The Low End of the Stupidity Spectrum   [24 February]

I'm a dimwit. I'm a dufus. I am not a Clever Man. Sometimes I'll be sitting round a table with people cleverer than I, and as their conversation wanders into the realms of *Roget's Thesaurus*, I find myself struggling to keep up, so instead I nod and smile and stare at the fruit machine and pray they'll find their way back to discussing a topic I can relate to, like 'Battle of the Planets' or things that would hurt if you sat on them accidentally.

Many, many things go clean over my head. But *Jim Davidson's Generation Game* (BBC1) is the first thing that's ever gone under it. As a child, I watched Larry Grayson's tenure, and found the programme dull but easy to follow. Now it's transformed into something I simply don't understand. In trying to appeal to the lowest common denominator, the entire show has managed to drop off the low end of the stupidity spectrum, to a point where the human brain is incapable of interpreting its signal.

Once the cacophonous signature tune has died down, cheeky

Jim scampers onstage, winking and twitching like a man with a fishhook in his glans, and immediately launches into a fractured comic pantomime of such awkward, ill-conceived clunkiness, you can't help but wonder whether it's been scripted by a human with a laptop or a dog with a Fisher-Price Activity Centre.

Assisting him are gaudy assistant Melanie Stace (the pair crackle with the kind of instant chemistry you'd more readily associate with a meeting between Peter Sissons and Roland Rat) and loveable pratfall king Mister Blobby (swear to God, stick your ear out the window the moment he bounds into view and you can hear the faint, descending murmur of a nationwide moan of dismay).

Of course it doesn't help that the frontman brings so much baggage with him. Even forgetting the hateful, hackneyed nature of the opening comic skits for a moment, it's hard to warm to this widely demonised comic – unless of course you're an imbecile, in which case you're probably too busy gurgling at Blobby, and the show could just as well be hosted by a bit of rag on a stick for all you care.

Actually, that's not a bad idea, for three reasons: 1) A bit of rag on a stick would be 100 per cent less likely to saunter around the set casually patronising women (last week, virtually the only occasion he resisted the urge to call a female contestant 'love' or 'darling' it was to call her a 'stupid woman' instead). 2) It would also be easier on the eye. If you ask me, Davidson's got a creepy head, all tight and desiccated, like a length of vinyl 'woodgrain effect' wall covering, topped with a haircut that seems to have taken place by accident. 3) A bit of rag on a stick would be funny.

But enough about Davidson himself. The whole concept of the *Generation Game* feels spiteful and cold. Skits and challenges exist as an excuse for Z-grade celebrities and grubby salespersons to plug themselves; presumably the reason they agreed to stand next to Jim in the first place, although it's hard to believe anyone could consider this effective advertising – it's like glimpsing a commercial flyer bobbing in a cesspool. The hapless contestants are rarely asked to speak – they're just jostled and humiliated, grinning like dunces, their dignity round their knees, all for the chance to sit in front of a conveyor belt watching the contents of the Argos catalogue scroll by. This junk doesn't belong on TV a moment longer: it should be stuffed down a hole and destroyed.

On the other side, *Popstars* (ITV) is eating itself, as it charts the effect its own success is having on the five dullards that maketh the band. But all the suspense has vanished. They're even trailing it with the words '*Popstars* – it's far from over', when it quite clearly is. Doesn't look like they'll be using any of your suggested band names, either: I've chosen the final winner: Dad Erector. Congratulations to Mellors Karloff, who suggested it, although I suspect that isn't your real name. This correspondence is now closed.

Oh, before I go: just realised that Nigel Lythgoe is the absolute spit of Admiral Ackbar from *Return of the Jedi* – you know, the lobster-headed one in the Rebel control room during the battle at the end. It's true. Tell your friends.

Inadequate and Miserable [3 March]

There's this theory that television is depressing us all. By pumping images of successful, beautiful, witty people into your home around the clock, it forces you to compare your humdrum existence with the knockabout lives of the onscreen funsters, even the fictional ones. Since real life can't compare to fantasy life, you wind up feeling inadequate and miserable – and the more inadequate and miserable you feel, the more television you watch, and the more boring your life becomes. Plus, you're inert, so you start to get fat. Before you know it, your fingers are too chubby to successfully stab the 'off' button on the remote control, and you're doomed to spend the rest of your days slumped in front of the box like a semi-deflated hot-air balloon, occasionally breaking into a sweat as you struggle to open the day's thirtieth packet of bourbon creams.

If this is the case, our ongoing obsession with handsome celebrities starts to look downright masochistic. It also explains why over the last two years I've become a) averse to watching slim, good-looking people, b) pudgier, and c) sick to the tits of bourbon creams. It's self-defence.

One unexpected side effect is that I've started actively warming to any unconventional-looking humanoid who makes it on TV. With more and more presenters being chosen on the basis of their looks alone (the only logical explanation for Donna Air), the homely ones are getting rarer, and therefore easier to spot. You can also guarantee they're going to be good at their job; after all, with a face like that, they'd have to be.

Take Alan Titchmarsh; he may look like something looming unexpectedly at a porthole in a Captain Nemo movie, but he's friendly, engaging, and he knows his subject matter inside out. But you won't be seeing his photograph on the cover of *Heat* magazine – partly because it'd curdle the milk in the newsagent's tea, and partly because customers might mistake it for 'Hobbit Monthly', but mainly because he isn't young and attractive enough. Oh, and because they don't cover gardening either. That might have something to do with it. But I digress.

As I say, for the last few years I've avoided watching anything peopled with pretty faces, on the grounds it might make me weep down my gut. One show I swerved away from in particular was *Dawson's Creek* (C4), but recently I've found myself 'getting into' it, seemingly by osmosis.

First it just happened to be on in the same room as me. Someone else was watching, while I pottered around, grumpily hunting for an Ab Roller Plus, pausing every so often to snort disdainfully whenever someone said something heartfelt. Then I discovered I'd accidentally learnt the names of several key characters. Then one day, somehow, I realised with a start that I'd sat down and watched the entire programme from start to finish, without an ironic sneer cracking across my head for a second. Now it's a guilty pleasure. And you know what? I don't care. Naturally, I still despise Dawson himself, for the following reasons:

1) He looks precisely – precisely – like the featureless lead in any bland Disney cartoon you care to mention. In fact, I suspect he's actually a piece of incredibly sophisticated computer animation

developed to play the lead in 'Toy Story 3'. He's probably got a hidden 'cheat mode' where his head spins round and breathes fire. Still, he's obviously a work-in-progress; with any luck once they've finished beta-testing he'll actually be capable of pulling facial expressions.

2) His character is boring. So boring in fact, they could replace him with a damp oven glove, and call it 'Oven Glove's Creek', and it would probably liven things up a bit. Thankfully, even the other characters have noticed how boring he is, and started deserting him for his best friend. Well, one did, anyway, and that was his girlfriend, so ha ha ha, Dawson! Take that, dullo!

3) Everyone else who watches *Dawson's Creek* dislikes Dawson as well, and I'm trying to fit in here, OK?

Still, I think the programme is helping me overcome my aversion to anything popular that features a good-looking cast. Emboldened, I've recently started re-appraising *Shipwrecked* (C4), which I laid into a few weeks ago in these very pages.

I say 're-appraising'. What I actually mean is 'unironically watching'. Yes: that's sucked me in as well, and I can only hold my hands up and apologise to all concerned.

So now I'm not just developing the viewing habits of a teenager, I'm an appalling hypocrite to boot. And that's depressing me. You can't win. Where are the bourbon creams?

An Exciting Journey into the Unknown [10 March]

Glance through the TV schedules and you might mistake present-day TV producers for a pack of coked-up jackals happy to sling any old hoo-hah at the screen so long as their cheque arrives on time and they're still in with a shot at that good-looking 22-year-old runner they've had their eye on for the past six weeks.

You couldn't be more wrong. In fact, TV people care too much about their output. They fret over the tiniest details: Is that word too long? Is this subject too dry? Have we got a higher-quality close-up of the blood leaking out? Why has the runner brought me regular Lilt, instead of the Diet Lilt I asked for? How quickly can I sack her? Will she still sleep with me afterwards? And so on.

In fact, they worry so much about the minutiae of the content, they often lose sight of the bigger picture. Instead of asking themselves, 'Is this new?', 'Is this ground-breaking?', they think, 'Is this suitable for our viewing demographic?', and creativity flounders and the world's joy supply trickles further down the drain.

But it doesn't have to be that way. There are still those willing to take a risk, to chance their arm on a show so original, so utterly innovative, it shatters the epoch, pushes the envelope, and heralds the dawn of a new era all at the same time. Ladies and gentlemen: *Touch the Truck* (C5) is almost upon us, and it will change the face of broadcasting for ever.

Finally, someone somewhere has twigged that it's entirely possible to transmit simply anything – absolutely anything – and boom! you've made a prime-time television programme. By default.

The concept couldn't be simpler. Gather twenty contestants. Drive them to the Lakeside Shopping Centre in Thurrock. Get them to gather round a brand new truck worth over £30,000. Then ask them each to place one hand on it. Tell them the last contestant to take their hand away wins the vehicle.

Oh, they're not allowed to sleep, of course, so by day three they might well be sobbing, collapsing or hallucinating. But that's all part of the fun. At this point, I'd like to interrupt this sentence to remind you that this programme is entirely real. And wait, it gets better: one of the contestants is a 42-year-old homeless man called Jimmy who plans to stay awake by 'singing Elvis songs in his head'. Woo-hoo. Other contestants include a zany vicar, a Kosovan refugee, a tattooed Cockney and a 'flirty clubber'. In other words, all human life is here. And it's standing round a truck.

The show is scheduled to run live over six days, starting tomorrow. There's a 40-minute update broadcast every evening, or you can witness the inaction unfolding live on the web, 24 hours. Why not keep a window open permanently on your computer desktop? Hopefully there'll be a live audio feed too, so you'll be able to hear them weeping softly in the background while you toy with Microsoft Excel.

Disappointingly, there are a few minor concessions to basic human dignity, presumably included to appease the United Nations. Contestants are allowed one 10-minute toilet break every two hours (we're in for a treat if someone gets diarrhoea), and one 15-minute food break every six hours. They also have a 'co-pilot': a friend who's on hand to offer encouragement and back-rubs. Thankfully, they're also allowed to try and put each other off by saying sarcastic things and generally annoying one another, which shouldn't be too hard, since chronic sleep deprivation tends to make people a bit irritable.

Our host is Dale Winton, who, according to producer Glenn Barden, 'brings an air of credibility' to proceedings. Dale reckons *Touch the Truck* is 'an exciting journey into the unknown'. He'll be chatting to sleep experts and interviewing the contestants, who, incidentally, should become increasingly incoherent as their minds attempt to cling on to consciousness, like a drowning man clutching at pieces of driftwood after five days at sea. Apparently we can expect the participants to start dreaming while awake – a feeling the audience at home should be able to closely empathise with, as they struggle to remind themselves that what they're looking at is real.

So there you have it. Don't know about you, but I've been rubbing my hands together with anticipation so hard I've taken the skin off my palms. After *Touch the Truck*, British television can go anywhere, do anything. Dale's right. This truly is 'an exciting journey into the unknown'. And you should be glad you're alive to witness it.

Why Am I Thinking about Knives in the Head?
[17 March]

I've never tried to stab someone through the skull with a knife, but I imagine it requires a great deal of skill. Without a steady hand, the aim of an Olympic marksman and, above all, an immensely powerful swing, it'd be all too easy for the blade to ricochet off a knobbly bit of skull, sending the dagger spinning out of your hand and leaving you looking like the biggest prick in the room come the next murderers' convention; worse even than that bloke in the corner who tried to batter his own brother to death with a handful of breadcrumbs.

Why am I thinking about knives in the head? Because it's hard not to after watching *Ouch!* (C5), a documentary that gleefully examines some of the most excruciatingly painful things that can happen to a human body. The knife-in-the-skull incident occurs early on, with the tale of Atlantan Michael Hill, whose life changed for ever the day a next-door neighbour decided to settle a dispute by turning up at the front door to plunge an eight-inch hunting knife into the top of Michael's head, burying it hilt-deep in his mind. Inevitably, a camera crew were waiting down at ER, so we're assailed by garish footage of him lolling about with the knife jutting out of his head, like a man going to a fancy-dress party as the sword in the stone.

The X-rays are remarkable, with the full length of the knife picked out with ghoulish clarity, looking as absurdly incongruous against its surroundings as a battleship in a cheese sandwich. Astonishingly, the blade somehow slid between vital arteries in the brain and Hill made a full recovery, although in his memory all numbers are divided in two and his friends have the top of their heads sliced off like poorly framed family snaps.

Now, people have different ways of dealing with gore and, provided it's fictional, I'll lap it up, from a bowl if necessary. I love video nasties: name any household implement, and the chances are at some point I've watched someone plunging it into a zombie's eye. I've sat through films so bloody, you could actually see scabs forming on the lens.

But put me in the real world, and squeamishness rules. I get giddy looking through the transparent pane on a packet of mince. I simply can't recall ever flinching so much at a single programme as I did watching *Ouch!* – especially since the tale of Michael Hill and the bloody big knife is only the tip of an undulating iceberg of blood-spattered sinew. Over the course of an hour, you'll meet a man who tangled his genitals in the whirring spindle of a cement mixer, a girl who fell from a bedroom window and impaled herself on the leg of an upturned table in the back garden, a man who got a door hook caught under his upper eyelid, and a woman who accidentally fired a 12-inch length of metal up her nose with an industrial rivet gun. The end result is almost impossible to sit through, but if you do, rest assured you'll have accumulated more than enough to appal co-workers with come Monday morning. Commit enough grisly details to memory and I guarantee you'll be able to make someone vomit. Right there. Right on their own shoes.

Elsewhere, on the evidence of episode one alone, it's hard to know what to make of *Happiness* (BBC2), Paul Whitehouse's mid-life-crisis comedy-drama. There's precious little happiness, and only brief smatterings of (genuinely funny) comedy in it, but there is plenty of angst. Whitehouse's character spends most of his time looking miserable and staring mutely into the middle distance; an entirely visual catchphrase that on the face of it seems unlikely to prove as popular with Joe Public as saying 'Brilliant!' or 'I'll get me coat!' although if you look out the window you'll see it's already caught on and simply everybody's doing it. Brilliant!

Switch Off Now   [24 March]

I'm not afraid of flying. I'm afraid of unflying. I'm afraid of that rare moment when an aeroplane malfunctions and is instantly transformed into a mode of transport approximately 200 times less secure than a Disprin canoe; a chillingly efficient air-to-ground death missile intent on delivering you and your fellow travellers straight to the heart of splatsville, no matter how loudly you scream into one anothers' ears.

Praise be, then, for the back-of-the-seat in-flight entertainment system. What better to distract a nervous passenger from the manifest impossibility of air travel than a nine-inch LCD display screen blasting a non-stop carousel of gurglesome blockbusters and over-lit sitcoms into the eyes?

Granted, it isn't perfect – last year I was subjected to the thrill-a-minute submarine actioner *U-571* (plot: men find themselves trapped within claustrophobic metal tube; many die) at 30,000 feet, and there are also regular interruptions when the captain comes over the intercom to say we're passing over Nova Scotia at a rate beyond reason and the starboard engine's just gone up like a bonfire – but on the whole that screen is a godsend. It shuts out real life until you're safely on the ground.

In other words, TV has the same properties as Valium. And if you watch *Counterblast: Switch Off Now* (BBC2), you could become convinced it also exhibits characteristics of heroin, nicotine, cocaine, alcohol and crack, blended together to form the single most addictive, destructive drug the Western world has ever seen, one that's painlessly administered through the eyeball, leaves no visible scars and is killing society dead.

TV-as-drug metaphors are nothing new, but anti-TV crusader David Burke, presenter of this persuasive 'televisual essay' (a phrase that would make him puke bullets) prefers to adopt Kurt Vonnegut's position: that our beloved gogglebox holds much in common with the lead pipes that poisoned the ancient Romans, sending them slowly round the twist. In the course of this single half-hour programme he aims to convince you to switch off your TV set and go out and do something less boring instead for the rest of your life.

He does this in a manner familiar to anyone who's read Allen Carr's *Easy Way to Stop Smoking* – by systematically debunking commonly recited myths about television: that it's educational, relaxing, a friend to the lonely, that it binds the nation together while providing a window on a wider world, that it entertains our kids and makes our daily lives more interesting, that it's 'just another medium' and finally that, yeah, sure, most shows are rubbish but since I only watch quality programming, I'm all right, yeah?

Not according to Burke you're not. With a combination of statistics, persuasion and simple logical reasoning, he puts a convincing case for the outright elimination of television; I won't reveal his methods here – you'll have to tune in, or scour around for a copy of his excellent book *Get a Life*, from which the bulk of this broadcast is lifted verbatim. Besides, you might agree with him, thereby putting me out of a job. In fact, ignore the guy. He's a liar.

Concise, compelling and refreshingly opinionated, *Switch Off Now* further benefits from the hilarious use of archive clips displaying TV at its most goonish and moronic; presented out of context, alongside facts about homicide, depression and alienation, they start to look very sinister indeed. He even makes the Teletubbies feel like something out of *Brave New World* (Junior Edition).

By the end you're likely to have agreed with at least 70 per cent of what Burke says. But you probably won't switch off (and you definitely won't follow his recommendations to the letter and crack your box in the face with a sledgehammer the moment the credits start to roll).

Why? Well, the unfortunate irony is that Burke sets about attacking the mere existence of television in such a vastly entertaining manner your initial reaction is simply to sit there and wish shows like this were broadcast more often – programmes that actually reaffirm TV's ability to inform (not educate) and entertain, as opposed to sedate and oppress. In fact, I could quite happily watch David Burke telling me to switch off the box for the rest of my life.

The single hole in his argument is this: maybe some of the audience, who aren't all staring at their boxes from within pits of lonely isolation, enjoy their addiction – particularly when there's opinionated, thought-provoking stuff like this on. They should give him his own series.

They didn't.

'Don't let someone else make decisions for you'
[31 March]

Outrage! This week's *Top Ten* (C4) deals in banned records, and is linked, wonderfully enough, by veteran pantomime dame John Lydon, who's been stuck on 'sneer' since 1977 and isn't about to snap out of it now. Before introducing the first entry, he treats us to a mini-lecture on censorship, which naturally he's opposed to. 'Don't let someone else make decisions for you,' he commands us, thereby causing logical short circuits nationwide.

Wafting towards old age, Lydon still has the most weirdly affected delivery since Frankie Howerd – he overemphasises every word, sometimes using audible italics; it's like listening to a man sarcastically reading aloud from a poorly translated instruction manual. As usual, that now-familiar range of accusatory facial expressions, ping-ponging between camp Kenneth Williams outrage and the boggle-eyed mesmerisms of a cheap stage hypnotist accompany his vocal performance. Whenever he tires of looking askance with an eyebrow aloft, he simply leans forward to peer through the lens as if trying to read an insult scratched on your forehead in letters one millimetre high.

The countdown itself contains few surprises – Frankie Goes to Hollywood turn up, as do Gainsbourg and Birkin, the Sex Pistols (naturally), Madonna, NWA and the witless 2 Live Crew. The recent surfeit of clip shows lends a slightly overfamiliar air to proceedings – the 'Relax' 'legend' was covered in *I Love the Eighties* a few weeks ago, for instance – but this is still immensely watchable, not least because most of the contributors have something of interest to say, for once.

Accompanying the music are clips from self-consciously controversial videos, from the calculated visual outrage of 'Smack My Bitch Up' (Drugs! Nudity! Violence! Dull twenty-something media tossbores calling it fantastic!) to the loveless S&M tinkerings of Madonna's 'Erotica' promo (as arousing as watching Metal Mickey being jerked off by a calculator). Yawn, yawn, yawn – most 'shocking' videos are more irksome than upsetting, akin to teenage Marilyn Manson fans who like to think they're undermining us all by getting their eyelids pierced. Incidentally, someone should tell them they've picked the wrong idol: Manson pops up tonight, like a ghost-train skeleton, but by far the most disturbing sight of the evening is the contemporary footage of Shane MacGowan, who looks like he's accidentally banged his face against a tree 657 times in a row.

Immediately after the X-rated *Top Ten*, there's a look at another corrupting influence on our youth, and one that coloured my teenage years more than music ever did. *Thumb Candy* (C4) may be billed as an exploration of 'the history of video games', but it's far from comprehensive, concentrating heavily on the early years of arcade gaming at the expense of latter-day amusements – PlayStations barely warrant a mention, Doom and Quake don't figure at all, and Sega have been airbrushed out completely. In fact, this feels more like the opening salvo of a potentially superb three-part series rather than a one-off; my guess is the makers had a lengthier run in mind. Still, until someone comes along to give gaming the full *Nazis: A Warning From History* treatment, this will do.

Thumb Candy won't tell unashamed games dweebos anything they don't already know, but they'll find it hard not to get a kick out of seeing the creator of 'Pac-Man' recounting the game's genesis. And while it may not cover everything, what is there has been admirably researched: they've even managed to track down Matthew Smith, author of legendary Spectrum titles 'Manic Miner' and 'Jet Set Willy'. Smith made a fortune overnight, blew it almost as quickly, then went a bit funny and ran away to live in a commune in Holland.

As a gawky teen I was so astounded by the brilliance of 'Manic Miner', I used to sit and watch the demo-mode loop over for hours on end, pausing only to go to the toilet or stare at the ceiling and sigh hopelessly about the girls in my class, most of whom were out having fun with older boys who didn't waste their evenings watching a pixilated miner leap over a thistle. Smith may have wrecked my adolescent love life, but for introducing Miner Willy to the world, he deserves to be immortalised on Trafalgar Square's spare plinth. The campaign starts here.

Come Out With Your Hands Up   [7 April]

The first thing that hits you about *Meet the Popstars* (ITV) is the screaming. It's truly hysterical: either the audience really loves

Hear'Say or a man has just chased them into the studio with a hammer.

Yes, you thought you'd seen the last of *Popstars*, but it seems The Man ain't through with us yet. Welcome to a watered-down cross between *This Is Your Life* and *Summertime Special*, hosted by Davina McCall, a woman who's become omnipresent to the point where you no longer notice she's actually there, like a clock on the mantelpiece that your ear filters out after two weeks of constant tick-tocking. She really is ubiquitous: last week I glanced in a mirror and was astounded to discover she wasn't hosting my reflection.

Not long ago, Davina was easy to warm to: she was dry, clever, strong. Now she just stomps about shouting about how great everything is. It's as though her brain's been spooned out and replaced with a rotating glitterball. Come on, McCall – we know you're in there. Come out with your hands up.

Anyway, back to the show in question, and Hear'Say in particular. Reviewing the first edition of *Popstars* back in January, I wrote, 'The final line-up is likely to consist of five fresh-faced interchangeables called Sarah, Sandra, Lorraine, Simon and Tom, and it's going to be [hard] to get wound up by them, in the same way that getting annoyed by S Club 7 is a bit like waving your fist at a Lakeland Plastics catalogue.' And sure enough, while it's easy to snort at the mechanics behind them, Kym, Noel, Danny, Myleene and Suzanne themselves are proving infuriatingly hard to fully despise. Funny-looking bunch, though. Noel's head distinctly resembles an obscure computer game character called Dizzy, a cheerful cartoon egg who appeared in a string of budget platform games in the late 80s. And then there's Danny.

Picture Danny in your mind's eye for a moment. Knead some mental plasticine around and ah! there he is! He really is astonishing to behold, isn't he? Each separate component of his head appears to be engaged in a no-holds-barred fight for your undivided attention. I'd leap to my feet and applaud whether he sang through it or not.

Just as well, too, since for the duration of *Meet the Popstars*

everything – absolutely everything – is greeted with thunderous
clapping. The sight of the band's mums walking onstage to show
off old baby photos triggers deafening applause, while each musical number the band performs provokes mounting hysteria,
despite the fact that most of the time they're belting out covers –
'Bridge Over Troubled Water' ('Beerrridge Ovah Ter-Ruh-Huh-
Bulled Wahahderrr Mmmyeah'), 'Monday Monday', and a dreadful
version of 'Boogie Wonderland' that sounds like a fairground ride
dying in its sleep. If Hear'Say came on and kicked a dog to death,
they'd receive the most roof-raising ovation since Live Aid.

There's also weeping. Tears of pride and joy, dripping from the
eyes of proud relatives and acquaintances, prodded on to yap
about the flabbergasting loveliness of each band member in turn.
The greater the flood of tears, the louder the applause from the
crowd. Blub, clap, blub, clap: it's a new form of hand-operated lawn
sprinkler.

The only participant who doesn't sob is 'Nasty' Nigel Lythgoe, off
shooting the British version of *Survivor* in Borneo. Davina and the
band chat to him via satellite and pretend it's live: chinny reckon.

Since his dalliance with tabloid fame, Nigel's lost weight and that
grim haircut's disappeared (it now vaguely resembles an orderly
bird's nest). He looks less like Admiral Ackbar and more like a million dollars: at least until he smiles, at which point he reveals a grin
like a second-hand mah-jong set.

Song lyrics aside, Hear'Say themselves don't say much. They're
just sort of there. Instead of *Meet the Popstars*, they should've
called it 'Look! Look! LOOK AT THEM! THEY'RE FAMOUS!' That or
'Grin Orgy'.

'They're like bits of rope, only angrier' [14 April]

Snakes! They're like bits of rope, only angrier. Snakes are feared by
millions because a) they've been demonised by the entertainment
industry, which portrays them as emotionless predators, and b)
they look weird and awful when they try to swallow eggs.

Oh, and c) they kill about 100,000 people a year. Snake popularity is currently at an all-time low, and with westerns also out of favour there's a lack of decent serpentine roles in contemporary cinema.

No one would have cared about the outcome of Lars Von Trier's *Breaking the Waves* if it had starred a pair of grass snakes. You'll never see a puff adder share the star billing in a kooky Meg Ryan rom-com. I did once glimpse a snake enjoying a romantic clinch on the front of a video, but that was in an Amsterdam shop window which doubled as a kind of pornographic zoological triptych (as far as I could make out – and I didn't stare for more than a couple of hours – the only animals that didn't appear anywhere amongst that menagerie of lurid video sleeves were giraffes and coelacanths).

But I digress. Most people despise snakes but Australian maniac Steve Irwin adores them, and in *Deadly Spitting Cobras* (ITV) he scours the African countryside on his hands and knees in a bid to prove it, grabbing gigantic cobras by the tail and cheerfully dangling them in front of the camera as they jerk about trying to kill him.

Only dimly aware of Irwin's existence prior to watching this programme, I am now an instant fan. Visually, he's a cross between Bill Hicks and a mad baby, all podgy cheeks and boggling eyes, his little round head bursting with joyful awe at the sheer wonder of it all. Then there's his gesturing – hands flying this way and that like a pack of startled crows. Animated? He makes Ainsley Harriott look like a lead bench. Kids must love him, although whether a man who deliberately provokes dangerous beasts for a living makes a suitable role model is open to question.

Still, who could combine childlike enthusiasm with suicidal bravery to such effect? The greater the threat posed, the happier Irwin becomes and the more compelling the result; it's like watching a circus clown pirouette across a minefield. In these days of po-faced I'm-cooler-than-my-subject-matter TV-presenter bummery, it's both rare and refreshing to see someone getting really stuck into an activity they genuinely love on TV, even if it does involve a cobra spitting acrid venom directly into their eyes.

'Cor, look at that! Right in me face!' Irwin says, indisputably impressed as an angry cobra scores a direct hit. These lethal creatures squirt poison at potential enemies in an attempt to blind them; each snakey throatful has the potential to permanently damage Irwin's vision, while a bite itself could kill – but he's loving every minute. 'What a grumpy lil' snake,' he says, venom dripping from his face, gleefully re-approaching a creature that's not so much grumpy as coldly homicidal. 'Isn't he a beauty?' Boom: another faceful. 'Woo hoo!'

Woo hoo? His bravery is remarkable, but what's truly astonishing is the way he's also capable of imparting solid zoological facts while in mid-wrestle. Even as he mops stinging poison from his face with one hand and snatches the tail of a lurching cobra with the other, Irwin maintains a constant level of lively and informative patter, pausing only to grin from ear to ear, or suddenly leap backward and concentrate extra hard for a moment when it looks like the damn thing might actually kill him.

In summary then: Steve Irwin is David Attenborough gone horribly right. I'd pay good money to watch him shoot a documentary in a violent urban environment, grabbing muggers by the ankle and cheerfully pointing out where their knife is. Hang on: that's Crocodile Dundee, isn't it? Ah well.

A Pastel Sketch of a Lonely Duckling   [21 April]

Sadism isn't simply wrong, it's also fun to watch. You know it's true. Nastiness trumps niceness every time. That notorious scene from *Reservoir Dogs* where Mr Blonde maltreats a policeman wouldn't be half as famous if instead of slicing off an ear and dousing the unfortunate cop with petrol he'd handed him a Lion bar and started kissing his legs. No, the reason it lodged in the collective unconscious was that half the cinema audience was thinking: 'Oh! How awful! How vicious! Perhaps he'll slice his nose off next! That'd be cool! Woo hoo!'

British TV was remarkably slow to pick up on the viewing public's limitless appetite for cold-blooded spite, but following the success of *Big Brother*, *Popstars* and *The Weakest Link* – all three of which relentlessly milk the sadogasmic thrill of watching everyday schmoes being shat on – they've suddenly grabbed hold of the concept of competitive cruelty with the delirious enthusiasm of an otherworldly Dobermann plunging its fangs into a choirboy's throat.

Hence, possibly, the canine theme of the latest 'cruel' offering – Ulrika Jonsson's *Dog Eat Dog* (BBC1), in which six contestants spend 24 hours getting to know one another on a mental and physical assault course, then attempt to exploit their new-found knowledge of one another's weaknesses in order to get their hands on a cash prize of £10,000.

Trouble is, it simply isn't dog-eat-dog enough. For one thing, Ulrika is about as menacing as a pastel sketch of a lonely duckling. She couldn't appear nasty under any circumstances – if she approached you in a dark alleyway waving a hunting knife, you'd assume she was going to carve a smiley face on the wall. Even after she'd stabbed you with it.

Another letdown: the contestants themselves, who spend most of the time smiling and winking at each other like it's all a big joke. For pity's sake, this is supposed to be a fight to the death: they shouldn't wink unless someone tosses a handful of powdered glass in their eye. Worse still, they're allowed to perform a group hug at the end, without a stormtrooper stepping in to break it up with a truncheon. Pathetic.

Listen here, BBC: you can't go building up our bloodlust, only to offer ice cream and free rides on the donkey instead of full-blown gladiatorial horror. It's grossly irresponsible. You want to bring us ruthless gameshows? Then do it properly or you'll have an uprising on your hands. Here are a few simple suggestions based on subtle modifications to existing programmes. They're yours for the taking:

Suggestion One:
Title: *A Question of Do That Again and I'll Smack You*
Synopsis: Two teams of sporting celebrities answer questions while twanging gigantic rubber bands at each other until all bonhomie disappears.

Pros: Cheap.
Cons: May result in the blinding of a jockey.

Suggestion Two:
Title: *Who Wants to Be a Deaf Millionaire?*
Synopsis: Contestants answer questions read with increasing volume directly into their right ear. A dormouse whispers the opening teaser; the final jackpot question is blasted through a loudhailer connected to one of Concorde's engines, producing a decibel level high enough to atomise the human skull.
Pros: No one will win.
Cons: People in neighbouring continents will start banging on the wall to complain about the noise.

Neither of those fit the bill? OK, since *Dog Eat Dog* is a shameless genetic splicing of *The Weakest Link* and *The Krypton Factor*, why not blend two other successful programmes together to create a brand new sado-quiz – like, say, a cross between *It's Only TV but I Like It* and *Son of God*, in which a contestant is led up a hill and crucified, then asked to correctly identify a selection of popular theme tunes whistled by Phil Jupitus. Or a combination of the *Generation Game* and the *Antiques Roadshow* in which Jim Davidson gets examined by experts and told that he's worthless.

Incidentally, that last one isn't a programme suggestion; just an idle fantasy.

In the meantime, I would encourage deflated viewers of *Dog Eat Dog* to make the proceedings seem more sadistic in their heads by imagining that instead of being asked to sit on 'the losers' bench', failing contestants are ordered to squat on a pine cone until their eyes water. And are then smacked in the face with a broom. Oh, go on. It's funny.

Conspicuous Dunces   [28 April]

Hands up if you're a teenage Limp Bizkit fan. It'll make you easier to spot as I scan the horizon through the sights of my high-velocity sniper rifle, in search of conspicuous dunces.

Sorry. It's just that I've been watching a lot of MTV recently, and simply don't understand what it is all these nu-metal pissbabies are getting so worked up about. There they are, living in the lap of luxury in the wealthiest nation on earth, and they're still throwing tantrums. Shouting, jumping up and down, punching the air, screwing up their faces like a pig shitting pineapples – what? What's wrong? What's the matter? I wish they'd just put down their instruments and tell us.

Ah, MTV. It's the angry, subversive videos I like most. You can tell them a mile off – they look like they cost $250 million to make, with funds presumably supplied by the Subversion Corporation. $1 million on a set resembling Nick Cotton's squat (because grime annoys 'The Man'), $1 million on a menacing helicopter that circles outside, waggling its floodlight and generally representing authority, $1 million creating a Force 9 gale for the lead singer to bellow into, and $247 million on the expensive post-production digital effects required to eradicate the minefield of zits on his forehead. After all, once you've spent a fortune making yourself seem as furious and alienated and forbidding as possible, you don't want to knacker your sales curve by revealing you've also got a face like an asteroid belt rendered in pus.

Pity Beavis and Butt-head aren't around any more to appreciate it. Speaking of B&B, MTV now offer their live-action equivalent in the form of the 'cast' of *Jackass* (MTV); stoners, frat boys, overgrown skate kids and suicidal maniacs, starring in a half-hour wrongcast of stunts, pranks and self-consciously gross acts of goofy derring-do.

Unlike most 'stunt comedy' shows, the majority of these pranks are self-inflicted – the participants fritz themselves with stun guns, hurl themselves off window ledges and gobble hard-boiled eggs until they vomit.

Ultra-lo-fi apocalyptic white-trash slapstick – all accompanied by the sound of a sniggering amateur cameraman. It's hard not to warm to a group of people so intent on seriously injuring themselves for our benefit, and laughing out loud as they do so – there's a perverse joie de vivre about it that's genuinely entertaining.

But the moment they pick on the public, it collapses. Head Jackass Johnny Knoxville (a punk Vince Vaughn) repeatedly performs a 'gag' in which he enters a restaurant, orders a meal, places a genuine dog turd on the plate, and calls the waiter back to complain, thrusting the offending matter under their nose whenever necessary.

Funny on paper, perhaps, but in reality you're ultimately watching a blameless wage-slave deal with a sneering prick waving shit in their face. Well, ho, ho, ho. In such spiteful moments, *Jackass* starts to resemble the spiritual cousin of those nasty websites filled with gory accident photography, run by US teens who confuse nihilism with rebellion. What's Johnny Knoxville going to do next? Fart in his hand and hold it over a paraplegic's nose? Hurr-hurr-hurr, dude. Hurr-hurr-hurr.

In other teenage news, Channel 4 have turned Sunday mornings into an angst marathon; first *Hollyoaks*, then the nifty *As If*, whose title might ironically refer to its shaky handle on realism. If you haven't watched it, do: it's far more addictive than it should be – like *Cold Feet* for kids, carried along by quickfire editing and an excellent cast. Finally, the daddy of them all: *Dawson's Creek*, back in a slot where it can be properly savoured by its most enthusiastic audience – hungover *Observer* readers.

There's been much hoo-ha of late regarding Joey and Pacey's inaugural romp, but for my money, the main focus of interest is Dawson's forehead, which seems to be expanding by the second. Dawson's Creek? Mekon's Creek, more like. Once you start staring at it, it's impossible to tear your eyes away.

It's just so big. It's the world's first IMAX forehead. They could project Pepsi ads onto it throughout each episode and really clean up. And it's not just wide, it's tall. Impossibly tall. To fit it all in, they'd have to rotate the widescreen signal 90 degrees or ask him to tilt his head sideways. It's a sheer drop. His hair must get vertigo. The cast probably call him 'Precipice Face' behind his back. But enough about the forehead – tune in and see for yourself. You can't miss it.

The 100 Greatest Attention-Seeking Reality TV Pricks [5 May]

Who will top the list of the *100 Greatest TV Characters* (C4)?

I'm not going to tell you – partly because I don't want to spoil the surprise, but mainly because I don't have a clue.

If preceding Top 100s are anything to go by, however, you can expect the voting public to have elected their current favourite as opposed to the genuine all-time best. In previous polls, the Guinness 'surfer' ad was crowned Greatest Advert, and Richard Madeley's Ali G impression (superbly accurate though it was) became Greatest TV Nightmare; voters had plumped for whatever they'd been watching that week. By this reckoning, the Greatest Character poll should see Yosser Hughes, Larry Sanders and Francis Urquhart being upstaged by the little yellow bleating thing from Pokemon.

The key to not getting enraged is to ignore the ranking and concentrate on the archive footage (oh, and if Paul Ross comes on to trot out a bit of blokey nostalgia, leave the room for a few minutes and concentrate on something less irritating, like pushing a spoon handle into your eye).

Actually, memory-challenged voters could run into trouble this time around, because with so many 'reality TV' programmes cluttering the airwaves, locating a decent contemporary fictional character in the schedules is harder than ever before. How long before we're being asked to choose the 100 Greatest Attention-Seeking Reality TV Pricks? Nasty Nick! Nasty Nigel! Maureen from *Driving School*! Whatsisname from that thing about traffic wardens! Vote now!

Personally I'd go for Matt Thornfield. You know – the chubby, smiling dancing man from the Halifax advert. The one who sings the awkward cover version of *Who Let the Dogs Out?* and dances like every embarrassing uncle in the world rolled into one. My favourite moment arrives at the end of the advert, when he stands on the spot performing a curious shaky jig, like a man with both feet in a glue puddle trying to dislodge a church mouse from his underpants without using his hands. It's strangely heartwarming.

With any luck nightclubs will be packed with people 'doing the Thornfield' before the end of the month.

It's the most bearable instalment of the bizarre Halifax 'karaoke' advertising campaign so far – previous entries have included a weird Penfold lookalike blinking his way through 'Sex Bomb' and a woman performing a version of 'La Vida Loca' that wandered so far away from any conventional notion of melody that it seemed to be single-handedly ushering in a new regime of dissonant noise. They should bundle them into one big variety show, with karaoke musical numbers interspersed with sketches performed by the gimps who pop up in DIY superstore commercials, pointing at a Black & Decker workmate and enunciating so awkwardly you want to lean into the screen and slap their mouths off.

Back to the week's schedules, and in the must-see stakes, the hilarious misery of *Surviving the Iron Age* (BBC1) – more on which next week – comes a close second to the latest instalment of the superb *Secret Rulers of the World* (C4) in which Jon Ronson follows David Icke around on a promotional tour of Vancouver.

In 1991, Icke suffered national humiliation after sensationally claiming to be the son of God during an edition of *Wogan*. The audience, convinced he'd gone insane, crowed with laughter – although why he should be considered any loopier than someone who'd travel all the way to Shepherd's Bush in order to sit in a studio audience and endure Jim Davidson (also on the bill that night) is unclear.

Since then, Icke has transformed himself. He's ditched the turquoise shellsuits and now resembles a dapper, retired Tarzan, with eyes so piercing that you duck involuntarily whenever he looks to camera. He's also jettisoned the whole 'I am the son of God' shtick (it was never going to catch on – there's too much competition) and reinvented himself as a successful New Age conspiracy theorist, explaining to appreciative audiences that he believes our world is run by a sinister cabal of 12-foot, shape-shifting lizards – including among their number the Queen, George Bush, Bob Hope and Boxcar Willie. The burning question is whether Icke's use of the word 'lizard' is a coded reference meaning 'Jew' – as the Anti-Defamation League believe.

This series is shaping up to be a masterpiece of even-handedness, with the added bonus of being bloody entertaining. Don't miss it.

Surviving Reality TV [12 May]

Camping holidays: I spit on you. Camping holidays are about as much fun as eating a stranger's bathtowel. At gunpoint. The whole point of taking a break should be to relax and pamper yourself a little, not waste your free time mired in the kind of rural hardship a medieval serf would consider excessive.

Unconvinced? Then consider the typical camper's itinerary:

4.20 a.m.: wake, suicidal, inside canvas triangle. Traverse hectare of wet grass en route to grim communal shower block. Inadvertently crush snail underfoot while quaking beneath merciless freezing spray.

Noon: squat before portable Calor Gas stove, stirring beans in dented pan. Pick bits of hay from damp woollen socks. Watch gathering rainclouds.

10.30 p.m.: cocoon self within unbearably restrictive sleeping bag. Jettison book in frustration as torch batteries dwindle. Spend 200 hours trying to sleep with rock jutting into back, spider weaving hammock inside right ear and imbecilic tent-mate repeatedly breaking wind and giggling. Drift off at 4 a.m., to be woken 20 minutes later by painful frost forming on surface of eyeballs.

See? Camping is rubbish. Still, if people who deliberately subject themselves to the standard vanilla camping expedition are mildly unhinged, the seventeen members of the public who volunteered to 'go hardcore' for *Surviving the Iron Age* (BBC1) must be utterly deranged.

The trailers claim they're 'ordinary people', but let's be honest: anyone prepared to spend seven weeks up a hill re-enacting life in 300 BC is about as 'ordinary' as a horse with gills.

Sure enough, in Thursday's opening episode they came across as grinning New Age do-gooders; the sort of sanctimonious know-alls who brag about how much organic food they eat (scoff all the corn-fed equal-opportunity couscous you like – you're still going to die) and could bore the legs off an oil rig with their dreary bleating about how we take the luxuries of modern life for granted. (Of course we do, stupid – what's the alternative? Jerk with astonishment each time we catch sight of a toaster?)

Listening to their enthusiastic predictions about the incredible freedom of it all, it was obvious reality was bound to fall short of expectation. What's remarkable is how far and how quickly it fell. Within four days their starry-eyed gushing was washed away by a tsunami of misery.

First, the weather conspired against them. The series was filmed last year during the wettest autumn on record. I remember it well because it looked miserable enough from where I was sitting: indoors, in a warm, dry flat, playing 'Petrochemical Destructo Wars' on a radioactive Sony Killstation, while they waddled through organic mud in their organic rags, soaked to their organic bones.

Then they undercooked some chicken and got severe food poisoning – bad news when you haven't invented toilet paper yet. Forced to intervene, the crew called in twenty-first-century medics to deal with the crisis. In a distinctly inauthentic Iron Age scene, the Hillfort residents accused a BBC producer (in jarring modern dress) of piling on too much hardship, too quickly. The conversation took place in the main hut and was rudely terminated when his mobile rang.

In that moment, the focus swung from 'Surviving the Iron Age' to 'Surviving reality TV' – with the inhabitants looking less like the Iron Age civilians of yesteryear and more like hapless inmates tethered to a pointless conceit.

Things get worse (and therefore funnier) in this week's edition. There's yet more illness and intervention, and the absurd sight of one of the volunteers using a mobile phone (still, in the interests of realism, at least he isn't shown exploring its WAP capabilities). Plus there's the bonus of watching all remaining community spirit go up in flames during a bitter argument.

So what's the point of *Surviving the Iron Age*? It's not a game show, as there's no overall winner. It's not really a docusoap either, because the setting is contrived. So is it educational? Well, there's loads of information on how Iron Age society functioned, but all we really learn is this: make their day-to-day existence as difficult as possible, and people get narky.

Ultimately it's just entertainment. So why not ditch the historical silliness altogether and simply crank up the discomfort?

This time next year: 'Surviving the Centrifuge', in which seventeen volunteers spend two months living inside a steel drum revolving at 1500 r.p.m.

'It's now week nine and the inhabitants are still pinned helplessly to the walls. Six are begging the production team to kill them; the remaining eleven are too busy weeping and vomiting.'

Not bad. Still beats camping.

Beautiful Boys with Big Issues to Tackle   [19 May]

New! Tonight! From the makers of *Dawson's Creek*! It's *Young Americans* (C5)! And it's set in prestigious all-male boarding school Rawley Academy – although as far as realism goes, it might as well be set inside a gigantic tin banana slowly orbiting the sun.

Rawley Academy is stuffed with Beautiful Boys with Big Issues to tackle. First up is our leading character, the Dawson of the series: local working-class kid Will Krudski, who's cheated his way into Rawley in a desperate bid to escape an abusive father. Whilst his dad is clearly a nasty piece of work – we see him snarling in the first 15 seconds – Will closely resembles the sort of freckle-faced scamp you see pulling awestruck expressions on toy packaging, making it hard to believe he's ever suffered anything worse than an un-included battery. It's early days, but already Good Will seems like a prime contender for TV's Blandest Teen Idol 2001 (although he'll have to work hard to overtake old forehead-face himself, the legendarily insipid Dawson).

Within 20 minutes of arrival at Rawley, Will's made himself a new best buddy in the form of chiselled senator's son Scout Calhoun; the pair quickly bond during a remarkably homoerotic sequence which sees them wandering lazily through a forest wearing nothing but their boxer shorts, trading innermost secrets like Top Trumps.

As for Scout, he threatens to rival Will in the dullard stakes until he meets a local girl called Bella, who works on the pumps in her daddy's garage when she really ought to be out doing something more suited to her appearance, such as advertising Timotei. Scout and Bella fall in love with suspicious haste; nervous chit-chat one second, slobbery kisses the next, moon-eyed talk of lifelong commitment three minutes later – until the discovery that they're actually blood relations hurls a considerable spanner in the works. Expect to spend the next seven episodes being disturbed by the sight of them staring hungrily at one other, like athletes awaiting a starting pistol that never fires.

Actually, they'll probably be too busy staring into the lake to look at each other: Rawley Academy sits beside a vast expanse of calming water, strategically placed so troubled teenage souls can stand on the shore and gaze meaningfully at the wonder of it all, to the accompaniment of some timid acoustic guitar. Huge though it is, the lake can only really accommodate a maximum of two troubled gazers at any one time; with the amount of angst flying around, finding an available time slot must be a nightmare.

The remaining central characters, blue-eyed Hamilton and the mysterious 'Jake Pratt', should probably block-book the shore for a summer of protracted staring now. 'Jake', you see, is actually a girl disguising herself as a boy – a flagrant breach of school regulations and narrative authenticity. Having undertaken the challenge of concealing her gender within an all-male boarding school (for reasons beyond normal human understanding), 'Jake' makes the small mistake of trying to snog Hamilton almost immediately. Hamilton, who has presumably never seen the episode of *Blackadder II* in which Edmund fell for 'Bob', finds himself reluctantly falling for 'Jake', prompting fears he may have turned gay. Within a few weeks they'll have to fly in a skilled negotiator to sort the mess out. Fortunately, such a negotiator already exists within the academy – infuriating 'inspirational' teacher and patriarchal linchpin Finn, who walks and talks like an absolute prick from the moment he appears. 'Just call me Finn,' he says to the assembled boys, 'no need for the "Mister".' Then, to their astonishment, he strolls straight into the lake fully dressed, to prove how unconventional he is. Combining the self-consciously eccentric traits of every 'inspiring' character Robin Williams has ever played, coupled with looks that hover somewhere between Harrison Ford, Ralph Fiennes and an understanding lion, Finn is the ultimate TV teacher. 'Spirit is the thing,' goes his subliminal message, 'but it helps to be tele-genic, like me.'

Young Americans looks slick and strangely golden, with the majority of scenes apparently shot on a warm, honey-coloured summer's evening. The formula is identical to *Dawson's Creek*: beautiful youngsters vapidly discussing complex problems. Emotionally compelling in the most anodyne way: an agony column crashing headlong into a Wrigley's commercial. So provocative yet so bland: consequently, the fiercest criticism and the highest praise I can muster is this: ''S all right, really.'

Las Vegas Swirling down a Plughole   [26 May]

Saturday evening, ITV? Not tonight, I've got a headache: is it my imagination or is some shadowy group of broadcast engineers applying an invasive audio filter to the entire Saturday prime-time stretch, transforming the mildest audience reaction into a massive discharge of ultra-compressed tinnitus that scrapes limescale from the inner walls of your skull as it blasts through your head?

No? Then perhaps I just need to fix the treble on my television. Last week I was reduced to watching ITV's Saturday offerings with a makeshift cotton-wool hood pulled tightly over my head. It took a while to pluck eyeholes in the thing, which meant most of *You've Been Framed* was hidden from view and had to be enjoyed in sound only. Still, once you've seen one blurry clip of a twirling prole fracturing their spine at a wedding reception, you've seen them all.

In fact, with the visuals obscured, *You've Been Framed* is much more fun; a simple guessing game in which you attempt to deduce the nature of the footage from the sound of the audience reaction. An 'aaahhh' indicates a kitten poking its head from a wellington boot; an 'ooohhh' signifies a man falling off a roof to land headfirst on the patio. Oh, and a high-pitched stilted burbling noise means you're in the middle of a piece to camera by Lisa Riley, a one-woman audio multi-tasker capable of sounding cheerful, terrified and condescending all at once – like a woman being forced to explain the alphabet to a class of remedial children at gunpoint.

Then: commercial break! Incredibly, the PG Tips chimps are still going, still miming their way through a series of excruciatingly unfunny half-minute exercises in dignity-theft at the behest of a teabag company, despite the fact that half the audience become dewy-eyed with shame at the mere sight of them, and the other half aren't paying attention and have forgotten these are real monkeys. They should ditch the ropey sitcom conceit and film a miniaturised remake of *Nil By Mouth* instead. That'd wake everyone up, although it might not shift quite as many teabags.

First came *Muppet Babies*. Then *Young Indiana Jones*. Now ITV are pinning their hopes on Reeves and Mortimer Junior, in the form of *Slap Bang with Ant and Dec*, a genuinely uplifting slab of excitable primetime silliness that only the most stonehearted, cod-faced curmudgeon could object to.

Slap Bang is essentially *Noel's House Party* minus the beard and the whiff of contempt: a mish-mash of strands and sketches performed with such palpable glee that even their lamest gags (of which there are plenty) are instantly rendered more endearing than embarrassing.

The humour is a curious blend of Whizzer and Chips and Roy Chubby Brown; groansome puns mingle seamlessly with absolutely filthy jokes about semen. The relentless spunk gags presumably dodge the watchdog radar on the basis that younger viewers won't understand them – although were the duo to deliver a 15-minute lecture on ejaculation, using explicit biological terminology and a series of close-up diagrams, the toddlers wouldn't get that either. Somehow – somehow – they get away with it. To watch *Slap Bang* as an adult is to be reminded how it felt to watch TV as a starry-eyed seven-year-old: quite an achievement. Still too sodding loud, though.

Then: commercial break! Jamie Oliver and a gaggle of Nathans lad their way through yet another strangely bleached Sainsbury's ad. Suddenly the PG chimps don't seem so bad (and they probably took less time to train).

Then: *Stars In Their Eyes*, with its songs and anxiety and garish, cavernous set (think Las Vegas swirling down a plughole). Why are the members of the public only allowed to mimic proper singers? Why not retain the musical numbers, but widen the celebrity net? I'd pay good money to see a Harrogate dentist impersonating Peter Sissons trying a cover version of 'Welcome to the Jungle'.

Back in my cotton-wool hood, the audience hubbub reaches a dangerous peak during the finale, assaulting my eardrums like a maniac armed with a white-hot knitting needle. I'm forced to switch off the set and crawl away in search of Nurofen. Next week I'll try watching with the sound off and the subtitles on – although I suspect *Stars In Their Eyes* might lose a little in the translation. Ah well.

An Everyday Schmoe Picking Their Nose [2 June]

Big Brother 2: The Next Generation. As a gang, they're a mighty improvement. Last time around, only Anna and Nick could be considered truly interesting and, Anna aside, the only agreeable candidates were Craig and Darren.

Craig was clearly a lovely human being, but not much to think home about: he dumboed his way through each conversation like a man born with a knee where his brain should be. Yet, astonishingly, he was twice as smart as Darren, who was even nicer, but spent most of his time frowning incredulously and asking people to summarise what they'd just said in terms a spoon could understand. The other six were brighter, but projected all the instant loveability of unrepentant seal cullers.

For the 2001 edition, either the calibre of applicants has been higher than before, or the producers simply couldn't stomach the prospect of spending the next nine weeks watching dullards work out which hand to wipe with.

Who you side with is down to you: on my personal 'Likeable' list are Bubble (hoarse, bright Jack-the-Lad with a laugh so filthy it sounds like someone flicking soil at a joke book), Amma (sassy), Dean (sardonic Brummie) and Brian (Graham Norton). In the centre of the Venn diagram, in the subset marked 'Undecided', lurk Penny (batty born-again Christian), Narinder (stroppy) and Helen (Courtney Love) – which leaves just three in the 'Overtly Objectionable' area: Elizabeth (quiet, boring), Paul (prat on crutches) and Stuart (Satan in a Gold Blend commercial).

Together the ten conspire to make *Big Brother Live* (E4), the most addictive piece of broadcasting in recent memory. For the duration, Channel 4's digital offshoot is spooling live footage direct from the house, affording us the opportunity to eavesdrop around the clock (minus breathers for the odd *Ally McBeal* or *Hollyoaks* omnibus). Once you tune in, it's hard to switch off.

Most people like to leave the TV on in the background while they go about their daily business, for which a more compatible programme than this is hard to imagine: the ultimate in ambient television. Nothing much happens; the housemates natter away, mill hither and thither and occasionally pick at their arses in close-up. Yet somehow the more mundane the action, the more riveting it becomes. It's infinitely more diverting than ITV's *Survivor*, whose overtly swish camerawork only serves to distance you from the contestants. Besides, it's easier to relate to an everyday schmoe picking their nose in East London than a mud-caked macho shitwit chewing maggots on a tropical island.

Plus, *Big Brother* doesn't suffer *Survivor*'s distracting musical soundtrack. The moments when the camera chooses to spy on a lone contestant silently wandering through the house are particularly haunting: all you're left with is raw, undiluted voyeurism – the Rear Window Network.

Intimacy aside, there's another advantage to the live edition: the contestants discuss things they're probably not supposed to – members of the production team, and gossip involving celebrities.

Of course, nothing illegally juicy makes it onscreen: to prevent a salvo of f-words battering the nation's ears during lunchtime, there seems to be some kind of time-delay system which ensures inappropriate language can be edited out by a scrutiniser armed with a blue button that dubs background noise over top of the speech – often the sound of passing trains, temporarily lending the exercise a seriously avant-garde air.

The scrutiniser's list of audible no-nos presumably consists of the following: pre-watershed smut, allusions to backstage personnel, addresses and phone numbers, libels and inadvertent product plugs. Must be nerve-racking – let a whopping transgression pass and the ITC will don horseshoes and dance on your fingers.

Still, bearing this list in mind, viewers at home can turn the live broadcast into a guessing game: the moment the sound of a train kicks in, use your judgement to ascertain which of the conversational rules has been breached (and in the case of a libellous statement about a celebrity, earn bonus points by imagining something horrendous involving a glue gun).

God knows what the scrutiniser would do if someone ran through the house at 10.30 a.m. sporting an erection: hopefully, activate a big red button that would replace the offending area of the image with the beaming, winking face of John Leslie. You wouldn't get that on *Survivor*.

Oh. Apparently you would.

Only Flirts and Dunces   [9 June]

Text messages! They're GR8! Actually, they're not – in fact, they're sixteen times less interesting than phone conversations, which in turn are sixteen times less interesting than face-to-face conversations.

Given their length, and the gnashing inconvenience of typing letter by letter like someone entering their initials in a Donkey Kong high-score table, there is little you can communicate in a text message beyond 'I LIKE YOUR BUM' or 'ME GO WEE PLOPS'.

Which is why only flirts and dunces use them. Oh, and teenagers, who fall into both categories by default.

Nevertheless, for some unhinged reason, BBC1 considers text messaging remarkable enough to devote this evening to *The Joy of Text* (BBC1), a broadcast that promises to be jam-packed with all the thrills and spills you've come to associate with the ASCII-based SMS mobile communications system.

They might as well broadcast nothing but a caption reading 'WE HAVE GIVEN UP'. Or simply tour the nation door to door, asking viewers to watch ITV instead. In fact, they're doing something only marginally less humiliating: bunging on a documentary that's simply one of the most desperate, worthless non-programmes ever to cross the airwaves.

How desperate? Well, for starters, it relies heavily on talking-head contributions from Vanessa Feltz, Steps, John McCririck, Ian Wright and Hannah Waterman.

Q: Hannah Waterman?

A: Yes, you know – Ian's wife in *EastEnders*. Dennis Waterman's daughter.

Q: Ah. So what's she got to do with text messaging?

A: Ummmm . . .

Despite clearly having been selected solely on the basis of their availability rather than any particular interest in text-based mobile communications, the nano-celebs in question gamely chirrup away about this astonishingly TV-friendly phenomenon.

'You know the rude ones where you get pictures on the screen? I can't get them on my phone for some reason, which is really disappointing,' reveals Waterman.

'When I'm angry, I write things like "What the bloody hell are you talking about?"' confesses Ian Wright.

On and on they go, occasionally pointing at their phones and smiling when there simply isn't anything to add. Worst of all, it's hard to shake the nagging suspicion that these pointless pieces-to-camera are being stored in a vault somewhere, to be resurrected in nine years when 'I Love 2001' hits the screens.

Perhaps the lowest point is when they're asked to input the

words 'I have discovered the joy of text' into their mobiles, against the clock, while the Formula One theme tune plays in the background.

Q: Why?

A: To see who's fastest at inputting text messages.

Q: Yeah, but *why*?

A: I DON'T KNOW.

Still, it isn't all celebrity typing. There's also a selection of true-life SMS stories (a man who met his future wife by sending a random text message, a woman who sent details of her sex life to the wrong number, blah-boring-blah) reconstructed in such plodding detail, chances are you'll begin to wonder what's making your chest wet, then realise you've been weeping for the last 10 minutes.

Perhaps the evening's live elements will cheer you up: we're promised an opportunity to 'interact' with Ulrika Jonsson via text message. And it's just possible they could make this bit interesting. Perhaps you'll be able to make obscenities appear on her forehead. Or rewrite her autocue so she ends up imploring the audience to hurl their first-born out of the window. I once had an idea for a live TV show called 'Text Message Theatre' where actors holding mobiles read dialogue supplied off the cuff by viewers at home: if they go anywhere near that, I'm suing. But don't hold your breath. According to the preview blurb, viewers will be encouraged to send in their own anecdotes and jokes, the best of which will be collected in a book.

Q: If SMS messaging is such an amazing means of communicating, how come these contributions have to be collected in a book – a centuries-old form of communication?

A: Because text messages are rubbish, and anyone vaguely interested in them should have their brain impounded.

The Joy of Text smacks of desperation; of taking an idea that might fill a passable 15 minutes on BBC Choice and stretching it right across the Saturday night schedules like a grubby tarpaulin. To tune in for 20 minutes, you'd have to be stupid. But to sit through two and a half hours? U'D HAV 2 B A RT CNT.

Bishi Bashi Special   [16 June]

Remember when it became legal for betting shops to have proper, clear windows you could see through? Made a huge difference to their image. For years they'd been secretive male hidey-holes with a whiff of sleazy mystique – and suddenly casual bystanders were afforded a glimpse within.

And what did we see? Invariably, a roomful of chain-smoking, ruddy-faced drunks chewing the ends of their stunted biros, staring grim-faced at a bank of winking televisions upon which their dreams got strangled on a daily basis. Failed betting slips and fag butts littering the floor around them like the dandruff of despair. In other words, a scene about as far removed from the glamour of *Casino Royale* as it's possible to get without lying in a skip lapping rainwater.

But gambling fought back. First came the Lottery, which turned widespread financial disappointment into a popular phenomenon. Then the white-trash aesthetic became hip, and twenty-somethings started flocking to Las Vegas to blend in alongside genuine US mullet-wearers, ironically pump coins into fruit machines and snap up authentically tacky $5 T-shirts that would set you back £85 in a Covent Garden prick boutique.

Now here comes the third and final stage of the Great Gambling Makeover – *Banzai* (C4), a pseudo-Japanese game show which gives a whole new meaning to the term 'odds' by shamelessly encouraging viewers to bet on the outcome of a relentless stream of absurd situations. Two geriatrics race towards each other in motorised wheelchairs – which will chicken out first? When a one-legged footballer takes on a one-armed goalkeeper, who will be the victor? How many helium-filled balloons does it take to lift a kitten into the sky? You could say *Banzai* prompts you to ask questions you'd never normally contemplate. You'd be right.

It's a con trick really – *Banzai* feels fresh and different, despite the fact that it's actually a compendium of the kind of self-consciously off-beat comedy stunts Chris Evans used to pull on *TFI Friday* week after week ('How many hotdogs can Anna Friel poke down her cleavage?' – that kind of thing), but given a late-night adult twist (i.e. it contains penises).

Three things make *Banzai* work. First, it's blessed with some of the finest TV graphics in years: hyper-kinetic idents which emulate the sensation of drinking too much wine, being smacked in the temples with a cricket bat, and left to wander through a Japanese typography exhibition searching for the exit. It's exceptionally close to the look and feel of 'Bishi Bashi Special', an obscure PlayStation game that could probably sue if it grew feet and walked to a lawyer.

Next, they've managed to talk a squadron of minor celebrities into participating in some spectacularly degrading games. In the first programme, we're treated to Harold Bishop knocking on doors and running away, Peter Davison voting on which other Doctor Who he'd most like to sodomise and erstwhile Channel Five chef Nancy Lam having her left breast hoisted in the air to find out how much it weighs. Good sports – but the true hero is surely the researcher who had to explain the idea to them on the phone.

Finally: the gambling. Originally on E4, the show came with an interactive option that kept track of your guesses and provided a final score – in effect turning it into a primitive computer game and making it infinitely more compelling as a result. Sadly, C4 either can't or won't retain that bit of high-tech hoo-hah for this mother-ship channel re-run, thereby forcing viewers to revert to old-fashioned interactivity – watching with a friend and holding discussions out loud. Damn them. And there is a slight aftertaste. Like so many other programmes these days, *Banzai* is tainted by a vague, sneering misanthropy directed toward anyone who isn't a middle-class twenty-something media git; it uses fat, old and disabled people as participants precisely because of their 'freak' value and prompts us to laugh at faded celebrities as though a lack of media exposure renders human beings worthless.

A quick recommendation: watch *Alt TV: The Lift* (C4), in which film-maker Mark Isaacs stands in a council block elevator for days, starting brief conversations with everyone who gets in. Unless someone lends you a copy of *Kes* or you get a job beating newborn kittens to death with a hammer, odds are it's the most heartbreaking thing you'll see all week.

Licked to Death by Cows   [23 June]

Being neurotic has plenty of drawbacks, but on the positive side you never get bored. I, for example, am completely paranoid about accidents. As far as I'm concerned they're lurking everywhere, waiting to strike – and this constant sense of impending doom imbues every second of my life with exciting nervous tension. Sit me on a train and I anticipate a crash. Stand me on a balcony and I imagine a freak gale gusting me over the edge. Leave me in a meadow and I picture myself being licked to death by cows. In its own way, my everyday existence is just as thrilling as the climactic scenes of *Die Hard*. Even now, sitting here typing, I'm acutely aware of danger: you never know, the 'M' key could fly off and lodge in my eye. It could. It could.

You may say I'm a dreamer. But I'm not the only one. There must be similarly morbid cowards all over the country – hence the widespread appeal of real-life It-Could-Be-You horrorthons such as *999* (BBC1) – now in its tenth series.

Tenth. That's a lot of broken bones and sudden impalements. It shouldn't be called *999* at all, of course. No. It should be called 'Fuck!' because: 1) that's precisely what you'd shout if any of the things detailed in the programme actually happened to you; 2) such a title would complement the dimly pornographic nature of the reconstructions, which share plenty in common with the average video skinflick – voyeur-friendly activity, a cast of unknowns, seasick camerawork, gasps, grunts, and the occasional slow-motion shot of bodily fluid arcing through the heavens.

The best accidents, of course, are the ones you can easily imagine happening to you – which makes this week's show a slight disappointment, featuring as it does an unusual yachting boo-boo, a freak electrocution involving farming machinery, an earthquake, and an arresting sequence in which a charity skydiver dressed as Santa Claus shatters his bones against the roof of a football stadium before landing comatose on the pitch, thereby earning himself a place in the *Guinness Book of Records* as the man who disturbed the greatest number of spectating children in the shortest period of time.

The calamities are ushered into position, as ever, by Michael Buerk, a man whose head looks like its been whittled from a particularly gnarled tree stump by a demented midget armed with a sharpened spoon.

And what's up with his eyes? He permanently squints at the camera as though it's a small sun. Squint back and he starts to vaguely resemble Clint Eastwood – until he opens his mouth and starts pouring out his links with the same kind of mock-sympathetic timbre Simon Bates used to employ during *Our Tune*, albeit with the additional gravitas that goes with a) being a widely respected television journalist and b) knowing he doesn't have to play 'Too Many Broken Hearts' by Jason Donovan immediately afterwards.

George Best's Body (C4) tells the familiar tale of the footballer's slow-motion plunge from grace, but does so in an innovative way – by charting the toll his lifestyle has taken on various parts of his body, from his legs (relentlessly hammered by brutal tackles – the only chance the opposing side had of stopping the light-footed genius) to his liver (which probably resembles a screaming walnut by now). Taking a historical tour around your subject's body is an interesting way of presenting a biography – there's scope for a series of these, surely. They might even be able to explain the origins of Michael Buerk's squint. Should they bother, the results would probably be more entertaining than *American Vampires* (C4), an isn't-this-nasty shockumentary about 'real-life blood drinkers', which contains footage of people in eyeliner standing around drinking small amounts of one another's gorejuice.

Amidst the yuks we're offered mind-boggling statements such as 'Teens are attracted to the vampire scene because it offers stability' in an apparent attempt to convince us vampirism is a burgeoning social phenomenon, instead of being precisely what it looks like: a tiny subset of goths trying to be scary. If they dressed up as ghost-train skeletons and ran around going 'whoooo' I'd have far more respect for them.

'Personal ads on the Internet suggest there are blood drinkers all over the world,' concludes the narration. And with reliable sources like that, who can argue?

Not me. I'm far too busy prising this 'M' key from my eye socket. Can you injure yourself dialling 999? Bet you can.

Whassup? [30 June]

The dot.com crash has had unforeseen consequences. First, and most importantly, the price of novelty mousemats has plummeted. Then there's the effect it's had on our advertisers, who have lost their minds.

Eighteen months ago they were sitting pretty, handling huge accounts from huge online clients. It was 'branding' and 'identity' and 'massive fourth-quarter spends' all round. Huge sums were blown creating high-production TV commercials that only served to make already baffling online ventures appear twenty-six times more baffling. Take the epic ad for breathe.com in which a miserable-looking couple stood on the beach making the tide go in and out with their breath. Cost a fortune. Explained nothing. Looked great on a showreel.

Now the dot.coms have limped offstage, taking their marketing budgets with them, and the only 'massive fourth-quarter spends' most agency creatives are going to encounter this year will be in the form of psychoanalysis fees. Like the cast of *Alive*, they're turning to cannibalism to survive. TV commercials are eating themselves.

Take Budweiser. First came the Budweiser frogs. Then came the Budweiser lizards, discussing the Budweiser frogs. Then came 'whassup'. Now the lizards are back, discussing 'whassup'. It's enough to turn you to drink. Which is presumably the idea.

Weirdest of all is the current ad for some male-oriented skincare glop, in which two men are shown sitting at home scowling at a TV commercial for Nivea. 'It's ads like this that irritate me,' mutters a Johnny Bravo lookalike with gigantic floppy hair, apparently oblivious to the fact he's appearing in an advert himself.

The overall effect is unsettling, like watching scientists tamper with the natural order of things. If they bring out a follow-up in which a further two men take the piss out of the first pair, it might cause a rip in the time-space continuum. And with Doctor Who out of action, who's going to save mankind?

Not BBC 1, which intensifies an already frenzied air of cannibalism by summoning up *A Question of TV* (BBC1), a new television-themed spin-off from *A Question of Pop* (BBC1), which in turn is a spin-off from the original *A Question of Sport*. Ladies and gentlemen, we are approaching critical mass.

Let's not beat about the bush here – *A Question of TV* makes for excruciating viewing, thanks largely to the unmistakable stench of desperation hanging round the entire affair. Stranded in a set apparently modelled on a particularly cut-price motorway service station cafeteria, Gaby Roslin appears haunted and ill at ease from the outset – rigidly sporting the kind of forced grin usually adopted for those moments when a friend's baby burps a gutful of puke down your shoulder. The team captains are Lorraine Kelly and Rowland Rivron (testing his innate likeability to the limit), while the guests are massive prime-time draws to a man – Bradley Walsh, Max from *Brookside*, Angela Rippon and, ridiculously, Trude Mostue, who, having been born and raised in a fjord, displays little knowledge of classic British TV.

It gets worse. One question is simply an excuse to give the antiquated footage of Lulu the elephant crapping on the *Blue Peter* studio floor, yet another unwelcome airing. They've even got the gall to acknowledge that it's been shown 'hundreds of times before' – as if admitting you're hopeless makes hopelessness less of a crime.

And for a light-hearted quiz this is astonishingly dreary. The contestants seize on the meagre laughs with the same mindless desperation of the flesh-eating zombies in a George Romero flick, and the results are equally gruesome – stumbling gags stretched way beyond breaking point, strangled, swallowed, regurgitated. It's the very definition of strained joviality – like watching people pull crackers on a crashing plane. Lord alone knows what's up with the guffawing studio audience – perhaps a sound engineer fed their reaction through a digital filter capable of replacing loud sighs of dismay with shrieks of enjoyment.

But it's the overwhelming pointlessness of it all that really grates.

What's next? 'A Question of Themes'? 'A Question of Questions'? 'A Question of Diddle-Dum-Doo'? After all, there's already one TV-related quiz on BBC1 (*It's Only TV but I Like It*) – why inflict another? Perhaps they think we don't care any more. And as long as they carry on like this, they'll have a point.

A Fascist Chorus Line [7 July]

Terror! It springs from nowhere. Sometimes triggered by something tiny, like an unexplained whispering that wakes you in the dead of night, sometimes by something altogether more palpable, like a bearded stranger chasing you round the garden with a grin and a dildo and a big sharpened spoon. *Fear Factor* (Sky One) is all about terror. And greed. Oh, and ratings. It's a truly remarkable US game show in which six contestants undertake a series of 'extreme stunts' in a bid to lay their hands on a prize of $50,000.

The challenges range from the scary (get dragged through the mud by a pack of wild horses) to the gross (lie in a box filled with 300,000 writhing maggots), and the whole thing is overseen by a sleazy, leering host called Joe Rogan, who'd look equally at home slowly breaking someone's fingers in an alleyway, and indeed probably did precisely that on his audition tape.

Sounds great, doesn't it? Sounds like a new high in lows. But it's boring. For one thing, the participants are made out of plastic. The six droids on offer in this week's edition seem to have wandered from the set of 'A Fascist Chorus Line'. One has a face so impossibly bland, shop windows probably forget to reflect it when he strolls past. Another somehow manages to resemble the entire cast of *Friends* all at once. In any sane world this would qualify as a disability. In America, it's a TV requirement.

Not only is it impossible to care whether these synthetic dicks live or die, there's the tedious rigmarole of watching them all perform the same stunt, one after the other. Once you've seen one Tupperware cretin jump a crevasse, you've seen 'em all – and it certainly doesn't get any more exciting by the tenth slow-motion replay.

Of course, genuine terror springs from unexpected sources, so forget *Fear Factor*, and instead tune into *Animal Park* (BBC1). On the surface, there's little promise of dread – it's a daily post-Kilroy blandcast in which Kate Humble and Prince William (played by Ben Fogle from *Castaway*) wander around Longleat pointing at lions and smiling: the kind of transmission that could be replaced one morning by a static photo of a kitten emerging from a flower-pot without anyone really noticing. But hang on in there and the horror surfaces, in the form of gruesome artworks and murals produced by King Longleat himself, the Marquess of Bath, showcased in a report with its tongue so deep in its cheek it could lick the man next door.

First, the Marquess leads us through a nursery he's transformed from agreeable playroom to fearsome hellbox by the simple act of daubing garish demonic-looking figures all over the walls and ceiling. He says his intention was to 'trigger [the children's] imaginations in a fantasy vein' – presumably a fantasy involving hunting down and murdering the bastard who invented paint.

It's nothing compared to the portraits. The Marquess mixes sawdust with oil-paint to create textured, slightly three-dimensional paintings: the sort of thing you might win during a visit to the worst fairground in the world. Imagine the ugliest painting you've ever seen. Then punch it. Puke on it. You're still nowhere close.

Seventy-three of these lumpy monstrosities hang on the walls of an otherwise agreeable stairwell, each depicting a past romantic conquest. And if they're accurate likenesses, the man must have slept with the entire cast of the *Muppet Show*.

'Some people have notches on the bedpost, but I think this is much more flattering,' he claims, standing in front of a particularly horrid example with the number 34 beneath it, placed flatteringly between paintings 33 and 35 in the stairwell of love.

Finally, a quick but enthusiastic nod in the direction of *The Office* (BBC2) – it might be another spoof documentary series, but it's a spoof documentary series distinguished by superb performances and regular belly-laughs, and is not to be missed. Even if a bearded stranger really is chasing you round the garden with a grin and a dildo and a big sharpened spoon: set the video beforehand.

More to it than Meets the Eye   [14 July]

Busy? Of course you're not. It's a Saturday. You're probably still lolling around in your pants. I wrote this several days ago, so technically speaking I've been up for hours. Slobs like you make me puke.

Still, it's a different matter during the week, when you're an absolute flapping pterodactyl of activity. Monday through Friday, your life's a whirlwind of phone calls and appointments, e-mails and car alarms, spooling through the calendar at a thousand miles an hour. Can't keep up, can you?

Fortunately, the nice people at BBC Choice know how busy you are. This week, they're introducing ultra-fast news bulletins aimed at people who don't have time to read papers and are feeling vaguely guilty because they only discovered Neil Kinnock was no longer leader of the Labour Party two weeks ago.

60seconds (BBC Choice) aims to 'quench modern viewers' thirst for news in an instant'. It's so efficient, even the title's been compressed for easy consumption: there's no space between the '*60*' and the '*seconds*' because that might waste valuable nanoseconds of your time.

Quite how it's going to pack 'the main national, international, sports and entertainment news headlines' into less than a minute isn't yet clear, but with any luck, it'll consist of a series of flashcards upon which the day's main stories are represented by simple geometric shapes and colours (a red hexagon means there's been another train crash; a green rhombus indicates controversy at the UEFA Cup). That or Peter Sissons bellowing single-word summaries of the top six stories at gunpoint.

It's a sign that broadcasters have realised viewers don't have much time to invest, which is why the BBC's new cop drama *Mersey Beat* (BBC1) collapses the period it takes an audience to familiarise itself with a range of new characters by making the officers of Newton Park incredibly simple to understand and hiring a gallery of recognisable faces to play them. Thus the station is populated by a veritable Déjà Vu Patrol, including That Nice Bloke from *Casualty*, That Nasty Girl from *The Lakes*, Thingybob from *Brookside*, and God He's Been in Loads of Things from, well, from loads of things. Within five minutes, *Mersey Beat* automatically feels like a series that's been running for five years – thereby saving you years of repeated viewing at a stroke.

In the lead is Superintendent Susan Blake, played by Haydn Gwynne (aka Oh It's Her from *Peak Practice*). Blake never takes her coat off, and rarely sits down. In fact, she seems to spend her entire day on foot, walking in and out of corridors, frowning, issuing instructions and generally looking pained and knackered. And why? Because she's not just a hard-working cop, she's a mother of two; something the script strives to point out with metronomic regularity, as though the notion of a police superintendent with a functioning womb is an epoch-shattering concept. According to the producer, 'Blake knows the score: if she has to leave her daughter's birthday party because there is a murder inquiry – she does.' Way to go, Superintendent Blake: that's just the kind of steely, selfless dedication we viewers admire.

The plot follows the time-honoured *Casualty* formula – it lifts emotive storylines from the tabloids and gives them a gentle twist in a faintly patronising bid to point out that, hey, there's more to these things than meets the eye.

So, for this opening episode, a schoolboy appears to be playing truant, but there's more to it than meets the eye: he's been abducted. For a while a suspected local paedophile is in the frame, but there's more to him than meets the eye too: he's not a paedophile. 'I was named and shamed by a newspaper,' he complains, as a brick flies through his living-room window courtesy of a hastily assembled mob (who doubtless heard about him in a *60second* news bulletin, but haven't yet learned that there's more to these things than meets the eye because the newsreader didn't have time to explain that bit).

Thus, we are sternly instructed that believing in crudely

demonised stereotypes can lead to hysterical knee-jerk behaviour – although in order to make this point, the anti-paedo mob leader is portrayed as a one-dimensional cartoon thug who gets excited at the prospect of beating up a female officer.

Still, never mind, eh? You're too busy for subtleties: at least it gets the point across quickly. Besides, who's got time to complain? Or listen to me moan about it? Not you: you're still in your pants. Put some clothes on.

You Are Nothing   [21 July]

Got a lava lamp? Then pick it up, unplug it, and hurl it into the nearest bin immediately, because *Space* (BBC1) has just rendered it pathetically obsolete. If you enjoy sitting in the corner of your living room dribbling and staring, this is for you.

Space, you see, is an all-new BBC spectacular in the *Walking with Dinosaurs* mould, permeated with magnificent computer-generated visuals from beginning to end. Almost too magnificent, in fact. Despite being clearly aimed at 'all the family', there really ought to be a parental advisory warning at the beginning. This is going to make children's tiny minds pop like cherry tomatoes on an overheated griddle.

Why? Because it's possibly the most hallucinatory programme ever broadcast.

Sam Neill is our host, standing in front of a 'Virtual Space Zone' – a sort of notional cubic viewing portal in which computer-generated images of the universe appear. With it he can conjure up brain-bending images of black holes and billowing nebulae, or reach inside to pluck entire suns from the heavens and toss asteroids around like pebbles, all in a bid to educate us in the ways of the cosmos. Jon Snow would kill to use one on election night.

It's all genuinely impressive stuff, with one potentially negative side effect: an entire generation of kids is going to grow up convinced that Sam Neill is a colossal soothsaying deity with the power to manipulate all universal matter, so if they ever catch him in a late-night showing of *Attack Force Z* (1981), it's really going to mess with their heads. Still, the content itself should do enough damage anyway. This first episode deals with the origins of the universe, and is impressively information-heavy. Plus there are more extravagant CGI simulations of interstellar phenomena than you can shake a joss stick at. At one point I got up to go for a piss and missed the entire creation of the Earth.

The programme does a fine job of sprinkling awe-inspiring croutons of information throughout the soup of intergalactic visuals, courtesy of a few interjections from real astronomers based in the real world. (You know they're proper astronomers because, like all astronomers in all space documentaries ever, they're introduced with a brief clip which shows them staring into the sky. Because that's what astronomers do, see? Thank God they're not proctologists or there'd be some tough calls to make in the edit suite.)

Anyway, the astronomers do a sterling job of blasting your cranium apart in a pop-science wow-factor kind of way, nonchalantly pointing out that every single atom around you was created within an exploding star, in a manner that makes you feel strangely exhilarated and dismally insignificant all at once. It's a bit like staring at a beautiful 1,600-foot flaming neon sign that reads 'YOU ARE NOTHING'.

Space is aimed unapologetically at the home-cinema crowd; the hordes of viewers who've used digital widescreen TVs, DVD players and bone-shaking surround-sound systems to turn their living rooms into the domestic equivalent of a theme-park ride. And this is no bad thing: most of the time these cathode-ray wonderwalls are being used to spoon-feed thundering Hollywood thickotainment into the eyes of gurgling dimwits; at least the high-tech majesty of *Space* might prompt the upcoming generation to ponder the heavens for 30 minutes (which isn't to say Tinseltown's DVD blockbusters can't also have a profound effect on the viewer – *Gone in 60 Seconds* in particular forced me to seriously question God's sanity).

It's surprising ITV hasn't latched on to the public's thirst for state-of-the-art eyeball thrills: given the same technology it would create an impossible edition of 'The World's Scariest Police Chases' in which blazing cars, driven by long-dead Hollywood superstars, swerve in and out of giant lap dancers' backsides. In 3D. On the moon. Which then explodes. Twice.

It's only a matter of time. But meanwhile, before such corruption arrives, families across the nation can enjoy the far-out hoo-hah of *Space*. And it really is far-out. At the end, Sam Neill turns to camera to blow younger viewers' minds one last time with a neat summation. 'Next time someone asks where you're from,' he intones, 'tell them you came from outer space – created in the heart of a star.' Then the screen goes all wobbly and he freaks out to some wild psychedelic guitar.

No, not really. But almost.

'What's in kidney beans?' [28 July]

It's over. Now it's time for the *Big Brother* awards. Without further ado, the results are as follows:

Biggest Time-waster: Josh.

Before being voted in, Josh promised to make sparks fly. In the event, he proved to be as effective a catalyst as a lump of cotton wool in a bowl of milk. What a waste of premium-rate phone calls: simply tossing a plank over the fence and asking the contestants to give it a name could have generated a more notable eleventh contestant. Prick.

Most Ubiquitous Humdrum Image: the sight of Dean, mudslide of apathy, slowly osmosing into his deckchair.

To be fair, whenever Dean actually made the effort to open his mouth he was consistently amusing, but most of the time he seemed to exist on a different plane to the others; in attendance yet somehow invisible – like the omnipresent cameramen behind the glass.

Lord alone knows what he's going to do after leaving the house. Given that he's universally viewed as an inexhaustible source of suffocating, enthusiasm-sapping indifference, there's little chance of him cashing in on his 'celebrity status'. Can you imagine Dean opening a supermarket or posing for a Rear of the Year photo alongside Denise Van Outen? Of course not. In fact, it's easier to imagine Peter Sissons doing it. Go on, picture it. See? See?

Still, Dean can always find employment as a Cadaver-Gram. He's welcome round here provided he leaves that poxy guitar at home.

Most Mesmerising: Helen, whose sweet-natured dimness was a miracle to behold.

An e-mail collecting Helen's dumbest utterings is currently sweeping the nation's inboxes – favourites include 'I probably sound Welsh on the telly' and two stunning food-related questions: 'Is there chicken in chickpeas?' and 'What's in kidney beans?'

Here's an exchange that didn't actually take place, but easily could have:

HELEN (pointing at the sky): What's that?

DEAN: The sky.

HELEN: Ahhhh. (*Pause.*) That's clever, inn-titt?

Quickest Fall from Grace: Bubble.

In the house, Bubble quickly became one of my favourites, thanks to his unapologetic lack of glamour. The best thing about Bubble was pointing out to horrified *Observer*-reading, Alessi-owning friends that although he sounded like a yobbanoidal Club 18–30 sperm generator, if you actually listened to the words, his intelligent wit shone through. But not for long. Once evicted, he was immediately transformed into an icon of despair-inducing tabloid mediocrity, courtesy of the *Sun* (who seemed to own him so completely it's tempting to believe he was a News International stooge all along, grown in a Petri dish beneath Dominic Mohan's desk prior to broadcast).

There he was, on the front page every day, waggling his tongue around like a gigantic leering bumwit, turning his own face into visual shorthand for tits-and-lager buffoonery, when in reality he could chair a debate amongst the nation's wiliest politicians and easily come out on top. Hope he got paid handsomely before they tired of him.

Plummiest Emma Thompson Lookalike in a Stupid Purple Jumper: Elizabeth.

Special Award for Services to Dreariness: Paul (pronounced 'Po').

Po was so dreary, his mouth acted as a gateway to an entire dimension of tedium – a dimension swirling with blank observations, dull anecdotes and self-centred pronouncements. Plus he resembled a fish. Almost silent to begin with, at some point around week three he finally opened his expressionless mouth and lifeless words began spilling out like molten tarmac, eventually coating everything in a thick layer of mundane cheerlessness. No wonder they kept nominating him: nine weeks in a house with Po must've felt like being slowly pummelled to death with boredom mallets.

Ach. Whatever. *Big Brother*'s over, but it's not the end of the world. Is it?

Actually, yes: you can watch Earth being vaporised by the Vogons in a welcome repeat of *The Hitch-Hiker's Guide to the Galaxy* (showing all week on BBC2), or for old-school cataclysm fun, catch *Ancient Apocalypse* (BBC2), this week investigating the spectacularly miserable demise of the ancient Minoans, who apparently became so psychologically disturbed by the aftermath of an almighty volcanic eruption they took to killing and eating their own children – eventually becoming so depraved they didn't even bother adding seasoning.

Disgraceful.

An Animated Dustbin   [4 August]

For God's sake, watch *Cheaters* (C5), because it's absolutely flabbergasting. As trashy experiences go, it's on a par with staring into a dustbin full of used contraceptives. An animated dustbin. With its own theme tune.

Here's the idea: members of the general public who suspect their sweethearts of sexual disloyalty contact the show, which then runs a covert surveillance operation on their behalf, tracking their partners for several weeks in a bid to uncover the grisly truth.

And it's certainly a grisly truth, of course: conveniently enough, the undercover camera crew always seems to end up following a love rat with a penchant for open-air fumbling. Not that the resultant shakycam footage is in the slightest bit titillating, mind: the wrongdoers in question are, by and large, unspeakably ugly – so ugly, it's sometimes hard to tell which way up they are. You have to look for the teeth and work it out from there. Seeing them paw each other up is like watching two warthogs slowly melt together in a microwave oven.

To be fair, their deceived partners tend to be even uglier: in the very first week there was one that looked like John Merrick in a wig. Her eyes were pointing so far apart in opposing directions, she could probably see in 4D. Plus she had a goatee beard. And a blow-hole.

Prodding the ugly-buglies in front of the cameras is our esteemed host, a fittingly sleazy, cupboard-sized scuzzball called Tommy Grand. Grand is truly awesome to behold: creeping through proceedings dressed in black, looking for all the world like a cross between Tom Hanks and a Las Vegas magician gone bad, practising a neat line in pretending vaguely to give a shit about the whirlwind of emotional distress he's unleashing. He probably lives in a cave lined with leather and chains. Bet he walks on all fours when nobody's looking.

Anyway. Once the adulterous evidence has been assembled, it's time to arrange the programme's main event: a confrontation in which the cheater gets caught in the act. This is the moment when the production team rolls up its sleeves and gleefully plumbs levels of nigh-on apocalyptic tackiness.

First there's a 'pre-bust briefing' in which a humourless gung-ho director called Jaaaahrrrn, who looks like he'd be more at home unleashing napalm, meets with the camera crew in order to map out the forthcoming 'sting'. Everyone (Grand included) wears ear-pieces, in a peculiarly successful bid to make themselves look all hard and important. Then, accompanied by several burly security guards with log-sized forearms, Grand, Jaaarrrhn and the camera-gimps meet with the deceived partner in order to confront them with the videotaped evidence.

'I hate to show this to ya,' Grand mutters, shaking his head with feigned dismay, simultaneously shielding the camcorder display from the glaring sun so the weeping victim can get a better look at a shot of her husband's backside rising and falling in the back seat of a pick-up. Once the victim's stopped crying (and their phlegm-encrusted blowhole's been unclogged and wiped clean), Grand pulls out his ace: he offers them the opportunity to catch their partner in the act.

'They're actually together right now,' he mutters. 'Do you wanna go see 'em?'

Inevitably, the blubbering wretch nods. And if they didn't, you half-suspect Grand might pull a gun and force them to take part anyway. An inevitable car-crash of emotions follows, generally ending with one or more parties wandering lost in the wilderness of a sun-baked car park, while the camera crew circles around like a shoal of cycloptic piranha fish, gobbling up every tiny frown and shudder.

Channel Five can get their imports right: take *CSI*, for instance. CSI stands for Crime Scene Investigation, and it revolves around a police forensics unit in sin-soaked, sun-baked Las Vegas. Judging by the number of perfect jawlines and cool contemporary haircuts in attendance, 'Funky Corpse-Prodding Squad' would've been a better title, but never mind: *CSI* may be needlessly glamorous, but it's also nimble and slick, and as efficient an entertainment engine as you'll find on any network. Give it a go: it's worth it.

And if you find the cast unbearably good-looking, you can always stare at the cadavers instead. They're great: all green and gnarled and knobbly, with their eyes popping out and their tongues hanging down like wet socks. Much like the sad sacks on *Cheaters*, in fact.

Phantom Flan Flinger for a day   [25 August]

You want to reminisce about the *100 Greatest Kids' TV Shows* (C4)? Go right ahead. But don't be surprised if I don't join in. Don't be surprised if I sit smugly in the corner, listening to you jabber your memories at anyone who'll listen. You're small beer, sunshine. I was in the thick of it. I was there, on the ground. I *was* the *Tiswas* Phantom Flan Flinger. For a day.

The occasion was a photo shoot in Trafalgar Square for the launch of a *Tiswas* compilation video. I'd been roped in to 'be' the Flinger by a PR company who'd called the student bar asking for volunteers. Turn up, they said, and bring loads of friends and you'll meet Sally James and you'll get to throw water and custard pies around – it'll be amazing. As a child who licked the screen with excitement whenever *Tiswas* came on, I couldn't refuse. Plus they were offering £20, and at the time I was living off those chocolate-flavoured milkshakes that come in a can – not the diet drinks, but the 'healthy' ones full of minerals that exist solely to stop students starving to death in our cities. (Pros: they're cheap, they contain all the basic nutrients you need to prevent the onset of scurvy, and they fill your stomach for hours. Cons: After four days you start belching bubbles of sugary vomit whenever you move. And your piss turns the colour of a fluorescent-yellow highlighter pen.)

Anyway, there I was, standing in Trafalgar Square, posing for photographs with Chris Tarrant, Sally James and Bob Carolgees. Nirvana. Except I was a rubbish Flinger. I was far too skinny: the milkshake diet had left me resembling a ghost-train skeleton, so the skin-tight costume dangled forlornly off my bony limbs, like an outsize condom engulfing a Twiglet. Worse still, Tarrant took me gently aside at the start of the photo shoot and, after insensitively mocking my slenderness, muttered that if I actually coated him in 'flan' (as the assembled paparazzi demanded), my bollocks would be 'hanging from a lamp post'. As a result, I was the most pathetic creature imaginable: a quaking, undernourished Phantom Flan Flinger too frightened to actually Fling.

This all took place ten years ago. *Ten years ago*, when pub conversations about *Tiswas* and *Swap Shop* and *Mr Benn* and *fingerbobs* were still a relative novelty. *Ten years ago*, and the same nostalgia engine's still running, still maintained by the same box-mad generation who've spent the whole of their 20s dementedly remembering *Bagpuss* and aren't about to stop now every kids' TV show in memory has been discussed, dissected, debated and double-penetrated to the point of hospitalisation. We should grow tails and chase them. Actually, drink enough of those milkshakes and you *do* grow a tail.

Anyway, from vestigial tails to fascist regimes, and *Secret History:Television in the Third Reich* (C4), a spooky documentary collating footage shot by German television crews between 1935 and 1944. What's remarkable is how similar to today's television it all is. The coverage of the 1936 Nuremberg Rally, in particular, with its endless tracking shots and embarrassingly servile whispered commentary, falls eerily close to the BBC's interminable live broadcasts of dull and pointless royal ceremonies (the sort of programme that, if it had an aroma, would invariably smell like musty books and colonels' trousers.) There are also cookery programmes (recipes provided by the Nazi Party), light-entertainment shows (largely feel-good ditties celebrating hare-brained Nazi schemes), early stabs at televised drama (not bad, but not a patch on *Heartbeat* either, and rather distractingly full of Nazis), and a haunting programme showing amputee soldiers hopping through an assault course that was insanely supposed to *cheer people up*. There's even a bland daytime TV lookalike broadcast from a roof garden – it's a bit like *This Morning*, but the hosts say 'Heil Hitler' quite a lot. Hypnotic.

Like *Derren Brown: Mind Control 2* (C4). Derren Brown, who looks like a man playing the Master in 'Doctor Who: The Soho Years', is a psychological street magician who wanders around bending minds: a kind of David Blaine for the brain.

Brown pulls astonishing tricks, such as guessing a PIN number by staring into the cardholder's eyes, and talking a group of girls into suffering collective hallucinations. Clearly the greatest dinner party guest in history, he's either a balls-out con artist or the scariest man in Britain.

The Winsome Lens of Haiku   [1 September]

Writing television listings – it's a bit like writing poetry, isn't it?

Well, no, obviously it absolutely isn't, in any way, shape or form, but bear with me because I'm trying to go somewhere with this, and if you're not prepared to suspend your disbelief (and your critical judgement) for 10 minutes this is going to be embarrassing for both of us.

So then. Surely there's no doubt that writing accurate listings is something of an art form. Squeezing a precise description of a potentially complex programme into a single sentence is a rigorous test of anyone's prose skills, and the end result is often more functional than emotive – a mere explanation of events rather than a flavoursome portrayal. How, for instance, could anyone hope to convey the unique tear-jerking magic of *This Is My Moment* (ITV) in just twelve words, without hand signals?

The answer is this: television listings writers really ought to turn to poetry. Or, to be more specific, they should write their listings in the form of haiku. Yes, haiku – the wistful, 17-syllable Japanese art form that's as delicate as a bone-china teacup and almost twice as beautiful. What better device to evoke the mood of a broadcast than a five-seven-five-formation stanza?

And so, with this in mind, and in the spirit of wild experimentation, this week, in place of the usual guttersnipe sneering, I bring you art. I bring you poetry. Ladies and gentlemen – I bring you the week's television highlights, as viewed through the winsome lens of haiku.

Don't snigger. They'll be doing this next week in the *Radio Times*. Just you wait and see.

The National Lottery: Winning Lines (BBC1)
> Applause detonates
> as bubblegum balls fall in line;
> you have won fuck-all.

The Weakest Link (BBC2)
> Disgraced, her target
> eats ginger malevolence.
> Now, the walk of shame.

Ally McBeal (E4)
> Sugar-pop high-jinks
> fouled by haunting appearance
> of skeletal lead.

Midsomer Murders (ITV1)
    Bergerac returns
    but this time round there is no
    Charlie Hungerford.

Kilroy (BBC1)
    Anguish spluttered
    into antichrist's mike: next it's
    Garden Invaders.

TOTP 2 (BBC2)
    Spangled archive fun
    sneered at pornographically
    by DJ Steve Wright.

A Touch of Frost (ITV1)
    Didn't the force once
    exclude dwarves like Frost? They did?
    No wonder he's cross!

The X-Files (Sky One)
    The truth's *still* out there?
    Stuff your UFOs: we don't
    give a flying one.

ITN News (ITV1)
    Dermot Murnaghan –
    crazy name, crazy guy? No:
    I'm sure he's quite sane.

The Bill (UK Gold)
    Officer arrests
    actor running amok with
    criminal accent.

Changing Rooms (UK Style)
    Here's a makeover –
    brand new title, free of charge:
    'Brighten Your Prole Hole'.

Top Gear (BBC2)
>   Cars and penises:
>   if I can tell them apart,
>   why can't Clarkson?

Real Sex (C5)
>   Don't pass the Kleenex:
>   you'd get more aroused in a
>   helicopter crash.

Emmerdale (ITV1)
>   Who watches this farm?
>   Resolutely undiscussed:
>   mud and soap don't mix.

Newsround (BBC1)
>   Gruesome news reports
>   quickly made palatable
>   thanks to pleasant shirt.

So there you go. We've laughed, we've cried, but most of all we've come away with a far better sense of how it feels to sit down and watch these shows, haven't we? Try writing some of your own. Right now. Send them to me and I'll print the finest examples in a forthcoming column. Together, we can change the face of TV listings.

Throw Them a Fish, Someone   [8 September]

Do you trust fish? I don't. It's the tiny bones. I can't taste fish without simultaneously picturing myself choking to death, hands clawing desperately at my throat, wheezing purple-faced into the afterlife. No amount of tartar sauce can disguise that. I know. I've tried.

Fish apologists like to point out that they're only full of tiny bones because they're intrinsically tiny creatures. I disagree. I think the fish are just being bloody-minded. But then I've had it in for them ever since a friend told me I had the face of a bloated, disconsolate cod. Now each time I look in the mirror I feel like a man staring at a doomed aquarium. Bitter? Of course I'm bitter.

Still, if you think cod are ugly, you clearly haven't seen some of the deep-sea yuksters dredged up in *Blue Planet* (BBC1). There are things down there that would make Captain Birdseye shit his beard through his arse: living, wobbling hallucinations, with big bug-eyes and gleaming tentacles, quivering around in the darkness like the inmates of some ghastly biological ghost train.

Fortunately, the programme also contains enough magnificent beauty to render the more unattractive moments palatable.

If you thought the computer-generated majesty of *Space* was impressive, you'll be astonished by the quality of the graphics Mother Nature has thoughtfully provided for this series. Swirling tornadoes of fish, colossal blue whales with hearts the size of automobiles, incoming squadrons of eerie hammerhead sharks – it's all here, and there isn't a pixel out of place. There's even the unsettling sight of an entire coastline engulfed by a mile-wide slick of discarded herring semen; the by-product of a mass underwater love-in. Delightful.

Far less impressive creatures shoal their way through a different kind of Bluewater in *Shopology* (BBC2), which sets out to disclose the devious means by which shopping mall architects and snivelling brand-management succubi induce the entire population of the world into blowing its wages on superfluous pap, but instead spends so much time flitting around the globe gathering sound-bites that you wind up none the wiser.

It also contains the gruesome spectacle of Trevor Beattie (hair by Michael Hutchence; facially, a cross between Jim Broadbent and notorious pornographer Ben Dover) blathering on about his deeply tedious French Connection 'fcuk' campaign, which convinced idiots nationwide to spend their Saturday afternoons trotting up and down the high street decked out in grubby slogans, when they really ought to have stayed home doing something constructive, like plunging screwdrivers into their own thighs.

And once Trevor's finished Explaining His Art, it's over to Joe Public for the people's say. 'I love all this fcuk stuff; it's crazy,' gurgles an impressed imbecile, instantly condemning himself to three hours of vividly imagined blowtorch torture in a corner of my head.

If I were king, anyone who'd ever so much as smirked at an fcuk billboard would be drowned in a giant bucket during a live Christmas broadcast.

Seriously: what does someone that dim actually *do* when they're not out consuming or trying to mate with other dunces? My guess is this: they lie slobbering on their backs, clapping their hands together and barking like seals. Throw them a fish, someone. We'll gather round, watch them choke on tiny bones.

Last week's Stilgoe-style request for TV-listings-as-haiku prompted an unexpected deluge, which I shall trawl through at leisure, selecting the primest examples for your future enjoyment. In the meantime, I'll leave you with my two favourite entries thus far.

The Tweenies (BBC2)
> Bright terratomas
> Nightmare heads scream, your children
> Wet collective beds.   [Karen McDonald]

Neighbours (BBC1)
> To impress a girl
> Toadie catapults himself
> Through a French window.   [Mark Griffiths]

Keep them coming – with any luck I'll eventually receive enough to compile one of those hateful 'Little Book of . . .' things, the profits of which will go towards some pioneering plastic surgery.

I'm having a set of gills installed. The way I figure it, if you already look like a cod, you might as well go the whole hog. Wish me luck.

The Miracle of Outside Interference   [15 September]

Six things you shouldn't do on a date: 1) pick your teeth; 2) pick your companion's teeth; 3) cry and smash plates over your head; 4) confess to murder (of course it's been eating away at your conscience all these years, but for God's sake save it for later); 5) dab a finger in your armpit and ask if they think your sweat smells like fried onion; 6) bring a camera crew and a team of 'dating experts' to dissect your every move in minute detail.

The latter, of course, is precisely what happens in *Would Like to Meet* (BBC2) and *Perfect Match* (C4), two programmes this week aimed at curing singletons of their isolated status through the miracle of outside interference.

Both shows are abysmally watchable, of course, because they relentlessly tickle the throbbing voyeur tonsil that dangles somewhere in the centre of your brain. Or maybe that's just *my* brain I'm referring to – I've been told I'm the nosiest person in Britain (I don't like the term 'nosey' – I prefer 'aggressively observant').

The two shows have opposed points of view. *Perfect Match* operates on the assumption that, hey, people should just be themselves, then it sets about finding them an ideal partner in a bid to create a couple so compatible they'll quickly osmose into a single two-headed creature. *Would Like To Meet*, on the other hand, simply encourages its subjects to lie in a desperate bid to make themselves seem more attractive. OK, I'm exaggerating: it doesn't actually encourage them to lie but it does fling them at the mercy of three irritatingly confident 'gurus' – a 'body-language guru' (top tip: don't spend the entire date sitting on your thumb and squealing), a 'conversation guru' (top tip: never try to slip the word 'infanticide' into casual conversation), and a 'style guru', who, somewhat bizarrely, dresses more like a pharmaceutical rep than a fashion editor (top tip: don't turn up with glue in your hair and a crude biro swastika on your forehead).

Together they aim to turn dowdy sadsacks into dynamic sexbags, through the simple method of relentlessly picking apart their subject's unattractive qualities (slumping, self-deprecating, gargling phlegm in mid-conversation, etc.) and demanding change within six weeks. Overseeing this somewhat bullish transformation process is the aggressively mumsy Lowri Turner, bubbling about like a cross between Bridget Jones and a boxing coach, practically turning pink at the life-affirming niceness of it all.

Irritatingly, their combined advice seems to work, apparently having a positive effect on their quarry's confidence level – and therefore their attractiveness – by the end of the programme. Of course, it's possible that as soon as the cameras leave they will make a clumsy bid to harm themselves with a teaspoon before slumping to the floor in a shuddering heap.

Perfect Match is altogether creepier, except this time there's only one professional guru on the panel (in this case an orange, vaguely Beppe-like 'relationship guru' sporting a micro-beard). The other two instant experts are friends of the singleton in question (a 25-year-old Essex-born subeditor for the *Sun*, no less, who alarmingly peppers his conversation with grammatical errors). Together the trio audition potential partners on his behalf, à la *Popstars*, whittling an initial flurry of fifty girls down to one, who then 'wins' the opportunity to move into the *Sun* sub's house for three weeks to see if the pair hit it off (i.e., have sexual intercourse). It all goes wrong before it goes right, of course, and therein the voyeurtainment value lies.

So, two more programmes that feed Ordinary Joes through the public scrutiniser. A good thing? No, but anything that distracts nosey parkers like me from peering at the neighbours for an hour shouldn't be dismissed out of hand. At least these saps signed release forms first.

Finally, on a totally different note, two last examples of the TV listings haiku you've been sending me:

Pingu (BBC1)
    Plasticine wasteland
    Proof that even wildlife go
    Mad without some friends.   [Ann Cooper, age 14]

Absolutely Fabulous (BBC1)
    Patsy and Eddie
    Once lined faces with laughter
    But the Botox smoothed.   [Carol Barron]

It's *Emmerdale*, for God's Sake   [22 September]

Equity, the actors' union, called it 'an insulting affront to the men and women in our profession'. But you know it better as fun-filled

Soapstars (ITV1), the show that aims to do for *Emmerdale* what no amount of fictional sex and skullduggery can: make at least four people in the country give a toss who's in the cast and who isn't.

I don't think I've ever sat through an entire episode of *Emmerdale*, although I've walked out on plenty. The moment that signature tune rolls in I'm out of the room quicker than you can think the word 'knife'. It's like a bloody starting pistol.

Have you ever met anyone who actually watches it? Me neither. *Emmerdale*'s one of those things whose existence you're dimly aware of but rarely witness first-hand – like early-morning milk deliveries or sex between your parents. They could sack the entire cast and replace them with spinning postcard racks with pages of script taped to the front and the odds are no one in Britain would notice for at least six months, and even then they'd only shrug indifferently and change channels in search of something less rural. It's the TV equivalent of a Turkish Delight (come on, do you know anyone who likes those things either? They're like a refrigerated internal organ dipped in chocolate). It's *EMMERDALE*, for God's sake.

Nonetheless, some persist in labouring under the delusion that *Emmerdale* Matters. Former cast member Jean Rogers isn't happy with *Soapstars*, claiming 'Most performers are in the business because they want to entertain, inform and enrich the culture of the country, not to be "rich and famous"' – a statement containing more bullshit than all the cowsheds in *Emmerdale*'s 29-year history put together.

Of course, some members of the public clearly think *Emmerdale* matters too, swarming to the *Soapstars* auditions, queuing for a chance to land a regular stint on the show. Not, repeat *not*, that there's anything inherently wrong with this – why push a pen all your life when there's a possibility you could be paid to stroll round a make-believe farm spouting bollocks? – although if it's fame they're after they'd stand more chance of being recognised if they photocopied their faces and stuck them in a local newsagent's window.

Anyway, the selection panel. Easily more entertaining than their

Popstars equivalents. For one thing, there's Cold Yvon, who resembles Miranda Richardson's Queen Liz from *Blackadder II* and is more effortlessly abrasive than 'Nasty' Nigel Lythgoe ever was. Nigel looked faintly goonish and colloquial, as though he'd be equally at home judging a rude-vegetable contest beneath an awning in some rain-sloshed backwater; Yvon has the benefit of a mean, angular, glamorous face – the kind of face you'd expect to see on a woman accused of murdering her high-society lover with a poisoned olive. Also, she's funnier.

Nigel aside, the remainder of the *Popstars* panel were so pointlessly anonymous, they may as well have stayed at home or worked behind the bar of the Woolpack. Yvon's supporting players on *Soapstars* are far better value. First there's the camp and vaguely futuristic Paul De Freitas, swooning with proprietorial glee like a steward on the first cruise liner bound for Mars. Then there's scruffy scriptwriter Bill Lyons, who looks like all seven Doctor Whos rolled into one and marched at gunpoint through Man at C&A.

Least interesting by far are the wannabe performers, who, when they're not doing predictable things like crying and crying some more, just sort of shuffle around awaiting their moment of drama – skills that should serve them well if they eventually land the part.

At heart, of course, it's a dignity-stripping contest. So is Equity right?

Are they heck. Half their members would dress up as a dancing turd in a bog-roll commercial if it helped pay the rent, so to start cracking on like the anointed guardians of some ancient craft is clearly nonsensical. Besides, *Hollyoaks* pulled a similar stunt last year (recruiting Joe Publics in a desperate bid to prove they don't simply grow their own cast in a Petri dish), and last time I checked most of our theatres were still in business (and up to their usual tricks – showcasing airless tedium for the benefit of eggheads dumb enough to believe what they're doing is somehow more worthy than sitting at home playing 'Bollock Wars' on a Dreamcast).

Whatever. It's all irrelevant. Everyone knows the best soap on TV right now is the AA insurance website ad with the sulky Asian couple. Stick that up your Woolpack.

Orchestrated Heartbreak   [29 September]

Glimpse the news and you'll agree: what the world needs now is love, sweet love. Instead it gets the UK version of *Temptation Island* (Sky One). Tough luck, world.

I've never looked up the word 'evil' in an encyclopaedia, but I'd guess the creation of *Temptation Island* figures somewhere in the entry. Where was this hatched? Whose coal-dark, hardened little pig's knuckle of a brain dreamt up this despicable affront to human kindness? Why is it here? Why? Why? Why?

You know the premise: four committed couples are flown to a Caribbean island for a luxury holiday. Once there, they are separated: the boys spend their time surrounded by and dating a selection of predatory single women; the girls do the same with a group of single men. Will they be tempted to cheat? Hyuk hyuk: pass the Doritos, Mikey, we's a gonna watch us some screwin'. Yee-haw.

We're all tempted to do things we shouldn't. Right now, I'm tempted to smoke a cigarette. Later, I might feel like drowning a cat. I shall of course do neither: not because I'm a model of restraint (ask anyone who's seen me eat – I can engulf an entire pack of bourbon creams in the time it takes a clown to clap his hands) but because like most people I've got a single molecule of lucid reason inside my skull, preventing me from doing anything rash. It tells me avoidance is the key to resistance. I don't want to smoke so I bought a course of 24-hour nicotine patches (which give you astonishing dreams, incidentally), and I don't want to drown any more cats so I've drilled a hole in the bucket and smashed up my taps with a hammer. See? Common sense, pure and simple.

As pure and simple, in fact, as the couples arriving on Temptation Island. This being the UK, they don't seem quite as computer-generated as their American counterparts (every single one of whom resembled a Hollywood lead), but that just makes it all the more squalid – like amateur Internet porn.

First up, Anna and Damien from Wales. They're engaged but aren't entirely sure they trust one another: what better way to test their neuroses than to venture into a camera-studded flirt-pit?

Next, there's Kate and Greg, two absolute plums, who instantly lose your support by allowing themselves to be filmed browsing for aspirational breads in a fashionable Chelsea supermarket, a place so snooty the Battenberg cakes sneer at your shoes as you walk by.

Behind them, Dawn and Adam. She's a model, he's a 'third assistant director' who initially 'wasn't sure if she only wanted me because of what I do' – although third assistant directors rank lower in the movie-industry food chain than the guy who irons George Clooney's toilet paper.

Finally, Helen and Jamie, and with them the first glimmer of sympathy – because Helen seems uncomfortable with the whole thing. With any luck she'll bolt.

The island itself looks genuinely gorgeous. Unfortunately the production team has populated it with two gangs of gurning simpletons – thirteen boys, thirteen girls, all of them as sincere as a Claims Direct commercial. The men are particularly hateful – half resemble leering uncles, and the rest are dullard goons, one in particular sporting a nose designed by Jim Henson. If you've ever fancied being violated by an imbecile, fill in those application forms now.

There's an argument that says the participating couples deserve all they get. Wrong. Genuine heartbreak is like a death, leaving genuine grief in its wake. Whatever their motives for taking part in the first place (a free holiday, a little excitement, 15 minutes in the spotlight), none of these couples deserves to have their relationship ripped up and pissed on for the delight of us dribbling dunces back home. They may be idiots, striding open-eyed into the teeth of a booby trap, but it's the ghouls that built the trap, and the ghouls who blob around watching the carnage, that truly deserve contempt.

But they signed a release form, you say? Since they're now fair game, perhaps once we've done breaking their hearts we can up the ante by smashing their knees with a hammer and making them run an obstacle course? Dub 'Walkin' Back to Happiness' over the top and lob in a few slow-mo replays each time their legs bend the wrong way.

Or in other words, shut up and be human. Once again: what the world needs now is love, sweet love. Not orchestrated heartbreak. Tough luck, world.

Insomnia Takes Hold   [6 October]

Sometimes television is your friend. When you're lonely, when you're sitting in a bedsit eating microwaved bachelor slop (Spicy Cow-Hoof Scrapings in Tear-and-Onion Gravy – For One), the box comes into its own, blocking it out, soaking up time like a sponge. But like all friends, it sometimes lets you down. Just when you need it most.

Example: Few things are as depressing as insomnia taking hold when you've got to be up early the next day. Each passing minute underlines your failure. Suddenly you're the world's biggest loser. A dunderhead who can't even lie down and close his eyes properly. Panicking motionlessly in bed as time drags by, neurotically calculating how many hours of sleep you could get if only you could go under right now – you need something crazy to distract you. Or you'll go crazy. Reading won't help: it strains your eyes and forces you to think. Perhaps a slug of TV is the answer.

So on goes the box. And suddenly you're gazing at an ocean of shit.

The simple fact is this: for all the talk of us being a 24-hour society, once you go past 3 a.m., there's nothing worth watching. BBC1 becomes News 24, absolute insomniac hell; the same scary stories being told over and over again, transforming your box into a recurring nightmare simulator. The Learning Zone on BBC2 is only slightly better; educational programmes by nature are intent on shaking your mind awake, but at 3.30 a.m. you need it shut down.

Channel 4 generally torments you with a subtitled film (eyestrain again), Channel Five is full of ponderous American sport (less exciting than watching a shop-window dummy play chess) and as for ITV – ITV is just hopeless. Often it's showing soccer – and I use that term deliberately in a bid to enrage dullards – old, repeated soccer which I'd rather drink a trough full of tramp phlegm than sit through.

Failing that, there's eerie video-game-review show *Cybernet*, a mind-addling combo of blurry in-game footage, repeated loops of an animated robot, and a stilted offscreen presenter quaking about polygon counts.

And then, around 4 a.m., just as gnawing psychosis sets in and your eyes begin to dart around the room in search of either a Bible or something sharp to kill yourself with, you're abandoned completely and thrown to the mercies of ITV Nightscreen – static pages advertising forthcoming shows, accompanied by wallpaper music. Suddenly you're no longer at home: you're near an A-road somewhere in Middle England, watching the in-house information channel in a gaudy hotel chain (to complete the illusion, phone a neighbour and ask them to bring a decaying steak sandwich to your room for £14.95).

Here's what should be on in the middle of the night: shapes and colours. And soothing music. And a voice telling you to close your eyes and breathe deeply. Anything else is torture.

LA Prick Convention [20 October]

Fascinating fact: your remote control has a button that can magically transform your TV into a muckspreader. It's true. All you have to do is push the '1' button on Friday night, pin back those eyelids, and gape in astonishment as it fires handfuls of molten crap directly into your eyes – in the form of *LA Pool Party* (BBC Choice).

It shouldn't really come as a surprise to anyone; if there's a Most Ill-Conceived Twatcast BAFTA up for grabs next year, *LA Pool Party*'s going to walk away with it, because the concept must have looked bad on paper. Take three TV 'babes' with pretty faces and dubious interview skills – Jayne Middlemiss, Tess Daly and Lisa Snowdon. Hire out an LA mansion with its own pool and fill it with scores of buff airheads. Plonk a DJ in the corner and generate a 'party atmosphere'. Add some who-the-heck celebrities. And hey presto. Trying to convey the resulting awfulness is like trying to describe the smell of sewage to a man with no nose.

OK – that's mean. We can assume no one actually *knew* it would turn out this bad. For one thing, basing the show in Los Angeles was a shrewd gambit for a British chat show; the logic, presumably, being that it's easier to get A-list US celebs to put in an appearance if you're shooting ten yards down the road from their homes. Cunning ruse, but uh-oh – show one featured such huge, happening stars as Ozzy Osbourne and Carmen Electra – as relevant to today's yoof audience as Prince Albert and Wat Tyler. In the show's defence, they did also bag an up-and-coming young actor whose name and face escape me, but since he a) stars in a movie as yet unreleased in the UK and b) spent his time sucking a lollipop with studied nonchalance, we'll discount him completely.

Osbourne, at least, has tales to tell, although hearing them was rendered impossible by three obstacles: 1) he was being interviewed by Jayne Middlemiss, 2) he talks in an incomprehensible, melted slur and 3) any digestible words that *did* manage to crawl out were hopelessly lost in the ever-present clatter of background 'party ambience'. To make matters worse, the interviews are intercut with footage of the 'poolside guests' – chosen on the basis of their looks rather than their conversational abilities – blathering inanely or simply grinning and leaping into the pool. After ten minutes of this, you pray for the unscheduled arrival of a misanthropic gatecrasher armed with a hammer and a deranged sense of justice.

There's an intensely patronising hypothesis amongst TV farmhands that goes something like this: build a show around glamorous people in glamorous locations and the proles will switch on in droves; wishing they were there, wishing they were like them. Perhaps that's true of the nation's most imbecilic viewers, but those bozos would probably tune in to watch Tania Bryer ride a goat around a funfair, and that's no justification for inflicting it on the rest of us. Any rational human exposed to *LA Pool Party* is going to wind up despising everyone onscreen – don't sit too close, or you may catch sight of your own reflection and feel like smacking *yourself* in the teeth. *LA Pool Party*? LA Prick Convention, more like.

If you still haven't been force-fed enough tinsel, watch *FANatic*

(C4) an absolutely terrifying programme in which various Barry Bulsaras-in-waiting are granted the once-in-a-drudgetime opportunity to meet their celebrity idols. Already in this series we've seen a girl blubber like a bereaved parent at the prospect of stroking Jennifer Lopez's hair, and another girl confess to vomiting with nerves prior to sitting opposite irradiated mantis Victoria Beckham. Last week, a whooping buffoon who worships the Red Hot Chilli Peppers almost kicked himself to death with excitement en route to an audience with his heroes.

Why such a big fan? Because, he claimed, their music is 'about being an individual, about being yourself'. And how can he best express his own individuality? Well, other fans have tattoos, so in order to be different, he had the band's logo burnt permanently onto his chest with zinc oxide. Then, to further underline his uniqueness, he reveals his favourite hobby – slavishly impersonating the band's bass player.

In the meeting itself, the Peppers seemed appalled and embarrassed (as do most of the other stars in the show), at one point earnestly trying to dissuade him from scoffing a bagful of *genuine* red-hot chilli peppers in an attempt to impress them.

Saddest of all is that now, having achieved his greatest dream, his remaining existence will be one long ride downhill. Celebrity worship – just say no, kids.

Punched in the Face by Father Christmas [27 October]

In order to contain my excitement at the imminent return of *Monarch of the Glen* (BBC1) – and that's not irony, I am genuinely excited by this – I've been sitting through *Pop Idol* (ITV1) agape with astonishment. I haven't witnessed so much crestfallen weeping since I last caught sight of myself naked in a changing-room mirror.

Enough Bob Monkhousing already: *Pop Idol* is, of course, little more than an exaggerated version of *Popstars*. Realising that the main draw of that show lay in the sadistic thrill of seeing eager young hopefuls having their dreams torn apart, they've trimmed away most of the fat and concentrated fully on cranking up the humiliation. The result is a bit like watching a programme in which young children queue up to be punched in the face by Father Christmas. Absolutely riveting for all the wrong reasons.

'Nasty' Nigel Lythgoe, perhaps tiring of the abuse he suffered at the hands of tabloid newspapers and *Guardian* 'Guide' columnists, has sensibly opted to concentrate on his backstage role this time around, leaving the role of chief abuser to A&R man Simon Cowell, who's instantly made a name for himself by behaving like an unpardonable bastard, unafraid to stare a contestant in the eye and overstate their uselessness with the sub-zero precision of a misanthropic character from a Neil LaBute movie. It'd be easier to forgive Cowell's deadpan cruelty were it not for his track record. He's been responsible for such musical luminaries as Girl Thing and Westlife – the former a hideous failure, the latter a finely honed joy-crushing machine – it's hard to believe he even understands pop music, which is surely supposed to make people feel better, not like diving beneath the nearest juggernaut. Perhaps he's just following orders. Perhaps he was issued an instruction sheet with the words 'Be Cruel' printed on it in 72-point Arial Black. Whatever: he's overdone it by about 5,000 per cent, and as a result looks less like an expert and more like a man clawing at fame with even more sad desperation than the hopefuls anxiously awaiting his judgement.

And the rest of the panel? Well, alongside mumsy Nicki Chapman (previously in *Popstars*) there's Dr Fox (last seen hammering a nail through a crab in the *Brasseye Special*) and Pete Waterman (no introduction necessary). It's hard to imagine a more cast-iron guarantee of blandness. In between their blatherings, official court jesters Ant and Dec are on hand to arse about and console rejected hopefuls, as though they're somehow not as involved in the programme's casual nastiness as everyone else.

The whole thing's on a hiding to nothing of course; you might be able to get away with manufacturing a band from thin air, but solo idols rarely appear overnight. Lasting pop megastardom takes years to ferment; in dramatic parlance, it requires a 'back story' –

preferably one that involves a deprived upbringing (Elvis/Eminem) or a ruthless struggle to the top (Madonna/Glenn Medeiros). It also requires a distinctive voice, and since 95 per cent of the contestants simply adopt the characterless transatlantic warbling of the average pseudo-soulful pop puppet rather than actually doing anything interesting with their throats, their potential careers seem destined to closely resemble the lifespan of a mayfly. Perhaps they should have called it 'Pop Patsy' instead.

There are exceptions, although they're clearly doomed to be weeded out before the final push: the quietly spoken fat guy (surely destined to be jettisoned once they've stopped toying with him for the novelty value), and Danny, the lad with the cleft palate and by far and away the finest voice in the contest. And then there's the most deserving winner: Darius, who deftly combines undeniable vocal talent with more unfortunate back story than the rest, and has thus far displayed more quiet dignity than anyone else in the programme.

Still, everybody's talking about it, so ITV must be cock-a-hoop. Next year, expect a further escalation of humiliation and brutality: male contestants forced to sing with their testicles in a cup of hot coffee, perhaps, or live DNA sampling, with results sneered at by Simon Cowell ('I have medical proof you will never amount to anything. You'll balloon in size once you pass 27, and you've inherited at least three debilitating diseases from your ancestors. In all honesty – you are awful'). And I'll doubtless tune in like everyone else. Provided it doesn't clash with *Monarch of the Glen*.

Stop Spoiling the Vikings! [3 November]

The clocks go back. The nights draw in. Cadbury's Christmas selection packs deck the halls of Safeways. It's winter. And what we need of an evening is comfort television; the brain's equivalent of a warm bowl of leek-and-potato soup – something bland and reassuring requiring minimal digestion.

In TV terms, that means countryside and quirkiness, and shows that feel like an elongated Mr Kipling commercial crossed with a widescreen reproduction of *The Haywain* – shows like *Monarch of the Glen* (BBC1), the most shamelessly pleasant series since *Ballykissangel*.

As I mentioned last week, I was genuinely excited when BBC1 began running trailers for this latest series, which must be as sure a sign of encroaching age as a grey pubic hair or an inexplicable urge to place a doily beneath every object in the house. Quite why I enjoy the programme is a mystery – perhaps my hate receptors are at their lowest ebb on a Sunday evening.

Nothing much happens in *Monarch of the Glen* – at least, nothing unpredictable happens – and therein lies the appeal. Each character is a mild eccentric, from Richard Briers' batty laird (signature move: dressing as a pilot and shouting 'Tally-ho!') to dimwit Duncan (signature move: getting tangled in a hedge). The exception to the rule is Archie, the world's dullest man, around whom the programme revolves.

Every week, against gorgeous scenery, Richard Briers gets up to some vaguely potty antics, a guest star tumbles down the glen, and the omnipresent incidental music chortles away to itself like a senile pensioner reading a saucy postcard. Ideal viewing if there's nothing else on and you're curled up on the sofa, massaging the feet of a loved one; absolute hell if you're single and bad-tempered.

I haven't caught its competitor, *My Uncle Silas* (ITV), yet, but judging by the trailers, it has twice as much scenery and stars Albert Finney as a sentient toby jug. Perfick.

Later in the week, *Blood of the Vikings* (BBC2) is a slight letdown, thanks to its pretty insistence on sticking to the facts. Opening with footage of cinematic Vikings on the rampage, it sadly soon turns studious, and sure enough, within 10 minutes we're in *Time Team* territory – watching archaeologists scrabble about in the mud.

Who'd be an archaeologist? Spending months methodically scraping dirt from a thighbone with a brush thin enough to paint eyebrows on a Barbie – Indiana Jones never bothered with all that shit. I'd snap after 10 minutes and hurl it in the bin where it belongs.

To be fair, the producers do attempt to liven up the dig by playing sinister chords and punctuating each find with recreations of people having their throats hacked open. But these brief glimpses aren't enough: show us more 'mad Viking' stuff, you bastards. We want a big bloody Viking with a big bloody axe, crashing through the fens, hacking limbs off peasants. Dispense with the dull quest for accuracy and simply make it up! Make it bloody up! Don't stand there telling us they didn't really wear horns on their helmets – you're spoiling it! Stop spoiling the Vikings! Tell lies! Exaggerate! It's not like the Vikings are going to rise up and sue, so fib your teeth out. Pretend you dug up some primitive Viking porn video. Tell us they were 100 feet tall and could fly and shoot lightning from the tips of their fingers. Show us a computer simulation of a Viking beating up John Lennon. Anything but bookworms scrabbling about in the dirt, pissing their pants with delight each time they unearth a bit of old tin. Please.

Walking with Bearded Animals on Fire [10 November]

'This is a world where birds eat horses,' booms Kenneth Branagh, as a giant dodo-like creature chomps on a vaguely equine creature with the face of a dog, and you realise you've either dipped your face in a bowlful of dream juice or woken up to the crazy, mixed-up world of *Walking with Beasts* (BBC1) – *Walking with Dinosaurs* v2.0.

Walking with Beasts shines its computer-generated spotlight at the bizarre mammals that walked the earth after everyone's favourite giant lizards had been wiped out by a bit of celestial clumsiness with an asteroid. Sabre-toothed tigers aside, it's doubtful whether the fuzzy creatures on offer here are going to fire childish imaginations to the degree that *Walking with Dinosaurs* did. Adults may enjoy seeing prototype horses trotting through the undergrowth, but kids will probably miss the scales and the fangs.

As with *Walking with Dinosaurs*, it *feels* educational, but afterwards you realise you haven't actually retained any information whatsoever, because you can't help spending more time assessing the visuals than listening to the commentary (Branagh might as well be saying, 'Ooh, check out this next bit, it took ages'). And when you're not gasping at the graphics, it's impossible to stop yourself obsessing over their minor flaws: they haven't quite mastered realistic 'hopping' motions yet.

Still, early mammals are largely uncharted territory, and this is a show that couldn't have been made at any other point in history: in 1983 they'd have been reduced to using ZX Spectrums to create a series called 'Walking with Single-Colour Blocks on a Black Background'.

Walking with Beasts' menagerie of early mammals couldn't have appeared three years ago because the software routines that simulate hair and fur weren't up to the job. Now they are – and CGI boffins can't resist showing off. Hence the sudden appearance of dancing mice in Aero commercials and the shaggy cast of the forthcoming Monsters, Inc. And this.

So, having mastered fur, what's next on the animators' wish list? My guess is beards or flames, both of which are notoriously difficult to pull off. Come 2003 we'll be settling down to watch 'Walking with Bearded Animals on Fire' ('As the blazing Friesian herd makes its way through Hair Canyon, a group of mustachioed dachshunds hurls makeshift petrol bombs directly into their path').

Actually, forget that: the latest in cutting-edge computer animation is already here, and it's hosting *Shafted* (ITV1). It looks a *bit* like Robert Kilroy-Silk, but somehow more evil, and with shimmering skin made out of woodgrain. Last week, he spent so long explaining the rules of this new psycho-terror gameshow, I felt in danger of evolving into a primordial mammal myself.

The accent is on stitching up your fellow man – just what's needed in the current climate and – and it's particularly disturbing to watch him ask the contestants whether they want to 'shaft' one another – close your eyes and he could be hosting a particularly lurid 'incest' edition of his morning angst show.

Horror of a different kind later in the week as Edward Fox promises an exciting glimpse at *The Secret Lives of Ghosts and Werewolves* (BBC1) and then spoils it all by sticking to the facts (just like *Blood of the Vikings* last week). Sounding like a man providing the voice-over for a cartoon starring an upper-class cat with a cigarette holder in its hand, Fox lolls in the back seat of a car explaining that werewolves are probably just lunatics and that ghosts are . . . well, it's too dull to go into here, but it's something to do with magnetic fields. Zzzzz.

What with this and *Blood of the Vikings*, I'm thinking of starting an official Campaign Against Realism for shows like this. Why schedule an exposé of ghosts and then tell us there's no such thing? Lie, for God's sake: pay a silver-haired actor to dress in a lab coat and point at a chart and say they're real and JESUS CHRIST there's one behind you RIGHT NOW. Even *Walking with Beasts* could be improved with the judicious use of fibs: lob in a few shots of dodo-monsters walking around in monocles, puffing on cigars, and bingo – you've got a runaway hit on your hands.

'You're stepping in brains'   [17 November]

Think your job's rubbish? Think again. Neal Smither mops up human brains for a living. He's a *Crime Scene Cleaner* (C4).

While you spend your days toying idly with paperclips, he's up to his elbows in putrefied intestines and discarded hunks of scalp. He'd raise the roof on *What's My Line?*

In the state of California, where Neal's self-owned company is based, there's no government agency devoted to disposing of the bodies of the deceased: if your sister blows her brains out in the bathtub, or your misfit room-mate fills himself with enough heroin to mong a blue whale, the cops simply turn up to take notes, then leave you to sort out the mess. They won't even leave you a souvenir squeegee. And unless you've got an iron constitution and a huge supply of Mr Muscle, you'll end up dialing Neal's cellphone. And doubtless getting the busy signal: Neal's cellphone rings a lot.

It rings, in fact, right at the start of this fascinating documentary. 'Shotgun suicide? You're looking at $1,500 bucks,' he explains to a client, '$1,800 max.' And then, snapping the phone shut with a grin, he heads off to work. Minutes later he's singing impromptu songs about money to himself as he scrubs blood from the wall of a grimy apartment.

'This is your brain on carpet,' he grins, holding aloft a rug soiled with the deceased's headguts. It's hard not to warm to him after that, and indeed throughout the rest of the programme he takes obvious delight in grossing out the film crew at every possible opportunity. 'Look out, you're stepping in brains,' he says at one point, as a cameraman accidentally does just that at the scene of a car-park suicide. As you'd expect of a man who spends his working day tossing strips of decomposing flesh into bin bags, Neal's world-view is pretty bleak. 'Eighty per cent of people are dirtbags,' he explains, with considerable authority.

'Most people live like animals, and behave like animals – violent, territorial animals.' He has zero sympathy for the victims, and only a few soft ebbs of compassion for the ones they leave behind. If he ever quits the gut-swabbing trade, he'll make a fortune penning greetings-card mottos for Hallmark.

Not that he'll quit. As far as Neal's concerned, he's just a man with a job to do – but while he claims it doesn't turn his stomach, I bet he doesn't eat much spaghetti Bolognese of an evening.

Hideous though *Crime Scene Cleaner* is, in the gruesome-spectacle stakes it's not a patch on the moment in *One Night with Robbie Williams* (BBC1) when Our Rob 'hands over' to a recording of Sinatra halfway through a counterfeit rendition of 'It Was a Very Good Year', and as Frank's spellbinding vocals fill the Albert Hall and show the audience precisely how it *should* be sung, Rob closes his eyes, mouths along with the lyric and feigns an agonising teeter on the verge of tears. Ickkkk.

This experiment in Rat-Packery is a curious thing: not an absolute failure, since Williams has the requisite showmanship, but his voice is pure Tupperware. When he sings, the words melt into one another, and not in a good way. Pass it through the Williams filter, and a simple couplet like 'let's face the music and dance' liquefies into a messy transatlantic 'lezface-thermusic-undens', devoid of any discernible emotion. Expect an 'Aloha from Hawaii' Elvis special some time in 2003. Probably.

More rock-idol indulgence in *Being Mick* (C4), an astonishingly boring hour-long commercial for Mick Jagger's solo album, Mick Jagger's recent movie (*Enigma*), and – well – for Mick Jagger himself. If the point was to prove that Jagger's life isn't nearly as exciting as the tabloids make out, it's a resounding success. We watch as he wanders around the globe with a face like a wet flannel hanging off a doorknob, attending dull meetings, dull recording sessions, and yakking to lots of dull paunchy men in coloured sunglasses, until your brain starts craning its neck in search of something interesting to chew on.

It even manages to make a party at Elton John's house seem boring. I always imagined a party round Elton's would involve carnival streamers and copulating Minotaurs, but no: on the evidence of the one Mick attends, it's all awkward chit-chat and dry white wine. Perhaps the fun took place off camera. Officially sanctioned celebrity documentaries are always a bad idea, but rarely do they make their subjects seem dreary: you'd have more fun following Stephen Hendry through a branch of MFI.

Tinsel and Idiocy   [24 November]

Following a brief lull, the dumbing-down debate has flared up again, leaving those of us who are dumb already more confused than ever. The question: is TV getting worse, or is it getting better? Curmudgeons would have you believe the former, while optimists (who, it has to be said, tend to have careers in television) insist on the latter. As for me, I'm sitting dizzy-faced on the fence, chewing a hayseed while spitwads fired from both directions sail clean over my head. We thickos never get a proper look-in in debates like these.

The complainants' argument runs roughly as follows: British TV is becoming a hotbed of tinsel and idiocy, obsessed with youth and sex; intellectual nourishment of all kinds is nudged embarrassingly to the sidelines in the blinkered quest for ratings. The optimists say there's nothing to worry about – far from having our options restricted, today we have more choice than ever, with entire channels devoted to our every whim (usually with names like Soup Network, or Puppeteer 24). There may be more crap than ever before (and make no mistake, it's always been there), but there's also more quality.

And the view from this fence-sitting doofus? Well, miss, I think both sides have a point. But it seems to me the main problem is the human race itself.

The majority of the human race prefers crap to gold; subsequently, we now have entire networks devoted to it. That's just natural efficiency. Trouble is, over the past few decades, crap technology has steadily improved, leaving us with crapper crap than ever. We now have vicious, blank-eyed, multicoloured crap; crap with lungs, crap that shouts louder and harder than ever before. The good stuff (and there *is* just as much as there's always been) can't, by its very nature, raise its cultured voice above the bellowing. It hasn't disappeared – it's just easier to ignore. Of course, no one likes being ignored, so even the more heavyweight programmes try a bit of yelling now and then, with embarrassing results.

Case in point: this week, a fairly grim documentary about the exhumation of the dead finds itself lumbered with an atrociously gimmicky title – *Changing Tombs* (C4) – in a bid to attract vultures. This is a curiously placid look at the grim business of corpse relocation, following workers from the London Necropolis Company (I kid you not) as they dig up a disused graveyard in Islington and replant the coffins elsewhere – out in the countryside, where the rent's less expensive and the quality of life is better by far.

Ghouls won't be satisfied: there isn't much footage of dripping human mulch, and at no point does anyone crowbar open a coffin lid to uncover a boggle-eyed skeleton clutching a silver pentagram. Instead there's lots of mud, some tatty clumps of corpse-hair, and a chilling snap of a freakishly well-preserved body unearthed at a previous dig (which wouldn't look out of place in a Dazed and Confused photoshoot, particularly now the 'Edwardian look' is in).

Disappointingly, the workers are not exactly heaving deadsters out of the soil and tossing them cheerily into the back of a van either. No. Corpses are afforded far more respect than us breathing plebs, with officials on hand to ensure they're not upset by the move. Typical: you wait your whole life to be pampered, but only when you're too decomposed to appreciate it will anyone actually indulge you.

More corpse action in this week's *Kenyon Confronts* (BBC1), in which Paul Kenyon investigates people who've faked their own deaths in a bid to collect insurance money. And again, it's a disappointment: no Reggie Perrin-style hilarity, just a bit of clumsy fraud involving a bogus death certificate, and not enough conflict by half. Kenyon (who looks more like an ex-choirboy or a sweet-faced orderly from *Holby City* than a journalistic Force to be Reckoned With) should ditch the detective work and concentrate fully on the confrontation, which, after all, is the reason you've tuned in in the first place. Perhaps he should just stand on Oxford Street, obstructing passers-by, tripping up pedestrians with a mike lead.

It'd make a great Christmas special.

An Ageing Thundercat [1 December]

Just like the artefacts it showcases, interest in the *Antiques Roadshow* (BBC1) accumulates with age. When I was a child, the *Antiques Roadshow* was a televisual Sahara I had to cross on hands and knees; a slow-motion assault on the boredom cells, physically painful to withstand. Every Sunday evening I'd writhe like a pig glued to an armchair, huffing indignantly at the tedium of it all, eventually sliding broken to the floor, close to tears.

At least that's how it used to be, back in the days of one-box-per-household, with four terrestrial channels and bugger-all else, when youth had no option but to sit there and suffer. Plonk a twenty-first-century whippersnapper in front of *Antiques Roadshow* and they'll merely shrug for a nanosecond before whipping a Game Boy Advance from their back pocket and tucking into level 98 of 'Borstal Oblivion X'. The little bastards have a portable escape hatch.

Having flown the parental nest, you doubtless swore never to glance at the *Roadshow* again, but over the years it wears you down. Pass 30 and it seems like quite a charming little programme, a pleasant diversion over coffee and biscuits.

This is a danger signal: you're a gnat's pube away from becoming your parents. Before you know it you'll be hopelessly infected with a sincere interest in antiques and no one will ever want to sleep with you ever again. Here's a tip: fight the urge to succumb by concentrating on the onlookers skulking in the background during each evaluation. Really *look* at them. Ashen-faced, sunken-eyed cadavers haunting the rear of each shot like lost spirits trapped inside your TV set, anxiously craning their necks in search of a way out. Carry on watching the *Roadshow* and that's how you'll look, age 50. Just you think about that.

But if the *Roadshow* is a guilty pleasure, daytime antiquefest *Bargain Hunt* (BBC1) is an innocent joy, largely on account of host David Dickinson, the most dapper man on earth. Dickinson is sometimes referred to as 'the real Lovejoy', but he's actually more like Lovejoy squared, Lovejoy to the power of 10. He surfs into view on a wave of liquid polish and is impossible to dislike from the moment you slap eyes on him.

It's the hair you notice first; a bushy helmet dimly reminiscent of Patrick Swayze's swirling mane circa *Roadhouse* – but darker, woven with grey and infinitely more distinguished. Then there's his skin – shiny, terracotta – and his eyebrows, which seem to have been applied with a chisel-tip marker pen.

He looks like an ageing Thundercat. He also dresses with genuine panache, and throws continual glances to the camera, generating a palpable erotic charge. My girlfriend fancies him more than any other man on earth, including me.

The show itself works thus: two pairs of punters have £200 to spend at car-boot sales and antique fairs, with experts on hand to provide advice and gentle bullying. Then it's off to the auction room to see their purchases go under the hammer – a nail-biting, unpredictable finale as they discover the haul's true value. The team with the largest profit (assuming there is one) gets to keep their winnings – on a good day as much as £40. The losers go home with a pat on the back and a good-natured chuckle from David. No one gets hurt, shot or belittled; it's all clean simple fun, and why it isn't broadcast in an early-evening slot is a mystery on a par with the origins of Dickinson's sexual charm.

Also this week: *Cold Feet* (ITV1), which is whipping past at a bewildering rate, like a soap opera viewed from the side of a fairground ride. Worth watching to see how many additional storylines they can plough into before the whole thing collapses beneath the weight of its own angst – and because the little girl Adam and Rachel are adopting looks precisely like Neil Hannon from *The Divine Comedy*.

Then there's the increasingly hilarious *Taboo* (BBC2), in which Joan Bakewell examines the forbidden by placing it in a stark white studio and squinting at it, in the vaguely disapproving manner of *Antiques Roadshow* bystanders discussed earlier.

In week one, she peered at an erect penis; by week two she'd graduated to watching full sexual intercourse. This week's topic is violence, so expect to see her pacing around, glaring over the rim of her spectacles at two transsexuals thumping each other to death with their own johnsons. Possibly.

'We'll have to get you a proper bra' [8 December]

Fashion terrifies me. It's the fear of the unknown. Once it was so easy: a pair of slacks and a vaguely ironic T-shirt and I was perfectly acceptable.

Now I've crossed the divide: too young for cardigans; too old for anything vaguely attractive. There it goes: my sense of style, vanishing into the distance at 10,000 m.p.h., leaving me floundering in a sea of crap trousers. I'm stuck here. And unless the 'oblivious buffoon' look comes in, I'm screwed for life.

I dislike clothes, although the alternative is unthinkable. But, Christ, how I loathe fashionable young men, with their skinny frames and their streetwise attire and their understated self-confidence. I feel like taking a baseball bat to the lot of them, although even then I'd probably pick an unfashionable brand of bat, or somehow manage to knock their brains out in a cluelessly passé kind of way – using an underarm swing when the overarm swipe's more 'now', perhaps – and everyone would sneer at me, including the arresting officer.

The rage is motivated by jealousy, of course, since I'm too homely to pull it off myself. I've got a face like a punctured beachball, like an arse that's fallen downstairs, like a rucksack full of dented bells. The coolest shirt on earth becomes a nondescript rag the moment you add my Tolkienesque features to the equation. Put me in a suit and bingo: Gollum in his Sunday best.

Hence my sudden interest in turd-polishing exercise *What Not To Wear* (BBC2), the new 'makeover show' hosted by wilfully catty double act Trinny Woodall and Susannah Constantine. The format: find a frumpy prole with the fashion sense of Tony Martin, then send Trinny and Susannah in to point out the myriad faults in their attire. They don't pull punches. If that skirt makes your backside resemble a bloated pumpkin, if your choice of collar turns your entire head into a gruesome accident, Trinny and Susannah will tell you, gleefully and on camera. Once all remaining dignity has been stripped clean away, said prole is suddenly given £2,000 and commanded to buy a new wardrobe, with two provisos: 1) they must follow a set of fashion 'rules' handed down by Trinny and Susannah, and 2) their shopping expedition takes place on camera.

It's all just about entertaining enough, with the hosts walking a fine line between likeable and annoying. Trinny's a rake; so thin she could crawl through an empty biro casing if the mood struck her, while Susannah's plump and mumsy and obsessed with other women's boobs, lurching at them like Sid James in *Carry On up the Tribunal*. 'We'll have to get you a proper bra,' she says, eyes agleam, kneading the subject's mammaries, sometimes heaving them apart and hoisting them aloft for good measure. Curiously, she dresses rather badly; a glaring flaw in a show like this.

Another flaw: both of them have posh accents – always off-putting. The upper classes really shouldn't open their mouths on television. Whatever it is they're saying, all your brain actually hears is 'Tra la la, I live in a bubble, tra la la, murder a fox, tra la la,

Conde Nast Traveller, tra la la, Kensington High Street, tra la la.'
They should know their place and keep quiet.

That aside, *What Not To Wear* does dispense useful advice during its half-hour duration, and the transformation of frump-to-flower is authentically heartwarming, more than can be said for anything in *It's a Girl Thing* (C4), a misguided hybrid of catwalk and sitcom, clearly inspired by *Sex and the City*, but with fashion dilemmas in place of sexual ones. Trouble is, it's *Sex and the City* minus the wit. And the budget. And the sex. And the city.

The result is a bit like finding yourself trapped inside one of those Z-grade Bridget Jones-like chick-lit novels that make you want to kill people; all kooky cover art and characters who say 'Crumbs!'

I can't remember much of the script, but it goes something like this:

GIRL #1: Durr, umm, durr, ugh durrr um durr.

GIRL #2: Durr? Durr umm durr!

GIRL #3: Does my brain look thick in this?

GIRL #4: Crumbs!

This week's episode centres on a guide to buying swimwear: just what you need in December. And it doesn't even offer concrete guidance: come the episode's end, the girls conclude, 'It doesn't matter what you wear, so long as you feel comfortable.'

Novelty slippers all round, then. Cheers for the advice.

Opportunity Nots [22 December]

Finished? Good. You were awful. You stank like a drain full of skunk guts. Close the door on your way out. And thanks for nothing. I sincerely hope you kill yourself. Yes, 2001 was the year of the nasty talent show – programme after programme in which aspirants had their fragile dreams torn apart in front of a nation. 'New Faces with Bollockings'. 'Opportunity Nots'. First came *Popstars*, a desperate search for the kind of stellar talent that could redefine pop – or, at the very least, pad out Hear'Say. Of course, panel member 'Nasty' Nigel Lythgoe (played by Admiral Ackbar from *Return of the Jedi*) was the real star, oozing Partridge glamour as he poured cold piss on the flames of enthusiasm.

Not that most of them didn't deserve a verbal kicking. Was there a more unpleasant spectacle this year than the sight of countless spoilt Britney wannabes tearfully brushing off their rejection with bratty blubs of 'I *will* make it one day – somehow. I will, you'll see. I'll be famous. It'll happen. It's my destiny.' Listen carefully: No it isn't. Your destiny is to sit in multiplexes watching sequels to *The Mummy Returns* for the next 200 years, so forget fame and get on with it.

But Lythgoe was a breeze compared with what followed. By September, *Soapstars* had arrived, and with it came 'Nasty' Yvon (aka Ilsa, She-Wolf of the SS), whose caustic put-downs generated a palpable chill, like a voice at a séance predicting imminent doom. All quite unnecessary when you contemplated the prize at stake: a three-month contract to appear on *Emmerdale*, the invisible soap. I've still never seen it, although according to the latest long-distance reports it's got something to do with cows and there's a McGann in the cast. More information as and when we get it.

No sooner had the *Soapstars* 'winners' been dispatched to the TV equivalent of a missing person's helpline than *Pop Idol* sprang up to accelerate their removal from our minds. Suddenly, our hopefuls had Simon Cowell to contend with. A walking definition of arrogance, Cowell was the Osama bin Laden of talent shows (minus the dreamy eyes). He was the tightest man on television – tight muscle, tight T-shirts and tight trousers, haunched all the way up to his big tight tits – firing staccato proclamations that crossed the line between constructive criticism and malicious abuse, thereby achieving the impossible by making both Pete Waterman *and* Dr Fox look dignified. He can tuck into his turkey safe in the knowledge that he's the king of breaking butterflies on wheels. Way to go, Simon, and goodwill to all mankind.

So what else happened on our screens? Avant-garde inactivity, that's what, in the bewildering form of *Touch the Truck*. Tune in and you could gasp in astonishment as a bunch of bozos stood round a 4x4 in Thurrock, keeping a hand on the chassis and their eyelids open. The rules were simple: last one standing wins the vehicle. The world of chronic sleep deprivation has rarely felt so glamorous. Let's just hope the winner didn't immediately drive away with the prize, swerving snoozily past railway lines all the way back home.

And if the sight of ten people standing motionless round a stationary vehicle wasn't mundane enough, you could always tune into the continuous live feed from the *Big Brother* house. Look! There's Dean, scratching his nuts. And does Bubble have a spoon in his hand? Can't quite tell from here. Hang on. Yes, it is. It's definitely a spoon. Brilliant. Ah, *Big Brother*. Or more specifically – ah, Paul and Helen. What a love story – 'When Knuckleheads Collide'. Half the nation on tenterhooks, wondering whether Dimbo #1 would get to nudge his tinker up Dimbo #2's foo-foo before the cameras went away.

Germaine Greer denouncing the ghastliness of it all in the *Observer*, while Dominic Mohan encouraged *Sun* readers to 'grab a beer and pull up a seat' in the event of penetration. True obsessives could even sign up for text-message updates of the latest developments. Middle of the night, and your mobile starts beeping: 3 A.M. LATEST: HE'S STUCK IT IN. Thank God for the twenty-first century.

As *Big Brother* was drawing to a close, the *Brass Eye Special* on paedophilia appeared. Several viewers were upset by the broadcast, but thankfully the press was on hand to ensure their views received an effective airing in the form of unintelligible pandemonium. I had some involvement in the programme, and consequently found myself 'named and shamed' alongside other evil conspirators in the *News of the World* for the benefit of readers who'd just finished masturbating over paparazzi snaps of topless pop starlets and fancied a bit of orchestrated outrage. The *Star* covered the furore opposite a photo of 15-year-old Charlotte Church in a low-cut top (caption: 'Charlotte's looking chest swell'), while the *Mail* spent an entire week exploring the outer limits of fury, occasionally lightening the mood with delightful snaps of Fergie's pubescent offspring frolicking in bikinis. No review of the year's TV is complete without some discussion of 11 September, when raw horror bled from every screen. Like many others, I spent the day nauseous and shaking, wandering dizzily from one location to the next, suddenly aware of just how many TV sets there are in the world. For weeks, the news exerted a pornographic hold on my interest. A grimly bizarre sight sticks in my head: an American journalist reviewing the English tabloids on News 24, saying: 'Real nice layout on this page, big headline here, great photo of a guy jumping from the building.'

Anyway. Where were we? Of course – 2001. There were good and bad programmes.

Among the good: Jon Ronson's *Secret Rulers of the World*, *Linda Green*, *The Office*, *The Blue Planet*, *Faking It*, *Sex and the City*, *Space*, *Extremes* – and *Cold Feet*, which contained 50 per cent too many storylines, but redeemed itself by turning David, superbly played by Robert Bathurst, into its most sympathetic and dignified character. And the bad? *LA Pool Party*, *One Night With Robbie Williams*, the UK version of *Temptation Island*, *Jim Davidson's Generation Game*, *'Orrible*, *It's a Girl Thing* and *Metrosexuality*.

That's it. Happy viewing over the Yuletide period. Don't OD on David Jason.

Alternative Christmas Day TV Listings [24 December]

6.00 a.m. Get Up and Scream Like a Demented Bloody Banshee
Children's Morning Fun. Three solid hours of uninterrupted hollering, impenetrable cartoons and Westlife videos designed to wind every child in the country into a state of uncontrollable arm-flapping rowdiness before anyone else in the house is even awake.

9.00 When Louis Met Wallace and Gromit
Cosy middle-class claymation dream come true.

10.30 Auntie's 14:9 Unsafe Christmas Bloomers
Terry Wogan introduces a seasonal selection of incorrect aspect-ratio blunders from an assortment of popular programmes including *Casualty*, *Holby City*, *Holby City*, *Casualty*, *Holby City* and *Holby City*.

Contains footage of Charlie from Casualty *standing slightly too far to the left and rendering himself invisible to viewers without widescreen televisions.*

11.00 Straw Dogs CGI
Cheerful *Toy Story*-style computer-animated remake of Sam Peckinpah's notorious study of male violence.

12.30 p.m. Patrick Kielty's Christmas Streets of Yuletide Fundom
Light-hearted silliness as Patrick Kielty rides a pantomime reindeer through the streets of Gloucester, pulling a cart full of orphaned children banging tambourines behind him. Music by DJ Otzi and Atomic Kitten.

1.00 Robbie Williams: Aloha from Hawaii Christmas Special
The nation's favourite boggle-eyed yelper dons a white jumpsuit and floral garlands and sets about methodically erasing all traces of spirit from a selection of perennial favourites including 'Burning Love', 'Suspicious Minds', 'An American Trilogy', 'Can't Help Falling in Love', 'See See Rider' and 'It's Over'.
Ladies and gentlemen, 'Robbie Williams Has Left the Building' is available now on CD. An extended 8-disc DVD edition of this live broadcast, including out-takes and an ironic 30-minute documentary in which Cat Deeley dresses like a 60s housewife and pretends to be stalking 'the new King', will be available to buy from Monday from phone-booth-sized record shops that offer no diversity whatsoever and make you want to slash your wrists and spray blood in the assistants' faces the moment you walk in the door.

1.50 Yuletide Sing-Song Hurtle-Bench Mayhem
Astonishing programme in which an untethered cast-iron park bench is fired with immense velocity into a group of unsuspecting carol singers.

2.00 EastEnders
Characteristically uplifting seasonal edition of the popular soap. Zoe downs a pint of bleach and falls beneath an underground train in full view of a group of horrified schoolchildren, while Steve accidentally backs his Mercedes over a pregnant cat, which bursts, spraying guts and dead kittens all over the windows of the Queen Vic in the middle of Christmas dinner.

3.00 The Queen's Christmas Message
The world's most uncharismatic figurehead peers eerily into the living rooms of a nation, monotonously reciting a dreary speech of absolutely no interest or relevance to anyone whatsoever, save the occasional loud-mouthed delusional racist nut.

3.10 Zulu: Named and Shamed Edition
New version of the spectacular epic dramatising the Battle of Rorke's Drift in 1879, in which the Zulus' faces are digitally replaced with those of men on the sex offender's register, thereby enabling viewers to enjoy a cinematic classic while simultaneously memorising the features of convicted child enthusiasts-perverts that may be living next door, within finger-poking distance.
Lt. Gonville Bromhead: Michael Caine
Zulu 1: That bloke from next door
Zulu 2: That man who's always in the park
Zulu 3: Jonathan King
Zulu 4: Sidney Cooke

4.15 The Royal Institution Christmas Lectures
Some bespectacled old Doctor Who wannabe introduces this year's topic: 'Why Does Anything Connected with Science Always Seem Interesting for Ten Minutes before Descending into Bottomless Tedium?'

4.40 Utterly Irrelevant Eight-Hour Ballet
Destined to be watched under duress by the disgruntled children of patronising *Guardian* readers on the basis that it's somehow good for them.

5.15 The Snowman Redux
All-new director's cut of the classic heartwarming cartoon with over 58 minutes of additional footage, all of it boring.

6.25 Before They Were Demonised
Angus Deayton takes an amusing look back at Osama bin Laden's early appearances in daytime game shows and Slimcea commercials.

7.00 Countryfile Christmas Special
Unnecessary Yuletide edition of the overlooked rural-affairs

show, including a report on six pine cones covered in snow and a shot of some bracken near a fence post.

7.35 Weakest Link – Offender's Register
Special edition of the elimination quiz hosted by Anne Robinson. Nine of the nation's most reviled men battle against each other to win money for a leading children's charity – but who will be first to make the dreaded 'Walk of Name and Shame'?

8.00 Big Brother Yuletide Special
Six hours of footage of Bubble nonchalantly picking his teeth near a Christmas tree.

9.30 I Love the Succession of Glittering Images Which Distract and Amuse Yet Ultimately Do Little to Quell the Boundless Sadness at My Core
Curiously despondent talking-head clip show in which desperate celebrities standing on ledges punctuate footage from vintage Christmas editions of *Top of the Pops*, *Morecambe and Wise* and *Bruce Forsyth's Generation Game*.
Is there a black dog in your head, pissing misery juice all over your brain, drowning the joy cells and stifling your ability to do anything other than stare at the walls and cry? Would you like to talk about it? To a man who nods without listening? A nodding puppet accompanied by a cameraman who's eating sandwiches and concentrating on getting the focus right and can't hear a word you're saying? Our researchers would like to talk to you: call now on 0207 946 0006, and for Christ's sake try to stop sobbing long enough to keep your contact details intelligible.

10.25 Nathan Barley @ Christmas
Upper-middle-class London media scumbag Nathan Barley visits an overpriced Soho shitshack to waste £350 on a selection of ironic Christmas gifts including an A-Team nativity set, a clockwork Bin Laden, the 2002 Zapruder Footage calendar featuring a different still for each month, a set of furry dice with the heads of The Strokes replacing the dots, a bottle of Ron Jeremy Cream Shampoo (emulating the precise consistency of semen and manufactured in San Francisco by a company whose name is spelt out in a knowingly kitsch font), two packets of swastika-shaped

corn snacks and a Japanese digital camera that prints photographs on marzipan-scented recycled toilet paper.

11.30 **Planet Littlejohn**

Computer simulation show in which Richard Littlejohn is given a virtual planet of his own to run as he sees fit. *Day 34*: Having seen all human life wiped out by six consecutive world wars, Richard starts trying to get the vegetation to fight among itself.

PART THREE   2002

In which Jonathan King takes umbrage, Jack Bauer watches the clock, and Uri Geller eats worms in the jungle.

A Choir of Coughing Rectums [19 January]

Birds do it. Bees do it. Even educated fleas do it. Yes everybody, but everybody goes to the toilet now and again. Even the Queen does, although it's hard to imagine her wooden expression ever changes, even if she's constipated.

But, so the cliché goes, you rarely get to see people going to the toilet on television. You'd never witness, say, Phil from *EastEnders*, sitting resplendent on the throne (although that's probably because when he needs to go he just gets down on all fours in the middle of the street and lets it drop casually out the back, like a horse).

For too long, broadcasters have been afraid to confront the harsh reality of bodily functions head-on, but there's recently been some headway, notably from the Americans – first they set half the action in *Ally McBeal* in a unisex toilet, then followed it up with a truly spectacular open-door bathroom sequence in last week's *Sex and the City*. Now, in the spirit of solidarity, and to show support for this new world order, the British are following suit with *Toilets* (BBC Choice), an entire series about all things lavatorial, hosted by walking seal-of-quality Claudia Winkleman.

Isn't it exciting, living in a renaissance?

This week's edition is concerned with how to go to the toilet. Subsequently, it's jam-packed with information that absolutely everyone on the planet knows already. Here are just a few of the startling revelations uncovered.

Revelation #1: *Men behave strangely at urinals.*

According to the programme's exhaustive research, when having a tinkle, men eschew conversation entirely and concentrate instead on staring dead ahead like unfazed shop-window dummies. It then goes on to explain how peeing alongside one another gives some men the jitters, to the extent they dry up completely and have to stand in silent humiliation until the room empties and emission resumes.

What it fails to say is that, for a sure-fire cure for this kind of urinal stage fright, you have to look to the world of contemporary literature, specifically Nicholson Baker's *The Mezzanine*, in which the narrator explains how he overcomes his pee-pee nerves by picturing himself urinating on to the face and head of the person standing next to him. The astonishing thing is that this tactic actually works – precisely the kind of useful information this programme could have done with.

Revelation #2: *Men's toilets are dirty; women's toilets are clean.*

Now there's a surprise. Most public gents' look like the aftermath of a water-pistol fight at an incontinence convention. By contrast, women's toilets are kept ultra-clean, generally resembling a cinematic vision of an eerily anodyne future society.

There's the glimmer of some useful information during this section – a writer advises men appalled by the cave-like funk of public conveniences to nip into the disabled loos instead, on the grounds that they're spacious and clean. Plus it's easy to barge past the cripples on your way in.

Revelation #3: *People don't like other people overhearing their 'noises' – so they cough, flush, or run taps loudly in a bid to disguise them.*

Perfectly understandable this, because the moment your backside starts misbehaving loudly, you feel entirely stripped of all nobility – although in my experience, that's a very British trait. The Americans don't seem to suffer from it – on several occasions I've found myself standing in stateside craphouses reeling with amazement as cubicled rows of clean-cut, Gillette-model businessmen nonchalantly unleash a truly thunderous din – a choir of coughing rectums accompanied by the sound of plummeting mud. And as for the French – well, they're currently lobbying the Olympic Committee to make loud, undignified defecation a team sport.

Revelation #4: *People used to wipe their bums on old bits of corn on the cob.*

To give the show its dues, this did come as a genuine surprise.

So there you have it. I can't help thinking there's a good show to be made out of lavatories (perhaps a *Scrapheap Challenge* special), but sadly, this ain't it. Rather than providing any real insight into precisely why we're so anal about our anuses (as C4's *Anatomy of Disgust* did last year), it seems content to simply reiterate obvious facts, in the manner of a particularly uninformative retrospective 'I Love' nostalgia blast. Perhaps they should have called it 'I Love Going Plop-Plop' instead, and given us a clearer idea of what to expect.

That's it. Now wash your hands.

A Tin of Beans and No Can Opener   [26 January]

When the shit hits the fan, you'll wish you'd seen *Ray Mears' Extreme Survival* (BBC2). Sitting in an irradiated wasteland, longing to snare, skin and spit-roast a passing mutant rat – if only you knew how – you'll pause and kick yourself for not having paid attention while Ray was on our screens.

So why didn't you? Answer: because on the evidence of this week's edition, *Ray Mears' Extreme Survival* is actually rather boring, that's why. So if you don't tune in then maybe one day you'll starve to death up a hillside in a tent clutching a tin of beans and no can opener, but at least you enjoyed slightly more entertaining television before death swooped down to snatch you away.

Perhaps I expect too much, but when I see the word 'extreme' in a programme title, extreme is what I want. But this feels decidedly softcore. For starters, Ray looks more like a plump village butcher than a weather-beaten survivalist. I was hoping for more macho excitement – even some brutality perhaps. I wanted to see Ray snap the head off a swan, then use its beak to jemmy open a coconut. But no. Instead he seems to spend half his time trudging around New England, setting up tents and making tedious little fires. That may be survival, but it sure ain't living, and having spent many a miserable, uncomfortable night under canvas myself, I for one would sooner die than ever go camping again.

Still, in case you find yourself stranded in an emergency situation this week – marooned in your living room with the remote control out of reach and Ray Mears on the box – here's some tips on how to survive the programme itself:

1) Drink strong coffee. 2) Sit with your arms folded, staring straight ahead at the screen. 3) When your attention starts to flag,

simply imagine the programme is more exciting – and if that fails, try glancing at a more interesting object in the room for a few minutes (a rolled-up sock or coffee cup should do the trick) until you feel ready to leap back in.

Still thirsting for macho kicks, I was forced to take a look at *Have-a-Go Heroes* (BBC1), a pop-doc blend of real-life stories and psychobabble aimed squarely at the Tony Martin in all of us. The best bits are the almost shamefully unpleasant candid-camera stunts, designed to test the public's willingness to intervene when crimes appear to happen beneath their noses. Early on, two actors feign a road-rage incident in the middle of Primrose Hill, tossing each other around the pavement, swearing and swiping at one another in an increasingly violent manner.

If Ray Mears were in the vicinity he could doubtless fashion an impromptu bow and arrow out of some nearby railings and put an end to the carnage, but sadly he wasn't available. Instead, the fight takes place before an audience of gawping pedestrians, with all but one unwilling to step in. Afterwards, the camera crew nose around asking the inert civilians to justify their apparent cowardice.

'You just stand and watch, don't you?' says a man who did just that, before adding cheerfully that even if he'd lived in Ancient Rome he'd 'still watch the Christians being burnt'.

Once the eye-popping stunt footage has spooled away, impossibly glamorous rent-a-shrink Dr Sandra Scott (as seen on *Big Brother* and – well, pretty much anything else that requires an impossibly glamorous rent-a-shrink) is on hand to provide the analysis, helpfully bothering to explain why passers-by are more likely to come to the aid of a young woman in smart clothing than a dishevelled man clutching a bottle of beer. (Apparently it's because people make snap judgements about a person's appearance – something Dr Sandra Scott, who resembles an icy Bond villainess, should know all about.)

This is an overlong show which runs out of steam about 100 years before the end, so in all likelihood you'll have nodded off before the spectacular finale, in which the genuinely tragic tale of a man who died attempting to defend a stranger is turned into one of the most jaw-droppingly mawkish pieces of television you're ever likely to see. Do we really need to see staged shots of a murdered man's son climbing a ladder in a bid to catch a glowing star representing his late father? Answer: no – but they went ahead and filmed them anyway. It was a taste crime in progress, and someone should have intervened – but all they did was stand and stare.

Humanoids with Funny Foreheads [2 February]

Q: When is nostalgia not nostalgia? A: When it's set in the future. Which pretty much sums up *Enterprise* (Sky One), the latest mutated offspring of Gene Roddenberry's original *Star Trek* series, boldly going where countless men have gone before.

In the grand tradition of *The Phantom Menace* and, er, *Indiana Jones and the Temple of Doom*, *Enterprise* is a 'prequel', set in the days before Captain Kirk hauled his paunch around the galaxy in search of strange new worlds and alien hippy chicks hungry for some Earth-man lovin'.

It's a mixed bag. On the plus side, teleportation devices don't appear to have been invented yet, so there's no preposterous 'beam me up' nonsense on show. Nor is there any high-concept faffing around in a 'holodeck' to confuse matters. Instead the format is more stripped-down, more in tune with the easy-to-grasp original: visit alien planet; discover hostile species; teach them a lesson; kiss and make up; wave goodbye; captain's log; the end.

All sounds good on paper. But there are drawbacks. The retro touches (old-fashioned phaser effects, endearing nods to the 1960s in the spaceship design, a female Spock) feel at odds with the up-to-date production values. And just to further muddy the general sense of what-era-is-this-anyway? they cast Quantum Leap time-hopper Scott Bakula in the lead role. Sensors indicate Bakula's Captain Archer contains no character traits whatsoever; he simply walks around looking permanently constipated (presumably he's having trouble producing the captain's log).

Then there are the aliens, who in fine *Trek* tradition seem to be little more than humanoids with funny foreheads (generally shaped like someone's fired a handful of crab parts into their brow). In these days of CGI dinosaur fun, we deserve better than mere make-up – we want permanent crewmembers with the bodies of spiders and the heads of donkeys, sporting Jamiroquai hats.

And the theme music – Jesus. The worst kind of 1980s soft-metal wanking imaginable; a Gillette commercial from hell. I'm all for rock music in theme tunes – Channel Five's CSI benefits greatly from having the Who play out over the credits, and if I were in charge *Newsnight* would open with an uninterrupted three-minute blast of Motorhead's 'Ace Of Spades'. But the makers of *Enterprise* have commissioned an absolute dirge, whose unironic presence betrays an inherent lack of wit at production level. Sure enough, the programme itself is far too humourless for its own good; overall, it's got the feel of a bland motivational poster on the wall of a software house (you know the kind of thing: a photograph of some dolphins and a greetings-card motto extolling the virtues of teamwork – distract the worker ants with enough of them and you can reduce desktop wrist-slashings by 13 per cent a quarter).

Marginally more successful prequel confusion can be found in *Smallville* (C4) or 'Superman: The Pubic Development Years'. Telling the tale of Clark Kent's teenage existence – a sort of Dawson's Kryptonite, if you like – it's just as confusing as *Enterprise* in that it's set firmly in the present day, when in your head it should all take place on the set of *Happy Days*.

Clark himself looks like a young Rob Lowe, and as befits the future man of steel, he's nauseatingly pleasant. Any normal hyperpowered teenager would be abusing his abilities to pull off superhuman *Jackass*-style stunts – tossing live cows onto the roof of the local high school, that kind of thing – but namby-pamby Clark contents himself with tidying up at the speed of light and insipid do-gooding. Boo to that.

The young Lex Luthor is a far more interesting prospect – a slap-headed 19-year-old whose inexplicable baldness hasn't yet turned him bitter and evil. Instead, his wilfully unpleasant father is the Darth Vader of the piece, simultaneously spoiling and corrupting his offspring.

Staying on a retro tip, *Scrubs* (Sky One) is a medical comedy splicing elements of *M*A*S*H* with the stylings of *Ally McBeal*. There are plenty of good lines, but the whole thing's in constant danger of being undermined by the *McBeal* influence – an over-reliance on quickfire 'fantasy' sequences and self-consciously kooky cartoon sound effects.

And for a black comedy, it's not quite black enough – more dark grey with occasional neon flashes. Patients die left, right and centre, but the show tends to chicken out and turn mawkish at the very last moment.

Cuh. Americans.

Arrogant, Unrepentant, Ugly and Rich [9 February]

This week, Channel 4 brings you the tales of two notorious sexual predators whose names have become synonymous with iniquity and manipulation. One was an uncontrollably demented holy man who exerted a dangerous level of influence over the Russian royal family and inadvertently sowed the seeds of revolution. The other recorded 'Una Paloma Blanca'.

The latter is profiled in Jon Ronson's *The Double Life of Jonathan King* (C4). Anyone expecting a kooky Theroux-style stalkathon is likely to be disappointed, since the programme largely consists of sobering talking-head interviews with King's former friends and victims, intercut with grimly comic archive clips illustrating the maestro's oeuvre.

It transpires King used his celebrity status to dazzle a succession of under-age boys, befriending them, showering them with gifts, exhibiting interest in their opinions, and then, just as they began to trust their exciting altruistic chum, spoiled it all by bringing his erect penis into the equation.

Convicted sex offenders don't tend to arouse much sympathy in the general public – particularly when they're arrogant, unrepentant, ugly and rich – but King himself comes across as such a miserable wretch, it's hard not to sense a small mouse of pity gnawing at the edges of your mind. An insecure misfit, who developed his odious, grating persona specifically to provoke a reaction from an otherwise uninterested world, King's crimes seem motivated more by crushing inferiority – coupled with a deeply misplaced craving for acceptance – than simple tabloid malevolence.

More disturbing is the fact that he got away with it for so long simply because he was famous – despised by huge swathes of the population, but famous nonetheless – and this pathetic glamour hypnotized his victims into returning.

One interviewee, whose relationship with King spanned 18 months, explains how exciting it felt to ride around in a Rolls Royce, accompanying a star.

'But he was only Jonathan King,' remarks Ronson.

'He was the most famous person I knew,' comes the poignant reply.

While wonky mouthed, troll-faced King had to deploy a rainbow-coloured wig and a string of novelty records to impress his prey, mad monk Rasputin had more natural advantages, namely piercing eyes and the apparent ability to heal ailments.

Like many people, my knowledge of Rasputin has to date been based solely on Boney M lyrics – I knew he was 'Russia's greatest love machine', and 'a cat that really was gone', but little else.

Until now. *Masters of Darkness: Rasputin* (C4) is one of the most entertaining historical documentaries I have ever seen, partly because it deals with the nefarious deeds of an absolute shit, and partly because it's brilliantly put together – a genuinely thrilling combination of informative talking-head opinions, archive footage and creepy reconstruction, liberally swathed with horror-movie sheen.

Rather than leaping head first into his most unhinged period, the programme carefully charts Rasputin's evolution from childhood freak (apparently his parents were 'disturbed by his ability to heal horses by touching them' – try finding *that* in 'Parenting for Dummies') to influential lunatic, lending weight and momentum to what could have easily been a gaudy ho-ho at a shagging monk.

As it is, Rasputin's shenanigans were fuelled by warped religious logic. Believing that redemption was the ultimate spiritual experience, it followed that the only way to garner redemption was to commit sin first – and the bigger the sin, the bigger the redemption that came after. Spiritual bulimia, in other words.

Which is why, in his prime, Rasputin would have sex with anything. Toss a ham sandwich across the room and he'd fuck it twice before it hit the floor. Russian society, gripped by a craze for spiritual weirdness and convinced of his healing abilities, gave him free reign to indulge, even though he stank like a sink full of mouldy fur.

Just like Jonathan King, Rasputin got away with it because of the aura of celebrity surrounding him. Yet both cases took place some time ago – today, we're more fame-obsessed than ever, so I've got no idea what insane acts of depravity our modern A-list stars get up to.

Although if *you* have, and you fancy drawing me an accurate picture (in crayon), send it in, care of the 'Guide'. Most repulsive example wins a pack of bourbon creams and a shoe. Promise.

'I didn't "get away with it"' [2 March]

After his dissatisfying (and overlong) encounter with the Hamiltons, Bridget Jones pin-up Louis Theroux does himself no favours whatsoever in *When Louis Met Anne Widdecombe* (BBC2) pestering her about her virginity (or lack of it) in a downright unpleasant manner within the first few minutes. And when she objects – having consented to the documentary on the understanding that her sex life (or lack of it) would not be discussed – her gruff complaints to the offscreen producer are left in the edit, thereby making her appear guarded and unreasonable.

Theroux is at his best when pitching his blatant insincerity against that of an equally insincere subject – fighting fire with fire – but, unfortunately for him, Widdecombe doesn't appear insincere in the slightest. A distant, stunted control freak with a face like a haunted cave in Poland who espouses depressing political views, maybe – but so are half of the pricks in the House of Commons. And aside from her ghost-train looks, Widdecombe has little that is strange or weird about her. The end result is an uncomfortably sneery hour-long amble in the company of someone who doesn't warrant the effort of a sneer in the first place.

Speaking of which, no advance tapes of *Being Victoria Beckham* (ITV1) are available, presumably on the basis that the programme's content is so universe-poppingly mind-blowing, its release must be cautiously timed and controlled, lest epochs start shattering around our quaking ankles. Therefore, in a fit of nihilistic despair, I opted for *Michael Landy: The Man Who Destroyed Everything* (BBC2) instead. Landy hit the headlines in 2001 when he spent a fortnight systematically dismantling and shredding his every possession in a deserted C&A store in the middle of Oxford Street. Everything was torn apart and mangled, from the big (his Saab car) to the small (a pen he stole from a friend's house). A detailed roster of all the destroyed items is all that remains – a list of 7,226 deceased belongings.

This documentary follows him in the weeks immediately afterwards, as he stumbles around, trying to make sense of his actions and gingerly making his first post-shredding purchases. There's also background information on Landy himself, and comments from dealers, critics, relatives and artists.

Ah, artists. They're always good value for money, and there's plenty of them here. Hilariously, some cantankerous old autodestructive artist named Gustav, actually wearing a beret and pointedly sitting with his back to the camera (because he 'shuns all publicity'), explains that 'Landy demonstrated the artist should not be the centre of attention'. He's saying this to a crew making a documentary on artist Michael Landy, the man who destroyed everything, and you don't get much more centre-of-attention that that.

So why did Landy do it? Take your pick: it was either a brilliant attack on consumerism or a brilliant piece of self-promotion. Either way, a brilliant spectacle, and an unexpectedly touching piece of television.

Finally, an aside: a few weeks ago, writing about the Jon Ronson documentary on Jonathan King, I foolishly – and to be honest, somewhat lazily – invited readers to send in crayon sketches of A-list celebrities engaged in hypothetical wanton exploits. The response was disappointing. In fact, only one person bothered entering: Jonathan King himself.

Using prison notepaper, Belmarsh inmate FF8782 drew a stick man sitting at a desk, captioned 'Charlie Brooker at word-processor (A-list star in act of modern depravity)'.

He's a one.

'I didn't "get away with it" because of the aura of celebrity surrounding me,' he writes, 'I got away with it because I didn't do it – a terribly boring explanation, although true.'

He also takes issue with my describing him as 'ugly' ('very handsome, as your picture showed') and 'insecure' ('I don't feel the slightest bit insecure – in fact, at the moment, rather too secure,' before going on to mildly berate me for not describing him as an 'easy target' or the victim of 'delusions, exaggerations, compensation [or] false allegations'.

Quite an amusing letter, as it goes, and had you received it you'd probably find it hard not to warm to him – unless, of course, you were one of the under-age kids he once waved his dick at. Ah well. What a wonderful world.

A Sure-Fire Recipe for Chuckles [9 March]

Jesus pole-vaulting Christ, you absolutely MUST watch *All About Me* (BBC1). There are no words in the English language to adequately describe it, so I'll have to invent one: flabbertrocious. That's a combination of 'flabbergasting' and 'atrocious', and it's as close as I can get to conveying the programme's perverse car-crash appeal without resorting to wild gesticulations, donkey noises or daubing a six-foot illustration of a weeping swan on your living-room wall.

This is that most unlikely of things: a joint Jasper Carrott/Meera Syal vehicle, in which they play a multi-racial couple with children from previous marriages, one of whom is severely disabled. A sure-fire recipe for chuckles if ever there was one.

I'm extremely fond of tortoise-headed Jasper Carrott, largely on the basis of warm teenage memories of his stand-up routines – but a versatile actor he ain't, and his performance here single-handedly redefines awkwardness. He spends the entire half-hour looking about as comfortable as a horse trying to balance in the middle of a see-saw. Your heart goes out to him, and indeed to everyone else in the cast – thoroughly decent sorts who've found themselves unexpectedly shipwrecked on the rocks of Bumwipe Island.

Bad sitcoms are ten-a-penny, but *All About Me* transcends them all. It's not just the shoddy jokes (half-hearted gags that lie around like dying soldiers on a battleground; sample exchange: 'Does your son like football?' 'No – he supports Man United!'), but the inclusion of frankly astonishing 'poignant' interludes that render the programme unique. The final five minutes of this week's episode – a belief-beggaring laugh-free sequence in which Jasper Carrott revisits his childhood home, has a flashback, and leaves in tears – constitute the most awesomely misjudged piece of television I've seen in years. As I said at the start, words can't do it justice, and with every cell in my body I urge you to tune in and witness the mangle for yourself.

Speaking of incommunicable spectacle, after weeks of being urged by friends, I finally got round to catching *Club Reps* (ITV1), and – well, what is there to say? It's like staring at footage of a football hooligan spinning round on a plastic sheet, dribbling and soiling themselves while 'Sex Bomb' plays in the background. I felt like dressing up as Travis Bickle and wandering onscreen to dispense a little smoking-barrel justice.

Why, precisely, are they filming these ugly, self-aggrandising, slack-jawed, leering, drunken, pointless buffoons? Answer: so we can all have a good cathartic sneer. And naturally, the cynical gambit works – but lest we forget, you could create an equally effective Bickle-baiting hatefest by training the cameras on the kind of snide, boneheaded, bellowing, drug-pumped, upper-middle-class scum who populate the media and consider this kind of programme a worthwhile addition to the tapestry of contemporary culture. Morons filming morons for the benefit of morons: it's one big imbecilic circle-jerk.

Do I sound bad-tempered? It's not all hatred and despair. Thank the Lord for *24* (BBC2) – utterly preposterous and impossible to leave alone. The big gimmick actually works. Each episode takes place in 'real time', tracing the events of a single hour in one chaotic day, slowly building, in the style of a weekly Marshall-Cavendish part work, into one 24-hour, 24-episode whole. The sense of rising momentum and increasingly clammy claustrophobia has me hopelessly gripped, even though on reflection it all seems about as realistic as Willy Wonka's chocolate factory. I'm already looking forward to the end of the series, at which point some enterprising cable channel can run the entire shebang in its full, improbable 24-hour glory.

And Kiefer Sutherland: bloody hell, he's good. His famously buttock-shaped cheeks have diminished in size, so it's now possible to concentrate on what an assured performer he is without worrying whether his mouth is about to break wind. Mind you, I'm slightly worried about his character, a counter-terrorist troubleshooter who spends approximately 70 per cent of his screen time blabbing on his mobile to anyone who'll listen.

He's so cellphone-dependent, he'll have to have spent the whole of episode eight recharging the damn thing – assuming, of course, he hasn't been finished off by a microwave-induced brain tumour by then.

Casualty on a Cliffside   [23 March]

Quivering fool that I am, I'm petrified of heights – or, more specifically, tumbling off them. Perfectly rational really: if there's one thing the human body wasn't designed to do, it's plummeting.

Benevolently enough, my anxiety also extends to cover other people. I can't bear to watch builders standing on rooftops or window cleaners sitting on window ledges (it's only a smudged window for God's sake – get back inside and stop risking your life in the name of transparency). Rock climbers are the worst. In the suicidal stakes, clambering up a mountainside is an activity on a par with licking plug sockets or goading Mike Tyson with a brightly coloured stick (now there's an idea for a televised sporting event).

All things considered, I was expecting to sit through the BBC's new mountain rescue drama *Rockface* (BBC1) with one hand over my eyes and the other unscrewing a bottle of tranquillisers. Imagine my dismay when in this week's episode (the first I've seen), no one topples off anything resembling a perilous drop. There's no yawning-chasm action whatsoever: just a couple of kids trapped on a small rock in the middle of a disappointingly placid river, who get rescued in the most laidback way imaginable. Boo to that.

Presumably, *Rockface* is supposed to be 'Casualty on a Cliffside', but the setting seems a little too self-limiting. At least in *Casualty* there's a certain random variety to the injuries – one minute you're watching someone trying to prise the lid off a jam jar with a butter knife, and the next their arm's dangling from a single tendon. Where, precisely, is the diversity going to spring from in *Rockface*? Once you've covered plunging rock climbers and mislaid hikers, what else can happen? Someone choking to death on a mint cake? After six weeks, it's all going to seem as predictable as a programme called 'Frisbee Retrieval Unit' ('OK, team, we've got a Frisbee lodged up a tree in the park – let's be careful out there.') *Rockface*'s answer seems to be to take the *Holby City* route and ramp up the soap opera element until the mountain-rescue element becomes almost incidental, so we get to see more of the team's personal lives than is entirely healthy. Trouble is, not only are their personal lives altogether pedestrian (with nary a paedophile nor psychopath amongst them to spice things up), but since half the cast consists of vague celebrity lookalikes it's easy to get confused. There's one who looks like Robbie Williams, another who resembles Brad Pitt with dark hair, and a girl who could double for Sophie Ellis Bextor in a dimly lit nightclub. And the ones who couldn't open supermarkets for a living just look weird: there's a rugged bloke with fascinatingly tiny eyes (about the size of a bat's), and a balding guy who looks a bit like a cheerful potato.

Still, maybe I'm missing the point: perhaps the real appeal of *Rockface* is supposed to lie in the glorious scenery – although if that's the case they should just broadcast a still shot of *The Haywain* instead and have done with it.

The 'What the Fuck?' Factor   [30 March]

This week on BBC1: hardcore pornography! Hardcore BESTIAL pornography! And it's all pre-watershed, where the kiddies can see it! Quelle horreur!

But don't panic. We're not talking about a special edition of *East-Enders* where Phil falls off the wagon and violates a dog in the middle of the Square (although I'm lobbying hard for that storyline, ideally during this year's Christmas Special). No. The raw sex in question occurs throughout *Weird Nature* (BBC1), which this week pokes a lens at the bizarre world of animal copulation.

Fascinating stuff, of course, unless like me you've been recently singled, in which case it'll only serve as a ghastly reminder that there are wart-encrusted toads out there in the world enjoying more fulfilling sex lives than you.

It's a cunning programme, *Weird Nature*. The producers have latched on to what viewers enjoy most about nature shows – namely, the 'what the fuck?' factor – and decided to provide nothing but. Consequently, there's no breathy Attenborough commentary, lingering shots of majestic fjords or diagrammatic explanations of the way cormorants' beaks work – just one juicy piece of oddness after another, accompanied by as little background information as possible. It's the natural-history equivalent of binge snacking.

Human sexuality may be a garbled mish-mash of perversions (and I once read about a man who could only achieve orgasm by swinging a live chicken around so its panicked wings brushed the tip of his penis, so I know what I'm talking about), but we've got nothing on the average beastie. *Weird Nature* brings us a tiny rodent that literally shags itself to death, a female fish that turns itself into a male and a downright disturbing sequence in which a male praying mantis continues thrusting despite being decapitated mid-coitus (a tiny brain in his rear end keeps him going – look for a similar sequence in the next series of *Club Reps*).

Filthiest of all is the humble sea flare, which has a male front end and a female back end, thereby enabling unlimited orgies in which aroused passers-by latch on to whichever end is closest. They're even shown forming a snug sexual daisy chain at the bottom of the sea, each simultaneously humping the other like a pornographic synchronised-swimming team. So be humbled, fetish club regulars: next time you're congratulating yourself on your latest bacchanalian sexual encounter, bear in mind there are tiny slug-like monsters who can effortlessly outdo you – and *they* don't have to spend a fortune on clockwork bum machines in order to reach nirvana.

Anyway, back to the insanely addictive *24* (BBC2). Those of you who've missed it thus far have a chance to catch up tonight, when BBC2 screens the first four episodes back to back, prior to the fifth instalment on Sunday (helpful BBC scheduling for a quality US import – what the hell's going on? Progress?).

It's now 4–5 a.m., and finally someone actually goes to sleep (a minor character, admittedly, but at least it's a vague nod in the direction of realism). For some reason, the Noble Senator seems to think he'll be able to function on the most important day of his political career without enjoying a moment's shut-eye the night before. Didn't he see *Touch the Truck*? Assassination will be the least of his worries once sleep deprivation kicks in and he starts swatting invisible demons in the middle of a pre-election press conference.

Meanwhile Jack Bauer (Kiefer Sutherland) continues his ongoing quest to get himself sacked. In week one, he shot a superior in the leg with a tranquilliser gun, and then blackmailed him. In last Sunday's episode, he thumped an FBI agent in the guts and got a police officer killed. Having thus torn up the rulebook, this week he proceeds to piss on the tattered remains by trying to organise a jailbreak.

All this in the space of a few hours. By 7 p.m. he'll be constructing a death ray and threatening to demolish what's left of Manhattan.

The Relentless Tick of the Clock [6 April]

Assuming you bothered to read my jabberings last week, apologies for the déjà vu, but I'm still hopelessly fixated with *24* (BBC2), the 'real-time' assassination drama that's single-handedly transformed Kiefer Sutherland from a Droopy-a-like brat pack also-ran into a sturdy action hero, and is currently the best populist drama on television by a good six-metre stretch.

Somehow, the relentless tick of the clock distracts you from pondering the show's more ludicrous elements – at least while you're watching it. After each episode I can't help shaking my head in disbelief at what I've just witnessed, as though awakening from a distinctly implausible dream that seemed convincing at the time. Therefore, in a bid to retain my grip on reality, I'm compiling a list of the most absurd elements, which I present here as a public service.

1) Jack Bauer's Anti-Terrorist HQ

What's with this place? Frosted glass, chrome railings, tasteful lighting, glamorous employees draped in Armani – it looks more like the offices of a Hoxton-based fashion magazine than a top-secret quasi-military nerve centre. I keep checking the background, half-expecting to see Sophie Dahl eating a punnet of sushi, or someone in a pair of low-slung jeans slipping an imported DJ Shadow CD onto the office stereo. It doesn't help that no one present, aside from Action Jack himself of course, appears to be doing any work whatsoever: look closely and you'll see they're simply wandering calmly hither and thither, occasionally stopping to shuffle bits of paper around or gawp at a monitor (doubtless in order to languidly check their Hotmail or log on to 'Friends Reunited'). They're supposed to be thwarting an assassination attempt, fer Chrissakes! They should be running around chain-smoking and barking orders at subordinates, or at the very least rolling their sleeves up and sweating like hillbillies.

Actually, there is one exception to the no-sweat-in-the-workplace rule and that's . . .

2) Shifty Beppe Guy

You know the one: the patently sinister computer expert who's banging Jack's ex-mistress, and has a miniscule hint of black goatee beneath his bottom lip, like a Hitler moustache that's accidentally slipped down his face. His job seems to consist solely of demanding to know 'what's going on' every thirteen seconds, being out-wardly confrontational with his boss (i.e. Jack), and peering suspi-ciously at anyone within a five-metre radius. He's like a dark twenty-first-century 're-imagining' of the McDonald's Hamburglar, and as such it's hard to comprehend why the hell they employed him in the first place.

3) Bill and Ted's bogus kidnapping

Bill and Ted, who appear to have undergone a startling transfor-mation of attitude during their years away from the limelight, have kidnapped Jack's daughter at the behest of the terrorists. Quite why a ruthless cabal of ultra-organised killers would entrust such a haz-ardous scheme to a pair of loafing, nu-metal stoners has yet to be explained. Perhaps it's a work-experience thing.

4) Mandy the oversexed, overkilling plane bomber

And while we're on the subject of the terrorists, what the hell's up with Mandy? Her task in episode one: to steal a photographer's press pass. Does she break into his apartment and rifle through the drawers? Does she pick his pocket on the subway? No: she seduces him on a passenger jet, screws his brains out in the toilet, steals the pass, and then covers her tracks by blowing up the plane in mid-air and parachuting into the middle of the Mojave Desert. Perhaps I'm oversensitive, but to me that smacks of overkill. Never one to do anything by halves, she opened episode two by stripping naked in the desert and spices up episode three with a French kiss for her Alanis Morissette girlfriend. By episode nine she'll be doing that trick with the ping-pong balls. Probably as part of the assassination.

5) Jack's car

Jack's car is a thing of wonder. Not only is it capable of travelling to any location in under five minutes (pretty handy in a real-time show), it's also positively laden with handy gizmos. This week he makes use of a fingerprint scanner which seems to have been installed *specifically* to identify thumbs he's recently severed from dead assailants. It's like the Innovations catalogue on wheels: next week, expect him to spend ten minutes operating a dashboard-mounted air de-ioniser before opening the boot to reveal a combi-nation rotating tie rack/GPS satellite system.

I could go on, but space won't permit me. Send your own 24 implausibilites in and I'll add them to the roster. But hurry: the clock's ticking.

Frowning with Added Vigour [13 April]

He's a toff. She's a pleb. Together they're a crime-fighting force to be reckoned with. I speak, of course, of Lynley and Havers, currently solving *The Inspector Lynley Mysteries* (BBC1).

It's all creaky bunkum of the highest order, but curiously entertaining nonetheless. I can't put my finger on precisely where the appeal lies, but it's got something to do with Inspector Lynley himself – the least congenial law enforcement officer since Harvey Keitel in *Bad Lieutenant*.

Not only is he an absolute crashing posho (fourteenth in line to the throne, raised on a diet of fox chunks in pauper's tears, etc., etc.), he's also devoid of humour and physically incapable of performing any facial expression more complex than his standard three: 1) annoyed, 2) annoyed and frowning, 3) *very* annoyed and *really* frowning.

I'm not joking: his face never changes. Lynley seems to have taken the traditional British principle of maintaining a 'stiff upper lip' and applied it to his entire head. You could spend an afternoon flicking rice in his eyes and he wouldn't blink or flinch once. He doubtless maintains the same rigid appearance even at the point of orgasm, although it's as hard to envisage Lynley reaching a climax as it is to picture, say, Peter Sissons in a similar situation.

(Speaking of which, when are they going to give Peter Sissons his own detective series? Can you *possibly imagine* how great that would be? They could simply call it 'Sissons', cast Jenny Powell as his glamorous sidekick, and boom: instant ratings magic.)

Anyway, back to the Lynley Show. Two episodes in, and a pattern has already developed. Despite the fact that he's a *Metropolitan* police officer, and should really be spending his time picking incriminating fibres from heroin-soaked cadavers in the capital's gutters, each week Lynley is summoned to an archetypal British location (last week a public school, this week a whopping-great mansion) deep in the glorious countryside. He must be part of the Met's new Picturesque Murder Division. Having arrived in the middle of *The Haywain* to frown at a collection of absurdly shifty suspects (each with more skeletons in the cupboard than Ed Gein), he encounters an old friend who becomes enraged by his insistence on following basic procedure by questioning them. Meanwhile, common old Havers puffs along behind him, repeatedly bemoaning Lynley's personal involvement in the case or making barbed comments about the class system, while failing to uncover the faintest shred of evidence herself. Midway through the investigation, a second victim buys the farm, right under the collective nose of the local police force. This annoys Lynley immensely, causing him to spend the rest of the episode frowning with added vigour. In fact it messes his face up completely – by the time the killer (easily identifiable as the character with the least amount of screen time) is unmasked, Lynley's eyebrows are knitted together in a tangled snarl, like a man halfway through a werewolf transformation.

In other words, you know what you're getting with *The Inspector Lynley Mysteries*: the same story, week after week, with few troublesome facial expressions to interrupt your viewing pleasure. Its function is not to provide any genuine mystery, but something altogether familiar and comforting: the TV equivalent of a flask of warm cocoa and a big slice of Battenberg.

Oops: little space to discuss *24* (BBC2). I'm swamped by your e-mails regarding the mounting implausibilities, from the glaringly obvious (Jack's repeated cellphone use in the hospital, the terrorist's preposterous hijacking of every CCTV system in the world, Kim's astonishing grave-digging skills) to the insanely specific ('Jack's phone is a Nokia 7110e. After dialling a number, it takes around seven seconds to be connected, whereas Jack gets an instant connection,' writes Drew Jagger). And five of you questioned the decision to cast Cherie Blair as Nina.

As for me, I'm busy mourning poor Janet York, who in the space of seven hours got seduced, deceived, kidnapped, assaulted, injected with heroin, hunted, run over, revived, and finally murdered in her hospital bed. Still, at least she never learnt that her dad had been murdered, mutilated, stuffed in a trunk and replaced by a psychotic impostor.

Every cloud, etc.

Leaving South London   [20 April]

I'm going to kill myself. Don't try to stop me. It's all planned out. Just as Nicolas Cage drank himself to death in *Leaving Las Vegas*, I intend to commit slow-motion suicide by eating nothing but jumbo sausage rolls from Gregg's the Bakers on Battersea Park Road. Leaving South London, if you like. Come July my arteries will be so clogged, my heart will start knocking on my chest and demand to be let out for some air.

Still, I can expire safe in the knowledge that by stuffing my face with low-glamour lard I'm going against the grain. This week's *Food Junkies* (BBC2) examines how supermarkets have altered our eating habits, replacing the traditional notion of buying what you want to eat with an altogether more aspirational purchasing strategy.

The programme opens with a Waitrose honcho visiting Portugal to inspect some 'horned melon' – a bland fruit whose desirability is dictated by its out-of-this-world appearance: it looks like a triffid's testicle. More a talking point than a taste experience, it's doomed to nestle in the fruit bowls of smug colour-supplement Joneses, intent on expressing their sophistication by filling their po-faced homes with self-consciously refined crap. It's the latest hateful twist in a revolution that's seen traditional grocers (with their cheery overpricing and quaint rotting produce) usurped by out-of-town supermarket motherships (hawking snooty olive oil and frosty triffid bollocks).

No shots were fired, but it's still been a ruthless coup. Supermarkets have tried everything, from squeezing food producers until they snap, to engaging in demented price wars (the show covers the Baked Bean War, when rival supermarkets slashed prices to 3p a can – and kept going, in one case actually paying customers to take them away).

The current tactic is to hire a celebrity chef. Sainsbury's has Roy Hattersley Jr (Jamie Oliver), Waitrose plumped for Raymond Blanc. Just about the only TV pan-slinger without a deal is Antony Worrall Thompson, who claims he's not really interested in that kind of thing (which is good news for the trade – who'd want to shop in a supermarket recommended by the warrior dwarf from *Fellowship of the Ring*?).

Further entrepreneurial spirit in *Cannabis Cafes UK* (BBC2), which follows scouser Jimmy as he tries to open a Dutch-style 'coffee house' in Bournemouth – a plan only mildly hindered by the fact that it's against the law.

Stupid, really. All drugs should be legal, with the possible exception of Pro-Plus, and aside from the paranoia, memory loss, apathy, psychological dependency and disorientation, marijuana has few ill effects. Quite why any self-respecting stoner would bother venturing outside (as opposed to sitting at home in the dark playing 'Super Magic Rhino Party' on a Sony Wowbox 4) is beyond me, but, hey, if someone wants to pay good money to visit a New Age bongo shack and sit opposite some prick with a chillum, for God's sake let them.

Interesting stuff, but having sat through *Food Junkies*, it's hard to shake the suspicion that in five years' time Jimmy will be heading a national chain of out-of-town spliff bars, replete with designer hash and a saturation ad campaign starring celebrity toker Howard Marks.

So You Think You Want a Hand the Size of a Cymbal? [27 April]

It's not often you discover the truth behind a myth, but it happened to me today. I'd heard of radio DJs receiving crateloads of freebies whenever they 'inadvertently' mutter a brandname, but always dismissed such tales as cynical fable. Until now. Last week, I wrote of my life-endangering addiction to the 'jumbo' sausage rolls available from a certain high-street baker's, and lo and behold, four days later, an unsolicited assignment of piping-hot savouries arrives at my workplace, as though scattered by a benevolent god.

Do I feel corrupted? No. Just ill. I've never eaten so much mashed pig in one sitting. I can already sense the ingested calories preparing to distort my body in new and exciting ways. Soon I'll be the proud owner of a mighty set of man-tits: those wobbly little melted pyramids of flab that nestle above the planetoid guts of the nation's masculine fatties.

To prepare myself for the inevitable, I cocked an eye at *So You Think You Want Bigger Boobs?* (C4), an epoch-shattering 'TV experiment' charting the progress of a flat-chested Liverpudlian hairdresser (eerily enough, also named Charlie) as she dons a set of fake breasts for a week in order to ascertain whether top-heaviness will improve her life. In the opening half, Charlie is sent to Shepperton Studios, where special-effects artists take a mould of her existing chest and set about creating a decoy bust to drape over the top. So far, so good – but as soon as the fruits of their labour are revealed, it's clear the project will fail.

What they have produced is perhaps the largest and most unconvincing pair of breasts you'll see this side of a fairground hall of mirrors: two mammoth swellings lolling in opposite directions, each topped off with a nipple the size of a cork. The moment Charlie hauls them on, she looks like one of those inept Internet fakes purporting to depict a topless starlet – the porno equivalent of Frankenstein's monster, only slightly less arousing.

Before long, Charlie's complaining that they're 'heavy', that they 'get in the way' and, least surprising of all, that people are 'staring' at them. Of *course* they are – you look like you've got a Ford Ka reversing out of your ribcage, for Christ's sake.

Consequently, the programme tells you nothing, save the obvious: being an aberration of nature ain't exactly a barrel of laughs. Still, it's inspired a range of follow-up programmes that I intend to start pitching tomorrow: 'So You Think You Want a Hand the Size of a Cymbal?', 'So You Think You Want Moss for a Beard?', and most promising of all, 'So You Think You Want to Walk down Oxford Street with a Dick Grafted onto Your Forehead?'

The big TV event of the week is the return of *Auf Wiedersehen, Pet*

(BBC1), something I'm unqualified to comment on with any degree of authority, having been too young to appreciate the original ITV series, which at the time seemed to consist entirely of slightly frightening men standing in a Portakabin, bellowing at one another in a dialect I didn't understand. (Having just read that description back, I realise I've made it sound like the sort of thing avant-garde toffs pay £640 to see at the Royal Court Theatre, but never mind).

What to make of this twenty-first-century respray? Well, it's early days, but to this newbie it feels sturdy enough. For one thing, it's refreshing to see a cast composed of unsightly, unglamorous blokes (or 'blerks'). Jimmy Nail in particular looks like an identikit photo assembled by Picasso using nothing but close-ups of knuckles and spuds. You know you're deep within a true jungle of ugliness when Kevin Whately's the best-looking man on screen by a wide margin.

As for the programme, it's a slyly jumbled concoction: a cosily predictable cartoon about loveable rogues, interspersed with flashes of grit (one's dead, one's got a terminal illness, and another's been reduced to driving a drug dealer around local schools to make ends meet). I suspect fans of the original may scream blue murder (that's their job), but I'm sufficiently interested to turn up for episode two.

Oh, and in case any other PR agencies fancy following the marvellous example set by Gregg's the Bakers, I'd just like to mention Blaupunkt, Sony, Agent Provocateur, Virgin Atlantic, Budgens, Walkers French Fries (any flavour), Ikea and the Nintendo Gamecube.

No one sent me a fucking thing.

The Most Sour-Faced Person on Television [25 May]

What an appalling time this is for non-voyeuristic, unpatriotic, football-hating Britons. First the screens get clogged up with the World Cup and *Big Brother*, and then the Queen's Golden Jubilee comes along to really piss on your chips.

Unless you're Jennie Bond or a gee-whiz American tourist, it's hard to understand why you should care less about old Mrs Monarch. Consider the evidence. Has she ever done anything even faintly amusing? No. Is she a wonderful orator? No. Can she fly or shoot lightning from the tips of her fingers? Don't be ridiculous.

The Queen doesn't even look like she enjoys being queen – a state of affairs that might save the day by rendering her slightly pitiful and endearing, if it weren't for the leaden sulkiness she tends to radiate as a result. Now that Victor Meldrew's been killed off, Her Majesty is the most consistently sour-faced person on television, perpetually wearing an expression like someone's just cracked open a packet of shitbiscuits directly under her nose.

The annual Yuletide speech is a case in point – fifty years of practice, and she's still bloody hopeless at addressing the nation. Steely gaze, stilted delivery, surly awkwardness . . . come on! You're the Queen, for God's sake! You spend the rest of the year flopping about in outrageous opulence, so if we ask you to turn up on TV for a ten-minute chinwag once a year, couldn't you at least *pretend* to enjoy it? Honestly: the face she wears, you'd have thought she'd been asked to squat on a pine cone at gunpoint. Come to think of it, that would be a Christmas broadcast worth watching.

Yet despite all this evidence to the contrary, some of Great Britain's dimmest lightbulbs insist on behaving as though HRH Grumpybones is in some way special or interesting, and our TV stations are happy to accommodate their delusion – this week's one-off special, *The People's Queen* (BBC1), being a prime example.

Tune in and here's what you'll find: acres of amateur footage of Liz Windsor turning up at public events to smile and wave at her minions, interspersed with interviews with the enthusiastic patriots holding the cameras, and a select few fortunate enough to shake hands with her.

Their recollections aren't especially illuminating. 'She had such great skin and her teeth were gorgeous,' recalls a woman who met the big Q at a Silver Jubilee bash in Bootle. Of course she had great skin, thicko – she's spent a lifetime reclining in gold-plated baths dousing herself with the most expensive balms known to man, and at your bloody expense.

Whenever the proles' searing insight threatens to falter, the programme whisks the simpering interviewees back to the location of their epoch-shattering encounter, so they can relive the moment all over again – minus trifling ingredients such as crowds, bunting, fanfares, and the immediate presence of Her Majesty the Queen of England. Call me a cynic, but it's hard to relate to the genuine excitement some participants must have felt at the time when you're watching some old goon standing in a street circa 2002, muttering, 'There was a flag over there,' and 'I was standing here,' and 'The Queen's car slowed down round about there,' ad nauseam, until you feel like slamming his head against the pavement.

Absurdities aside, there are a few genuinely interesting clips on offer – footage of the Queen as a gurgling five-year-old, and a fascinating sequence in which Her 20-year-old Majesty runs around on the deck of a ship, flirting with sailors (remarkable for two reasons: 1) Hey, she's quite foxy, actually, and 2) It's just about the only time I've seen her smiling without looking forced).

As a final aside, I'd recommend *Spooks* (BBC1), if only because any drama series that's prepared to build Lisa Faulkner up as a major character, then shove her head first and screaming into a deep fat fryer . . . and *then* blow her brains out . . . and put all this unexpectedly in episode *two* – deserves brownie points for sheer balls-out nerve alone. What next? Introduce Charlotte Church, then toss her in a threshing machine? At least she'd scream more harmoniously than poor Ms Faulkner, which might limit the number of furious complaints a bit.

Voice of an angel, you know.

It's not a 'Beautiful Game'   [22 June]

Think of something you don't like. Not necessarily something you hate, but something you're ambivalent about. For the sake of argument, let's say you're thinking about country-and-western music.

Now, picture a world in which country-and-western has become inexplicably popular. It's everywhere. It spills from every radio. When you buy a newspaper, a third of it is devoted to country-and-western (news, reviews, sales statistics, whopping great photo-graphs of Garth Brooks picking his bum, etc.). Pubs overflow with people in ten-gallon hats watching country-and-western concerts on a big screen, jubilantly yee-hawing along with every flick of the steel guitar. Taxi drivers insist on discussing classic Johnny Cash albums with you, even after you've told them you're not keen on the man. Television is filled with footage of cowboys and people eating 'grits' (whatever the heck they are), interspersed with professional analysis of their grit-eating technique and billion-dollar commer-cials for the latest tasselled shirts. And when Billy Ray Cyrus trips over a mike stand and sprains his ankle, fans riot through the centre of town, smashing up buildings with their fists and feet.

How would you feel? Alienated? Resentful? Furious? Probably all three. You'd also have some measure of how I (and the thousands of football-averse citizens like me) feel during the World Bloody Cup (BBC1/ITV).

It's not a 'beautiful game', all right? It's just 'a game'.

The matches themselves I could probably withstand were it not for the dull circle-jerk of punditry that surrounds and envelops them. It's like being locked in the greyest room in Boredom Hell, the air thick with sweat and violent aftershave, while paunchy sales reps stand around monotonously discussing sales figures.

I can't understand the need for such exhaustive analysis. Oh, I've asked people about it. People who care about football. They *love* the analysis. 'ITV's the best,' said one, 'it's like being in a pub, lis-tening to some blokes talk about football, except they're genuine experts.'

Really? To me they're just nerds (all football fans are nerds). And if there's anything worse than personally encountering a football nerd, blathering on until you can practically sense your lifetime joy supply being permanently depleted, it's watching an entire panel of them on television, day after day after mindbending day.

IT'S A GAME INVOLVING CHANCE, YOU IMBECILES! IT'S GOT A BALL IN IT, AND BALLS BOUNCE! THERE'S A HUGE RANDOM ELEMENT RIGHT THERE! STOP BLOODY SCRUTIN-ISING! SHUT UP!

But no matter how hard I bellow, they simply don't stop. On and on they blurt, boring for Britain: Bobby Robson, Ian Wright, Gary Neville, Martin O'Neill (the sourest man on television – he has the demeanour of a man who's just spent the last hour being spoon-fed earwax), Ray Winstone (Terry Venables) and, worst of all, Gazza.

Ah, Gazza. Perpetually gurning like a Cabbage Patch Kid that's just found a lollipop behind a mulberry bush, he slurs not just words but entire sentences, into one long incomprehensible gurgle. Analysis you can't even hear: genius.

Here's a typical exchange:

LYNAM: Well, the match ended five hours ago but there's still plenty for us to dissect, and mark my words we will, at punishing length . . . Paul Gascoigne, what did you make of it?

GASCOIGNE: Zwozzerbrilyntsnurtenfurten.

VIEWER: What?

GASCOIGNE: Izfluckederbelldunnersayedunnitsgonninnagull.

VIEWER: WHAT???

You're watching the English dictionary melt before your very eyes.

The players (and they *are* players, not 'lions' or 'heroes' or anything else – just men who are quite good at kicking balls around, like little children do in parks) aren't much better. So little of interest spills from their mouths (aside from the odd spectacular salvo of phlegm) it's hardly surprising there's been so much attention paid to their haircuts. Beckham's in particular is hideous. He looks like a damp osprey. It's only marginally better than David Seaman's 'fairground worker' abomination (at least that's *funny*).

Still, there is hope. I'm writing this prior to the England-Brazil match, which I sincerely hope we've lost by the time you read this. Maybe once we're out we can get back to normal. The nauseating football-centric commercials will become less omnipresent (is there a single player who doesn't routinely slurp corporate schlong?). Coverage will peter out. And best of all, it'll be possible to switch the TV on again without getting bored to death by a pundit's dribbling gob.

Especially one you can't even understand.

Crapping in Outhouses and Strangling Chickens

[6 July]

Dontcha just love Americans? They're so cute, with their pudgy faces and their pudgy brains, whooping, waving their flags, firing their guns, hauling their elephantine behinds into chain hamburger shacks to plug their hollerin' mouths with grease and mashed-up cow flesh. Ain't they the *neatest*?

That's mindless racism, of course. In my experience, Americans are among the nicest people on earth. It's not their fault they're governed by an eerie, apocalyptic dormouse – they didn't even vote for him, after all. Yes, there are plenty of lunatics and dickheads in the States, but before chastising them for that, I suggest you try walking around Britain with your eyes and your ears open for a few minutes, to build a clearer sense of our own scum-to-genius ratio.

Anti-Yank prejudice is often motivated by jealousy of course, because right now they're the most pampered folk on earth. But it wasn't always so, as this week's *The Frontier House* (C4) demonstrates. A stateside spin off of *The 1900 House* (a surprise hit over there), *Frontier House* takes the same surviving-the-past principle and relocates it to the US. Three families have agreed to ditch their all-American dream homes in exchange for four months fending off the elements in Montana, playing the role of pioneers in the Wild West circa 1883. Cue much hilarity as they sit around eating tastebud-punishing combinations of flour and cornmeal, crapping in outhouses and strangling chickens.

That's the idea anyway. But historical authenticity isn't the main draw – the fun lies with the almighty personality clash between the two main families, the Glenns and the Clunes. The Glenns are likeable, earthy, liberal types. The Clunes are a bunch of pricks. Heading up the Clune clan are husband Bordon and wife Adrienne. He's president of a manufacturing company, she's a pampered LA housewife. They live in a Californian mansion. Why participate? Gordon wants quality time with his kids. Ahhhh.

But hang on: Gordon's idea of 'quality time' consists of macho fantasies in which he and junior bond over firearms in the untamed West, and the moment he discovers that the programme's dedication to historical authenticity doesn't extend to overturning federal hunting laws – i.e. that he can't simply run around blasting every creature in sight – he turns into Michael Douglas in *Falling Down*.

'I'm very disappointed in how little this part of the West is going to be emphasised in this programme,' he mutters bitterly. Presumably he was also looking forward to forming lynch mobs, raping slaves and getting scalped by Comanches.

Even the provision of a genuine, loaded firearm (for shooting coyotes which might attack their livestock) fails to cheer him up. It's been made in Russia, and that really sticks in Gordon's craw, particularly since he's bought his own antique shotgun along to give his kids, and can't wait to show it to us.

'This gun was made in 1886,' he says, huffing with a scary combination of anger and excitement as he fingers his beloved weapon. 'Look at this engraving: pictures of rabbits and squirrels. This is a kid's gun. Kids in the West had guns. But what they've given us is something you'd better not do a close-up on, because it's *embarrassing*.'

Adrienne, meanwhile, is upset by a similarly outrageous infringement of her human rights – the ban on make-up, which quickly drives her into a flub of nigh-on suicidal tears. With any luck she'll find Gordon's shotgun and give herself a full cranial makeover before the series is over.

Amazingly, all the self-centred griping occurs during the initial preparation stage, before they've even moved into their 'frontier cabin'. As if to prove the existence of karma, the Clunes' luck continues to falter as the families set out via wagon for their new homes.

Some of the horses go nutzoid; Adrienne is almost trampled underfoot, while their eight-year-old son Conor gets thrown from the wagon, narrowly escaping death.

God alone knows what kind of indemnity forms the producers made them sign up before taking part, but it's clear that genuine risk of life and limb is seen as being all part of the fun – good news for the viewer, bad news for the luckless Conor, who is later mauled by a dog.

Personally, I can't wait for next week, by which time everyone's shouting or in tears, and Gordon's threatening to use his cherished shotgun for real. Oh, and Conor gets eaten by a buffalo. Probably.

Like Tipping Your Hat to a Prostitute [13 July]

Hello. My name is Charlie Brooker and I'm a hypocritical snob. Like millions of other hypocritical snobs, I like nothing better than settling down to a Sunday roast in the local pub, flipping through the papers with a mouthful of undercooked parsnip. Like millions of other hypocritical snobs, I buy two different papers – a broadsheet (in my case – the *Observer*), and a gaudy tabloid (the *News of the World* – the grubgasm of choice for any serious voyeur).

The broadsheet provides serious news, profiles of unheard-of sculptors, reviews of books I'll never read and jazz CD's I'll never buy, aspirational recipes and interminable think-pieces on male–female relations or parenting or a host of other things I really couldn't give a sun-blushed shit about. The tabloid provides scandal and photographs of celebrities with their chests out, both of which I pretend not to be interested in.

Why bother buying the broadsheet? Because it makes buying the tabloid feel somehow less shameful. It provides a veneer of civility, like tipping your hat to a prostitute. See: hypocritical snob. There are millions of us. Close down the Sunday tabloids and their broadsheet companions would collapse overnight – there'd be no point in buying them any more.

I bring this up in the light of *My Worst Week* (BBC1), a new series looking at the 'story behind the scandal', which opens with an exhaustive raking-over of George Michael's 1998 'toilet incident', and which, by interviewing tabloid editors, paparazzi and fans, seeks to hover somewhere above the grubbiness of it all, while simultaneously taking its shoes off to wade thigh-deep into the bog.

Let's get one thing clear – when I refer to 'grubbiness', I don't mean Mr Michael's rather endearing indiscretion. I've never committed a lewd act in front of a policeman (adjusting my crotch during an episode of *The Bill* notwithstanding), but it sounds quite fun, and certainly far less grubby than paying to ogle bum-shots of Britney spears taken by an overweight photographer hiding in a tree, before turning the page to tut-tut at the 'sordid' antics of somebody – anybody other than myself.

Anyway, back to *My Worst Week*. Naturally, since there's nothing to say about a teensy bit of rudeness that took place four years ago, the show takes half an hour to do so, padding the time with blurry, impossible-to-watch 'reconstructions' of the incident, interspersed with talking heads from paparazzi perverts (who, hilariously, don't want their identities revealed) and assorted tabloid prickerati (Piers Morgan, editor of the newly principled *Daily Mirror*, chastises the 'rank hypocrisy' of the public, before saying his gut instinct was to 'get as much salacious detail as you possibly can' on his good pal George, whose rubbish 'Shoot the Dog' single Morgan's paper recently touted as the pinnacle of genius).

Does the programme pick him up on this? Does it say, 'Hang on a sec – which is more perverted: waving your goolies around in a loo, or spending six days camped outside the home of a man who waved his goolies around in a loo?' No. Come the end there's no opinion, no conclusion – in short, no point.

It's just there, bunging a hole in the schedule, just one more tiny monument to celeb-obsessed needlessness. So why bother writing about it? Because I'm a hypocrite. And why slag it off? Because I'm a snob. But I told you that at the start so don't act surprised.

On to *Believe Nothing* (ITV1), Rik Mayall's new vehicle (and I'll leave a pause here for you to insert the quad-bike/vehicle joke of your choosing), which I rather enjoyed, even though (judging by episode one) it's not particularly funny. It's heartening to see a new, mainstream sitcom so completely hell-bent on being just plain silly.

Mayall, who now closely resembles Sven Goran Eriksson (who in turn resembles Professor Yaffle from *Bagpuss*), plays an egotistical professor called Adonis Cnut (the most brazen 'comedy' name since Kenny Everett's Cupid Stunt) entangled in a succession of absurd conspiracy theories. Utter pantomime, and nothing to do with real life whatsoever, but when it comes to sitcoms, I'd rather have Rik Mayall (a hero during my adolescence, even if his recent forays into anti-euro rhetoric have made him look like a genuine cnut) bellowing his way through surreal whimsy than a cast of interchangeable twenty-somethings with dating dilemmas.

In short: it may be a poor man's *Blackadder*, but at least it's not a poor man's *Friends*. And right now, that's something.

The Sleep-Deprived Mind of Jack Bauer [20 July]

If you've ever had to stay up all night, then go into work the next day, you'll know there comes a point around lunchtime when everything turns surreal, leaving you on the brink of nervous hysteria, prone to demented thought patterns. Before you know it, you're assigning an individual name to every pixel on your monitor or finding the concept of staplers inexplicably hilarious. You've lost your mind.

And this is what's been happening in *24* (BBC Choice). My new theory: the entire show is an avant-garde experimental drama, representing events as filtered through the sleep-deprived mind of Jack Bauer. Or maybe it's more *Vanilla Sky* than that: Jack has gone the whole hog and fallen asleep. Regular viewers may recall he nodded off for a few moments in a building-site Portakabin at around 11 a.m. I don't think he ever woke up.

Since that point it's all been random and disjointed, yet you're able to follow it, just like a dream. Characters appear and vanish without explanation, just like a dream. There are even recurring events – such as Senator Palmer's noble chinwags with his son Keith, a scene that replays itself every 25 minutes, like something out of *Groundhog Day*.

(Incidentally, while Palmer's trust in his wife dwindles, how come he hasn't asked her the most glaringly obvious question concerning their marriage – why his 'son' Keith is clearly of a different racial origin?)

My 'dream theory' even accounts for the latest development in

Jack Bauer's world: the appearance of familiar faces. Previously, his dreamscape was invaded by pop-culture doppelgangers (witness Kimberley steadily morphing into Jen from *Dawson's Creek* or the unexpected arrival of the late Michael Hutchence as a ruthless Serbian terrorist, who cheerfully emulated his lookalike by meeting an untimely end in a hotel room). Now, as Jack accelerates into REM sleep, in stroll a bunch of bona fide celebrities from Kiefer Sutherland's undistinguished movie career, back to haunt him.

Take this week's episode: first, exploding onto your screens, it's Lou Diamond Philips! Hooray! A chance for him and Kiefer to recreate the onscreen chemistry that made *Young Guns* one of the foremost cinematic achievements of the twentieth century. And then, before your excitement chips have finished processing this stunning development . . . look, it's Dennis Hopper!

Dennis Hopper: the rent-a-psycho with a face like a chunk of pumice stone the Incredible Hulk's just used to remove the rough skin from his feet.

Dennis Hopper: who starred alongside Kiefer in the 1990 movie *Flashback*, in which – get this – Hopper's a prisoner and Kiefer's an FBI agent named John Buckner.

John Buckner, Jack Bauer, John Buckner, Jack Bauer. I think it's part of the dream. Next week: the entire cast of *The Lost Boys* battle on the set of *Flatliners*. Most exciting of all, since it's now a dream, literally anything can happen, and the finale will consist of Jack being chased round a funfair by a visibly erect Honey Monster.

Anyway, there's more fractured reality elsewhere in the schedules: take *Headf**ck* (Sci-Fi), a self-consciously 'weird' programme apparently aimed at heavily stoned twenty-somethings – a collage of horror-movie clips, surreal shots and the occasional close-up of a lizard or something else equally 'mind-boggling'. The big draw here is meant to be David Icke, who pops in to babble about UFOs, although the most interesting thing this week is the woefully lame video for the latest Prodigy single: topless go-go dancers milking cows and being beaten with sticks while Keith bellows 'We love Rohypnol! She love Rohypnol!' for the benefit of *Daily Mail* readers who need their shocks spelt out.

There's also the unmissable unfolding nightmare of *The Frontier House* (C4). Having whinged about everything from razors to the quality of tealeaves, gun-lovin' Gordon Clune has a new gripe: he ain't gettin' any.

Wife Adrienne, it seems, just isn't putting out. It's now surely only a matter of time before Gordon strips naked, smears mud on his face and runs through the village, firing at invisible communists.

Meanwhile, his luckless son Conor, who's already survived dog maulings and high-speed wagon smashes, now has starvation to contend with. And boy, did I chuckle as the tears rolled down his gaunt little face. Biggest laugh of the week, in fact. Altogether now: ho, ho, Conor. Ho ho ho.

Outrage for Dummies [27 July]

Picture someone stupid. Really impossibly stupid. Like, literally going 'durrrr' out loud, grinning, dribbling, clapping their hands together like a seal and wearing one of those little beanie caps with a propeller on top.

Keep that image in your mind's eye for the next 10 minutes, because unattractive though this notional moron is, he seems to be the kind of viewer ITV is courting shamelessly these days, as it sets off, USS *Enterprise*-fashion, to explore the furthest reaches of a strange new universe of dimwittery, beaming back transmissions which seek to provide an authoritative televisual definition of the word 'brainless' – out-and-out dunce-casts that don't so much insult your intelligence as bypass it completely.

First we had the ghastly *Elimidate*, in which Kerry Katona's stunt knockers bobble around a beach or shopping centre encouraging dunderheads to feel each other up; now, hot on its heels, comes *Wudja? Cudja?*, the show that by its own admission seeks to 'test the limits of taste, greed and self respect' by offering the public wads of banknotes in exchange for performing humiliating challenges.

Now, I'm all for watching people debase themselves, particularly if they're younger and better-looking than myself (a demographic that grows by the nanosecond), but *Wudja? Cudja?*, transparently misanthropic though it is, entirely fails to capitalise on its premise by displaying a downright offensive lack of imagination. The 'challenges' are predictable Club 18–30 shenanigans – like snogging as many strangers as possible, or letting a mob of baying lads lick ice cream from your bosom, or, at its very worst, simply flashing your bum for five pence. It's like flicking through a copy of 'Outrage for Dummies'.

Look, if you're going to get people to demean both themselves and the whole of humanity, do it properly. Have some balls. Here, off the top of my head, is a list of five challenges that *Wudja? Cudja?* shoulda hadtha nervta feacha:

1) Cut the end of your nose off with scissors (£500)

2) Crush a live dormouse in your fist, and then eat it (£80)

3) Squat in the street, pooing into a big bowl of flour, while a bloke dances around playing the accordion (£50)

4) Penetrate a sea cow (£20)

5) Break your elbows with a mallet, then riverdance in a tray full of sick until you lose consciousness (£400).

There. Put those on air and I'll tune in every week. In fact, sod that: I'll turn up and spectate, provided I'm allowed to bring firearms and dispatch the contestants at the end of each stunt. Bang: one less moron. Bang: one less moron. Bang bang bang bang bang: wee hee! You'd need a bulldozer to tidy the corpses away.

Come to think of it, why bother handing out money? Why not simply scour the alleyways in search of heroin addicts, getting them to flash their privates on camera in exchange for vials of smack? After all, testing the limits of 'taste, greed and self respect' *is* our aim, right? Think I'm being harsh? Think again: I'm displaying no more contempt for the public than the ding-dongs who nodded this through. Difference is, I've got the decency to be honest about it.

Aaaaanyway, if *Wudja? Cudja?* doesn't satiate your need for knuckle-dragging antics, there's always *Sex BC*, an in-depth investigation into the mating habits of our cave-dwelling ancestors – who were, the programme claims, far more sophisticated than we give them credit for.

Rather than sitting about all day grunting and poking their prehistoric genitalia in the direction of anything vaguely hole-shaped, there's evidence cave folk preferred to form loving relationships with one another. Women were afforded respect and played an active role in hunter-gatherer activities. In fact the main way they seem to differ from us present-day bozos is that infidelity was punished with a skewer through the penis of the offending cheater – which would liven up the Ricki Lake show no end.

Obviously, the makers of *Sex BC* have a slight problem regarding the lack of decent video footage shot during the Stone Age which might support their findings, but they've made up for it by getting modern-day actors to strip completely naked, then circle round filming them for ages and ages and ages. Which is clever of them. In fact, alongside *Wudja? Cudja?*, this makes two opportunities in a single week to watch cavemen getting their bums out.

Now that's progress.

Sick and Wrong, or Wrong and Sick? [10 August]

Attention, *Daily Mail* headline writers: on no account should you miss *Teenage Kicks: Drugs Are Us* (C4), because it provides countless opportunities to flex those outrage muscles to the very limit. In fact your only dilemma will be which line to take: is the programme sick and wrong, or wrong and sick? Should you gnash with fury, or shake your head with world-weary dismay? Questions, questions. It's a pity they couldn't have thrown in a few asylum seekers for good measure – but you can probably work out a roundabout means of blaming them nevertheless, and I don't want to tell you how to do your job because, let's face it, you already know how everything in the world should be done anyway.

In case you hadn't guessed, this is one of those scandalous documentaries in which something approaching everyday reality is portrayed in non-judgemental terms, thereby appalling Middle Englanders who'd prefer it if the world would just bloody well sit still and behave.

It focuses on three drug-guzzlin' teenagers: Johnny, 16, who puffs his way through more cannabis than an entire hall of residence on a daily basis; 17-year-old Sam, who spends his weekends navigating an obstacle course of Ecstasy, speed and ketamine; and Ashleigh, also 17, a disarmingly nonchalant Geordie girl with a penchant for garish blue eyeshadow. Oh, and heroin.

None of them slots neatly into a pre-determined pigeonhole: Sam, for instance, is a fresh-faced and articulate public schoolboy who, when he's not grinding his teeth to powder in a strobe-lit jiggle hut and using drugs as a chemical joystick to control his every mood, croons hits for Jesus in the local church choir; stoner Johnny's a good-natured Scot who disapproves of heroin (it's 'stupid') and cheerfully decides to temporarily curb his Cheech and Chong lifestyle to sit his exams.

They'll both be fine, particularly once they realise the grim truth about drugs: that their main purpose is to provide you with something fun to grow out of, and that people who go on about them are really boring.

Ashleigh's the one to worry about, because she's entirely blasé about her heroin addiction, discussing it as though recounting events from a particularly dull episode of *Holby City*, unconcerned that it's clearly going to blight her existence until she drops dead or kicks the habit.

And the parents? Irresponsible? Nope. They're all admirably realistic about the situation, begrudgingly accepting that they'd rather know what their kids get up to than simply bellow disapproval and force them to do it in secret. Ashleigh's mum Maureen is especially heartbreaking, balancing pragmatism with parental love as she deals with three teenage daughters who routinely steal from her to pay for their five-quid bags of smack.

Ashleigh, if you're reading this – which you aren't – for God's sake, give yourself a kick up the arse and do something, anything, to wean yourself off that life-crushing muck, because your mum deserves a breather. Oh, and ditch the blue eyeshadow; it makes you look like a smackhead or something.

Further follies of youth are on display in *Classmates* (C4), which is basically nothing more than the 'Friends Reunited' website (the online nostalgia site where you get to discover precisely how many of your school friends now work in IT – i.e. all of them) transferred to television, but curiously life-affirming nonetheless. In this edition – the first – a group of pupils from a vaguely bohemian mixed-sex boarding school in Surrey meet up after 12 years apart to compare jowls and job descriptions, and it's all rather sweet: teenage sweethearts are reunited, the school wallflower turns out to be a super-confident glamourpuss and the troubled wide-boy enjoys an amiable chinwag with the headmaster who expelled him.

The arrival of school heart-throb Adam Donald is especially gratifying, since in his youth he had the uncannily handsome looks of a Hollywood superstar, but now resembles a slightly cheeky potato (and is infinitely more likeable as a result).

By the end of the programme I was on the verge of boo-hooing like a baby, mind, simply on account of the soundtrack, which to my ears sounded almost contemporary until I realised it consisted of music from 12 years ago – Screamadelica-era Primal Scream et al. – thereby proving I'm officially old.

And if that isn't a *valid* reason to start knocking your brains out with pills and spliffs and smack, then I don't know what is.

Teenagers: they don't know they're born.

Ethically Right?   [31 August]

In the good old days (you know, back when we all lived in fear of nuclear extinction and greed and bigotry were rife, utterly unlike the present era), there were only three or four channels, so it was easy to keep tabs on what was showing where. Kelly Monteith on BBC1, snooker on BBC2, Cannon and Ball's 'Madcap Snooker Chucklehouse' on ITV, or subtitled 'Disabled Lesbian Snooker with Extra Pubic Hair' on Channel 4. Simple.

Today there are 1,500,000 channels, growing at an exponential rate, and you can't flip open the *Guide* without noticing a new addition to their ranks: one minute there's an Open University programme about hills on BBC2, and the next there's the Discovery

Hill Channel (documentaries about hills), Hill 24 (24-hour hill news), The Txt-a-Hill Network (teenagers communicating via text message captions superimposed over footage of hills), and Fantasy Hill X Super Hardcore Plus (fat men having sex with hills).

It's bedlam out there. Hence the trend for 'Ronseal' programme titles – shows that explain exactly what they do right there on the tin, with names like 'Britain's Scariest'. The idea is that they stand out in the listings, so you're more likely to tune in. Why name your programme *A Touch of Frost* (which could be mistaken for a documentary on winter mornings), if you can call it 'The Shortarse Detective' instead?

ITV has honed this practice to such a fine art, you don't even need to watch the programmes any more, just read the titles: *Britain's Sexiest Builders*, *It Shouldn't Happen to a Game Show Host*, *To Kill and Kill Again*, and now the latest example, *I'm a Celebrity – Get Me Out of Here!* (ITV1), in which a bunch of vaguely famous people have been dumped in the Australian outback in order to suffer for Ant and Dec's amusement.

OK, so the use of the word 'celebrity' contravenes the Trades Descriptions Act, but the programme itself is a guilty pleasure, and everyone who's wearily grumbled about the bile-scooping tackiness of it all is wasting their time: this *is* vastly entertaining stuff; no amount of hand-wringing is going to change that. And I can sum up the appeal in two words: Uri Geller.

See, the big surprise about *I'm a Celebrity* is that most of the 'stars' seem quite nice: Tony Blackburn, Tara Palmer-Tomkinson, Nell McAndrew, and Rhona Cameron. Heck, even Christine Hamilton's grown on me. Nigel Benn you can keep, and Darren Day could annoy me just by breathing in and out, but Uri Geller . . . CHRIST.

Don't know about you, but I always assumed that behind closed doors, once the cameras had been put away and he'd finished spoonbending for the day, Geller magically transformed himself into a normal person – but no. For him it's a lifetime gig. I wouldn't be able to stand in the same room as him for five minutes without feigning a fatal brain haemorrhage, just to make him stop banging on about spirituality and his psychic bloody powers, which he's not going to use on this expedition because 'it wouldn't be ethically right'.

Ethically right? *I'm a Celebrity – Get Me Out of Here!* may be many things, but a noble contest of far-reaching import it is not. Sod ethics, Uri – prove your abilities. Go on. I dare you. Bend us a spoon. Float in the air or something.

I'll even watch you squatting on the outdoor toilet, curling out a turd in a supernatural trance. That beats ethical restraint any day. And if you can't do that, at least spill some Michael Jackson gossip. You must know loads, particularly since you can probably read his mind as well. But no. Uri's content to simply weird everyone out. The sequence in which he slimed around the camp attempting to ingratiate himself with the women (by patronising them) has to rank as the creepiest thing I've seen all year. Spoons are one thing, but this man has an innate ability to bend minds, and not in a good way; I'm guessing – hoping, praying – that by the time you read this, the public will have revolted en masse, and voted him into a whirlpool of misery.

And with any luck, next year we'll have a series called 'I'm a Celebrity – Get This Out of Me!' in which members of the public phone in to vote on which unwieldy object gets shoved up whose famous backside. I'm setting my telephone to speed-dial Uri's number already.

Footballers' Wives for Sociopaths   [21 September]

Wahey! The trailers say it all: action is back on ITV! And it's courtesy of *Ultimate Force* (ITV1) – *The Sweeney* with a hard-on.

Set in a parallel universe in which the SAS are called in to sort out problems at the drop of a hat, *Ultimate Force* is about guns and machismo and very little else. And we're talking gallons of machismo – the smug kind, the kind that shoots first and doesn't bother asking questions later, safe in the knowledge that anyone wringing their hands over the nastiness of it is simply Missing the Point.

In fact, describing this as an 'action' series is misleading. It's pornography, plain and simple, pandering to the fantasies of tire-some British bloke creatures – that wretched breed of style-free thickos who drive too fast and spend the weekend starting fights outside dismal nightclubs. With any luck, one glimpse of the gun-play in *Ultimate Force* and they'll all succumb to a Pavlovian urge to masturbate before bedtime, thereby reducing their risk of impregnating their girlfriends and spawning yet another genera-tion of insolent heirs – and if in 20 years down the line that means one less bellowing imbecile in the Friday night minicab queue, it'll all have been worth it. In fact, if ITV broadcast a new episode every night for a couple of decades, we might see the national average IQ treble in size by the year 2033.

So yes, it's macho and daft, but when you're dealing with a series starring Grant Mitchell, what else would you expect? Quaker Academy? Harpist Squad?

Of course not. We're talking about Ross Kemp here – ITV's stellar signing, who's thrashed around in search of a decent vehicle for so long it was in danger of becoming embarrassing. The sigh of relief is almost audible over the gunfire: finally they've hit upon the ideal showcase for him – something in which his ability to act is sec-ondary to his ability to stand around looking vicious.

Thing is, Kemp's never been a convincing hard man – he's more of a try-too-hard man. Bona fide toughnuts don't need to pull such obviously menacing facial expressions, at least not all the time.

Honestly, what's with all the furious glares? The moment Kemp walks onscreen he enters into a demented staring competition with everyone else in the room, including the viewers at home (if glowering ever becomes an Olympic sport, he's a dead cert for the gold – he could out-stare a man with two glass eyes). Presumably, Kemp maintains this unique wide-eyed frown because when his face is at rest it's actually rather baby-like and friendly, but the result is disturbing; he looks like a version of Nookie Bear that's had its fur shaved off and isn't happy about it.

Thankfully, there's more to the Kemp repertoire than mere scowling. He's mastered nodding as well, which is why every line is delivered with his trademark bob of the head, like a man auditioning for the part of a nodding dog in 'Toy Story 3: Playthings of Fury'. Squint and he starts to resemble a testicle bobbing in a bathtub. And a particularly hairless one at that.

Apart from Staring Nodding Man, what else does *Ultimate Force* have to offer?

Bloodshed. Taking their cue from the recent trend for graphically violent combat in films like *Saving Private Ryan* and *Black Hawk Down*, the special-effects team has raised the splatter quotient well above the televisual norm. Hence a shoot-out in a suburban bank ends up resembling something out of *Dawn of the Dead*, with shot-off bits of scalp dangling from the lampshades and flambéed kidneys squelching underfoot.

But while the aforementioned movies all used shocking gore to hammer home the sheer hideousness of violence, *Ultimate Force* simply uses it to titillate, in the manner of a 1980s video nasty.

Regular readers will know I've got nothing against that, but I do think if you're going to dish up gore for gore's sake, you might as well go the whole nine yards and make it absurdly, unrealistically gory. Since *Ultimate Force* doesn't seem to convey any message besides 'The SAS are hard', let's see them ripping the bad guys' ribcages out with claw hammers, please.

Needless to say, despite all my griping, I rather enjoyed it. It's got a camp appeal, like Footballers' Wives for sociopaths. The trailers say it all: action is back on ITV! Wahey!

Reality Jokers   [28 September]

Today, fame is power and everyone wants to be a celebrity. It's become as ubiquitous a human requirement as the need for air, water and a decent pair of socks, which is why the world is full of bewildered people doing misguided and humiliating things in a bid for fame. Things that would make you or me curl up and wither to a desiccated husk of embarrassment, like singing Bodyform jingles, or having sex with geese on the Internet, or performing onstage with the Stereophonics.

Pathetic sights, the lot of them, but none is as truly heartrending as the sight of a Reality Joker basking in his moment of glory.

A what?

A Reality Joker – it's a new phrase I've just coined, which refers to the type of person who turns up at the auditions for programmes like *Model Behaviour* (C4), knowing full well that a) they don't stand a serious chance, and also b) the production team won't be able to resist plastering their mugs all over the screen for a few moments, so we can all have a good laugh at their expense.

Hence the judges in *Model Behaviour* – a programme designed to pick out tomorrow's male and female supermodels – occasionally find themselves stifling smirks in front of some chubzoid clown (generally a fat moron named Barry, or something similarly Woolworths) who comically insists he's got the making of a cover star.

Blimey! He's bonkers! Barry is bonkers! Of course he won't be chosen – he's obese and disgusting! Har har har!

The judges are happy, because they look like good sports, the production team are happy because they've got a few more easy moments of sneersome air time under their belts, but most of all Barry's happy because his mates will see him on the telly and roll around guffawing at how downright daffy BONKERS!!!! he is. Well, hooray hooray. Enjoy your 1.5 nanoseconds of fame, Barry – then shove off back to Doncaster so we can concentrate on the meat of the programme: encouraging teenagers nationwide to work on their eating disorders.

This second series of *Model Behaviour* has clearly been taking notes – or more accurately photocopying instructions – from *Popstars* (a show which has not one, but *two* Reality Jokers, in the form of the 'touch my bum' girls). As a result, it seeks to pressurise and degrade its participants at every turn – 'cos that's good telly, innit? Jettisoned wannabes aren't just gently informed that they're no longer required – no. Despite already having been picked from the line-up and ordered to parade around in skimpy underwear for our titillation, they haven't been puppeteered enough. So they're separated into groups.

You, you and you – stand on the pink carpet. The rest of you, stand on the blue.

Drum roll, please. Let the maximum tension build – we want to see anguished looks on faces, please. OK. Now then. Pink carpet. Congratulations, you're through to the next round. The rest of you: your dream is over. Go on, shoo. And try to cry into the lens on your way out.

Still, there's a case for arguing that the spoilt little yelpers who turn up to undergo this sort of humiliation deserve everything they get. Particularly when you compare them to the dashing breed of old-school celebrities profiled in the engrossing *Showbiz Set* (C4); bona-fide stars who secured lasting fame the old-fashioned way: by actually being good at something.

Oh, except Simon Dee – the here-today, gone-tomorrow 1960s chat-show host whose sudden disappearance from the nation's screens is often referred to as a complete and utter mystery, although interviewee Jimmy Tarbuck's explanation of the reason for his downfall – 'Well, he was crap wasn't he?' – sounds plausible enough to me.

Good programme this, although in some ways it's enough to make you weep, outlining as it does an age when Britain's TV stations were unafraid to court controversy for a reason other than empty controversy itself. In its own way, the 1960s BBC was a veritable punkfest, unapologetically delivering shock after shock – the establishment-baiting of *That Was the Week That Was*, black comedy in *Steptoe and Son*, outrageous social satire in *Till Death Us Do Part*.

Where are their counterparts now? Answer: nowhere. Unless the imminent *Fame Academy* (BBC1) turns out to be a piece of coruscating satire in disguise.

Which it won't, of course. Pass the napalm.

Steamy Lesbian Romps   [5 October]

Before the tragic death of England's Rose (and that's Princess Diana I'm talking about, not Roy Kinnear), I'd had an idea for a short story, which went something like this: two demented pranksters kidnap the Princess of Hearts, then contact Scotland Yard and announce their 'ransom'. She will be released unharmed, provided Terry Wogan goes on live television and has full sexual intercourse with a sow. The act must be broadcast in blistering close-up on all five terrestrial channels, uninterrupted and entirely unexpurgated. Cue plenty of soul-searching for Wogan as the deadline draws ever nearer. Finally, after much pressure from the tabloids, he gives in. The horrendous act is broadcast live, the Princess is released, and the nation's television is never quite the same again: the bar for what's acceptable onscreen has been raised to unthinkable levels; Wogan's career has been revitalised – the ratings were so good, he repeats his performance on a weekly basis. At teatime. And everyone's happy.

See, I've often thought that if something like that were to actually happen, no one could ever complain about programmes like *Tipping the Velvet* (BBC2) again. You've probably heard about it already – according to the tabloids, it's set to 'shock' viewers with 'steamy' scenes of lesbian 'romps'. 'The most explicit sex sequences ever broadcast!' they screamed. Graphic! X-rated! Adults only!

Is it bollocks. Speaking as someone who recently watched a video entitled 'Strap-On Sally: Face Dildo Frenzy' (not mine, I hasten to add, and it belonged to a lady, so that absolves me of all blame twice over, OK?) I can quite confidently state that the sex scenes in *Tipping the Velvet* are not 'explicit'.

Good-natured and charming maybe, but not explicit, and if they involved a heterosexual couple no one would raise an eyebrow. Instead, *Tipping the Velvet* is a light, fluffy and fairly disposable romance; stylised in the *Moulin Rouge* mould with a vaguely Christmassy air (the scenes backstage at the music hall have the feel of one of those trailers promising 'a feast of entertainment' over the Yuletide season). The lesbian imagery is laid on in a coy, tongue in (cough) cheek manner; the very first shot is of a young girl slowly prising open an oyster, and the filthiest exchange goes like this: 'You smell.' 'I know! Like a herring!' Although I've quoted that out of context.

That's this week's sex quotient out of the way, so for violence we have to flip channels and locate *The Shield* (C5), an excellent US import starring Michael Chiklis as Vic Mackey: a cop who doesn't play by the rules of basic human decency.

Yes, he's corrupt, but it doesn't end there: he's merely the rottenest apple in a whole barrel of bad 'uns – a sort of Bad Lieutenant Squad. The show delights in confounding the audience with a tangled maze of moral dilemmas: the pilot showed Mackey beating a confession from an arrogant paedophile (ah, so he's bad but he gets results), passing bribe money to a hooker so she can buy her son some toys (he's bad but he's got a heart), then coldly shooting dead one of his own officers (oh – he's just bad). It's relentlessly brutal throughout – the sort of programme where everyone greets each other by saying 'Hey, asshole' instead of 'Hello', and even the 'nice' cop (a nerdy homicide detective) is shown commenting favourably on the breasts of a murder victim – with violent action sequences (of which there are plenty) cut in time to an angry numetal soundtrack for added hard-on value.

The main distraction is that Chiklis resembles both Mitchell brothers crossed with Bruce Willis; often he manages to look precisely like all three of them at the same time (no wonder he won an Emmy).

What with this and *CSI*, Five is rapidly becoming a plausible competitor to Channel 4, at least in the populist stakes. Consider the similarities: quality US drama, quirky home-made products, a daily *TFI Friday* clone and a selection of mainstream-baiting movies (they've broadcast *Natural Born Killers*, *Boogie Nights* and last week they even showed Harmony Korine's rubbish and unwatchable *Gummo*, fer Chrissakes, and films don't get much more Channel 4 than that).

All Five needs to do now is commission several hundred documentaries on the 'history' of porn and they'll be as indistinguishable from Channel 4 as Michael Chiklis is from Willis and the Mitchells.

Or how about a look at the 'history' of lesbianism? 'The Real Tipping the Velvet', anyone? I give it three months.

Strawberries and Bream [12 October]

He's orange. She's Mancunian. Together they're a force to be reckoned with.

I speak, of course, of Des O'Connor and Melanie Sykes, united at
last in *Today with Des and Mel* (ITV1) – either the best new daytime
TV show since *This Morning* or a nightmare of ghoulish obscenity,
depending on your point of view.

Like its obvious inspiration, the successful US daytime show
Regis and Kathy Lee, *Today with Des and Mel* is a blend of aimless
waffle and obsequious celebrity chat (so obsequious, it should
really be called 'Toady with Des and Mel'). But while their American counterparts have genuine chemistry, Des and Mel go together like strawberries and bream – and the resulting
awkwardness feels a bit like the forced, polite bonhomie between
a parent and their offspring's latest sexual partner during a Christmas dinner.

Nevertheless the sheer banality of it all is quite appealing – it's
akin to eavesdropping on the thoughts racing through the mind of
a doily, particularly during the pre-guest banter when Des babbles
away like a man in a fever (the other day he actually referred to his
backside as his 'bimbo bumbo'). His anecdotes never reach a conclusion, but simply wander around looking lost and confused for a
while before mutating into an anecdote on an unrelated subject.

Mel's even better. While Des uses his anecdotes as a platform for
endearingly corny gags, Mel butts in with conversational cul-de-
sacs; observations so crashingly pedestrian, they're either intended
as a sly satire on the mundanity of daytime television or part of an
ominous one-woman quest to redefine insipidness.

It certainly stops Des in his tracks. Here's a genuine, typical Mel
interjection, during a jovial discussion about cars: 'My husband
always shouts at me when I take the car to the car wash, because
apparently they can get scratched. He always says, "You should go
and get it done properly." [Pause.] So I do.' That's it: no point, no
punchline. Just a short, awkward silence, until Des changes the
subject and starts prattling away again.

Today with Des and Mel is so trite, it feels genuinely cutting-edge; it'll be a cult student hit by the end of the year, guaranteed – as will *The Psychic Show* (ITV1), which directly follows it. *The Psychic Show* is, to put it bluntly, aimed at idiotic women (and before anyone writes in to complain, consider this: we men might be arrogant, war-mongering rapists-in-waiting, but you'd never catch us dialling a premium-rate astrology phone line).

The opening sequence depicts a gigantic rotating healing crystal – enough to ward off all but the most gullible dunderheads, which is just as well since things go downhill from there, as we enter a rationality-free zone of horoscopes, dream analysis, palm reading and all the preposterous bummery that goes with it. It's ideal subject matter for a cut-price daytime show, of course, since anyone who believes in astrology is a fool by default, so the producers don't have to try too hard to keep the audience happy.

The best part is a segment in which the resident 'psychic' fondles an object belonging to an unseen member of the audience and makes a few vague predictions about them. They then bound onstage and shake their head in amazement at his remarkable supernatural powers. Me, I'm amazed by the shamelessly generic nature of his proclamations – favourites include 'This is someone who lacks self-confidence' (obviously, or why else would they bother asking a prick like you for advice?), 'I'm tempted to say this is a man' (while handling a large, manly piece of jewellery), and 'If I burble enough hazy generalisations about this person, some of them should stick' (of course he didn't actually say that last one – I just read his mind). You see, I've got incredible powers of my own – and I'll demonstrate them now.

If you're a regular viewer of *The Psychic Show*, simply place your palm firmly on the opposite page, and I'll give you a personality reading *and* predict your future into the bargain. Ready? Here I go.

Right, I'm getting something. I can tell this is a gullible person, a scared and stupid individual, terrified by the notion of a random, godless universe – someone who desperately wants to believe there's more to this life than daytime TV and celebrity gossip magazines, although sadly in their case, there isn't.

And the future? That's easy. They're going to spend the next five minutes rubbing ink off their palm. Magic.

Human Nature is Inherently Rotten [19 October]

Our basic human instincts get a terrible press. They stand accused of causing everything that's wrong with the world: pollution, corruption, obesity, sexually transmitted diseases, football hooliganism, racism, war and Dunstable. Mention the words 'human instinct' and even the world's biggest optimist weeps bittersweet tears (you can prove this in a laboratory, especially if you squirt lemon juice in their eyes as you say it).

Captain Kirk was regularly sentenced to death by egghead aliens who'd studied footage of the Second World War and decided human nature was inherently rotten (thank God their space transmitters never picked up *Jim Davidson's Generation Game*, or they'd have come down and kicked us all to death). Earthbound thinkers agree that our very humanity is our downfall.

Kurt Vonnegut's oeuvre deals with little else, and after decades of research no less an authority than Gary Clail and the On-U Sound System concurred that there was indeed 'something wrong with human nature'. Thus it was I slid my review copy of Dr Robert Winston's high-profile investigation into *Human Instinct* (BBC1) inside my VCR with a sense of clammy trepidation. And almost immediately, I breathed a sigh of relief: this isn't a despair-inducing trawl through the inescapable cruddiness that lurks within us all – it's cheery knockabout edutainment, plain and simple. Fashioned in the achingly slick style of a megabudget commercial for a global corporation, *Human Instinct* is a snack-science programme that, unlike 90 per cent of the TV schedules, provides something to think about.

This week's instalment deals with our survival instincts – the set of hard-wired subconscious responses that lead us to recoil from the smell of something potentially hazardous, cause lifelong cowards to heroically toss the infirm behind them when running from charging tigers, and can provide an 8-stone mother with the strength to lift a 10-tonne truck off her baby's head, once she's finished laughing.

Speaking of finding joy in the misfortunes of children, there's an immensely entertaining section in which Dr Winston demonstrates our inbuilt aversion to unpleasant tastes by spoon-feeding globs of offensive mush to a baby until it cries itself insensible. Elsewhere, we're informed that a baby's incessant wailing can equal the din created by a pneumatic drill penetrating concrete – although the programme inexplicably fails to mention that if you place the baby beneath the drill, the noise from both is diminished.

Of particular interest to me was the segment on spiders and snakes. As an unashamed arachnophobe I've had to endure years of spider apologists informing me that: 1) Spiders won't hurt you; 2) Spiders are more frightened of me than I am of them; and 3) You're only scared of spiders because you learned to fear them during childhood.

Now, thanks to kindly Dr Winston, that all-round good guy with the face of an approachable Stalin; Dr Winston, the cuddlesome uncle who could play the lead in 'Santa Claus: The Early Years', I now have televisual proof of what I've always suspected: we arachnophobes are simply slaves to an obsolete, uncontrollable primal instinct to run like funk whenever something creepy crawls near. Now, next time some gurglesome joker cups a spider in their hands and chases me round a table with it, I can gouge their stupid eyes out safe in the knowledge that no jury could reasonably convict me – I was only acting on instinct. People who are afraid of snakes, though, they're just wussy.

There's a hilarious archive clip in *Fame, Set and Match – Breakfast TV* (BBC2), in which Jeremy Beadle attempts to brighten the morning of several million *TV-am* viewers with his 'Today's the Day' slot. 'America's worst nightclub fire erupted in Boston on this day in 1942,' he chirps. 'People were literally beaten to death in the fight for the exits.'

Ah, those wacky survival instincts.

She's the Queen Mum of Telly and Blah Blah Blah

[26 October]

Blind Date (ITV1) has been running for ages, if not longer. In fact, it's been on our screens for so long, the original contestants have long since withered and died, leaving grieving offspring in their wake. 'So romantic, how they met,' sniff the children at their parents' graveside. 'Mother asked Father how he'd break the ice on their first date, and Father said "Darling, I'm so hot the ice'll melt the moment you see me." Then he did a Bobby Ball impression and pulled a moonie. The audience loved him. And so, after several drinks, did Mother.' With that, our imaginary mourners hold hands and walk sombrely through the churchyard gates, brittle autumn leaves swirling at their feet.

So much for the sepia-tinted days of yore. Now *Blind Date*'s been given a twenty-first-century makeover. Its previous format, for years considered the height of lows, simply wasn't shabby or cruel enough to keep a modern audience's attention.

Hence the changes: OUT goes 'Our Graham' (the announcer who always referred to Cilla as 'Cilla Blaaaaaaaah'), IN comes 'Ditch or Date', a new gimmick which allows contestants to change their mind once the partition goes back, thereby making a mockery of the title and robbing the show of whatever tension it once had. Brilliant.

One thing that hasn't changed, of course, is Cilla. Oh, the audience adores her and she's the Queen Mum of telly and blah blah blah. Ahem: pardon me for spitting in the punchbowl, but she's always annoyed the cogs off me, and the situation isn't improving as we both get older. For one thing, she's synonymous with barrel-scraping gaudiness: *Surprise Surprise*, *Moment of Truth*, *Blind Date* . . . For God's sake, the woman would *have* to be 'well-loved' or she'd have been lynched years ago.

Not that even the most demented angry mob would want to meet her in the flesh: either there's something wrong with my reception or she's starting to resemble the result of a unholy union between Ronald McDonald and a blow-dried guinea pig.

And that voice: Christ. The singing was bad enough – she sounded like an angry wasp trapped in a shoebox, butchering melodies with the ghoulish efficiency of Jeffrey Dahmer – but even though she no longer bursts into song, her incessant piercing squawk is still enough to make me want to slice my ears off and hurl them into another dimension.

Then we have the contestants. *Blind Date* has always attracted the very worst scrapings from mankind's petri dish – it works in the same way as one of those sticky-floored cockroach traps – but for the new series they've gone one better by inviting 'celebrities' to take part in the dates. Not proper celebs you understand (you won't see Ralph Fiennes riding a jet ski round Ibiza with Karen from Bracknell, more's the pity), but the boy band Blue – a group whose core audience consists almost exclusively of easily impressed foetuses.

At the risk of sounding like a wizened old prude, when I was a whippersnapper, the only musical act aimed exclusively at children was the Wombles, and I can't imagine *them* singing 'Baby when we're grinding, I get so excited / You're making it hard for me', like the Blue boys did a full three hours before the watershed last Saturday. Ironically, I suspect any one of the Wombles would actually prove a far better shag. Those protruding orange snouts could perform sexual tricks Blue can only sing about.

Still, at least compared with the sort of gurning farmhands the show usually features, Blue are good-looking – well, all except one, who's got a face like a kneecap soaked in vinegar. He didn't get chosen: that honour went to the sexily named Duncan, who's a bit like Brad Pitt minus the talent and charm.

Tonight we'll get to see how the date went: £10,000 says the wuss doesn't utter a single disapproving word. In summary, then: the new *Blind Date* – you'll need Rohypnol to get through it. How very twenty-first-century.

A Pissload of Spaghetti   [2 November]

Loathed. Reviled. Pilloried. Ridiculed. And for what? For being a dopey-faced, fat-tongued TV chef. Say what you like about Jamie

Oliver, in the light of recent allegations regarding other TV person-alities, there's no denying he's ultimately harmless. His idea of a 'coke-fuelled threesome' is a glass of cola followed by a bacon, brie and avocado sandwich, and the only time you hear him growling 'You know you want it' is when he's holding a hunk of steaming roast lamb up to camera.

Yet huge swathes of the population despise him. Well, it's time for me to 'fess up: I don't. Oh, I grind my teeth at the supermarket commercials just like everyone else, but I can't get furious with him personally for the same reason I can't wholeheartedly despise Alan Titchmarsh. Commercial whoredom and irritating tics aside both possess genuine skill and are capable of communicating it. Titch-marsh and Oliver are responsible for inspiring thousands of people to actually get up and do something that improves their lives. It's all very well to sit there and sneer, but when was the last time *you* inspired anyone, huh? Well? Oliver's clearly been stung by the sheer volume of animosity he generates, which is probably why his new series *Jamie's Kitchen* (C4) feels almost like an apology, an attempt to make the public at large reassess their hatred for the Roy Hatter-sley lookalike-in-waiting. It's a reality show in which he sets about establishing a non-profit restaurant staffed by underprivileged youngsters, largely funded with Oliver's own cash. They should've called it 'Jamie's Penance'.

And that's not all: aware that the only people who actually think he's 'cool' are the sort of home-counties women who think Dawn French is cutting-edge, Jamie sets about alienating them with cal-culating efficiency.

His secret weapon: bad language. Fifteen seconds in, every Mid-dle England mum's favourite cheeky chappie opens his mouth and starts spitting out a wasps' nest.

'Fuckin' shit,' he blurts, tossing a burnt slice of toast across the kitchen. 'I've fucked it up. Fuckin' bollocks.' The air remains blue throughout the programme: I counted six uses of the f-word, sever-al 'shits' and 'bollocks', and a solitary, yet heartfelt, 'wanker'.

See? He's human! I can picture the spin-off recipe book – 'Jamie's Fuckin' Kitchen'. 'Here's a recipe I call "Shit-Hot Spag Bol" – 1lb minced cow bollocks, 2 onions, garlic, a tin of fucking tomatoes and a pissload of spaghetti. And if you don't like it, you're a c***.'

Once you've got over the swearing, the next surprise is the way the show tackles Oliver's public perception head-on: included is a sequence in which he visits Xfm to be jovially humiliated by breakfast host Christian O'Connell.

'He's absolutely loaded,' O'Connell tells his audience. 'He's come in here today wearing gold lamé trainers and trousers made from poor people's skin.'

Next week in 'Jamie's Penance': the pudgy chef dons sackcloth and flagellates himself with a piece of knotted rope while shouting 'I'm a stupid c***' over and over again. Probably.

My Growing Obsession with Davina McCall
[9 November]

Remember *Manimal*? It was an enjoyably appalling 1980s action series starring Simon MacCorkindale as an explorer-adventurer blessed with the peculiar ability to mutate himself into various animals at will, largely notable for its *American Werewolf*-inspired transformation scenes, in which MacCorkindale's flesh would unconvincingly contort itself into exotic zoological shapes. A ludicrous premise, of course, and as the series went on, the writers clearly became desperate to shoehorn in the animal action: in one sequence a woman fell in some quicksand, prompting Manimal to transform into a snake and allow himself to be used as a length of rope in order to drag her out. *I, Claudius* it wasn't.

I only bring it up because of *Popstars: The Rivals* (ITV1), and more specifically my growing obsession with Davina McCall, who appears to have been halted midway through a Manimal-style transformation into a crow. Or maybe it's a raven. So far I'm not sure, but with any luck she'll have completed the transition by the end of the series, and will introduce the finale perched atop a telephone wire, ruffling her feathers and dropping silvery crap on the stage (entirely fitting, since the *Popstars* stage is the nation's premier showcase for silvery crap).

In case you think I'm merely being fanciful, tune in and consider the evidence for yourself: the makings of a beak are clearly visible, rudimentary black plumage seems to be emerging from her scalp and, most damning of all, her voice patterns are starting to closely imitate an insistent, grating caw.

Speaking of which, is there a single more annoying racket than Davina's nasal caw (apart from the singers themselves, that is)? It doesn't help that ITV appears to employ some kind of secret CIA sound-compression technology throughout the entire Saturday evening schedule, which turns every noise into a white-hot shard of solidified tinnitus. Listen to a burst of applause and it's like having a rapid-fire nailgun unloaded into your ear, and when Davina starts SHOUTING, which is something she does at the end OF EVERY SENTENCE, it starts to sound less like an ENTERTAIN-MENT PROGRAMME and more like a bizarre torture method straight out of THE IPCRESS FILE.

Her technique is to speak quickly and quietly, then suddenly break into a caustic bellow – the audible equivalent of someone using capitals and multiple EXCLAMATION MARKS!!!!!! in a humorous e-mail in a desperate bid to underline their point.

'Welcome to another edition of *Popstars. THE RIVALS!!!!*' (Decibel level: Concorde crashing into a saucepan factory).

'Singing live on stage . . . IT'S JAVINE!!!!' (Decibel level: Jupiter exploding above a foghorn convention).

Well, enough is enough. It's time for us to have a whip-round and buy Davina a gag. A nice Burberry one with comfortable flock lining, because we wouldn't want her to suffer. We can have it delivered to her nest in time for Christmas; all she has to do is peck through the gift wrapping and get someone with hands instead of wings to help tie it in place. And BINGO!!!! Peace on earth.

Next, we should organise a Yuletide boycott of the *Popstars* singles, on the grounds that It Simply Won't Do for our nation's grand pop heritage to be repeatedly violated in this manner. With the *Popstars* and *Fame Academy* singles jostling for position, this year's Christmas Top 10 is going to look and feel like a musical interpretation of the Argos catalogue.

Where's our Culture Minister when we need him? Nailing procla-mations to the walls of the Tate Modern, you say? Quick: someone phone Lemmy and get him to re-release 'Ace of Spades' so we can buy it in protest and have a decent Christmas No. 1 for a change.

In fact, phone anyone: I'd rather see 'Star Trekkin' back in the top slot then have to digest another load of this oleaginous crap along with my turkey and stuffing.

There's still time. There's still hope. Together, we *can* save Christ-mas.

Judge John Grumpybones [16 November]

DVDs are good, aren't they? Not if you've only got a video recorder, obviously, but if you're that much of a Luddite you can always entertain yourself with spinning tops or lutes or something while the rest of us enjoy slam-bang entertainment in pin-sharp digital crikeyvision.

As a medium, DVD is ideally suited to the nimble repackaging of hulking great TV series. In the sepia-tinted VHS era, if you bought a box-set containing the entire series of *The World at War*, you'd walk out of the shop looking like someone lugging a coffin around in a carrier bag. Now you can fit it in the palm of a slightly exaggerated hand. It's intrinsically satisfying.

In fact, buying entire series on DVD is so addictive, I can't pass a megastore without picking up a 200-episode epic. I already have more digitised footage than I can possibly watch in my lifetime: some good (*Band of Brothers*, *Our Friends in the North*, *Reggie Per-rin*), some variable (*Sapphire and Steel*, *Tales of the Unexpected*), and some plain dull (*I, Claudius*).

I'll buy anything. I've currently got my eye on a compilation called 'The Complete Ceefax'; it's got an 18-year running time, Dolby surround, a director's commentary and 500 deleted scenes (including a hilarious incident in which 'John Selwyn-Gummer' was mis-spelt as 'John Winky-Bumpoo').

Anyway, the ultimate proof of the new format's victory over VHS arrived this week: my review copy of *Judge John Deed* (BBC1) came on DVD. All well and good, but it also means I can't tape over it, and in this case that's a disadvantage.

Judge John Deed? Judge John Grumpybones, more like: he spends so much time frowning, you'd think he was doing it on commission. I thought he was supposed to be 'the fun judge', the womanising wildman of the judicial arena, but on this tedious evidence, his gavel's gone limp. And in the absence of a compelling storyline, there's nothing left to do but marvel at the way the crystal-clear DVD image emphasises the tininess of Martin Shaw's eyes: I swear each one's a single pixel in size.

One thing the BBC wouldn't send me was a preview tape, disc, or zoetrope strip of the *Robbie Williams Show* (BBC1), which is a terrible shame because I was looking forward to heaving a copy into a gigantic burning bin, thereby doing my bit for the overall advancement of mankind.

Williams appears to be doing Elvis's career in reverse: first he got fat, then he went through his Vegas period (courtesy of his odious Albert Hall extravaganza, also broadcast by the BBC), and now he appears to be tackling the 1968 comeback special. With any luck this means he's about to be usurped by some cheeky young lads from Liverpool, but somehow I doubt The Coral are up to it (if they can ditch the 'unlistenably awful' shtick, they might be in with a chance).

Lord Potato Dauphinoise of Grand Guffawing Castle [23 November]

Corsets. Repression. Whopping-great stately homes. Yes, the costume drama season is upon us again: time for the annual heavy snowfall of royalty cheques onto Andrew 'Adaptation' Davies' doormat. And this year he's going to need a snowplough to clear them away: he's already banged out *Tipping the Velvet* for BBC2, and this weekend he's got two new epics leaving the starting gate – *Doctor Zhivago* (ITV1) and *Daniel Deronda* (BBC1). I'm all in favour of encouraging good writing, but really, that's just taking the piss.

And I don't know about you, but I find it impossible to get excited at the prospect of yet another sumptuously adapted classic. At the risk of sounding like a furrow-browed philistine, aren't they all the bloody same? Boy meets girl and struggles with stiff social mannerisms – then in episode three he rips his shirt off and everyone thinks he's a sex king. A bit of fainting, ruffled ballgowns and pleasant scenery, a quick burst of tragedy, and a nice happy ending. The average episode of *Quincy* is less predictable.

Daniel Deronda in particular ticks all the usual boxes.

1) Brattish heroine? Check: she's a spoilt heartbreaker called Gwendolyn who has toffs crawling over themselves just to touch the hem of her ballgown.

2) Handsome young gent? Check: Daniel Deronda himself, who's essentially just a posho Nathan bumming about on a gap year. 'I want to find my own way in the world,' he explains to Edward Fox. 'I want to travel . . . find out how other people live, understand their philosophies' – probably quite an original move in the 1860s, but today he'd simply be following in the footsteps of 10 billion other overprivileged Barnabys who've spent an idle summer smoking dope on Thai beaches or photographing kneeless beggars in Calcutta (then hotmailing the snaps to the Tobys and Susannahs back home) before settling down to university and a lifelong career in frictionless boredom.

3) Cold-hearted bastard with designs on aforementioned heroine? Check: he's called Henleigh Grandcourt, which is just about the poshest name anyone could possibly have, short of Lord Potato Dauphinoise of Grand Guffawing Castle. His chat-up lines may come straight from John Leslie ('Do you like danger?' 'Yes.' 'Good.'), but do people like this ever actually have sex? I only ask because I once overheard a pair of poshos going at it hammer and tongs in a hotel bedroom, and it was hilariously funny, particularly when she shouted 'Oh, Gerald!' at the moment of climax – I can't imagine anyone being able to shout 'Oh, Henleigh!' without immediately putting themselves off. Or throwing up. Or both.

Anyway, back to the subject at hand: *Daniel Deronda*. Don't get me wrong. There are surprises along the way – not least the remarkable Mr Lush, Henleigh's sinister assistant, who closely resembles Lemmy from Motorhead and therefore doesn't look quite right in a boater – and it IS undeniably entertaining, but . . . well. Isn't it time we called a five-year sabbatical on costume dramas and spent the money on more contemporary offerings? Oh, and *please* don't anyone argue that *Daniel Deronda* is 'still relevant to a modern audience' – you can bang on about that till you're blue in the face: fact is, he's still wearing a waistcoat and prancing through ballrooms.

Yes, less of that and more modern drama please. The money saved on costumes alone could fund a few extra hours of the next *Our Friends in the North*. And – ahem – let's not just concentrate on grisly crime epics either (*Waking the Dead*, *Silent Witness*, *Wire in the Blood* . . . how many more lives?).

What we want is surprise. And there's little surprise in a corset. No, really.

It isn't impossible. There's a new series of the BBC's excellent secret-service shocker *Spooks* currently in production – that's more like it. Now all we need is our own *West Wing*. One that, for once, isn't set in the west wing of Tossington Hall.

'This is not something we can test'   [30 November]

Last year he proved under laboratory conditions that Jesus Christ had the face of a *Crimewatch* e-fit. Now, Jeremy Bowen turns his attentions to *Moses* (BBC1) and embarks on another quest for truth.

Of course, Moses doesn't quite warrant an entire series on his own – he simply wasn't as cool as Jesus. Nonetheless, he had the decency to do a reasonable number of interesting things, like floating down the river in a basket and holding conversations with flaming bushes, so there's just enough for Bowen to investigate in an hour-long special. Thank you, God.

The show opens, hilariously, with our Jeremy wandering through a CGI recreation of the parting of the Red Sea and asking whether any of this actually happened. He then wisely switches focus and starts tackling the easiest questions first – such as did Moses really get lobbed in a basket and bunged in the Nile?

Apparently, yes. Well, OK, maybe. Academics and theologians are on hand to explain that people often did rid themselves of unwanted offspring by sending them down the river. It must have looked like an infant armada – if you were a bit of a bastard, you could amuse yourself by standing on the banks of the river trying to sink passing baskets with rocks.

And was Moses rescued and raised by a Pharaoh's wife? Possibly. That could happen, argue the experts. Not very likely, argue the sceptics. Shhh, reply the experts.

Having 'established' that these things might have happened, the programme hits shakier ground as it examines the claims regarding Moses' adult life. Take the whole 'burning bush' incident, in which God spoke to Moses via a flaming shrubbery, and told him to set his people free. Helpfully, Jeremy points out that 'this is not something we can test', before explaining that loners wandering around the desert often undergo strange religious experiences, so hey, it could've happened. What he fails to mention is that hearing the voice of God isn't an experience confined to ancient loners in the desert – he's also been known to tell Bradford lorry drivers to kill prostitutes. Whoever this God guy is, he's clearly got a penchant for mischievous prank calls.

The programme goes on, explaining how the biblical plagues might have happened, and skirting around the whole parting-of-an-ocean issue by pointing out that it's based on a mistranslation – he actually led his people across a Reed Sea, not the Red Sea. As in a sea of reeds. As in a swamp. Not quite as impressive, but it's feasible.

Ultimately, Jeremy decides that whether you believe the story of Moses is true or not comes down to a question of faith, thereby rendering the entire investigative process somewhat redundant.

Still, it passes the time, and if the BBC wants to give me a load of money, I'm quite prepared to travel the world trying to discover whether Sherlock Holmes really wore those hats or if 'Willy Wonka and the Chocolate Factory' was a documentary.

Sleigh Bells A-Shinking   [7 December]

Christmas is coming. The shops are full of gibberish and you can hear sleigh bells a-shinking in the background of every commercial on television. Even the ones for Anusol.

And, in TV land, they're doubtless putting the finishing touches to the traditional 'feast of entertainment' we've come to expect: even as we speak, somewhere in a Soho edit suite, someone's checking shots of French and Saunders pulling funny faces in a *Tipping the Velvet* spoof. The BBC will have shot special 'Yuletide' versions of those 'dancing' continuity links (my money's on a troupe of snowmen pirouetting round a Christmas tree), ITV should be dusting down their copy of *Die Hard 2*, and Channel 4 will have taken delivery of a set of Mark Kermode intros to a mini-season of Mexican wrestling movies.

In fact, everyone in television is so busy concentrating on the annual climax, they've neglected to fill this week's schedules with anything approaching decent programming. Take a look through this week's *Guide* and you'll see what I mean – it's like gazing at the shelves of a particularly threadbare Poundshop, one that sells nothing but bootleg 'Bobb the Bilder' toys and *Pop Idol* wrapping paper.

Here are the highlights: *Alistair MacGowan's Christmas Big Christmas Impression At Christmas* (BBC1) – a repeat from last year; *Time Flyers* (BBC2) – that's a bunch of archaeologists sitting in a helicopter looking at the ground; *The World's Greatest Oil Rigs* (C5) – does exactly what it says on the tin; *Scalpel Safari* (C5) – people travelling to South Africa for plastic surgery followed by, yes, a safari; and *Extreme Ironing* (C4), a documentary which purports to follow 'the progress of the UK team at the Extreme Ironing World Championship in Munich' but, disappointingly, turns out to be a none-too-hilarious joke stretched out for an entire hour.

Then there's the awards ceremonies: *Sports Personality of the Year* (BBC1) – generally about as much fun as eating a handful of dried yeast; the truly loathsome *Record of the Year 2002* (ITV1) in which Dr Fox congratulates whichever soulless bunch of Tupperware automata have appealed to the largest number of idiots this year; *The Turner Prize* (C4) – the pseudo-intellectual's equivalent of the above; and *FHM High Street Honeys: The Winners* (Sky One) – essentially the TV equivalent of a dirty old man masturbating at a bus stop.

These celebrations of nothingness reach their peak with *Kylie Entirely* (C4), a 90-minute brown-tonguing of Britain's 'best-loved entertainer' cluttering up the schedules of the UK's number-one 'alternative' broadcaster: further proof that Channel 4 have long since abandoned an imaginative agenda and are now committed to pursuing the lowest common denominator with all the dignity of a man with his trousers round his ankles chasing a Thai prostitute round and round a sofa.

Still, *Kylie Entirely* would be just about justifiable had they managed to secure an interview with Ms Minogue herself, but no: instead it's yet another mélange of archive clips and talking heads. *Kylie Entirely* reaches its nadir with a full 10-minute dissection of the Minogue arse, which unfortunately isn't carried out by Dr Bodyworlds, but a gaggle of pundits including – AAAARRRGGHHHH – Paul Ross, the Ghost of Rubbish Past, who talks soundbites in his sleep and indeed does so here, in a series of unflattering shots which make him look like a melted Benny Hill. Any show desperate enough to resort to Ross soundbites really shouldn't be on television at all – it should be out in the street, wearing an 'UNCLEAN' sign and ringing a bell. In fact I shouldn't even be writing about it – but there's *nothing else on*.

Still, everyone in the media will be out at their Yuletide parties, so what do they care? Come to think of it, I'll be out too – getting into the festive spirit by sitting in a skip at the end of my road, drinking meths till I bleed. And since it's Christmas, you're all welcome to join me.

Slam it in a Filing Cabinet   [14 December]

Last week I bemoaned the state of the schedules in the run-up to Christmas.

A week later, and guess what? Zero improvement. The main difference: instead of *The World's Greatest Oil Rigs*, this week Channel Five (oh, all right, 'five') brings us *The World's Greatest Cranes* – I confess I didn't bother ordering a preview tape since I suspect even the mightiest industrial hoist in existence couldn't raise my enthusiasm for the subject matter. Particularly when said programme is hosted by Tiff 'Quick, Turn Over' Needell.

So, barren viewing: what's to do? Obviously, writing for an upstanding publication such as the *Guardian* means I would never encourage readers to flout international copyright law by scouring the Internet for downloadable episodes of the next series of *24* (which I also wouldn't suggest are easily available, particularly if you hunt for them using a peer-to-peer file-sharing program like Kazaa or WinMX, and I *certainly* wouldn't suggest they're as nail-biting as the previous series and therefore well worth the lengthy download time – no siree).

Instead, I draw your attention to *Vain Men* (C4), a documentary examining the increasingly methodical preening regimes of the British male.

Speaking as a man whose idea of sophisticated grooming involves dipping a sock in the toilet to swab his armpits each morning, it all came as a bit of a shock.

For starters, according to the voice-over, 'the average man now moisturises daily'. What, really? Where was that survey held? Pussy-land? The Kingdom of Nivea? Nope: right here on earth apparently – and to prove it, the researchers have rustled up a collection of image-conscious males who blow far too much time and money on manicures, spray-on tans, diets, masochistic work-out routines and even 'pectoral implant surgery' (that's a tit-job to you and me) in a desperate bid to resemble the exalted male ideal. Look, I'm no expert on the rules of attraction, but I do know this: any man who spends half his life agonising in front of a mirror simply doesn't *deserve* to get laid. Not by a human at any rate, although I'd queue round the block to watch them take it from an undemanding Dobermann. I mean honestly. Lighten up and weather-beat yourself like the rest of us, you idiots: we're practically drowning in ladies here in Slobsville.

Still, *Vain Men* does provide the hands-down 'water-cooler' moment of the week: a cornea-warping close-up of a maniac having his bumcrack and testicles waxed with terrifying efficiency by a nonchalant beautician.

The scrotum is a sensitive area at the best of times. Tap it lightly with a pen and your eyes can water for an entire weekend; actively volunteering to have it stripped bare is demented. The accompanying noise would be excruciating enough (the sound of all those wispy hairs being uprooted en masse is like someone wearing Velcro gloves tearing a rice cake in half), but the aftermath is worse: the scrotum emerges crimson and raw, like a napalmed dormouse. If this is what it takes to be considered handsome these days, I hereby retire from the mating game. In fact, I can only think of five more painful things you could do with your scrotal sack, which I'll list for the hell of it: 1) Slam it in a filing cabinet. 2) Catch it on a lathe. 3) Place it inside a George Foreman Lean Mean Grilling Machine and repeatedly wallop the lid with your fists. 4) Tie one end of a tow cable round the Marble Arch monument, the other round your egg basket, leap onto a motorbike and see how close you can get to Hyde Park Corner before losing consciousness. 5) Declare it part of the 'axis of evil' and convince the Americans to wage a five-week bombing campaign against it (don't wax it first – it'll help your case if it's already wearing a beard).

Anyway, enough of this balls. Next week, the Yuletide broadcasting onslaught begins in earnest. Which means yet more painful bollocks on the telly.

An Appalling but True Story   [21 December]

Here's an appalling but true story. I was in a taxi on the day the John Leslie story finally broke. The cabbie, who'd caught talk of 'a mystery presenter' on the radio, without actually hearing the golden name itself, spotted my copy of the *Evening Standard*, and asked me who the culprit was. 'Says here it's John Leslie,' I replied.

'John Leslie,' he muttered, then ruminated for a moment before delivering his verdict: 'The lucky sod.' The Leslie debacle summed up our confusion over celebrity – the year's overriding televisual theme. Exalted one minute, tortured the next – we simply don't know what to do with our famous people. Watching Leslie blank-eye his way through a standard edition of *This Morning*, aware he was the subject of frenzied Popbitch speculation, but unaware *The Wright Stuff* had inadvertently fingered him hours earlier, was the year's most haunting image.

Of course, Leslie wasn't the only 'lucky sod' this year. So many TV careers were derailed by scandal you needed a metal umbrella to avoid being brained by falling stars, and when they hit the ground we tore into them like the confused, rage-fuelled zombies from *28 Days Later*. Angus Deayton discovered no amount of nonchalant smirking would prevent the tabloids from crucifying him, while Barrymore's career was as dead as the man in his swimming pool, even though he was cleared of any involvement: proof, if any were truly needed, that light entertainment and corpses don't mix. (The exception to this rule is Professor Scaryhat Bodyworlds, the walking Hammer Horror character who performed an autopsy for Channel 4 – I'd have loved to see him turn up on the now mercifully cancelled *Generation Game*, giving grandmothers from Preston marks out of 10 for the way they sawed a ribcage open – especially if said ribcage belonged to Jim Davidson, and he was still alive, and his feet were kicking about and everything.) The torturing of famous people never let up. Hit of the year was *I'm A Celebrity – Get Me Out Of Here!* in which we were treated to the sight of Uri Geller scoffing live grubs and Christine Hamilton falling down a waterfall and blacking her eye. No sooner had that finished (granting Tony Blackburn an additional 15 seconds of adulation before we all got bored of him again) than *Celebrity Big Brother* took up the gauntlet, affording viewers an opportunity to sneer at Anne Diamond's weight problem and publicly debate whether Les Dennis was going to commit suicide. And on BBC2, *The Entertainers* painted a sorry picture of Leo Sayer; oh how we cackled, even though his life to date has been 10,000 times more exciting than that of the average couch potato. Don't forget, this man sold millions of records, travelled the world and performed live in front of thousands of screaming fans. And what have *you* done? You've sat there, inert on your sofa, laughing about what a joke you think he is. So who's the tragic figure in this equation?

The end result is that celebrity has never seemed so second-rate. With all mystery removed, the cachet of fame is plunging so rapidly, by this time next year it'll actually be cooler to work down your local newsagent than to appear on telly.

Perhaps that's why, in a desperate bid to boost the dwindling ranks of the famous, TV companies pulled out all the stops attempting to transform regular Joes into megastars – *Pop Idol*, *Popstars: The Rivals*, *Model Ambition*, *Fame Academy*, all of them acting as gigantic blandness sieves, ruthlessly weeding out anyone of interest; art defined by committee. Even the very public implosion of Hear'Say – last year celebrated in an hour-long prime time special, this year spat at in the streets – didn't hamper the process.

The *Popstars* panel of judges pre-defined just how bland the end product would be: Louis Walsh, a squashed omelette of a man who wouldn't recognise soulful singing if it crooned at him from a deathbed; the curiously self-righteous Pete Waterman and gushing Geri Halliwell, a national joke who has to wear her heart on her sleeve because there's no room left for it in her sunken Belsen-chic chest any more. The end result is that, what with the combined cast of *Popstars* and *Fame Academy* AND Will and Gareth all releasing watery-bollocked singles in the space of a few weeks, we're left with the worst Christmas Top 10 since records began – a situation so dire, even the producer of *Top of the Pops* started publicly complaining. Which makes him my hero of the year: after all, he's the poor bastard who has to try to make this shit look interesting. And where were all our proper pop stars while this was happening? Liam got his teeth kicked out and Jarvis spent the year doing *Stars In Their Eyes* and dangling off lamp posts in a BT commercial.

The tragedy of it all is that while we amused ourselves watching mallrat crooners burst into tears and Rhona Cameron inspecting Uri Geller's pubic hair for lice, the Americans were creating some of the finest TV drama ever made – a veritable renaissance, in fact. In addition to the continued artistic successes of the *West Wing*, *Oz*,

The Sopranos and *Sex and the City*, they brought us *Six Feet Under*, *CSI*, *The Shield* and my favourite show of the year, *24*.

Ah, *24*: preposterous, over-stylised and occasionally schmaltzy it may have been, but it was also the single most tense television drama series ever made, insanely addictive once you got caught up in its unstoppable march toward midnight. It even provided a gutsy, unconventional ending: Jack Bauer, our hero, cradling the body of his pregnant wife, shot through the stomach by his traitorous ex-lover. The second series, already running in the US, hits our screens in February: I've seen the first six and incredibly, it's better.

The closest we've come to emulating the gritty new wave of American dramas is the BBC's spy drama *Spooks*, which demon-strated astonishing nerve by signing Lisa Faulkner as a regular char-acter, then killing her off in spectacularly grisly fashion in episode two. The moment her head was forced into the deep-fat fryer, view-ers reared on the formulaic, it'll-be-alright-in-the-end blandness of cookie-cutter populist dramas like *Casualty* and *Merseybeat* sat up and blinked in disbelief: here was a major BBC drama series that actually had the nerve to confound expectation. Perhaps the failure of ITV's *Doctor Zhivago* and the BBC's *Daniel Deronda* to set the world alight means my dream of a five-year moratorium on cos-tume dramas will become reality – if we get more programmes like *Spooks* in their place, then heaven be praised.

So what else happened? Comedy rose in popularity, thanks to the likes of *Black Books*, *Phoenix Nights*, *The Office* and *I'm Alan Partridge*, all on their second series. The latter two suffered from 'difficult second album' syndrome, but were still head and shoul-ders above the likes of *TLC* (essentially the Chuckle Brothers for morons).

The funniest show of the year, however, was unscripted and American, although it starred a British family. I'm talking about *The Osbournes*, of course – a real one-off success that simply can't be replicated (although God knows TV producers will try). A celebrity reality show that didn't invite us to sneer, it provided more laugh-out-loud moments than it had any right to.

So. That's the year in a nutshell. Now turn to the listings and plan your Yuletide viewing. Speaking of which, there's just time for my prediction regarding next year's Christmas TV – an Aardman animated version of *Only Fools and Horses*. Go on, picture it – I swear to God it'll happen one day. Oh, and merry Christmas. Unless you're a Pop Idol, in which case you can piss off. Quietly.

PART FOUR 2003

In which Chris Evans comes unstuck with Boys and Girls, *interactive TV turns out to be rubbish, and the world's first widescreen war is started.*

Metal-and-Flesh Pâté   [4 January]

I've always been deeply suspicious of people who are 'into' cars –
you know, the sort of overgrown adolescent who slaps Ferrari
posters on their walls and doesn't contemplate suicide when they
hear the *Top Gear* theme tune. Perhaps it's because they tend to be
the sort of person who'll think nothing of driving to within two
atoms of the car in front at 300 m.p.h. and, as the G-force starts
shearing your face off, will attempt to quell your cries of fear and
protest by repeatedly pointing out what a good driver they are,
shortly before ploughing head-on into a container lorry and turning both of you into a bloodied streak of metal-and-flesh pâté
smeared across ten straight miles of motorway. Perhaps it's
because I can't drive and I'm jealous. Either way, I'm right and
they're wrong.

Anyway, said motorphiles are going to love *Fastlane* (Sky One), a
frankly astonishing new US cop show which appears to be beamed
live from the brain of an excitable 14-year-old boy. I don't think I've
ever seen anything quite like it – eight times as puerile as *Gone in
60 Seconds*, with a concept and script you could scribble down the
edge of a beer coaster and *still* leave room for a dubious cartoon
sketch of a pair of breasts.

The set-up is as follows: Tom Cruise/Ethan Hawke-hybrid Peter
Facinelli *is* officer Van Ray Strummer (not so much a name, more a
masturbatory euphemism). He's ridiculous: the very first scene in
this week's pilot finds him hurling a sports car round a speedway
track while a glamorous female thief fingers his crotch. Moments
later, before the opening titles have had a chance to kick in, his
partner is gunned down in cold blood. 'Noooooo!' bellows Van Ray,
and spends the rest of the episode attempting to avenge his death
by getting his shirt off a lot and penetrating the blonde thief on a
bed covered in banknotes (in a daring move for mainstream US
drama, there's a slow-mo shot of him pulling down her knickers to
reveal some cavernous bum-cleavage – *Fastlane* pushes the artistic
envelope wherever possible).

Meanwhile, Bill Bellamy *is* Deaqon LaVelle Hayes, undercover

NYPD cop, and the brother of Van Ray's slaughtered partner. Deaqon is black and street and is therefore first encountered playing basketball with a bunch of toughs from the 'hood. He hot-foots it to LA to find out more about his brother's death and subsequently teams up with Van Ray who, by this time, has been signed up by Tiffani-Amber Thiessen, who *is* Wilhelmina 'Billie' Chambers, a sultry lieutenant in charge of the 'Candy Store', a repository of impossibly expensive seized vehicles, weapons and clothing the LAPD has thoughtfully provided in order to aid high-gloss undercover operations.

The Candy Store is also decked out with gigantic plasma screens upon which the faces of suspects can spin about futuristically, thereby assisting the fight against crime.

And that's about it: I couldn't really tell you what else actually happens because it makes no sense whatsoever – although it does involve several high-speed car chases, a bit where the bad guy beats up a girl on the beach, four explosions and a jaw-dropping sequence in which Deaqon wins the trust of a country-and-western-loving crime lord by performing a spontaneous line dance.

In case you hadn't guessed, *Fastlane* is a shameless attempt to 'do' *Miami Vice* for the twenty-first century (at one point they even have the nerve to include Phil Collins' 'In the Air Tonight' on the soundtrack). Dementedly glossy throughout, with flash cuts and apparently random forays into slow motion, the overall effect is like watching a Sisqo video, drunk, on a helter-skelter. This really shouldn't be on so soon after New Year's Eve. Nevertheless, I urge you to tune in, if only so someone can e-mail the *Guide* and explain precisely what happened. Because I'm still not sure whether I actually saw this or dreamed it, and if that indicates the way TV's going in 2003, I'm going to need all the help I can get.

Disasterporn [11 January]

It's funny, the things that stick in the memory. Many years ago I recall reading an NME interview with affable slap-head techno duo Orbital in which one of the Orbitees claimed he never smoked cannabis because he had 'an Alfred Hitchcock mind' – i.e. he was perpetually expecting something nasty to happen, even in the most serene surroundings. 'I can't even walk past a park railing without thinking, "Urgh, you could slip and skewer your hand on that,"' he said, and I practically leapt up and started pointing at the page shrieking, 'Me too! ME TOO!'

Well, I hope he's not been watching *Collision Course* (BBC2) of late, because it's a programme apparently designed to nurture your existing paranoid fantasies and generate countless new ones in the process.

Officially, it's described as a series 'on the science and psychology of fatal transport accidents, revealing the decisions made seconds or decades before that will determine who will live or die', but I reckon you could sum it up more accurately as 'extreme rubbernecking', 'untertainment', or perhaps simply 'disasterporn'.

Last week's edition examining the Southall rail crash is a case in point. Using a combination of survivor interviews, expert opinion (from rail-safety advisors through to psychologists) and – most upsetting of all – haunting computer-generated reconstructions of the accident itself, it picked apart the collision atom-by-atom, stretching an incident which lasted roughly eight and a half seconds into an hour of unrelenting terror.

In fact, the end effect is a bit like *The Matrix* for neurotic vultures: plenty of slow-mo 'bullet time' enactments of precisely the sort of calamity both myself and that bloke from Orbital spend so much time worrying about.

We learned how one woman's life was saved because she decided to move to a different carriage when a group of noisy people boarded the train. We learned how a doctor was spared one of the grisliest fates imaginable when the carriage fell on its side – he broke six ribs landing sideways on a table which prevented him from plummeting through a smashed window at the bottom and getting smeared across the tracks (other passengers weren't so lucky). And we learned that in moments of extreme terror, it's not unusual for victims to see in black-and-white – because the brain decides that the processing power required to replicate colour would be better employed doing something else, such as locating the nearest exit or kissing your arse goodbye. But mostly we learned this: There Is No God.

You see, for all its gory details and eye-popping computer simulations, the single most disturbing thing about *Collision Course* is the way it lays bare the random cruelty of fate – in fact, it positively revels in it. The Southall edition ended by explaining that many victims of rail accidents often choose to travel exclusively by car afterwards, then gloomily pointed out this is an even more unpredictably dangerous mode of transport. 'The decisions you make tonight could mean you die on the roads tomorrow,' boomed the voice-over (Charles Dance, who seems to have gargled with some kind of special 'doom pill' prior to recording). Cue lots of meticulous reconstructions of shattered windscreens and twisted gearsticks for this Tuesday's edition – a pile-up special. Thank Christ it's only a three-part series or we'd all be too scared to leave the house by week nine (when they'd probably be calculating the likelihood of a hot-air balloon crashing into your face, recreating just such an incident in photo-realistic pixelvision).

All in all, nasty but compelling – my only question is this: why don't they use all this moment-by-moment jiggery-pokery to create reconstructions of *nice* things for once? Like maybe an exhaustive hour-long recreation of a child being delighted by a jack-in-the-box? OK, so it wouldn't have quite the same voyeuristic pull as a spine-splintering motorway pile-up, but if it helps a troubled nation sleep at night, who's complaining?

Holby Prison   [18 January]

Heavens to Betsy, where did that come from? Just a few weeks ago I was bemoaning the embarrassing efficiency with which American TV drama was kicking our collective national arse: they make *The Sopranos* and *24*, we spew out identichangeable star vehicles for Ross and Martin Kemp (how long before they team up for a show called 'Shop Window Dummy Squad'?).

Then suddenly – bam! Channel 4 wheels out a fantastic new

series called *Buried* (C4). Set in the cheery confines of the British prison system, and hailing from Tony Garnett's ever-reliable World Productions (*This Life*, *The Cops*, um, *Attachments*), it's the polar opposite of the sort of bland-o-matic mush we're usually spoon-fed.

Had it appeared on BBC1, chances are it would've been called 'Holby Prison' and starred Leslie 'Sofa-Mouth' Ash and a cast of *Hollyoaks* deserters. The average storyline would involve a kindly old lag befriending a frightened young whippersnapper, inter-spersed with scenes of comic relief in which the prison pig goes missing and Officer Alan Davies has to track it down.

As it is, it's late-night Channel 4, and it's packed to the roof tiles with anger, violence, sexual assault and more casual usage of the f-word than the average south London school playground. Scathing and espresso-strong, then – but what's interesting about it is that it's very, very good: an intelligent script that constantly surprises and illuminates, coupled with uniformly excellent, entirely con-vincing performances from every single cast member.

It'd be a crying shame if *Buried* were overlooked by its native audience, so I urge you all to do your civic duty by tuning in and watching the damn thing. That's an order. Don't worry if you missed last week's opener – there's a quick recap at the start and once you're in, you're in (rather like prison itself, actually). It's a measure of how good *Buried* is that, despite being relentlessly grim, frightening and, yes, profoundly depressing, you won't want it to end. And if for some mad reason you feel the show itself fails to live up to my histrionic praise, I apologise – it's not often I find myself utterly blown away by a preview tape and it's nice to get car-ried away in a positive way for a change.

Another recommendation: *Without Prejudice* (C4) which on paper sounds like it could be incredibly rubbish, but in practice is jaw-dropping, infuriating, intelligent and hilarious. The format's simple enough – a panel of average Joes decides which of five other average Joes should receive £50,000 on the basis of whatever char-acter information they can glean from them. If this was ITV2, they'd be quizzed on their bedroom antics, asked to do impressions of Joe Pasquale, balance spoons on their nose or do something equally arse-minded. Instead *Without Prejudice* wisely concentrates on the kind of red-hot ethical issues that could provoke a furious argument between identical twins – animal rights, same-sex marriages and capital punishment. It's high-stakes Kilroy, in other words, but immeasurably better than that sounds (and minus Kilroy of course, which is always a bonus).

The interesting thing is that while the studio panel is judging the contestants, the audience at home can't help judging the panel – and the findings are usually unfavourable. If you're looking for televised proof that power corrupts, here it is – the torrent of self-righteous smuggery that pours from the temporary cash committee is astonishing. Ugly opinions, knee-jerk reactions and plain old-fashioned ignorant blatherings – all receive an exhaustive airing, and if this is how the average Brit behaves when handed even a fleeting taste of authority, we're clearly doomed. How Liza Tarbuck resists the urge to kick the table over and start slapping them around is beyond me.

Here's hoping they sell the format round the world, so we'll eventually get to see a demented South American version in which the host does precisely that. While dressed as a giant cat or something.

Pretty Bleedin' Pedestrian [25 January]

Q: When is a British Transport Police officer not a British Transport Police officer?
A: When he's a 'Rail Cop'.

'Rail Cop' sounds more exciting, you see – or at least the producers of *Rail Cops* (BBC1) seem to think so, because that's how their voice-over track routinely refers to the Transport Police. A clever ruse, with only one drawback – whatever you call them, the job itself is still pretty bleedin' pedestrian. Drunkard pissing on the line? Send in the Rail Cops. Person under a train at Bethnal Green? Here comes a Rail Cop with a body bag and a mop. And when a commuter snaps at Liverpool Street station and starts screaming and crying and defecating on the floor, it's the Rail Cops' job to contain the situation before everybody else joins in. Woo and hoo.

It isn't a patch on those documentaries about American police – the ones with cars flipping over and people blowing their own knees off with shotguns. For instance, much of this week's episode concerns the efforts of a Welsh Rail Cop who's spotted some kids trespassing on the line. Now, if this was America, he'd abseil from a helicopter, bundle them to the floor and start kicking them in the spine or something – y'know, being inhumane but entertaining. Instead our British Rail Cop drives around ponderously, talking to camera in a Welsh accent until it eventually dawns on you that you're essentially watching *Marion and Geoff*. To cap it all, when he eventually catches up with the kids in question, they don't even get a clip round the ear, just a mild talking-to.

To be fair, there is one interesting bit where a Rail Cop-in-training loses the plot during baton practice and almost beats a man to death on camera, but since his 'victim' is wearing heavy padding we don't even get any blood or anything. Boo.

The BBC should invent a whole new branch of the police, and film that. How about 'Tiger Squad' – a unit that uses specially trained tigers to maul suspected paedophiles to death. Or a team of homicide detectives who force-feed suspects LSD and interrogate them wearing masks, on a trampoline.

Anything but bloody *Rail Cops*, basically.

Ho Ho Ho   [8 February]

In 1965, the critic Kenneth Tynan made history by saying the f-word on *BBC3*. Civilised society was stunned; a Norfolk farmer punched his entire herd to death with disgust. Tynan was sentenced to 48 decades in prison and had his gob washed out with soap by Prime Minister Disraeli. The *BBC3* in question wasn't a channel, but a satirical comedy show starring Bird and Fortune. Only now, 38 years later, does the BBC dare to launch an actual channel with the same name, largely because Tynan's no longer around to fuck it up with his potty mouth.

BBC3 replaces BBC Choice, the digital station that forged a name for itself as *the* place to come for *EastEnders* repeats and rubbish Ralf Little vehicles. Choice was undistinguished, sullied by a demented belief that what the viewers wanted was an endless torrent of vaguely 'yoofy' B-list celebs fronting ill-thought-out programmes – *Mark Owen's Celebrity Scooters*, *Dermot's Sporting Buddies* and possibly the worst programme ever broadcast by the BBC, *LA Pool Party*.

To be fair, Choice also endured low budgets, which explained the reliance on cheap-to-make schlock like the above (a lack of funds was also responsible for leaving one of Choice's potential stars – Simon Munnery, aka *The League Against Tedium* – floundering in a sketch show whose budget couldn't keep pace with his imagination). Now, with a fresh cash injection, Choice is about to transmogrify into BBC3 – but is it any good? Well, it's certainly more watchable: while you *can* use cheap DV cams to knock out a broadcast-quality TV show, the content needs to be of *Jackass*-level stun value to make it worth sitting through, and most shows aren't that interesting. More money equals proper DigiBeta crews and proper programmes.

On TV, surface quality makes a huge difference. Bigger bucks also equals bigger scope, which means in come a slew of new shows on a diverse range of topics: twenty-something drama *Burn This*, documentaries on Vinnie Jones and Fatboy Slim (the latter rendered somewhat haunting thanks to repeated scenes in which Zoë and Norm coo all over each other) and *Body Hits* – a series in which telegenic Dr John Marsden 'investigates the culture of excess'.

Body Hits number one tackles booze, and includes a bit in which Marsden downs seventeen shots of tequila and ends up flailing around on the floor. A forthcoming edition investigates cocaine, so maybe we'll get to see him joining the snaking queue outside the toilet cubicles at the next BBC 'wrap party' he's invited to. Or maybe not.

Then there's *Dreamspaces*, a new architecture show presented by Charlie Luxton, David Adjaye and – weirdly – Justine from Elastica. Essentially *Top Gear* for building fetishists, *Dreamspaces* is almost ludicrously glossy, shot like a cross between *Gattaca* and *The*

Matrix: the overall effect is like having a copy of *Wallpaper* magazine slowly injected into your eyeball while listening to a Royksopp CD.

Most promising is BBC3's commitment to comedy shows, which have lacked a decent home at the Beeb since BBC2 decided to concentrate on lifestyle makeovers and cookery instead.

The launch night alone features five new comedies: Lucas and Walliams' excellent *Little Britain, This Is Dom Joly* (which, er, might grow on me), a new Paul Calf one-off from Steve Coogan, *Monkey Dust* (a disappointing, self-consciously 'dark' cartoon sketch show) and, to round things off, *3 Non-Blondes*.

The latter is a female *Trigger Happy TV* with a rather dispiriting reliance on pussy jokes. If they can ditch the lame shock tactics and concentrate on the good-natured absurdities (such as the skit in which a street altercation turns into a dance routine), there'll be a better show at the end of it.

Mind you, for a supposedly shocking, 'streetwise' show starring three black comedians, they could at least have had the nerve to call it either 'Black the Pony' or 'Ho Ho Ho'.

Peril and Cleavage   [15 February]

Rejoice! Time for the second series of *24* (BBC2). And here's where things stand at the start . . .

It's one year on and following the murder of his wife, heroic Jack Bauer's gone off the rails. In case we're in any doubt about just how far he's fallen, there's a hideous ginger beard sprouting round his chops, which makes him look like a piece of Shredded Wheat impersonating Kris Kristofferson. Clearly, any sane man would've reached for the razor some time ago, but Jack's so despondent he probably doesn't keep sharp objects in the house in case he's tempted to slice up his forearms for funnies.

Jack's daughter Kim (hobbies: peril and cleavage) doesn't want to see her dad because the mere sight of his beard dredges up memories too painful to contain. Besides she's busy working as an au pair for a too-good-to-be-true Californian husband-and-wife team and their whiny blonde daughter (whom Kim presumably relates to on a fundamental level). All very idyllic . . . but wherever Kim goes, contrived danger is sure to follow, and before long we sense there's something not quite right about the daddy of the household, a Gillette-model type who spends rather too long ogling Kim's body – as indeed will every heterosexual male in the nation, since she helpfully starts the episode clad in a tight vest and skimpy knickers. FHM readers and/or chronic masturbators will be relieved to hear that, just like last time, Kim is destined to spend most of this series running around in a low-cut top.

Meanwhile, there have been a few changes over at CTU. Jack's left, Grumpybones Mason is in charge and they've hired Darlene from *Roseanne* to clean fluff off the mouse balls. Most significant of all, smoulderin' Tony Almeida has shaved off the bizarre little Hitler moustache that used to live below his lower lip (presumably because he's upset about Nina's deception and because, like Jack, he tends to signal changes in his emotional state by altering his facial hair). This being a high-octane thriller, it isn't long before the tranquillity of the office (which, as before, looks more like the HQ of a poncey Hoxton lifestyle magazine than a government agency) is shattered – courtesy of a hot bit of intel claiming that terrorists are planning to set off a nuclear device! In Los Angeles! Today! Professionals that they are, the CTU team manage to take this impending Armageddon in their stride and focus on the important things: preventing the tragedy and casting meaningful looks at one another.

So far, so good. But I know what you're thinking. Since the end of the first series you've been lying awake at night, worrying about the relationship between Senator Palmer and his son Keith. You tossed and turned, unable to contain your excitement at the prospect of more scenes in which Keith gets upset and Palmer says he loves him and Keith says he doesn't and Palmer says he does and they make up.

Well, sorry, bad news: we do see Keith at the start, enjoying a fishing trip with Pops (who's now President Palmer), but he's soon nudged out of the storyline – I fear we won't encounter him again;

pity, because I just couldn't get enough of those mutual-respect chinwags they had last time. Here's hoping Fox produce a spin-off series called 'Keith's Fucking Problems', in which the drippy-eyed jerkwad sits on a fence post pouring his heart out to passing strangers.

So Keith's out, but don't hang up the bunting just yet – there's an irritating subplot involving a wedding which provides ample opportunity for agonised heart-to-hearts between a pair of blonde sisters. You'll know when to put the kettle on. That gripe aside, it's a case of more, more, more. More intensity, more brutality and, best of all, more George Mason. Oh, and episode one lasts a full hour thanks to a product-placement deal with Ford, which meant it played minus ad-breaks in the US. The most addictive show on TV is back, and it's better.

Of course the real world's probably going to end before the series does, but you can't have everything.

Human Suffering Equals Big Guffaws [22 February]

OK, before launching into the coming week's telly, a quick word about a programme that got me all angered-up last Saturday – *The Luvvies*, ITV's light-hearted anti-awards show, which doled out joke gongs to celebrities for categories such as Most Likely to Turn Up for the Opening of an Envelope and the like. An epoch-shatter-ingly hysterical concept, I'm sure you'll agree.

What specifically enraged me was the section in which awards were shelled out for 'going off the rails' – a category in which Barry-more, John Leslie and Matthew Kelly were conspicuous by their absence. No, instead the award went to easy target Les Dennis, whose wife – ha ha! – has left him, leaving his personal life – tee hee! – in tatters. This was hilariously illustrated with footage of him in the *Big Brother* house crying his eyes out. Hoot! Just in case that wasn't rib-tickling enough, it was followed by a *Cook Report*-style sequence in which a *Luvvies* camera crew chased Les down the road, up to his front door, and – please, my aching sides – tried to give the award to his housekeeper.

Perhaps I'm a wuss but I think harassing the heartbroken for funnies is disgraceful. Clearly, the producer, Dan Clapton, believes that human suffering equals big guffaws, so if anyone out there has any first-hand accounts of him having his heart broken, send me the juicy details and I'll reprint them here so we can have a good hearty ho-ho together. After all, it's just a bit of fun, right Dan? Right?

Anyway, onto this week: Larry 'Seinfeld' David's *Curb Your Enthusiasm* (BBC4) – which takes the comedy of discomfort into previously uncharted territory. If you thought *The Office* was good at making you wince, you ain't seen nothing yet. Honestly, it's like sitting on a pine cone for half an hour – but in a good way.

Shot entirely with handheld cameras, apparently using natural light and semi-improvised dialogue, *Curb Your Enthusiasm* is like a sitcom take on the Dogme 95 movement. The resulting 'ambient' tone is initially disorientating, but stick with it: it's a major grower.

Larry David plays himself: a pampered, embittered misanthrope wandering dazed, through the LA celebrity circuit, digging absurdly deep holes at every opportunity. And while there aren't any 'jokes' as such, there's an almost obscene level of enjoyment to be had watching him doggedly convert a minor inconvenience (such as a pair of bunched-up trousers that make him look aroused) into a full-blown social catastrophe. David surely can't be this big a dick in real life (no one would employ the man) and the masochistic relish with which he's made himself the butt of every situation raises serious questions about his mental state – but thank God he's out there, and thank God the BBC are showing it, albeit on a digital offshoot (presumably so unsuspecting BBC2 viewers won't get confused by unexpectedly encountering a bit of golden comedy amid all the lifestyle makeover shows).

Speaking of embittered misanthropy, have you seen former *Double Dare* presenter Peter Simon on the live auction channel *Bid-Up TV* recently? I swear to God, the man's turning into Howard Beale from the movie *Network*: sighing audibly on air, describing himself as 'sad' and muttering about how lonely he is – half the time I'm not even sure if he realises he's speaking out loud.

It's surely only a matter of time before he starts shuddering, or crying, or urging viewers to hang themselves with their trouser belts – and, if they obey, he ought to be given some kind of award for services to the national gene pool. I do hope it's all a massive put-on; if not, you can bet Dan Clapton and his camera crew will be nipping round to stick their gongs through his letter box some day soon.

Imbecility Event Horizon   [8 March]

Attention, attention. This is not a drill. I repeat, this is not a drill. Go to your shelters. Do not stop to retrieve belongings. Do not venture out until instructed to do so. We have reached Imbecility Event Horizon. Clouds of noxious thickery are billowing across the nation: do not risk exposure. If you have a television, smash it now. It is acting as a conduit. On no account switch it on. On no account watch *Boys and Girls* (C4).

Even a fleeting glimpse can cause inoperable brain damage. A nightmare vision of the future, folks, but one I fear could come true at any moment. Let me explain. The shelves of Waterstones are littered with breeze-block-sized sci-fi novels with the following premise: a group of scientists attempt to create a black hole in their laboratory. They succeed. Planet Earth is engulfed by an out-of-control vortex of nothingness. The end.

Well, that's what's happening with *Boys and Girls*, Channel 4's new Saturday night bozo-cast. It's not so much a TV show, more an organised attempt to create a newer, more toxic form of crap; one that can eat through the screen and pollute the human brain within minutes, leaving the victim unable to perform anything but the most basic motor functions, such as chewing cud or masturbating.

And it's in danger of going wrong. I'm scared. They're meddling with things so far *below* the realm of human comprehension, they may inadvertently create a swirling portal to a whole new dimension of stupidity. All solid matter in the universe may get sucked in. For God's sake Blair, send the troops in now.

What follows is an excerpt from notes I made during last Saturday's edition.

Please excuse the scrappy nature of the text; I was undergoing heavy exposure at the time.

Boys and Girls: awful. No, worse: possibly illegal. Vernon Kay must be liberated. Man looks lost. Send search and rescue team immediately. Audience consists of opposing teams of 100 men and 100 women. Bellowing cow people. Mass outbreaks of hollow-skulled whooping. The noise, the noise. Going to be sick. Going to [text unintelligible]. Please God stop the noise. Taliban definitely right. Is this an al-Qaeda recruitment film? Sheer level of witlessness terrifying. Quantities of tackiness not balanced by equal quantity of sly intelligence, leading to potential China Syndrome of Shitness. Reminded of difference between *Wayne's World* and *Dude, Where's My Car?* – both puerile, but the latter rendered unwatchable by utter absence of clever: *Boys and Girls* even worse. Getting worse. Jade Goody cackling, 'Sex or beer, sex or beer?' as audience bellows around her. Consider possibility this is live-action version of Hieronymus Bosch triptych.

Cannot believe this cost half a million pounds. Must call Hans Blix and request immediate dismantlement. More cackling. Can sense idiocy piercing own brain. Must look away. Must look away. [Remainder of text obscured by blood.]

The time has come to protect yourself and your family from the *Boys and Girls* menace. Collate a survival kit: you'll need books, magazines, paper, pens, an old Nirvana CD and videotapes of *24* and *Curb Your Enthusiasm*. Detach the aerial lead from your television set and establish a protective cordon around it on Friday and Saturday nights. If anyone goes to switch the TV on during this time, shoot them.

Fortunately, early data indicates far fewer innocent viewers than anticipated have been exposed to *Boys and Girls*. Best-case scenario is that this trend continues until it withers away, at which point field operative Vernon Kay can be scrubbed, defumigated and returned to active service. Do not be fooled. This is not, repeat *not*, a harmless exercise in feelgood nonsense. It is a cynical, hateful, nauseating and witless insult to humankind. It is sub-ITV. It is sub-ITV2. We *must* act now, lest it destroy us.

Return to your shelters, beloved populace. And may God be with you.

The Greasy Horror of it All [15 March]

Fact! There's a saucer full of extra-terrestrial pod people lurking behind Jupiter, intercepting our TV transmissions, collating information on human culture. And over the last 18 months they've reached three unusual conclusions. 1) Earth people sit on specially designated park benches when upset (*EastEnders*). 2) Earth people settle arguments by seeing who can bellow their point of view the loudest (*Kilroy*). 3) Earth people loathe celebrities and enjoy watching them suffer (every other programme on TV). The third conclusion is correct, of course. We've watched them huffing their way through *Fat Club*, sobbing in the *Big Brother* house and eating maggots in the outback. Now we're subjecting yet another gaggle of faded stars to something even worse: total career humiliation, courtesy of *Reborn in the USA* (ITV1).

Usually, my last remaining scrap of human decency means that I find it hard to join in the collective sneering whenever a has-been celeb is publicly ridiculed, but there's something so damn perfect about *Reborn* that it leaves me rapt with admiration at the workings of this infernal machine. Here's the mechanism: ten former British pop stars are flown to the USA, where they're even more unknown than over here. They perform live in front of American audiences, who vote for their favourite performer. The two with the lowest scores are separated from the pack; the British public phones in to decide who gets drowned in a bucket before the next episode. On paper, another format; on screen, a hypnotic cross between *Pop Idol* and *Alan Partridge*. Before a note had been sung we were subjected to a spectacular tantrum courtesy of Mark Shaw of Then Jericho, who managed to single-handedly redefine the term 'wanker' by a) sleazing over a potential groupie at the airport, b) flicking ash in Michelle Gayle's food because she thought he was childish, and c) announcing that he wouldn't have any more to do with these 'fucking has-beens who couldn't hold a note if their lives depended on it'.

Previously, I'd never even heard of Then Jericho but now I'm half-tempted to seek some of their albums out, if only to see if the percussion section consists of a baby hurling toys from its pram. Then there's Dollar: not so much a car crash, more a 200-vehicle pile-up with massive loss of life. Physically, David Van Day has turned into a precise replica of William Petersen from *CSI*; Thereza Bazar has been replaced by a Kafkaesque locust. Together, they resemble the ballroom-dancing couple from *Hi-De-Hi*, and, accordingly, their performance last week came straight from the end of a recently bombed pier. I recently saw an uncut copy of *Cannibal Holocaust*, in which a live turtle is torn apart; sitting through that was a breeze compared to watching Dollar inflict equally horrific injuries on 'They Can't Take That Away From Me'.

And Sonia: Jesus Christ. Astonishingly, she possesses a powerful singing voice, but like a nuclear bomb in the hands of a madman, that's not a Good Thing. During her nightmarish rendering of 'The Greatest Love of All', she shuddered, howled and shook her fists, like Shirley Temple in a remake of *The Exorcist*.

The rest are less interesting. Leee John could pass for the bloke from the Halifax commercials if you gave him a pair of Penfold specs; Gina G has the weakest voice but the pertest arse; Tony Hadley looks like a stage magician; Michelle Gayle is great; Go West's Peter Cox (heroically replacing Shaw) seems pleasantly unassuming; Elkie Brooks could be your best friend's mum; Haydon from Ultimate Kaos was unknown to everyone beforehand but seems destined to succeed. In other words, most are likeable performers who stand a decent chance of reinventing themselves.

Ignore the insanely ubiquitous Davina McCall and concentrate on the greasy horror of it all: *Reborn* is great Saturday night TV. And it'll utterly trounce C4's despicable *Boys and Girls* – another reason to love it. Fact!

The Truth is Out There   [22 March]

At the time of writing, the world's first widescreen war has yet to
begin in earnest, so there's still time to contemplate the important
things in life, namely *Reborn in the USA* (ITV1) and more specifically, the moment at which David Van Day and Thereza Bazar lashed
out at humankind (in the guise of Sonia) for thwarting their
inevitable return to power. Sonia left the show, only to return,
which gave rise to a conspiracy theory in Van Day's head: she had-
n't just flipped out in the wake of her ridiculous performance in
show one, oh no: the devious minx had done it deliberately in
order to, er, win. Cue tears from Thereza ('I only wanted to sing,'
she wailed, prompting sofa-bound cynics everywhere to bellow
'You tried that already, and look where it got you' at the screen),
while David fumed that disparaging remarks about them on Sonia's
website proved their imminent ejection was due to 'dirty tricks'
from a shadowy Liverpudlian cabal – as opposed to, say, Dollar
being rubbish. Things reached a head when Van Day, clutching his
smoking gun evidence of Sonia's duplicity (a print-out of the web
page) hectored the ginger chanteuse backstage until she begged
him to leave her alone. Later, Dollar were kicked out, Sonia com-
pounding their defeat by taking the stage and giving a decent performance (surely the ultimate treachery). Now they've got some
free time, Dollar should become professional conspiracy theorists.
Among the mysteries they might be able to clear up: what happened to their recording career? Why was 'Mirror, Mirror' so irritating? Why do people laugh whenever Van Day appears on
television? The truth is out there.

They could be the new Mulder and Scully – perfect timing, since
the old Mulder and Scully have vacated the position. Yes, after nine
years, *The X-Files* (BBC2) has come to an end, an event celebrated
with a feature-length finale that purports to clear everything up. I
loved the first two series of the X-Files, but stopped watching
around the time it turned to shit – i.e. when they stopped investigating fun Scooby Doo-style mysteries and concentrated instead
on interminable uber-conspiracies involving alien DNA, shape-

shifting agents and anything else they could think of. But ignorance on my part doesn't excuse this ludicrous final episode, which is easily the most incomprehensible slice of TV I've seen since the day I accidentally banged my head on a door frame and tried to watch an episode of *Pobol Y Cwm*.

Mulder is on trial for murder, and the only way to clear his name is to prove the existence of 'the conspiracy' in a military court, prompting a procession of witnesses from throughout the series, each of whom triggers a string of flashbacks that attempt to tell the entire story of *The X-Files* in bullet-point form – an exhausting load of bum wipe about 'super soldiers' and meteors and conspiracies within conspiracies, all of it impossible to follow without a three-dimensional diagram to back it up. Harry Knowles lookalikes might cream their jeans when, say, Harris the Moleman from season 52 episode 96 puts in a cameo, but everyone else is going to shrug and flip channels.

The X-Files stands as a stark reminder of what happens when a series passes its sell-by date and starts lazily satiating the most rabid fans: average viewers couldn't give a toss whether Mulder's sister is a clone or not, they just want to see the duo chasing bogeymen through the woods. The *X-Files* finale is the equivalent of one of those terrible live tour versions of popular comedy shows, in which beloved characters simply walk onstage and utter a catchphrase, prompting 15 hours of rapturous applause from an audience of imbeciles – instead of actually telling some jokes.

The Third World War in Low-Res JPEGs [29 March]

They say the first casualty of war is truth, but actually it's picture quality. I'm not being callous . . . it's just that this being the twenty-first century I thought we'd get a digitally perfect, Dolby Surround kind of war, with swooping Michel Gondry camera moves and on-the-fly colour correction. But no. It's all shots of empty skylines and blurry videophone bullshit. Most of it isn't even in widescreen, for Christ's sake.

I'm writing this on Tuesday morning, so apologies if things have changed: I know it's a war, and I've been as horrified by the 'Shock and Awe' bombardments as anyone (well, less than the average Iraqi, but you get my point), but the fact is our modern news channels are so obsessed with bringing us live images they've failed to notice there often isn't anything to show: all have broadcast hours of an unchanging skyline, while the newsreader apologetically explains that you probably can't see the explosions from this angle because it's a fixed roof-top camera and blah blah blah, but the moment we get a shot of someone's leg coming off we'll let you know.

With my Freeview box I can pick up three dedicated news channels, each carrying 24-hour war coverage. You'd think one was enough, but no. Before long, you develop a distinct channel-hopping routine. Here's mine: I keep it on Sky News most of the time, because its absurdly over-excited 'BREAKING NEWS!' ticker tape tends to break the most sensational (i.e. inaccurate) stories first. If something particularly juicy comes up, I hop to ITV News to see if they've picked up on it, before alighting on BBC News 24 to see if they'll confirm it (like most British viewers, I don't believe anything until the BBC says it's true).

Apparently, they're aware that viewers are flipping about like maniacs, which is why they keep trying to cram as much onto the screen as possible. Ticker tapes, banners, constant split-screens and replays – it's like a cross between an episode of 24 and the impenetrably busy Bloomberg channel.

But since they're constantly claiming something's *about* to happen, it's hard to switch the mess off: you know whatever occurs, you'll see it unfold live on air. They're willing you to think like a ghoul.

This obsession with live coverage reached a ridiculous nadir last week on the ITV News Channel: Alistair Stewart breathlessly announces incoming live footage of behind-enemy-lines conflict; cut to an indistinct green blur with the odd dark blob wobbling around, like a plate of mushy peas behind a layer of gauze. But the viewers' bafflement was nothing compared to Alistair's – because he's got to explain what's happening. 'And there you can see . . . uhhh . . . well, it's hard for me to make out because my monitor is situated quite far away, but I'm sure at home you can see more.' Nice try, but all I could see was my own bemused reflection. Sod the Second World War in Colour – this is the Third World War in Low-Res JPEGs.

Still, the fuzzy pictures are nothing compared to the fuzzy language. I've lost count of the number of times I've heard military pundits ending a discussion with the phrase 'but this is all mere speculation'. In which case, why talk about it at all? You might as well speculate over what would happen if Saddam suddenly turned into a shoebox, and Charles Dance arrived on the back of a clockwork dog and kicked him into the ocean.

But they keep yapping because there's air time to fill. Hence the constant repetition of custom 'war' idents. Sky's ident takes the piss, frankly: a pompous barrage of CGI tanks, fighter jets and fireballs, with the Sky News logo emerging victorious at the end. Of course, if they wanted to accurately reflect what's happening, they could superimpose their logo over a long tracking shot of an overflowing graveyard, or that footage of an Iraqi boy screaming in hospital – hey, they could even make the logo spin out of his mouth!

But that won't happen, because viewers might start to think war is horrific. And not just another TV show.

Skull-Flaunting Cueballs   [5 April]

Hooray! We've achieved equality! For years it was rubbish being a woman. Now it's equally rubbish being a man! Hey, gals – let's join hands and celebrate the erosion of the gender gap together! What's that? You don't want to hold hands? You're calling the police? Oh. Sorry.

Really, it feels rubbish being a man at the moment – assuming you base your self-perception on the images pouring from your TV set, that is. I know I do, and I'm beginning to feel like scum simply for owning my own testicles.

Take adverts. I don't recall attending the meeting where it was decided that all male characters in adverts should be portrayed as pitiful figures of fun, but, nevertheless, that's precisely what's happened: every other commercial on television seems to feature a sassy female character rolling her eyes in dismay at the buffoonish antics of an imbecilic man. In advert-land, boyfriends and husbands are routinely ditched, cheated on or, in the most offensive example, literally traded in for a sleeker model at a dedicated showroom.

Of course the implicit message is as patronising to women as it is to men – it's saying, 'Hey, you're a modern woman, yeah? You're cleverer than most men, right? Brilliant! Now buy this. Go on, bitch – buy it.'

It's odd, though – the insidious nature of this continual chap-dissing – because if I'm anything to go by, it works on men themselves. To let you in on my cynical way of thinking, I ordered a preview tape of *Bald* (C4) – a documentary about the desperate measures to which men with premature hair loss will go to disguise their cueball status – specifically because I thought it'd make a nice 'light' subject. My reasoning went thus: last week I got all miserable covering the war, so this week I'll lighten things up with a savage attack on an easy target. Using a sledgehammer to crack a walnut never fails to cheer me up, y'see – that's why I spend most weekends kickboxing children to death in a barbed-wire thunderdome in my back garden.

Anyway, a funny thing happened. I actually started feeling sorry for these people. Even though they're bald! Slap-headed, shiny-bonced, skull-flaunting cueballs to a man, and yet I couldn't help but empathise. Curses.

Little wonder, though, that so many baldies feel they're perceived as a 'joke'. Most say their discomfort stems from society's obsession with youth and looks and vigour – a world in which naked noggins don't cut it. It's the TV-fuelled image-perception problem women have had to wrestle with for years, in other words – the sole difference being it's currently de rigueur to mock men who don't conform to the mythical hunky norm. There's no reason why a man smearing hair-growth lotion on his scalp should be any 'sadder' than a woman rubbing anti-ageing moisturiser on her crow's-feet, but he is.

Likewise, the sight of a toupee prompts chuckles galore, yet a prosthetic breast masking a mastectomy is about as funny as, well, as cancer. Ah, well. If you're a bald man yourself, the advice from the programme is 'For God's sake just get a grade-one crew cut.' The only interviewees who felt they'd 'come to terms with their baldness' were the ones with a set of clippers at home. And a quick checklist of celebrity slapheads – Vin Diesel, Bruce Willis, Ross Kemp, Pacman – bears this theory out. Oh, and there's another famous baldie to add to the list – Peter 'Go West' Cox on *Reborn in the USA* (ITV1), a man clearly on his way to becoming the next Robson and Jerome (except there's only one of him, and he can actually sing).

Follically challenged he may be, but when he lets that roaring voice out of its cage, you need a mop to clean the auditorium afterwards. I'd fancy him myself, but that weird face he pulls whenever he approaches peak volume – a sort of cross between Joe Cocker and a man trapping his testicles between the cogs of a gigantic machine – sorta puts me off. Well, that and the fact that he's bald.

Modern Life Isn't Rubbish   [12 April]

Modern life is rubbish, right? Go on, flick through the newspaper. Nothing but depressing headlines: TEEN THUGS ROB AND EAT 84-YR-OLD MAISIE; BIONUCLEAR TERRORIST APOCALYPSE 'INEVITABLE' SHRIEKS MINISTER; CHILD MISSING ON INTERNET, etc., etc. – it's enough to convince you the world's going to hell in a handbasket.

Well it isn't. Things are better than they used to be, and if you don't believe me, try counting the number of dead babies littering the streets next time you go for a stroll. Unless you're really unlucky, you won't find any – which is a pretty good yardstick of how civilised we've become since ye olden tymes. Back in the Georgian era, it wasn't uncommon to come across decomposing illegitimate offspring lying around the pavements like doggy doo, a situation that so upset a man called Captain Thomas Coram, he established Britain's first Foundling Hospital to care for them. The big wuss.

Coram's story comprises the first episode of *Georgian Underworld* (C4), a series hell-bent on convincing us that although the past may look more genteel from where we're standing, it stinks to high heaven the moment you get too close.

We could do with more of this, because the past is steeply overrated, especially by bitter old goats who blame society – i.e. everyone else in the world – for their current dissatisfaction with life. Goats who think music and films aren't as good as they used to be, despite mounting evidence to the contrary. Who think video games are a mindless distraction for infants, but consider chess – essentially a very dull beat-'em-up running on an outdated wooden system – to be the pastime of gentlemen. Who think costume dramas are worth watching.

I've never liked costume dramas, largely because I'm not particularly interested in watching some spoilt doily-wearing bint sob down her harpsichord because the horse-riding Jeremy she's had her eye on betrothes himself to another, while around her, her subservient handmaidens (whose combined annual wages wouldn't buy two of their mistress's pubes at auction) tug their forelocks in sympathy.

The BBC, of course, churns them out regardless, presumably because they've got a warehouse full of bodices that need a regular airing. Having failed to win me over with their countless Austen adaptations and Sunday evening boredom festivals, they've now changed tack, by inventing *Servants* (BBC1), a warts-and-all youth-oriented costume drama that purports to show life in an 1850s mansion house from the staff's point of view. It's *This Life* meets *Upstairs Downstairs*, in other words.

They've got off to a good start by hiring Joe Absolom – a likeable performer so weird he somehow manages to resemble 100 different things at once. One minute he looks like the lead singer in a meerkat version of Supergrass, the next he's like a cross between Malcolm McDowell and the Cat in the Hat.

Trouble is, the programme he's stuck in is as heavy-handed as a robot with lead fingers. *Servants* tries so hard to prove it's a costume drama for YOUNG PEOPLE, it becomes a parody of itself – quite an achievement for an opening episode. Staff say things like 'Fancy a shag?'; there's nudity, drinking and swearing; the master of the house has a crafty wank over some nineteenth-century equivalent of *Razzle*; one of the footmen pulls some eye-popping flip kicks on the half-pipe in the courtyard (I made the last one up, but you get the idea). Once you get past the jarring clash of old and new school, the drama beneath is as predictable as a pub-style steak-and-ale pie.

Servants won't please anyone except the most bovine viewers: it'll scandalise the goats, who'll see the inclusion of sex and swearing in a period piece as further proof of the decline of everything, while simultaneously disappointing anyone looking for something genuinely diverting. But that's the true way of the world. Modern life isn't rubbish. It's just as shit now as it's always been. Happy trails, gang!

The Lawn-Sprinkler of Doom [19 April]

Apologies if some hideous Columbine-style tragedy has occurred in-between the time I wrote this and the time you're reading it, but hasn't it been simply *ages* since the last mass slaying? I'm discounting the war, obviously: instead I'm talking about those grisly incidents when someone goes 'postal' – usually an under-achieving, under-endowed American mailman with a gun collection Ted Nugent would consider excessive, who wakes up one morning and thinks, 'I feel like doing something out of the ordinary,' and winds up stomping round a former workplace spraying bullets about like the lawn-sprinkler of doom.

Since no one gets a second shot at that kind of glory – after all, it's traditional to turn the weapon on yourself at the end – it's best to achieve a higher body count than the last trigger-happy nutjob, or you'll end up consigned to the footnotes next time Colin Wilson brings out one of those 'Complete Histories of Murder with Big Colour Photos and Everything'.

You certainly want to end up claiming more than two victims, which these days is scarcely a minor misdemeanour, let alone a massacre. Unless of course, you've used a bandsaw to slice up the bodies afterwards, in which case you'll get an entire hour-long documentary called *The Real Texas Chainsaw Massacre* (C4) devoted to your exploits.

I have a couple of problems with this programme – not with the story itself, which is fascinating in its own right – but with the title, which is clearly misleading, since the case in question doesn't involve either a chainsaw or a 'massacre'.

A bandsaw does seem to have come into play, but only when the victims were already dead. Admittedly, that's pretty unpleasant by itself, since it was used to slice the corpses' heads up like so much Battenberg cake, but it hardly competes with a man clad in a leathery mask of human skin swinging a chainsaw around his head and carving people up willy-nilly, which is what you get in the film.

Still, like I say, the story itself is undeniably interesting, particularly when the man responsible for the apparent atrocity moves to a sleepy English village, gets married and starts amassing a terrifying collection of firearms. Perhaps most discomfiting is the ease with which he obtained a gun licence, despite using his real name, and despite having recently arrived from Texas, where his premature release from Death Row made him the lead news item for an entire week.

It seems the authorities were blissfully unaware of all this, until a suspicious local looked up his name on the Internet and his gruesome history came to light. Another case solved by Inspector Google.

Then another astonishing thing happens: with his cover blown and his wife in hiding, our bandsaw maniac attempts to flee the country, and is arrested in the company of another woman set to become his fifth wife. Now this man is an elderly, overweight, wheelchair-bound ex-Death Row inmate accused of shooting two men and cutting up their heads with a bandsaw – yet he doesn't seem to have any problem scoring with the ladies. What's he using? Some kind of spray-on pheromone shit? I mean I can understand the appeal of a 'bad guy', but Christ, get a grip.

Anyway, having brought us a 'Real Texas Chainsaw Massacre' that isn't, Channel 4 also offers *The Real Winona Ryder* (C4), who is. This is a look at the troubled star who is troubled and ran into troubles, but still engenders more than her fair share of sympathy because 1) she appeared in *Heathers*, which was really cool and 2) she's got big watery eyes and porcelain skin. You know, a bit like Gollum.

As an even-handed celebrity portrait, you won't learn anything astoundingly new – only that Winona's godfather was Timothy Leary, that she's not happy and that her Hollywood nickname is 'Rock'n'Roll Hall of Fame' because she keeps getting entered by famous musicians.

I made that last one up, by the way.

The New Robin Hood   [26 April]

The pursuit of money makes gimps of us all. Some labour for years in jobs they despise, toiling for the benefit of faceless bigwigs, each day waving goodbye to yet another small portion of their precious unique lifespan, slowly degenerating into dispirited husks, devoid of hope, devoid of love, or pity, or the release of laughter; living cadavers with nothing but death to look forward to. And some attempt to defraud *Who Wants to Be a Millionaire?* with an arse-witted coughing scheme.

Last week's disappointing *Tonight* special on the throat-clearing caper failed to shed any light whatsoever on the mindset of the culprits, concentrating instead on second-by-second analysis of the unbroadcast episode, as though we were looking at a previously undiscovered reel of the Zapruder footage instead of a daft incident on a quiz show. Meanwhile the major and co. were painted as a pack of pathetic, sweating sneaks.

Was it really so wicked, this childish attempt to bamboozle the nation's no.1 pub quiz? This is a television show we're talking about here, not a hospital fund for the blind and footless. Lest we forget, the prize money itself is drawn from the proceeds of the show's premium-rate phone lines – money drawn from wannabe contestants, the vast majority of whom earn considerably less than the average TV executive. Besides, TV tries to wring money out of *you* at every turn. In fact, you might as well instal a cash point and attendant beggar in the corner of your living room.

Think about it: you have to pay a licence fee to watch the BBC channels, while the commercial channels carry adverts, the cost of which is met by you whenever you go shopping. Then there's all the optional expenses: satellite subscriptions, pay-per-view events and, yes, premium-rate phone lines – usually supporting a multi-ple-choice question so simple it's clearly designed to be easily solved by any life form on the planet from the potato upwards.

Here's a typical TV phone-in question:

Which of the following currently plays James Bond?

A: Pierce Brosnan.

B: Superman.

C: A sycamore tree.

Of course, everyone knows they only make the questions simple so more button-punching cow people will phone in. But there's more to it than that.

Ever wondered why they bother setting a question at all, instead of simply running it as a lottery? Because that's a breach of broad-cast regulations. They'd have to supply a free alternative entry method if they were going to do that (which is why reality shows allow you to vote via the Internet as well). To run a premium-rate TV phone-in, you have to prove it's supporting a contest requiring some degree of skill – even if said skill is as cursory as knowing the difference between James Bond and a tree. In other words, the nice TV folk are cheerfully doing the *barest possible minimum* in order to avoid a slap on the wrist, while simultaneously raking in as much money as they can. That's how much they respect you. Make no mistake; to the TV brigade you really are just a number. It does-n't matter how pretty you are, how many press-ups you can do, or how much your children love you – you're naught but a potentially exploitable blob of matter in the dark.

Factor all this in and the major starts to look like the new Robin Hood – albeit a nervous, absurd and incompetent one. If there's any justice in the world, he'll rake in a fortune from personal appearances, reality TV shows and a long run in panto. And the Sars virus will explode across Britain, filling the *Millionaire* studio with so much background coughing, Tarrant'll end up bellowing questions through a loudhailer. At a corpse with a runny nose.

Speaking of Sars, anyone noticed the striking similarity between the Stella Artois commercial with coughing paupers and the Sars outbreak? How long until they pull it, do you reckon? A: Three days. B: Four days. Or C: Five days. Calls cost £1,000,000 a minute. All proceeds to the major's appeal campaign. Get dialling.

Ten Years of Awful Television   [3 May]

'Hell is other people,' said Jean-Paul Sartre. But the egghead wuss never had to sit through ten years of awful television. There's a problem with trying to recall the worst TV shows you've seen: your mind tends to blank them out, like some kind of repressed abuse memory. Initially, you have to strain to remember them, but once you've started, the floodgates open and the memories pour out like tears, or vomit, or some unholy combination of the two. Ever puked through your brain? It's not pleasant.

Which brings me to my next problem: how to corral these recollections into some kind of coherent order. After much deliberation, I've decided to simply spew them onto the page in whatever order my reeling mind dictates. After all, we're talking televisual dreck here. You can't treat it respectfully. That'd be madness. So then, without further ado . . .

Hotel Babylon
Synopsis: Heineken-backed, late-night untertainment with additional ethnic cleansing.
Comments: Lager-sponsored take on *The Word*, complete with Dani Behr, that caused a stink when a fax from a Heineken representative in Holland came to light, requesting more shots of their product and complaining about the 'proportion of negroes' in the

audience. The resulting furore almost masked the fact that the show itself was as much fun as eating a bowlful of milk and mud. Almost.

Trisha

Synopsis: Daily bellowing festival in which a sorry collection of confused and inarticulate commoners air their dirty laundry before an audience of self-important, loudmouthed hags.
Comments: *Trisha* is the most depressing programme on earth, regularly leaving me bereft of any hope for mankind. There are no sympathetic participants, the audience is hateful and Trisha's mannered insincerity could be mistaken for mental illness if it wasn't so sinister. Furthermore, everyone in that studio is incredibly ugly: it's like staring at a cave full of trolls from *The Dark Crystal*. They should brick up the exits and fill the room with killer bees.

Goodnight, Sweetheart

Synopsis: Novelty 'time-travelling' sitcom in which Nicholas Lyndhurst discovers a side street that allows him to visit wartime London and lay a bit of pipe supreme on a 1940s chick behind his wife's back.
Comments: In time-travel scenarios, it's traditional to avoid meddling with the past, but Lyndhurst's character actively molests it. You can't relate to a man who cheats on his wife with a woman who's probably dead by now: what is he, some kind of necrophile? It's just stupid. No one ever watched *Goodnight, Sweetheart* and said admiringly: 'It's funny . . . 'cos it's *true*!' Inexplicably, it ran for years before finally suffocating under the weight of its own paradoxes.

Harbour Lights

Synopsis: *Heartbeat*-on-Sea.
Comments: You want bland? Here's bland: a series in which Nick Berry sails around gently solving wharf-related crime. Each punishing episode of *Harbour Lights* seemed to last nine weeks – which means somewhere, in another dimension, it's still going on, right now.

Selina Scott Meets Donald Trump

Synopsis: Doe-eyed husky (aka the poor man's Princess Di) meets the man who can afford everything except a plausible hairstyle.

Comments: Trump started the show by introducing Scott to his buddies as 'the legendary Selina Scott from Europe'. But the admiration dried up when he saw the finished product: a hatchet job. Viewers could only sit there and argue over which of the two was the least likeable.

Jim Davidson's Generation Game

Synopsis: End-of-the-pier meets end of days.

Comments: What do you do when you've got a tired old variety format that's dying on its arse? Why, hire no one's favourite comedian to host it, of course. The result was a hideous collision of bafflingly witless sketches, clumsy pratfalling and gor-blimey condescension that made *Chucklevision* look like *Frasier*.

H&P@BBC

Synopsis: The show that killed off Hale and Pace.

Comments: You think that title's bad? Trust me, things went downhill from there. It was hard to work out just what *H&P@BBC* was supposed to be. Sketch show? Audience participation cabaret? Sorrowful requiem? Hale and Pace didn't seem to know. Viewer reaction was so negative, the show got pushed back further and further in the schedules until it was virtually appearing early the following morning.

Anything Hosted by Steve Penk

Synopsis: The only man in Britain who makes you appreciate Denis Norden.

Comments: Despite being cursed with the kind of demented, boggle-eyed stare you'd expect to find on a haunted doll in a Hammer Horror quickie, the erstwhile Capital Radio prankster has forged a sturdy televisual career as the 'racy' alternative to Denis Norden. He now fronts hour-long 'naughty' clipfests in which the single gag is that someone from *Emmerdale* fluffs their lines and says 'fuck'.

LA Pool Party
Synopsis: California Uber Alles.
Comments: Take Jayne Middlemiss, Tess Daly and Lisa Snowdon, an LA mansion, some low-grade celebrities and about 100 Californian pod people and what have you got? A talk show in which you can't hear what anyone is saying coupled with a *Stepford Wives*-style nightmare vision of the future. The standard viewer reaction was to smack the screen in with a bloody big spade, which may or may not have been the whole idea.

'Adult' *Hollyoaks*
Synopsis: Racier, late-night version of the soap, starring Chapman Brothers' dummies.
Comments: Ever watched *EastEnders* and thought, 'Wouldn't it be funny if, like, Phil suddenly got his winky out, or Dot said "bollocks" or something?' Late-night *Hollyoaks* proved the answer is 'no'. Forced to justify its 'red light' slot by tossing in the odd swearword or flash of buttock, things reached a nadir when a character absent-mindedly tried to brush their teeth with a vibrator. Please, we're not this stupid. And if we want to see the *Hollyoaks* girls in their underwear, we only need glance at the blokey shelf in the newsagents. You can't build a show around a fleeting masturbatory fantasy. Well, not unless you're Dennis Potter.

Doctor Who the Movie
Synopsis: Crazy Like a Who.
Comments: And you thought things had gone downhill with the introduction of Sylvester McCoy. In 1995 the BBC joined forces with the Yanks to make a pilot for a proposed future series of big-budget Who-jinks that foolishly replaced the original series' eccentric charm with cookie-cutter action bullshit. Paul McGann as the Doctor? OK! Eric Roberts as the Master? Hmmm. Doctor Who bombing through an American city on a *motorbike*? Piss off.

They Think It's All Over
Synopsis: Boorish pub jabbering brought to you at the licence-payers' expense.

Comments: I hate sport, and I hate blokes shouting in pubs, so *They Think It's All Over* was always going to leave me cold. What I couldn't have foreseen is what a thumping big success it'd be. What are they up to now, series 85? Somehow, this self-satisfied prick parade always conspires to be on television at the precise moment I desperately need something to watch in order to stave off the suicidal despair that's been hanging around since that morning's *Trisha*. I've lost count of the times it's nearly killed me.

Dishonourable Mentions . . .
You could fill an encyclopaedia with this rubbish. Space prevents me from going into detail on the following, but simply reading the titles alone should be enough to set sickbombs bursting in your head: *Dotcomedy*; *The Girlie Show*; *Crocodile* Bloody *Shoes*; *Metrosexuality*; *Bushell on the Box*; *All About Me*; *Bonjour La Classe*; *Blind Men* (brilliantly, a sitcom about men who *sell blinds*), *Temptation Island*; *Pie in the Sky*; *Rockface/Merseybeat/Holby City* et al.; *Soldier, Soldier*; *Days Like These*; *'Orrible*; *Sam's Game*; *Babes in the Wood*; *Married for Life* (Russ Abbot takes on *Married with Children* and loses); *The Vicar of* Bumming *Dibley*; *TFI Friday*; *The House of Eliott*; *Peak Practice*; *Robot Wars*; *Airport/Airline/The Cruise/*any fly-on-the-wall doc set in a shoeshop etc.; any cheapo, CGI effects-fest, e.g. *Timegate*; *Littlejohn*; *Boys and Girls*; *Model Behaviour*. Oh – and the *Late* Bastard Bastard Bastard *Review*.

   There. Think that about covers it. Here's to the next decade.

Another Dignity-Shredding Festival [3 May]

They said it would never happen. Actually, that's not true – they said it most definitely would. And it did. *I'm a Celebrity – Get Me Out of Here* (ITV1) is back, packed with people going mental, screaming and getting wet down under, just like the front row at a Blue concert.

   I'm a Celebrity was the surprise hit of 2002, so with the thudding inevitability of night following day, ITV has pulled out all the stops (well, OK, three or four of the stops) for this year's new, dramatically unimproved sequel.

For starters, we've got more celebrities to choose from: ten to be precise, which is too many for the human brain to process all at once, which means you're surprised every few minutes – it'll cut to a shot of Wayne Sleep and you'll hear yourself going, 'Ooh, I'd forgotten he was in this.' Sleep's probably the most famous one in there. The rest are a motley collection whose stars glow so dimly in the showbusiness firmament, they're 50 per cent less famous than the red laughing cow that appears on a range of dairy products. So who are they? Here's a handy cut-out-and-keep list:

1) Antony Worrall Thompson. Fresh from his success playing the dwarf warrior in *The Two Towers*, Worrall Thompson has already made a mark in the *Celebrity* camp by smuggling in a sachet of cooking spices strapped to his inner thigh, which means his scrotum's going to smell like a pair of greasy dumplings with cumin for the rest of the series. He's also lost weight, and now looks less like Henry the Eighth and more like an ageing Kiefer Sutherland.

2) Chris Bisson. A huge non-entity. Such a personality vacuum, in fact, his presence gives rise to an interesting philosophical question: if a tree falls in the rainforest when only Chris Bisson is there to see it, does it make a sound?

3) Sian Lloyd. Flirtatious Welsh weather girl with a hint of Wallace and Gromit round her chops. She's a close pal of Huw Edwards, apparently, so if a freak tornado whips through the camp and everyone dies, his face during the news afterwards should be an absolute picture.

4) Phil Tufnell. A cricketer, which means I've no idea who he is, and on the evidence thus far, I haven't missed anything. They should replace him with Ray Mears, who'd construct a jacuzzi out of bark within 10 minutes of arrival, then brew up some funnel-web-spider beer and watch them all get nekkid. Yee haw!

5) Catalina. Famous for playing the 'sexy girl' in *TFI Friday*'s 'Ugly Bloke' segment and . . . that's . . . it. Still, at least she can open her mouth and make sounds come out, unlike Nell McThingbags last time round.

6) John Fashanu. My flatmate is convinced Fashanu's voice occasionally becomes a perfect replica of Frank Spencer. Once you've noticed it, it's impossible to take Fashanu seriously – just as well, since he seems to be undergoing some kind of frightening mental collapse, and it's nice to be able to distance yourself from it a bit through the miracle of laughter.

7) Linda Barker. A glorified B&Q assistant who might as well be replaced by a mop for all I care. The same goes for number 8, the eerily feline Wayne Sleep. Vote 'em off.

9) Danniella Westbrook – it's traditional for *Celebrity* to feature an ex-cokehead, and Westbrook's this year's candidate. With any luck a community of cockroaches will start nesting in her nose and liven things up for all of us.

10) Finally, Toyah Willcox, more scary now than during her punk days. At the risk of sounding cruel, she resembles a 98-year-old woman in pigtails, and every time she comes onscreen I think I'm watching that scene in *The Others* where Nicole Kidman's daughter turns round, revealing a terrifying, prematurely aged fizzog.

Who'll win? Who cares? It's another dignity-shredding festival, and none the worse for that. Besides, it's already nearly killed Worrall Thompson, who narrowly avoided being crushed by a falling lump of tree within minutes of arrival. And any show that does that deserves the support of the entire nation.

The Australian Revolution   [10 May]

We've had the French Revolution. We've had the Russian Revolution. But both pale into dull insignificance compared to the great Australian Revolution of 2003. Years from now, our descendants will make a pilgrimage to Trafalgar Square to lay flowers at the feet of Antony Worrall Thompson's memorial statue. And, as the bugler sounds his reveille, they'll lower their heads in respect for this inspirational rebel, this rotund colossus – he who taught us to rise up, stare the forces of reality television in the eye and say, 'Enough!'

Seriously though, last week's *I'm a Celebrity – Get Me Out of Here* (ITV1) revolt – aborted though it was – could bring about a new phase in the ongoing advancement of reality shows. For those who missed it (and being a *Guardian* reader, you were probably off on BBC4 watching a harpsichord masterclass, like a great big ponce), the ten-strong group of celebrity campers reached snapping point and threatened to walk out en masse if they didn't get a decent meal.

The producers, who only had themselves to blame for stirring things up by issuing a 'meal' consisting of nine single sausages and a bit of old bark, were at pains to make it look as though the 'stars' were being a bunch of precious whingers – but the fact is the producers were in the wrong, and if the entire camp *had* walked, the programme would have ended there and then. ITV would've had the production team lined up against a wall and shot. Probably in a Saturday night special hosted by Ant and Dec (two men who magically remain blameless whatever the circumstances – even if they hosted a live show in which sick children were torn to ribbons by wolves they'd somehow come across as likeable).

Accordingly, the producers caved in, bent over and took it like suckers, right there on the telly – on their own *show*! Never mind their face-saving bullshit about providing an alternative meal of 'identical calorific value' – we saw the replacement with our own eyes, you cowards: steak and potatoes, a whopping great feast by comparison. A victory for the inmates, and hopefully an inspiration to all subsequent reality contestants – direct action works!

It's just a shame the campers merely issued threats. If I was in that group, I'd have grabbed Ant or Dec during the live section and held them to ransom by holding a jagged piece of flint to their throat. Never mind steak and potatoes – I'd demand a helicopter, 50 per cent of the show's production fee in cash and a blow job from every single member of the crew, even the no-nonsense Australian safety instructor. In fact, *especially* the no-nonsense Australian safety instructor. And, under those circumstances, I'd probably get it.

Anyway, the upshot of it all is that Worrall Thompson has now gone up in my estimation by about 10,000 per cent. The same is also true of Danniella Westbrook, who showed Fashanu up as the oddball faux-ninja chicken he is by gamely undertaking her 'bush tucker trial' with palpable relish. Cockroaches crawled in her hair, maggots frolicked in her cleavage, and this ass-kicking survivor simply laughed it all off. Fashanu would've screamed, hyperventilated, punched invisible samurai assassins and generally squealed like a pantomime dame being goosed by Dick Whittington. Danniella, by contrast, has gone from a national joke to the next Lara Croft simply by being game for anything. Better still, in the end, she didn't even give a toss about winning the damn programme. Missing her kids, missing her boyfriend, and literally bored to tears, Westbrook did the sensible thing and bolted. Perhaps if they'd given her more to do she'd have stuck around, but they didn't, and I admire her ah-well-bollocks-to-it attitude.

Worrall Thompson and Westbrook – recast as heroes. Proof that we're living in unpredictable times. And equally possibly, proof that I need a good lie-down. I'm off for a week. See you in a fortnight.

The Spanish Inquisition with Cooler Haircuts
[24 May]

Tick tock, tick tock . . . I've held off writing about *24* for weeks on end now, largely because last time round I became so obsessed with it I rarely mentioned anything else, and readers who weren't following the series got so bored with each column they'd nod off in the middle, wake up with backward newsprint all over their foreheads, then spend the rest of the day wondering why strangers were squinting at them in the street.

That said, now seems like a good time to assess where this second series of *24* (BBC2) is heading. Or 'Carnival of Torture', as it might as well be called, given the amount of violent interrogation going on. You can't go 10 minutes without bumping into a torture scene – it's like the Spanish Inquisition with cooler haircuts.

So far we've had electrocution, scalpel hi-jinks, finger-breaking and a particularly touching interlude in which Kate Warner's private detective had his spine carved out with some kind of rotating-blade power tool. Product placement for a new range of Black &

Decker gizmos aimed at oppressive regimes? I wouldn't discount it.

Jack Bauer's a particularly efficient inquisitor, ready to extract even the most trivial information via gruesome means – clearly, Jack's suffering from horrendously chapped lips, probably incurred during the plane crash he survived a couple of hours ago, because he spent most of last week's episode threatening to shoot a suspect's entire family, starting with the kids, unless he told him the location of 'the balm'. 'Tell me where the balm is!' 'Where's the balm!?!' At one point he even claimed that 'millions will die unless you tell me where the balm is' – the man's lost his mind.

And he's not the only one. Even mild-mannered President Palmer's got the torturin' bug, sanctioning the repeated electrocution of the head of the NSA – a decision that initially caused Palmer no end of soul-searching (as indicated in traditional Palmer fashion, i.e. by flaring his nostrils and lolling his head around like a punch-drunk bull), but obviously grew on him, because he spent the next hour watching the proceedings on a private video link in his office, in a manner not entirely dissimilar to a man illicitly viewing pornography in the basement while his wife sleeps upstairs.

If Palmer keeps this up, by the end of the series he'll be stalking the corridors of the Mexican restaurant that seems to double as his HQ, wearing a long dark cloak, wielding a scimitar and insisting on being addressed as 'His Dark Highness Torquemada the Pitiless'. At which point Radioactive George Mason, who by then will have mutated into a lesion-covered Hulk-like monster, will fight him to the death on the roof of the White House.

None of which would be any less preposterous than Kim's ongoing 'storyline', which increasingly resembles an entire series of 'The Perils of Pauline' reduced to the length of a diet Coke commercial and starring Britney Spears. Things reached a ludicrous high with the whole chased-by-a-cougar sequence, something I suspect was written into the script as a joke while the producer was on holiday; you can tell by the way it was abruptly done away with in the very next episode – as though the boss had gone away saying, 'Don't do anything stupid,' then came back and said, 'You did WHAT?'

So what happens next? Being a downloadin' Internet smart arse-stroke-bore, I already know, of course . . . but hardened *24* addicts alarmed at the prospect of 'spoilers' can rest easy, because I'm not about to spoil what's *still* the best show on the television by spilling the plot beans . . . although I will tantalise you with the following question: which of the following names genuinely, honestly joins the cast of *24* to play a major character in later episodes?

1: David Yip, the Chinese Detective. 2: Ex-WWF star 'Rowdy' Roddy Piper. 3: Jim Robinson from *Neighbours*.

Answers on a postcard please. First 200 correct entries win a car, a knighthood, and a set of official CTU thumbscrews.

The answer was Jim Robinson from Neighbours, *who played the vice-president.*

Like the Doritos Friendchips Crew, but Worse

[31 May]

Whenever I tell people I'm a misanthrope they react as though that's a bad thing, the idiots. I live in London, for God's sake. Have you walked down Oxford Street recently?

Misanthropy's the only thing that gets you through it. It's not a personality flaw, it's a skill.

It's nothing to do with sheer numbers. Move me to a remote cottage in the Hebrides and I'd learn to despise the postman, even if he only visited once a year. I can't abide other people, with their stink and their noise and their irritating ringtones. Bill Hicks called the human race 'a virus with shoes', and if you ask me he was being unduly hard on viruses: I'd consider a career in serial killing if the pay wasn't so bad.

Thank God, then, for *Big Brother 4* (C4/E4), which provides the perfect cathartic vent for all this pent-up rage, in the form of a shack full of absolute squawking scum.

True misanthropes reserve their sourest bile for anyone younger and better-looking than themselves; consequently I *really* hate this year's inmates, the *yoofiest* selection yet. They're like the Doritos Friendchips crew, but worse.

(Speaking of the Friendchips berks reminds me: I'm looking forward to an entire spin-off series based around their rib-tickling antics – something like *This Life*, but with a greater emphasis on fried corn snacks. It'd run for nine years, and the final season would depict them as depressive mid-30s fatsoes, their bodies ravaged by years of nachogulping, dropping dead one by one of heart failure. Ratings dynamite!)

The *BB4* house contains not one, but *two* finheaded Nathans in the form of Federico and Scott. The fin haircut is visual shorthand: it screams *dingwad* as efficiently as a flashing icon hovering above the head of a pixilated character in *The Sims*. Scott's 27 and has apparently written a play for Radio 4, an achievement that should impress anyone who's never had to sit through one. Of the two, Federico is the more fashion-conscious, which naturally makes him the bigger arse: the man loves himself so much he probably sends a Valentine's card to his own right hand each year. I hate him. I hate him so much I'm already fantasising about killing him. (Here's how: I sneak into the *BB* house in the dead of night armed with a saw and a mallet; I swipe at his eyes with the saw, and while he's crawling around blinded, finish him off with 15,000 blows to the back of the head. In all honesty, would that be such a crime?)

Next there's Jon and Ray, two dullard Roland Gift lookalikes, one of whom (I can't recall which) has long, revolting hairs sprouting from his back, like a foul animal. It's enough to put you off your Friendchips.

Cameron, the eldest at 32, is a gentle Scot straight out of *Two Thousand Acres of Sky*. Doomed to be described on his own headstone as 'nice' and by anyone else as 'who?' Cameron's so bland he probably shits papier-mâché.

Then there's token lardarse Gos, who thanks to his bulk commands more screen space than anyone else, yet selfishly does nothing to justify it.

The women are an amorphous mass of low-slung denim and hair gel, somehow high-street and vaguely upmarket at the same time, like Girls Aloud drinking white wine in a gastropub. The terrifyingly self-absorbed Anouska (played by Jenny Powell) seems destined to be this year's chief gobby irritant *and* tabloid dream since she's happy to walk around with her bum hanging out. She'll be chief pin-up on a thousand one-handed websites.

Justine, Steph, Nush and Sissy seem – tragically enough – just about bearable.

But Tania – isn't she actually, genuinely, one of the Friendchips posse? I'm sure I've seen her gobbling snacks and working out her porn-star name round that lanky blond prick's kitchen table. Or am I just confusing mundane fantasy with mundane reality? I just can't tell any more.

Anyway, that's the new, improved *BB4* housemates – now 50 per cent more hateful than ever. Let's follow their progress together. Pass the salsa.

A Man of Logic Trapped in a World of Emotion
[7 June]

'A man of logic trapped in a world of emotion' – to whom is psychologist Dr Gareth Smith referring? Abraham Lincoln? Sir Clive Sinclair? Professor Yaffle from *Bagpuss*?

Nope: Jon Tickle – the hilariously named 'household pet' from *Big Brother 4* (C4/E4), and quite possibly the most boring man in the universe. At first glance, with his shaven head and exotic good looks, he could easily be mistaken for an up-and-coming DJ, lifestyle journalist or TV presenter. But beneath the chill-out-zone exterior beats the pale damp heart of a monotone nerd; a man whose conversation is so violently dreary, military scientists could harness its joy-withering energy and create some kind of ennui-based death-ray.

Whenever Jon opens his mouth, out rolls a 200-foot granite ball of tedium that crushes everything in its path. And there's no escape. His high point so far: sitting on the pedalo listing all the words in the realm of physics that begin with the letter 'p', while a horrified Cameron struggled to retain consciousness beside him.

'Photon, proton, particle . . .' On and on he went, turning the air grey in the process.

The *other* famous Mr Tickle (the one invented by Roger Hargreaves) was renowned for having two long orange arms that reached round corners and made people laugh: *Big Brother*'s Mr Tickle comes equipped with infinite invisible tendrils that reach across a nation and make people yawn. Is that progress?

No. It's not.

Still, it's fun watching him bore the other housemates into the ground, banging on about how much money he earns or tirelessly recounting the entire plot of whichever breeze-block-sized sci-fi novel he read last. At the time of writing, the inmates have yet to make their nominations, so I'm hoping the King of Snoozeland won't have been evicted by the time you read this.

The same goes for Federico, the biggest arsehole this side of a guide to anal fissures. Last week I was fantasising about killing him, but by now I've gone beyond even that – in my head I'm already chasing him through the afterlife, wielding a sabre, a club and a bloody big hook. Just as Jon had a high point, Federico had a low: the excruciating Avid Merrion impersonation he inflicted on an offscreen female 'voice of *Big Brother*' from the confines of the diary-room chair. 'What are you wearing? Can I watch you do a shit?' he asked repeatedly and, according to him, hilariously.

Federico failed to consider two salient facts: 1) Even in its original form, Avid Merrion's 'funny foreigner' shtick is about as funny as shattering your teeth on a kerbstone, and 2) When someone doesn't laugh at a 'jokey' come-on, repeating it again and again until the producers castigate you for harassment isn't the wisest course of action. Still, it was one of the few diary-room encounters when Federico didn't employ vocabulary he doesn't understand in a doomed bid to look clever. A glance at his misspelled entry on 'Friends Reunited' reveals him as a dim pseud of the highest order.

'In all it's entirety an overview of my own experiences since my insertion into the civilian landscape would not only render any reader unfairly incomparable, moreover the banality in which you contrive to exist in your futile landscape implicates to one's own that indeed I must strive to march forth with my own avant garde approach to life,' he dribbles, thesaurus in hand. 'I wish for you all the justification of your own endeavour.'

Almost as impenetrable and meaningless as the *Matrix Reloaded* script. Almost.

The other house-dicks are less despicable than last week. Scott (played by Damon from *Brookside* or the leprechaun-sized prison psychologist from *Buried*, depending on the angle) now seems quite a decent chap; Cameron, Nush, Steph, Sissy, Justine and Flabbo are equally inoffensive. Ray and Tania, on the other hand, have all the impact of a margarine hammer. It might help if they'd *do* something. Like walk away from the cameras. And never ever ever come back.

Safe Beneath the Watchful Eyes [14 June]

A series of posters promoting CCTV on public transport recently appeared across London. Resembling old Soviet propaganda, they depicted a fleet of buses trundling through the capital underneath a galaxy of hovering eyeballs, accompanied by the slogan 'SAFE BENEATH THE WATCHFUL EYES'. The overtly Orwellian tone was alarming; for a campaign designed to provoke reassurance, it's quite breathtakingly sinister. But it's nothing compared to the current anti-benefit-fraud TV commercials, in which cheaters are pursued by glowing rings of light. Sod CCTV – the government's just unleashed the Mysterons to hunt you down, and they don't care who knows it.

'We can track your every move,' booms the voice-over. 'We're on to you.' Pardon me, but since when was it acceptable for 'The Man' to openly brag about his omnipotence? At this rate, I give it two years before we get a licence-fee campaign in which a single mum is raked with machine-gun fire by armoured stormtroopers.

No wonder mass paranoia is in – and the BBC is right at the forefront of it. We've already got *Spooks* with its surveillance and terrorism, *State of Play* and *24*, which – bless it – had the nerve to actually detonate its nuclear bomb mid-series. Now the terror continues with the cheerily titled *Death by Home* (BBC1) in which 'Handy Andy' from *Changing Rooms* does his level best to convince you that if you even *think* about leaving your sofa, you're dicing with death.

Billed as a 'light-hearted guide to household accidents', it's a full hour of scalding, electrocution and bloody big shards of glass slashing arteries open, intercut with rib-tickling clips from *Some Mothers Do 'Ave 'Em* in which loveable imbecile Frank Spencer fractures his spine on a banister. Highlights include celebrity chef Kevin Woodford recounting how he severed a finger while excitedly chopping herbs before an Elton John concert (just a finger, unfortunately; he didn't lop off his head with a spade, more's the pity) and an uplifting reconstruction in which three women almost succumb to fatal carbon-monoxide poisoning (while sitting on a sofa, no less – so even *that* isn't safe, folks).

Having taken all this on board, I simply don't know what to do: I can't go outside because the Mysterons and stormtroopers will get me, and I can't stay indoors because some awful fate might befall me – like ripping my neck open on a tin lid or accidentally catching sight of *V Graham Norton* (C4).

It's clearly time to put Norton to bed now. Sure, he'd be a great dinner-party guest – but would you want him in your house every sodding night of the week?

Here's tonight's guest – the late Judy Garland. First of all, Judy, tell me about your latest film. Mmm. Really? Out on Friday you say? Gosh. Hey, look at this – it's a website run by a 48-year-old American pervert who likes to dress up as you and poo on the floor. And he's on the phone now! Crazy! I wonder, has anyone in our studio audience ever done a poo? Hands up! Yes, you, the bloated, cackling sea cow. What's that? You once pooed on a willy?!? Outrageous! Look, Judy, I've got a Polaroid of a willy here! Hold it up! Ha ha, look everyone, Judy Garland's holding a willy! Tee hee! Chuckle! Snort! (Repeat to fade).

It's not as though there aren't enough penises on Channel 4 anyway. After all, they're currently showcasing the nation's biggest dick on a nightly basis – Federico from *Big Brother*.

I know I keep banging on about him, but 'Fed' really is abnormally twattish: a freak occurrence, like one of those giant squid that occasionally get hauled from the deep by a crew of Spanish fishermen and held in a cage while villagers gather round excitedly taking photographs to send to Ananova.

Yep, that's precisely what he is: a harnessed idiot, held in captivity for our study and amusement. A unique zoological specimen – safe beneath the watchful eyes.

Perhaps CCTV isn't so bad after all.

There's Somebody at the Door [28 June]

There's somebody at the door! And in Rod Hull's case, it turned out to be the Grim Reaper of Death, calling unexpectedly early to whisk him off to deadland. Adjusting his roof aerial during a football match, Hull slipped – ending a life of ups, downs, and countless feathered assaults in a thrice. And when the master died, Emu died too: no Sooty-style persistence of dynasty for him. Yet another creature rendered extinct by the follies of man.

A Bird in the Hand (C4) tells the story of Hull's bizarre career, starting with his early days in Australia's fledgling television industry, where he enjoyed modest success before hitting on his winning formula: playing the bumbling straight man to a demented, punch-drunk bird. Before long, he'd returned to his native Britain and found fame by simply beating the shit out of Parkinson with a glove puppet. Roy Hudd (whose name sounds like an anagram of Rod Hull but isn't) pops up to explain how Emu 'put the violence back into comedy' and watching the vintage maulings it's hard to disagree. For a one-joke act, it was bloody amusing: sociopathic aggression rendered weirdly acceptable via the use of a cartoon fabric bird. Perhaps if Fred West had offed his victims while dressed as the Honey Monster we'd view him more fondly.

The show is rammed with fascinating Hull tidbits, chief among which is the revelation that he had an almighty johnson. The very words 'Rod Hull' imply a cross between a pole-shaped object and the prow of a tanker, and by all accounts that's precisely what was swinging between his legs. Yep, Hull was packing serious meat. And the ladies knew it: that puppeteer tore through more women than Jason Voorhees. Veteran producer Michael Hurll claims Rod was often serviced by 'starfuckers'; even plump green witch Grotbags asserts that 'It was always on offer, and Rod was a man.' In other words, a bird on the hand bagged him loads in the bush. Whether he ever employed his feathered sidekick in the bedroom is left to our imagination, although it certainly conjures up some deliciously appalling imagery, particularly if you use Photoshop, an old *Look-In*, and a collection of porn shots to build a visual reconstruction, which is precisely what I'm going to do the moment I've finished typing this.

Hull's moment in the sun didn't last, however, and having made his fortune prancing round a pink windmill, he blew it all on an overpriced mansion. Unable to get work, he grew to loathe Emu, who represented both the pinnacle of his success and its limitations. With pathetic naivety, he tried appearing in public sans bird only to encounter disappointment: an uncomfortable clip from around this time shows a birdless Hull reacting with a face like thunder to a 'hasn't-had-much-work-of-late' crack by Jonathan Ross during a comedy awards show.

This is a peculiarly touching documentary that doesn't attempt to hide its subject's weak points (it seems Emu wasn't his idea in the first place), yet still paints a sympathetic picture of an eccentric, unique performer who brightened the lives of millions.

That he looks hilariously similar to Camilla Parker-Bowles throughout is an unexpected bonus.

Like Waiting for a Bus [5 July]

Morning has broken? Good. I hate morning. You wake, soaked in your own filth, your face raw from last night's tears, shards of shattered shot-glass peppering the bedspread, and you ask yourself what difference it would make if instead of going to work you spent the day banging your head against the kitchen table and howling till your skull bursts open and the pain flops out. Or is that just me?

Whatever. TV doesn't help. Breakfast shows are one thing –

they're so insipid I often catch myself wondering if I've died in the night and come round during a particularly bland coffee morning in heaven – but what follows is worse.

Take *Kilroy* (BBC1). Why start the day with an interminable wallow in the worst life could possibly throw at you? Death, disease, abuse, betrayal, Robert Kilroy-Silk. It's all there, and it's all about as life-affirming as a handful of shit for Christmas. The show's single laugh comes during the pre-credits intro, when Kilroy (played by Judge Death from the old Dredd strips) floats toward the camera like an undersea monster looming at a porthole, and sums up the day's agenda with a single rhetorical question, inevitably broken in two by a camp dramatic pause in the middle.

'Your son was a choirboy. Now he's wanted for murder?' 'Your husband left you for a blow-up doll. And it's male?'

The all-time classic Kilroy opener is: 'It's 9 o'clock in the morning. And you've already got a bottle in your hand?' I know people who use that as a catchphrase.

Once that's out of the way, we're treated to a short title sequence of Kilroy grimacing like a man with his scrotum caught on the business end of a coathanger – and then the real fun begins: the crying, the shouting, the constant interruptions.

I once awoke blearily on a sofa to hear the Kilroy audience bawling each other into submission and I swear to God I thought there was a real-life fight going on in my living room: imagine my disappointment when I discovered the truth.

And it isn't just the content that's disheartening: the finest synopsis of *Kilroy* I've ever heard came from Peter 'Look Around You' Serafinowicz, who described the studio as looking 'really cold . . . it's like waiting for a bus'.

Awful though *Kilroy* is, it's got nothing on *Trisha* (ITV1), which bypasses 'objectionable' and hammers towards 'despicable' with metronomic regularity. Sneering ratboys, wizened harpies, gum-chewing spitbags of every description – that's the subject matter. And 'Who stuck it in who?' is the daily question; a conundrum that's often settled with the help of on-air DNA and lie-detector tests. Cheers for that, world of science.

But the studio audience is worse. I've got nothing against fat, ugly women, until they stand up and bellow moronically on television, at which point I dream of kicking their teeth down their throats (a doomed fantasy – the gobblesome warthogs would immediately digest them and demand pudding). There's a lot of pent-up rage in that studio, and it's unswervingly directed at whichever man happens to be on stage. Granted, the men are arseholes, but the sight of one arsehole being shouted at by another arsehole – one whose arms are so blubbery they're still undulating five minutes after she's finished shaking her ham-sized fist – does not fulfilling television make.

My advice? Lie in till 11, when the *Terry and Gaby Show* starts on Five. Clearly inspired by the USA's *Regis and Kathy Lee*, it's what the *Des and Mel Show* is trying to be but isn't.

Wogan – whose name sounds more like a Norse god each time I say it aloud – is a genuinely funny man, and the relaxed format gives him plenty of opportunity for cynical asides and amusingly dark mutterings. Yes, it's just a cross between *This Morning* and *TFI Friday*, but I guarantee it won't drive you to suicide. And, for morning TV, that's high praise indeed.

And Then You're in France! Amazing! [12 July]

Holidays! They're fantastic. You get to travel the world, encounter unfamiliar cultures and experience chronic diarrhoea on outlandish toilets.

Drink cocktails! Lie on the beach! Feel your skin blister beneath the punishing Mediterranean sun! Don sunglasses and pretend not to stare at topless 19-year-old Italian girls! Laugh at the stern faces on brightly coloured foreign banknotes! Marvel at the hardcore goat pornography openly on sale beside the kiddies' inflatables in the mini-supermarket! Get your bag pinched! Holidays! Yaaaay!

But holidays weren't always this brilliant. Phone up someone from the 1950s and ask them to describe their average holiday and they'd paint a picture of crowded Margate beaches, warty-faced landladies who ruled their B&Bs like Ilsa, She-Wolf of the SS, monochrome skies and bracing sea winds. So why did our habits change? Two reasons: 1) We realised that British holidays were inherently rubbish, and 2) Television started broadcasting foreign-holiday shows.

The Way We Travelled (BBC2) is a fascinating trawl through the history of TV travel shows. Back in the 1950s and 1960s, the general population viewed a foreign holiday as a deadly serious undertaking, as pioneering and dangerous as piloting a UFO through the rings of Saturn: consequently to modern eyes the shows appear to be aimed at imbeciles. Look! An aeroplane! It goes up in the sky! And then it lands! And then you're in France! Amazing!

Basic stuff, yes, but there's a genuine charm to these antiquated holiday shows that's sadly lacking from today's gaudy travelogues. Perhaps it's the sense of class, personified by Alan Whicker, whose dapper dress sense and smooth nasal delivery never faltered for a moment, whether he was ascending Mount Fuji, exploring Ayers Rock, or beating a monkey to death with a stick on the Great Wall of China (he never did the last one, obviously, but you get the point – this was one unruffled hepcat).

So unchanging was Whicker's look, in fact, he became an instantly recognisable 'brand' almost overnight: the stiff but personable Englishman abroad, utterly incongruous yet somehow right at home against an ever-changing background. (The one time he looked out of place came during a report from hippy-packed San Francisco – as he stands in Haight-Ashbury surrounded by moon-eyed junkies, it's hard not to feel sorry for him.)

The excitement in Whicker's early reports is palpable: even a simple act such as boarding a foreign bus was a strange and fascinating adventure for most viewers, so God alone knows what they made of his more demented excesses – such as the time he flew through the Alps in a glamorous heiress's jet, then joined her in a speedboat for some outrageous on-camera flirting which proved so efficient they ended up engaged to one another.

But while slick Whicker lived the life of an international playboy, it was down to paunchy Cliff Michelmore to cover more attainable locales. The BBC's *Holiday* series launched in 1969, just as cheap package deals started taking off. At the time, the whole notion of a fortnight in Majorca was such a mind-blowing prospect, the show was presented à la *Crimewatch* – with a panel of experts on hand to answer questions from curious callers. Is the sun the same colour in Portugal? Do they have bread in Greece? What is 'Spain'?

By contrast, we're spoiled today. Holiday shows have lost their charm and are little more than a bland whizz through a world of cliché, replete with quasi-porno shots of female presenters enjoying naked back-rubs and pan-pipe music accompanying 50 per cent of the footage. And the viewers themselves demand more from a holiday, hence the rise of idiotic Holiday from Hell shows in which pale whingeing killjoys burst into tears at the memory of cockroaches on a Jamaican shower curtain. Where's the excitement? Where's the joy?

Answer: it's gone. The past really *is* a foreign country. And you can't book a flight there.

The Uzi of Folly   [19 July]

Television specialises in images that are easy on the eye: soothing set design, rolling landscapes, presenters with faces so Formica-bland they make the Stepford Wives look like Slipknot. After all, it keeps the populace docile, which is what the infernal thing was invented for in the first place.

But every now and then, and apparently just for the heck of it, the box spews up something hard to watch. Televised operations, for instance. Lord knows how anyone can sit through them without puking into their lap. I once saw a gruesome hip replacement on *Your Life in Their Hands* that resembled someone rummaging through a bag full of mince in search of an ivory walking stick; I was dizzy for four days.

But even the grisliest operation, even close-up eye surgery with a lemon squeezer – it simply can't compare to the arrgh-no-God-make-it-stop horror of Victoria Aitken's freestyle rap performance on this week's *Young, Posh and Loaded* (ITV1), which is by far the most painful sight you'll encounter this week, even if you spend the rest of the time walking round an anal trauma ward with a magnifying glass. Ms Aitken is intent on launching a career in hip-hop and nothing – including public opinion or common sense – is going to stop her. 'People keep saying, "You can't do that," but why not?' she asks, displaying the kind of self-awareness deficit normally associated with inanimate objects and root vegetables.

Her logic dribbles thus: despite being raised as a blue-blooded posho, she's down wit da rap world because Daddy was a jailbird, even though he ended up there for being a greedy arrogant liar rather than a crack dealer. Well get hip, Vic: Papa was no rolling stone; he was Jonathan Aitken MP, the slimy Tory gonk who famously vowed to clear his name with the Sword of Truth and ended up popping a cap in his own ass with the Uzi of Folly.

Still, at least Victoria can rely on her firm grasp of black-American street culture. 'I suppose instead of going to the theatre, people in the ghetto stand around rapping for hours,' she explains, before setting out to take part in an open-mic freestyling contest during which she achieves the impossible by piling far more disgrace on the family name than Pater ever did.

It's all staged for the cameras, of course – this is one of those cut-'n'-shut ITV sneer-u-mentaries whose sole purpose is to make you despise everyone onscreen – but that doesn't detract from the overall nausea factor; if anything, it makes it even worse. Just how dim do you have to be to willingly take part in a programme called *Young, Posh and Loaded* anyway? Would it have made any difference if they'd called it 'Hateful Shitheads' instead?

Judging by the programme's other subjects, it wouldn't: we're also introduced to fat-arsed party organiser Jonny (specialist subject: guffawing at his own jokes) and wormy little princess Donatella (specialist subject: wanting to be famous).

Naturally, none of these coin-sodden bozos are actually doing anything of merit: when not bragging about how much money he's making, Jonny runs dull club nights for braying Mayfair swan-munchers, while Donatella is simply shown failing her driving test – not that this little mishap dissuades Daddy from buying her a £45,000 customised Mini Cooper replete with an on-board DVD system and custom-dyed lambswool carpets, which with any luck she'll plough headlong into a concrete wall before the end of the year (sole drawback: if only it were a people carrier, she could pack more of her friends inside prior to impact).

All in all then, an unremarkably despicable half-hour of television. Short of not actually broadcasting this crap in the first place, I can only think of one improvement – tie it in with some kind of high-tech video-game light-gun technology, so incensed viewers can blow the heads off the onscreen participants. 'Young, Posh and Shot in the Face' – now there's a concept. Are you listening, ITV?

More White than Black   [26 July]

I'm not entirely sure why, but the term 'aspirational' really gets my goat.

Take the 'aspirational' broadsheet Sunday supplements: are they aimed at human beings? Here's the average content: a po-faced profile on some arse-bound artist you've never heard of, a 10-page photo splurge on limbless Angolan babies, a recipe for summer pudding, a page showcasing designer potato mashers costing £85 each and a column by some supercilious woman explaining What Men Think and Where They're Going Wrong in joyless and punishing detail. If that's what you aspire to – reclining in an Olaaf Dynstiblanq chair tutting sorrowfully over reports from Korean sweatshops while sipping a nice glass of Shiraz – I'd suggest you alter your mental trajectory now, before it develops into full-blown madness.

Aspirational TV drama is equally laughable: from *Thirtysomething* to *Attachments*, tasteful lighting and pretty faces always leave me cold. This week, just to annoy me, BBC3 premières another slick-but-soulless example in the form of *Platinum* (BBC3), a US drama series revolving around a pair of brothers running a New York hip-hop label. Two things separate *Platinum* from previous aspirationfests. First, there's the setting: starring a largely black cast, it follows the life of Jackson and Grady Rhames, owners of an ailing rap label called Sweetback Records. Then there's the production: John 'Undercover Brother' Ridley and Sofia 'Virgin Suicides' Coppola have devised it; Francis Ford Coppola serves as executive producer.

There's no denying that initially, with its rap-speak dialogue and absurdly slick visuals, *Platinum* feels different: the problem is that it takes just 10 minutes for you realise it isn't. In fact, the whole thing is little more than a conveyor belt of standard, formulaic blubber: the chalk and cheese siblings (Jackson's sensible, Grady's a wide boy), the childhood friends drifting apart, the noble suffering wife, the highs and lows of 'living your dream'. You could plot the future story arc on graph paper with your eyes closed. Then there's the script, which is 90 per cent rap cliché: pseudo profundities that occasionally rhyme. Hence there's much empty yap about 'taking it to the next level' and 'stepping up' for your buddies, but precious little else.

So far, so irritating. But your ears have it easy: it's the constant visual masturbation that seriously grates. Absolutely every scene is rendered in the style of a Craig David video, with immaculate colour co-ordination, slow-mo pans across nothing much occurring and blurry cutaways. It's like falling asleep inside Trevor Nelson's head.

All of the above might just be forgivable, but just as you're coming to terms with the safety-scissor blandness of it all, *Platinum* delivers a fatal shot to its own skull by trying to make Sweetback Records' financial performance the single most important aspect of the show. Well intentioned, maybe – drama serials about black-run businesses are pretty thin on the ground – but storylines about takeover bids and sales figures don't exactly set the pulse racing and besides, no matter what colour your lead actor is, he becomes a dull amorphous blob the moment he double-clicks on an Excel spreadsheet.

With any luck, future episodes will concentrate more on the absurdities of the hip-hop world rather than Sweetback Records' shareholder concerns, and it'll all pick up as a result (and, to be fair, episode one does contain a sequence in which a bit of inter-company rivalry is settled by a belt-wielding thug – although since even that scene is rendered in slow-mo Craig-David-O-Vision, it looks curiously serene, like the gangsta equivalent of Constable's *Haywain*).

A mainstream black drama with genuine crossover potential is long overdue. Sadly, *Platinum* ain't it. By chasing the widest audience possible, it feels more white than black, more software than drama. And who can aspire to that?

They're Better than Us at Everything [2 August]

Don't like the Americans much, do we? We're jealous, because they're better than us at everything. They've got better cars, better food, better scenery, better shops, better serial killers, better manners, better teeth and better faith in their own inherent superiority. They take everything we do and then improve on it, from farming to empire-building. Thank God they currently rule the world with an iron fist, because they do a far better job than we would. Can you imagine how a modern global British empire would function? It'd be like Railtrack with stormtroopers. Brrrrr.

For years we were better than the Yanks at making television, but they've recently overtaken us on that front, and I defy anyone to name a single TV genre in which the finest contemporary example is not of American origin. Drama? *Six Feet Under*. Comedy? *Curb Your Enthusiasm*. Reality TV? *Big Brother USA* (which contains more intrigue in five minutes than Cameron and co. could ever manage, even if they'd been goaded with cattle-prods – a tactic I'd recommend for the next series). And so on and so on. We currently lead the world in antiques shows and sheepdog trials, but that's about it.

Since Americans enjoy talking almost as much as they enjoy benign global oppression, they've always been masters of the chat show, although since their late-night yapathons were rarely screened over here, we Brits have been ignorant of the fact for years. Now, however, it being a glorious age of multi-channel digital cathode, we can finally catch up. Most of the major US talk shows are screened in some form or another: *Late Night with*

Letterman turns up daily on ITV2 in the dead of night, and the *Tonight Show* with Jay Leno airs regularly on satellite.

Of the two, Letterman's show is by far the most watchable, although it takes a bit of getting used to: once you understand that the first guest won't be called until Dave and co. have slooped their way through what feels like six months of enjoyably laidback shtick at the top of the show, you can settle down and relish the proceedings.

Leno, on the other hand, is simply one of the most punchable men you're ever likely to encounter – facially, a cross between Pop-eye the Sailor and a bloated throw pillow; vocally, a mosquito trapped inside a harmonica. But he's worth catching now and then, if only to see just how many times a man can kiss arse within the space of 10 minutes without visibly bruising his lips.

Both Leno and Letterman, however, feel altogether stale compared to the latest US import: *The New Tom Green Show* (C4). The spiritual successor to the Letterman show (which in turn succeeded the *Tonight Show*), it's an utterly idiotic slice of joie de vivre that you'll find yourself laughing at against your will. Channel 4 already has a homegrown Letterman pretender of course, in the guise of Graham Norton, but his one joke (shocking innuendo) outstayed its welcome several hundred centuries ago. And besides, Tom Green's one joke – that he's an obnoxious arsehole – is funnier.

Annoyingly, C4 are only showing a heavily edited 'Best of' compilation, rather than screening each edition in its entirety, so what we're left with is a dissatisfying, thumbnail sketch of the full Green experience. Nevertheless, there's plenty of laugh-out-loud material here – witness the pig-headed stupidity of the sequence in which our host borrows a super-expensive Segway scooter and uses it to repeatedly crash into things against the owner's express instruction.

Until we can come up with something as relaxed and carefree as this ourselves – a situation that'll probably only come about the moment TV stations stop plopping their collective pants over every half-percentage of a rating – we really shouldn't bother. And in the meantime, let's be big enough to just admit defeat: put Norton back to one show a week (on the basis that a single dose is just about palatable) and run Tom Green in the slot left behind. Please?

Fame Rehab   [16 August]

Young adults: they're everywhere. They're a virus. And they turn everything they touch into dog dung. I know precisely how brainless young adults are because I used to be one myself. Throughout my 20s I was a selfish, clueless, clumsy, ignorant jerk. As were all my contemporaries. It's safe to assume that subsequent generations of young adults are equally bone-headed: the sole difference is these days, their every squeak, squawk and belch is broadcast on television.

In this torturous summer we've already endured *Big Brother 4*, which featured the youngest set of contestants yet and was therefore the most boring household to date. Tellingly, the oldest contestant won. Undeterred, the Stormtroopers of Youth return, courtesy of *Fame Academy* (BBC1) and *Pop Idol* (ITV1). Two talent shows separated by a gigantic class divide: *Fame Academy* is stiflingly middle-class, while *Pop Idol* is sheer Asda-economy-range plebbish. But weirdly, the musical output from both is identical: music with all the interesting nobbles and rough edges smoothed away. These are people who earnestly admire Robbie Williams, which in the mind of any sane observer is akin to earnestly admiring the My Lai massacre.

Pop Idol's big draw, of course, is Simon Cowell, a fool who knows everything about selling music and zilch about what makes it touch your soul. He's a walking fart cloud of poor taste: poor taste in music, poor taste in clothes, poor taste in women . . . he probably thinks Chicken McNuggets are bursting with flavour. In fact his brain probably *is* a Chicken McNugget, held in place with two strands of tinned spaghetti, generating just enough power to keep his eyes blinking. He's an idiot. And he's an idiot who's made a name for himself by being 'nasty' to the contestants. But, as with everything else about the programme, Cowell's 'scathing' comments are bland and misguided. Why pour scorn on someone who clearly can't sing? Just be nice to them. Reserve your insults for the more demented Robbie Williams wannabes, the ones who've studied his every move and honed their voice into a shiny plastic bum gasp.

In fact, sod insults: just get up from behind the desk and hit them. Get me on that show; I'll do it myself. I'll take a cricket bat to the bastards. Dash those talentless brains right up the wall. They could use a lingering shot of grey matter splattering across the *Pop Idol* logo for the break bumpers. A hundred security guards couldn't hold me back. That's genuine bile, Cowell, not your piss-weak excuse for venom. Get off my screen or I'll sue. In fact, I hereby challenge you to a duel. Fought with shoes. Come round my house and I'll kick you round the garden like the fey rag doll you are.

Fame Academy doesn't have Cowell; its gimmick is round-the-clock live coverage of self-satisfied dullards, courtesy of digital television.

Hilariously, they're all so boring, they were sitting around the other day holding laminated cards with topics of conversation printed on them, presumably handed out by the production team in order to spark some signs of life (this is also how *Hollyoaks* is made, fact fans). Just how much of a blank sheet do you have to be to require that kind of prompting? A quick check on the contestants' biogs reveals the answer: among their 'musical idols' they list legends such as Celine Dion, Lenny Kravitz, George Michael and of course Robbie Williams. THESE PEOPLE BELONG IN HOSPITAL, FOR GOD'S SAKE, NOT IN A TALENT CONTEST. In fact, that's a good idea: 'Fame Rehab', a show in which the academy is turned into a kind of psychological deprogramming unit, in which teams of psychiatrists and talented musicians work round the clock to knock some artistic sense into these simpering dumb-bells.

And Simon Cowell undergoes ten weeks of electric-shock therapy. Not to cure him of anything, mind. Just for a laugh.

Robot Wars with Ghosts [23 August]

Here's a great idea for a TV show. You find an unsuspecting member of the public who's about to have an operation, and secretly research their background. They go into hospital, have the op, and when they come round from the anaesthetic, they discover they've died and woken up in heaven, where they're surrounded by dead relatives and angels playing harps. Except of course it isn't *really* heaven – it's a set-up, and you're filming it with hidden cameras. And the dead relatives aren't *really* spirits – they're actors wearing painstakingly accurate prosthetic masks. Hilarious! And a bit cruel, perhaps, but you could hand out prizes for anyone who susses out what's going on before the end of the day.

What really happens after death is a mystery of course. Lots of people believe we appear in the afterlife and sort of float around like wispy humanoid clouds, which is a charming image but not really very likely, if you sit down and think about it for more than nine seconds. I'm a cynic: I reckon if there really *is* an afterlife, chances are it's a bit like a small, clean town in West Germany.

It also seems the afterlife has phone lines, given the number of patently dishonest psychic mediums doing the rounds. Communicating with the dead has never been so popular – in fact, next week Nokia are launching a new mobile phone that lets you exchange SMS messages with deceased relatives (this is a lie). C4 are reacting to the fad by hosting a dedicated *Psychic Night*.

First up, *Living with the Dead*, a fascinating, even-handed potted history of séances, spirits and mediums (albeit one that's a tad too reliant on filmed 'reconstructions' and abstract imagery of cadavers to spice up the narrative, but since it's impossible to send a camera crew into the afterlife and interview ghosts first-hand, we'll let it go).

Chief among the highlights is a chunk of footage from *The Spirit of Diana* the infamous pay-per-view US TV special in which 'professional mediums' Craig and Jane Hamilton-Parker attempted to contact Princess Di. They start by visiting Paris to retrace her final steps, in the belief that this will bring them closer to her spirit.

Once they've finished goosing Di and Dodi's anguished spirits at the point of impact, it's back to the studio for the séance itself. Or rather it isn't, because the ITC have barred its transmission, presumably on the grounds that it might cause the opening of a portal to the spirit world, swamping the nation with asylum-seeking spectres.

The show also features a flatly ludicrous 'medium' called Derek Acorah, who tours the UK foisting his unique brand of supernatural bullshit onto grieving people in exchange for money. Naturally, he claims to be a serious spiritualist, in which case he really ought to hand out tickets for free and tell the audience they can settle up in the afterlife. Using 'ghost coins'.

He also makes regular appearances on UK Living, the channel that's rapidly becoming the deranged housewife's network of choice, thanks to shows like *Antiques Ghostshow*, in which Our Derek handles heirlooms and gets possessed by the ancestors who once owned them – side-splittingly funny, until you remember he's essentially exploiting someone's fond memories of a loved one.

Living with the Dead is followed by the tacky *Ultimate Psychic Challenge*, in which GMTV presenter Kate Garraway (dressed, for some reason, like she's auditioning for *Chicago*) invites psychics and sceptics to battle it out before a studio audience, who get to vote on whether they 'believe' or not.

It's 'Robot Wars with Ghosts', in other words, but 200 times less interesting than that makes it sound.

Remarkably, despite a rigorous unveiling of many of the tricks so-called 'psychics' employ in their acts, by the end of the show, the number of people believing in séances actually goes up. Well, pah. I'm not convinced. But if any dead readers out there want to get in touch and put me right, be my guest.

A Poor Man's *Bargain Hunt*   [30 August]

It's madness, the sheer amount of television there is out there. Hundreds of channels, filling hundreds of hours. No wonder the majority of programmes are churned out like sausage meat: unloved swathes of videotape whose sole purpose is to bung up the schedule. They used to call TV 'chewing gum for the eyes', but most of the time it isn't even that good any more. Modern chewing gum has flavour; it's constantly updated in new and exciting ways (like the new 'melt in the mouth' gum strips that turn your tongue blue and your breath fresh, then vanish like a benevolent menthol ghost). Most modern TV is uniformly nondescript, the equivalent of oxygen-flavoured gum.

Apologies if I sound despondent and cathode-weary, but I've just sat through an episode of *Boot Sale Challenge* (ITV1), and it's left me violently disillusioned. Don't get me wrong. I love television. I grew up licking screens with delight. Maybe I was young and impressionable. Maybe I never noticed how boring the majority of TV shows were back then. Or maybe these days I'm bitter . . . but when you're confronted with meaningless 'will-this-do?' dregcasts like *Boot Sale Challenge*, it's hard to shake the notion that things never used to be this clawingly, embarrassingly *desperate*.

Because unbelievably, *Boot Sale Challenge* is a poor man's *Bargain Hunt*. Read that phrase again: 'a poor man's *Bargain Hunt*'. Let it sink in. Pop that notional gum strip on your brain and feel it dissolve. Got it? Understand the full horror we're dealing with here? Good. Let's continue.

As you've probably deduced from the title, it's a show in which two teams of dull viewers dawdle round a car-boot sale seeking out bargains. At the end of the show two 'experts' evaluate their purchases: the team whose purchases are judged most likely to turn a profit win a prize (generally, a big hunk of chintz). And. That's. It.

Ever been to a real-life boot sale? They're like *Dawn of the Dead*, but bleaker. Row upon row of Kajagoogoo albums, board games with pieces missing, Franklin Mint atrocities and pieces of furniture so ugly they'd defile a skip, all of it covered in a fine layer of grit and dust and bubbling fly eggs, put up for sale by yellowing cadavers whose eyes point in different directions. The best you can say for *Boot Sale Challenge* is that it brings this experience kicking and screaming into your living room.

The air of desolation is hard to convey with words alone. These people are foraging through a swamp of refuse, paying 50p for a battered old tray, and then whooping for joy when the expert values it at £1.50. You could turn a bigger profit sitting by a cashpoint offering blowjobs for pennies. The show's sole atom of fun is provided by resident expert Paul Hetchin, and that's only because he's the spitting image of Ron Jeremy, the flabby porn star with a penis the length of a window cleaner's ladder – a man who makes more money getting his dingle out in one afternoon than any of the *Boot Sale Challenge* participants would make in a million years of scavenging. Still, if bleak rummaging is 'in', let's see a show called 'Canal Dredge Challenge', in which contestants don wetsuits and drag whatever old shit up to the surface to have it valued.

'The blue team found an old Asda trolley, valued at £9 – but the red team have capped that with their discovery: the body of a missing schoolgirl, the reward for which could earn them as much as ten grand and an interview on GMTV.'

Or how about 'Warzone Scavengers', in which viewers crawl through recently ravaged Chechen villages hunting for valuable trinkets amongst the body parts and rubble?

Give it a year, and they'll both be on. At which point you can blame me. Until then, blame *Boot Sale Challenge*.

D'You Remember Spangles? [6 September]

There's a great deal of talk about the current generation of 'kidults'; millions in their 20s and 30s who refuse to 'grow up', shunning traditional 'adult' pursuits such as theatre and bookkeeping in favour of listening to Justin Timberlake and completing 'Twitty Bum Wars' on the Xbox; ditching suits and floral dresses for a pair of low-slung Levi's with 10 inches of thong-strung arse crack peeking over the rear. It's a hideous prospect: if things carry on like this we'll wind up a nation of Nicky Haslams; wizened cadavers playing Game Boy Advance on a stairlift.

Since we're all simultaneously refusing to acknowledge the ageing process, it's hardly surprising nostalgia has become such big business. The TV schedules heave with 'D'you Remember Spangles?' shows, the Renault Mégane now comes equipped with a School Disco compilation album in the glove box as standard, and Bungle from *Rainbow* is set to be immortalised on the new £50 note.

The king of nostalgia cash-ins is the 'Friends Reunited' website, which has enabled millions to systematically check up on each and every one of their old schoolfriends, only to discover that 98 per cent of them work in IT and want to kill themselves. Worse still, it soon becomes clear that absolutely everyone you ever fancied is now happily married with eighteen kids.

Still, according to *The Curse of Friends Reunited* (C5), a little thing like that needn't dissuade you from attempting to rekindle the spark, the pubescent thrill that fizzed and popped back in the good old days when your skin still fitted and grey hair was an alien concept. A populist documentary cut from the same cloth as last week's cannily positioned *Curse of Blue Peter* sniggerfest, it's chock-a-block with shattered relationships, jilted grooms and ruined lives – all manner of human tragedy, ostensibly made possible by the 'Friends Reunited' website.

It's all tongue-in-cheek because the central premise is nonsense, of course: when your wife runs off with an old flame 14 seconds after begrudgingly muttering her marriage vows, blaming the Internet for enabling the lovebirds to communicate is like blaming the sun for providing enough light for them to see one another in the first place. Demonising technology is more palatable than facing the ugly truth: that a large number of Britons are either fickle, or trapped in make-do relationships, or both, and consequently spend a sizeable portion of their time spooling through past romantic liaisons in their head, with particular emphasis on the ones which teased and tormented, yet never reached their full passionate conclusion.

More interesting than the tales of romantic woe is the story of the boneheaded coke dealer, who visited the site to brag to former classmates about the monstrous amount of 'charlie' he was shifting (much to the delight of the police force tracking his every move), and the sinister case of a man who described his job as 'drop-dead exciting' in a faintly sarcastic way in his profile, and got fired as a result (by a boss who presumably wouldn't think twice about using a mind-control device to scan his workforce's brains for signs of dissent, if only such a thing were available).

Gah. Fah. Pah. Anyway, speaking of teenage-related follies, this week sees the start of the BBC's contemporary update of Chaucer's *Canterbury Tales* (BBC1) . . . and the first episode ('The Miller's Tale') stars none other than BILLIE PIPER!!! Hooray! And in a piece of nakedly appropriate casting, she plays a young chanteuse married to a boozy old duffer twice her age (Dennis Waterman). Sadly, that's as far as the fun goes, because the programme as a whole is intensely annoying, not least because it largely consists of James Nesbitt reprising his cheeky Irishman role for the billionth time this year.

Fans of nightmarish imagery might be interested to know that he and Ms Piper can be glimpsed rutting feverishly on a sofa at one point. Bluuugh. I can still see it each time I close my eyes. My tip: turn the sound down and hang a tea towel over your screen during that bit. And keep it there till it's finished.

Clashing Neighbours in a Bad Sitcom [13 September]

Nothing will drive you insane faster than a relationship with someone who blows hot and cold at random, flipping from love to indifference like a hyperactive imbecile playing with a light switch.

One minute they're praying aloud for extra arms to hug you with, the next they're pissing in your cornflakes while you sob at the breakfast table. Then it's back to kisses and cuddles for a few days, followed by an inexplicable month-long sulk during which your every action provokes a 10-tonne scornful sigh. Saddle yourself to someone like that and you might as well ram a whisk in your ear and scramble your brains manually.

But when both parties are equally schizophrenic, equilibrium is achieved, and the relationship survives, despite constant detonations from within. It's the same with international relations: an identical balancing act maintains the bond between Britain and France, two pig-headed countries with eminently slappable faces, clashing neighbours in a bad sitcom, and the subject of *With Friends Like These* (BBC2), a new series chronicling Britain's postwar relations with key political allies.

Now before you yawn yourself unconscious, it's worth pointing out that *With Friends Like These* is better than you think. For a dunce like me, whose knowledge of Anglo-French relations begins and ends with the *EastEnders* special in which Ricky ate a croissant on the Metro, it's also downright educational, deftly explaining how personal clashes between leaders altered the course of history, typified by the battle of wills between Churchill and De Gaulle.

De Gaulle was a Frenchman so stereotypically arrogant he could have been invented specifically to annoy Richard Littlejohn. Following the Nazi invasion of France, he was whisked to our shores in a light aircraft, where Churchill installed him in a plush Westminster office, pledging full support. De Gaulle repaid our hospitality by sustaining a deep-seated resentment of the British to his dying day, refusing the UK entry to the common market on the grounds that our mindset was 'insular' – this from a nation that recently invented its own word for e-mail, just for the bloody-minded thrill of being surly and different.

But, as anyone in a stormy relationship knows, bitter rows lead to mind-blowing make-up sex: fast-forward a few decades and there's the gruesome sight of Ted Heath and Georges Pompidou practically rimming one another at a press conference, announcing Britain's entry into Europe like lovers at an engagement party. Following years of mutual animosity, Pompidou's head had been turned by the fine selection of French wines on offer at the British Embassy; once he discovered Heath shared his passion for immense helpings of expensive food, romance blossomed. The two men consummated their lust by building Concorde together, a totemic phallus symbolising their subconscious desire to tickle each other's winkies.

Right now, the Anglo-French relationship is going through a rocky patch: thanks to Blair's insensitive flirting with that brainless slut from the White House, Chirac's moved into the spare bedroom. Which is where you come in, dear reader. Because together, we can save this marriage. I have a bold suggestion which will a) improve international relations, b) provide us all with a holiday, and c) destroy David Blaine's career. It's simple: we all move to France for the next 44 days. There's plenty of room; we can camp in the hills, especially since their forests burned down.

Next, we launch a charm offensive with the locals, providing Best of British festivals in which we sing Kinks songs and cook Sunday roasts for entire villages. Then we'll get drunk on their wine and watch them hit on our women. Our nations will fall in love all over again.

Best of all, back in London, freshly deserted London, there'll be no one to greet Blaine when he finally slithers from his Perspex cell. He'll have to drag his skeletal remains into an abandoned Prêt A Manger and make himself a sandwich with his wizened, shaking hands.

And that, my fellow Europeans, will be truly magical.

A Film about Peace. Or Music. Or Both [20 September]

John Lennon – aintcha sick of him? More specifically, aintcha sick of the endless procession of dickwits who bang on and on about how bloody great he was and how if only the entire human race would sit down and listen to his lyrics there'd be no more war or suffering, and the rainforests would grow back, and all our children could grow up in a carefree world full of flutes and rainbows and tepees?

There's no denying Lennon wrote some of the most fantastic music ever committed to vinyl, but he also produced his fair share of dreck – a fine example being 'Imagine', the song recently voted Britain's bestest pop song ever, and the subject of tonight's *Arena: Imagine Imagine* (BBC2), a programme which could serve as a text-book example of what happens when you ask a Mojo reader to create a documentary.

The song itself is the musical equivalent of one of those air-brushed paintings of dolphins they sell in tabloid magazines, which manages to outstay its welcome despite being little more than three minutes long: *Imagine Imagine* lasts 88 minutes and contains more lumpish padding than an outsize Muppet factory. This is a prog doc – a long, slow, bloated fart of a programme; pretentious and pompous enough to include everything from Lennon's inarticulate ramblings about chocolate cake to footage of the Twin Towers exploding in the mistaken belief that the whole unfocused mess will somehow transcend the subject matter to become a powerful statement about . . . er . . . something or other. Oh, peace. Yes, that's it: it's a film about peace. Or music. Or both.

Along the way, we're accosted by all manner of talking-head morons: chief offender Yoko Ono on hand to smugly guff out her standard pseudo-deep bullshit.

'There are only two industries in the world – the war industry and the peace industry,' she says. Really Yoko? What about the textile industry then? Come to that, what about the John Lennon industry, which, under your guidance, markets a range of branded Lennon products including duvet covers and baby wear?

Cut to some ponderous footage of babies and clouds. Cut to the opening of Liverpool's John Lennon Airport (at which a marketing expert gushes that 'the slogan "Above Us Only Sky" isn't just a beautiful sentiment, it's a strong corporate message reinforcing how John Lennon Airport has risen above its competitors'). Cut to archive clips of John and Yoko exhibiting artworks consisting of everyday objects from their opulent home sawn in half and sealed in signed jars (an act of self-aggrandising celebrity chutzpah even Victoria Beckham would balk at). Cut to a gathering of hateful American hippies blubbing over the Lennon memorial in Central Park.

Cut to ethnic children performing the lyrics to 'Imagine' in sign language. Cut to – arrrrrgh. You get the picture. And there's an hour and a half of it.

By the end you'll want to imagine this programme was less abysmal. But that'll be difficult. Imagining the cynical, caustic John Lennon spinning in his grave at 5,000 r.p.m., however, is surprisingly easy.

Before I go, a quick command: move heaven and earth to catch *Turn on Terry* (ITV1) – Terry 'The Word' Christian's late-night TV review show, and a car crash of considerable force. It consists of Terry Christian sitting in a Manchester nightclub incoherently 'reviewing' the week's television ('So, like, what's this *I, Claudius* all about then, eh? Romans and that, innit, right?') while a bored-looking audience stands around in the background wondering why they're there. Best of all there's a house band, fronted by Shaun Ryder's brother, whose job seems to consist solely of introducing each item with a bit of plodding, Madchester dirge.

If you can sit through 10 minutes of this without wanting to lean forward and rub a big blob of dog muck into Terry's rictus grin, you're far more compassionate than me. Or John Lennon. Or the both of us combined as one, living life in peace, above us only sky, etcetera etcetera et-bloody-cetera . . .

Dean Gaffney as Derek Hatton   [27 September]

It opens with Tony Blair and Gordon Brown sitting down to dinner in an Islington restaurant. It ends with a shoot-out in a hall of mirrors.

You'll GASP – as the two leading Labour stalwarts wrestle naked by a fireplace! You'll SCREAM – as Mandelson holds his hand in a candle flame to prove his loyalty! And you'll HOOT – when Blair's trousers fall down unexpectedly, in front of Her Majesty the Queen!

I'm lying of course. *The Deal* (C4) should have been totally ridiculous, and quite frankly it's a miracle it isn't. The lack of ridiculousness is also, truth be told, a crashing disappointment for cynics everywhere. I was praying for a preposterous camp masterpiece, the real-life equivalent of the Comic Strip's *Strike!* film, in which a Hollywood studio attempted to tell the story of the miners' strike by casting Al Pacino as Arthur Scargill.

But no. Instead, *The Deal* is actually rather good – once you come to terms with the notion of actors in a straight drama playing Tony Blair and Gordon Brown, that is. And, thanks to David Morrissey and Michael Sheen, that utterly crucial suspension of disbelief doesn't take as long as you might expect.

Can you imagine the sheer balls it must take to accept a role like this? Playing Brown or Blair in a satirical comedy would be nerve-racking enough, but surely to do so in a serious drama is the thespian equivalent of volunteering to clear a minefield with a teaspoon – one false move and you're screwed. Wisely, neither Morrissey nor Sheen opts for Rory Bremner caricature, instead adopting a kind of semi-impersonation that leaves neither man looking stupid.

Actually, that's not entirely true: Blair still looks stupid, but that's because he is. With his goggle-eyed perkiness and supremely slappable fizzog, Sheen's Blair is a thumpingly massive twit – just like the PM himself. Reminiscent of a recently violated meerkat in a gay bouffant competition, skittering around wearing a hideous salmon-pink shirt tucked into his chinos, this fictional Blair cries out to be despised.

Brown, on the other hand, is a gloomy, complex potato of a man: serious and committed, stiff and dour, sensitive and slightly bitter. The other main players here are John Smith and Peter Mandelson: other MPs appear as themselves in interstitial archive clips. A pity, because I'd love to have seen, say, Joanna Lumley as Margaret Thatcher or Matt Lucas and David Walliams playing Neil and Glenys Kinnock. In fact, the list of dream casting opportunities is endless: Jamie Oliver as Roy Hattersley; Dean Gaffney as Derek Hatton; Animal from *The Muppet Show* as Robin Cook.

Still, by focusing tightly on the two main subjects, *The Deal* manages to keep snorts of derision at bay (although it's hard not to laugh at the sight of the young Mandelson's ridiculous Basil Fawlty moustache – but to be fair, that's his fault for having grown one in real life), and thus commands your attention. The scene where Brown and Blair finally sit down to tensely hatch the deal of the title is vaguely reminiscent of the pivotal Pacino/De Niro restaurant scene in *Heat*, and arrives on a similar wave of palpable tension.

Neither man comes out as particularly likeable, but you're likely to end up siding with Gordon because a) everyone loves the underdog and b) he's simply less of a twerp than Tony.

Anyway, it's comforting to find proof that C4 can still rustle up a decent slice of intelligent, solidly crafted drama. Can we have fewer property shows and more programmes like this, please? Oh, and how about a series of spin-off sequels using the same cast, in which Tony and Gordon find themselves having to pull together in a string of increasingly absurd situations, like going undercover in a convent, or trying to catch an escaped monkey during Paris fashion week? Because the comic possibilities of an odd couple like this are too good to pass up. And it'd be a damn sight funnier than watching them run the country.

Hitting the Red Button [4 October]

They said interactive television would change our lives. They said it would be TV's biggest technological leap forward since the introduction of K-9.

They said it would put the viewer in control, that we'd be able to alter storylines on the fly, hitting the red button if we wanted to see Dot sleep with Barry, or the blue button to see Ricky find a magic whistle. They said all of this and more. Reader, they lied to us.

The majority of 'interactive' programmes are actually long-running talent shows in which the public votes to save their favourite contestants. We're told this puts the viewer 'in the driving seat', but that's another lie: the audience's power is strictly limited – you can't text a number to sack Dr Fox or drown all the contestants in a gigantic bucket.

To date, the purest example of interactive broadcasting I can find is the ridiculous Friendly TV network (Sky 268). Described in its own literature as 'a new venture in digital television', it's an unbroken stream of yabbering 'presenters' responding to text messages from viewers – a cross between a help desk, a radio phone-in and a sign of the coming Apocalypse.

Later in the day, they cover video games and sex tips, but their most compelling show is the *Morning Chat* slot, in which two young women sit behind a desk talking about nothing in particular, apparently only semi-aware they're on television, fielding endless enquiries from lonely, desperate men. Despite the girls' constant pleas to 'keep it clean, or it won't go on screen', since the bulk of the messages are wretched stabs at daytime-friendly erotica – 'DO U LIKE BEING TICKLED?', 'WILL U BLO ME A KISS?', it's clear what sort of 'friendly' interaction the viewers have in mind, and if you needed two hands to send text messages, the channel would fold overnight.

The broadcast itself doesn't so much cut corners as deny their existence outright. You can phone in and speak to presenters live on air but, amazingly, other viewers won't hear your end of the conversation – they're just left staring at a girl going 'Yes', 'Really?', and 'Ha ha ha' or, more often than not, frowning and hanging up when the caller says something untoward.

Around lunchtime one of the girls will get up and go to the corner shop, asking her co-presenter *on air* if she wants anything. Ten minutes later she'll return to eat a sandwich right there at the desk. When things get quiet they flip through the latest *Heat* and discuss which shifts they're working. For some reason this is quite, quite terrifying.

But the true joy of Friendly TV lies in its interactivity: since the conversation is driven by whatever you text in, you can quickly steer it into preposterous territory. Or to really spice things up, sit around with a bunch of friends, firing confusing messages en masse. Some work chums and myself tried this the other day, and for entertainment you can't match it. Within minutes we had them discussing *On Golden Pond*, the death of the Pope ('I didn't know he was dead! It's not in the paper'), and whether they 'trusted' Trevor McDonald ('Yes . . . well, as much as one can').

We sent suicide notes, reading, 'So, so alone – just want out' ('You're not alone, we're here! But there's nothing we can do, so don't send that, it's just upsetting.')

We said, 'My dad's drunk again he keeps falling over' ('Oh, that's not nice, it's quite early') and asked if they fancied Lord Hutton. We quoted the Wearside Jack tapes from the Yorkshire Ripper investigation. Best of all, we asked, 'Philosophically speaking, when you wake up in the morning are you still you?', which prompted five minutes of debate before they reached the verdict: probably not.

Here's a suggestion, nay, a command: this Monday morning, at 11.30 a.m., I want as many 'Guide' readers as possible to bombard them with mind-bending philosophical queries, plaintive calls for help and Billy Joel lyrics. Interactivity: it's all about power to the people. Friendly TV is on Sky 268. The number to text is 86121 (it's £1 for four). Monday, 11.30 a.m.

B THR OR B SQR.

Do Spiders Live Alone? [11 October]

Reader, I thank you. Last week I asked you all to send mind-bending philosophical text messages to Friendly TV's *Morning Chat* show (Sky 268) and good crikey, God damn, you didn't disappoint.

Yep. Last Monday, at 11.30am, poor unsuspecting Friendly TV presenter Sara-Michelle was on duty when a string of dreamy queries began pouring in – courtesy of you, dear reader. Since the vast majority of Friendly TV texts seem to emanate from about-to-masturbate loners, the sudden rush of asexual cerebral probing took her unawares.

'Do spiders live alone?' you asked.

'If the earth is round, how come a table is flat?'

'Where do you think the soul goes when you are under general anaesthetic?'

Sara-Michelle fared very well, considering. I think she had a nasty cold. Well, she kept reaching for her nose anyway. But what a trouper. Despite all that, she was still quite animated. Wide-eyed with enthusiasm, you might say. And at that time in the morning! Incredible!

A special mention to the texter who insinuated that Billy Joel had died, prompting considerable distress from Sara-Michelle, although the grand prize awaits the anonymous reader who posed the question: 'Given that all matter is really energy condensed to a slow vibration, is there really any such thing as death or is it merely a transition to another plane?' That got my vote for text of the day: Sara-Michelle damn near swallowed her own brain searching for a coherent answer.

Not that I could hope to answer such a query with any degree of authority myself, of course. Nope, I was caught on the hop. In a freakish example of interactive television striking back, the Friendly TV 'babe' phoned me on my mobile live on air. There I was, just a-walking down the street, when my phone chirruped and Sara-Michelle herself said, 'Hi,' from the other end.

It seems that someone behind the scenes sussed what was going on, and deduced my personal number by checking the texts detailed in last week's column and phoning the mobile that sent them. Oops. I'd make a terrible serial killer – ol' fingerprints on the ribcage, that's me.

And there I was, outside Shepherd's Bush tube, when Friendly TV came calling. There wasn't much I could do except offer bland chitchat until Sara-Michelle got bored and hung up. Not that you'll have heard a word of it – Friendly only lets you hear the presenter's side of the conversation. So you won't have heard me enquiring how much they usually charge for one-on-one conversations. Or asking whether or not I could swear. It's not Sara-Michelle's fault, of course. She's pleasant enough, and like all the *Morning Chat* 'babes', she's simply doing her job, which is to sit there and look cute while clueless masturbators text in to say HELLO and I LUV U and I AM OUTSIDE STUDIO NOW WITH A HAMMER. In fact, as a concerned *Guardian* reader, you *owe* it to Sara-Michelle and her co-hosts to make their lives more bearable by sending a constant stream of thought-provoking, non-sexual enquiries to liven up their day. Don't be horrid – they're your friends! Let's drive the perverts away, back to the Internet where they belong!

And since Friendly TV already have my number, if there's anything you want to ask *me* directly, address the question to *them* and they'll pass it on. Probably live on air. (Note to Friendly TV: you can call me whenever you like, and unless I'm in a meeting, I'll respond right away. Really.) So, reader, let's do it again: Monday, 11.30 a.m. The number to text: 86121. Four messages for a quid. Unless you're on T-Mobile, in which case it's loads more. Sky Channel 268. And they *will* respond *live* to almost *any* query. Provided it isn't obscene.

Come on people – let's make this the UK's number one interactive TV channel before the end of the year. 2GETHA WE CN DO IT!

Coagulated Body Fluids   [8 October]

Noel Coward once said: 'I don't think pornography is harmful . . . but it is terribly, terribly boring.' What a dur-brain. Pornography is the only thing on earth more fascinating than sex itself. And that's precisely what makes it so undeniably, eternally popular.

Come on, own up: you secretly like pornography, don't you? Don't be embarrassed. Everyone does. If pornography didn't exist, the Internet would shrivel to the size of a single conker overnight. And you could print the entire contents of Google on the back of a chickpea.

Hardly surprising, because while yer average website, DVD or satellite broadcast could scarcely entertain a recently concussed farmhand, let alone a *Guardian*-reading cleverclogs like yourself, hardcore porn is endlessly fascinating to people of all varieties – particularly when the camera zooms in really close and it all ends up looking like a butcher's shop window hallucinating in the middle of a heatwave.

Thankfully, there's loads of filth knocking about the schedules this week. As a horrified world struggles to cope with the recent demise of *Penthouse* magazine, BBC2 highlights the sheer magnitude of our loss in *Sex Empires* (BBC2), a three-part documentary chronicling the rise and fall of traditional printed jazz mags. I can sum the entire series up in one sentence: you don't have to look a shop assistant in the eye while paying for online porn, and it's physically impossible to stick the pages together – so bye-bye, jazz mags.

Meanwhile, armed with the knowledge that all print erotica is now doomed, good ol' opportunistic C4 is peddling *Pornography: The Musical*, a textbook example of have-your-cake-and-eat-it television: part unflinching glimpse at the seedy underbelly, two parts nudge, wink titillation. With added songs. Yep, songs. Full-blown musical numbers, acted out by porn stars.

Pornography: The Musical comes from the award-winning tinkers behind last year's borstal rap-a-long *Feltham Sings*, hence the format: straight interviews interspersed with fantasy musical sequences enacted by the 'real' participants. If it were any more arch, it'd be a curved structure forming the upper edge of an open space.

Shakespeare once said: 'If music be the food of love, play on.' *Pornography: The Musical* isn't what he had in mind. As you might expect, it's a treasure trove of dreadful lyrics ('bring in the horse/then order a hearse' being just one mind-boggling example) and yet more dreadful vocals (particularly from professional phallus manipulator Rebekah Jordan, who really ought to contact her GP and check her larynx hasn't been permanently clogged by all those coagulated body fluids).

D. H. Lawrence once said pornography represented 'the attempt to insult sex, to do dirt on it' and, having witnessed the frankly jaw-dropping 'musical bukkake' sequence in this programme, it's hard to disagree. Or move. Or speak.

In case you don't know, 'bukkake' is . . . um . . . well . . . it's a term of Japanese origin that refers to the mass deposit of male reproductive fluids into and onto a solitary female recipient courtesy of a mammoth assembly of solemn-looking gentlemen. It's the sort of thing that's rarely discussed in *Razzle*, let alone the *Guardian*, so it's fair to say that by setting it to music and then televising it, C4 have a notable first. You might call it a 'Singing in the Rain' for the twenty-first century. If you're a prick.

Ultimately, *Pornography: The Musical*'s main flaw lies in its own novelty value. The songs aren't as interesting as the straight interview segments they're intended to embellish.

One talking-head sequence in particular, in which a male porn artiste gleefully recounts a cautionary tale about the perils of over-zealous rectal douching prior to intercourse, is worth the price of admission alone – even though a) C4 don't charge an admission fee and b) there's a very real chance it'll make you vomit.

Ready, Steady . . . Boo! [25 October]

Be afraid. Be very afraid. Tonight Channel 4 showcases the *100 Greatest Scary Moments*, which promises to be a decent evening's entertainment provided Paul Ross doesn't turn up and spoil it all with his big booming gob.

No word yet on which particular example of blood-curdling Channel 4 viewers have crowned the King of Brown Trousers but for a bit of fun, and because I'm an egomaniac with his own bloody column, I've decided to compile my own list of spooky moments, which favours TV instead of movies, and has the added advantage of being 14.26 times shorter than its Channel 4 equivalent.

Ready, steady . . . boo!

7 Diana eats a guinea pig (*V*, 1983)

Not the late Princess of Hearts – although that *would* be scary. I'm talking about Diana the alien dominatrix from the mini-series *V*, whose subhuman nature is first disclosed when Marc Singer hides in an air vent and spots her swallowing a giant rodent in true reptile fashion (i.e. by dislocating her lower jaw to fit it all in). I saw this scene again recently, and like most on this list, it now looks downright ridiculous, but at the time I was so scared I practically pooed a new substance consisting of raw, solid fear.

6 James Harries on *Wogan* (1988)

You know: the eerie antiques-expert kid who looked like a cross between Christopher Atkins from *The Blue Lagoon* and a squinting rat foetus. The creepiest boy since Damien from *The Omen*, with the added spook-value of being entirely non-fictional.

5 Doctor Who is virtually dismembered (1980)

Everyone has a favourite *Who* freak-out moment: mine came at the end of episode one of 'The Leisure Hive', when Tom Baker appears in some kind of primitive VR machine, gets his arms and legs torn off, and screams – the camera zoomed in on his bellowing mouth, the scream blended with the already-terrifying closing title music, and my spine scuttled out my backside and ran for the nearest exit. Couldn't walk for six months. Cheers, Doctor.

4 Charley the cat almost drowns (1970s–1980s)

Yes, Charley the cat from the Public Information films (as sampled by the Prodigy in the days when they made harmless rave tunes instead of violent commercials for spousal abuse and Rohypnol). In a short cartoon intended to alert kids to the dangers of playing near canals, he plunges beneath the waves to flail about in a terrifying subterranean hell, mewling bubbles as he does so. Result: I spend the rest of my childhood convinced that canals are portals to hell. Cheers, Charley.

3 Anything with a mushroom cloud in it (1980s)
That covers *Threads*, *The Day After*, *When the Wind Blows* and in particular *A Guide to Armageddon*, a 1982 episode of pop-science show *QED* which soberly explained the effects of a single nuclear bomb blast by intercutting close-ups of burning pork with pictures of human faces. Child psychiatrists experienced a five-year boom immediately afterwards. Cheers, BBC.

2 *Crimewatch UK* (any year)
What's so scary about that, you ask? Well, I reply, have you ever watched *Crimewatch UK* while spending an evening alone, in an isolated cottage, in the middle of winter, surrounded by dark skies, silence and the occasional ambiguous shadow on the horizon? No? Then shut up. Trust me, by the time the end credits roll, you *are* Tony Martin.

1 Any newsflash since 11 September
Newsflashes always used to put the wind up me – I assumed they heralded imminent nuclear apocalypse – but since 9/11 they've taken on an even more nerve-jangling significance. At least you knew where you were with nukes – flash, bang, frazzle and it's over.

These days, you see a newsflash and your mind starts racing – what'll it be? Dirty bomb? Smallpox? Plague of locusts? Al-Qaeda death-ray? Don't know about you, but when the Queen Mum died I breathed such a huge sigh of relief I knocked out the back wall of my living room.

I Don't Even Know What Rice Is   [1 November]

Take a good look around and ask yourself how much of the world you truly comprehend – and I'm talking about a true scientific understanding here. At a rough guess, I'd say you probably understand about 0.0002 per cent of everything. Thicko.

Even so, you're twice as clever as me. Earlier today I used a microwave oven to heat a saddo's instant meal-for-one, and shortly afterwards, as I spooned said molten slop into my downturned mouth betwixt guttural sobs of despair, it occurred to me that I have no idea how a microwave oven works. As far as I know, it warms the food by beaming it to Jupiter, where a herd of magic space goats breathes fire into the molecules, before knocking them back to Earth with a quantum tennis racquet.

Then I looked down at my plate and noticed the meal contained rice. And I realised I DON'T EVEN KNOW WHAT RICE IS. Not precisely. What is it? A type of vegetable? A tiny egg? What?

Well, I looked it up, and guess what? Technically, rice is a bloody *fruit*. Well, sort of. Apparently all grains are. So it says here. Look, I'm no expert. Besides, that's not important right now. The point is that to a bumwit like me, life is one big mystery, which is why *The Theory of Everything* (C4) has a seductive ring to it.

It's a pop-science series tracking the quest to arrive at a 'grand unification theory' – a hypothesis governing absolutely everything in the universe. Such a theory wouldn't just explain how microwaves work *and* what rice is, but also *why* they came to exist in the first place. It could explain the relationship between gravity and time and quantum physics and you and me and the bloke next door with the wonky eye. It could explain what would happen if you switched a time machine on at the precise moment British Summer Time ends and the clocks go back. It could explain the plot of *Mulholland Drive*, even if it had nipped out for a wee during the 'Club Silencio' scene. It could do anything.

Trouble is, you could go nuts trying to grasp the basics, which thus far run roughly as follows: everything in existence, including the space-time fabric itself, is assembled from an infinite number of minuscule, oscillating 'strings' which swirl around in ten dimensions. Yep, ten dimensions, six of which are apparently themselves curled into loops. Suddenly my 'space goats on Jupiter' theory of microwaved food doesn't sound quite so stupid.

Anyway, until string theory arrives in earnest, we'll have to rely on documentaries like this to explain things to us. Fortunately, despite a few mildly irritating 'zany' graphical touches, it manages to entertain as it does so, feeling for the most part like a cross between the animated sections of *Hitchhiker's Guide* and an old James Burke think-u-mentary.

Of course, if a little knowledge is a dangerous thing, it stands to reason that a grand unification theory could destroy us all. Ten minutes after its discovery, you can bet your sweet bippy the US military will write it down, glue it to the front of a missile, test-fire it in the desert and inadvertently turn the whole world into a massive tangerine or something.

Blame Einstein. He thought of it first. In his latter years, while the rest of the scientific world was playing with the newly discovered principles of quantum physics, Einstein was obsessed with rustling up his very own 'grand theory of everything'. Other scientists pitied him, partly because he seemed behind the times, and partly because he had silly hair. Only now can we see just how far ahead of his time Einstein was. Not only has 'string theory' become cutting-edge enough to form the basis for a Channel 4 pop-doc, but far more significantly, Albert's crazy out-of-bed haircut now makes him look like an eccentric uncle to one of the Strokes.

Sod string theory. That's *way* cool.

The Sneering Classes   [8 November]

OK, I admit it: I'm a fully paid-up member of the sneering class – that curious section of modern society that spends its time smugly guffawing at the foibles of all the other classes. The sneering class laughs at the plebs taking part in *Pop Idol* one minute, then snorts at the preposterous brayings of public-school gentry the next – pausing to pour scorn over *Daily Mail*-reading Middle-Englanders on the way. You see, no one's quite good enough for us – we hate everyone with equal vigour.

Joining the sneering class is simple: you're given a membership card the minute you start working in the media, log on to 'Popbitch', or find yourself enjoying sneering-class telly formats such as *Celebrity Wife Swap* (C4), which manages to be hilarious and brilliant yet essentially reprehensible, all at the same time.

In the red corner we have *Big Brother*'s Jade Goody and her boyfriend Jeff Brazier, two unapologetically scrubby diamonds from Essex; in the blue corner it's the ex-Major Charles Ingram and his wife Diana – the lying, cheating scum who had the audacity to pull a harmless con on *Who Wants to Be a Millionaire?*, whose makers, Celador, were so upset they cancelled his cheque and proceeded to wring their quaking, appalled hands at the effect a high-profile court case might have on the programme's dwindling ratings.

Chris Tarrant called it 'a very cynical plan, motivated by sheer greed', which sounds like a description of *Millionaire*'s premium-rate phone-line method of gathering contestants, but isn't. Mr Ingram was found guilty and forced to resign from the army; Celador limped from the courtroom with nothing more than a prime-time special and blanket press coverage to support them.

So, the Ingrams, then: a pair of cheating bastards who deserve everything we can throw at them. Which in this case is Jeff and Jade. Jade is a remarkable creature and almost impossible to describe, although throughout *Big Brother 3* some of Fleet Street's finest did their best, light-heartedly describing her as an 'oinker' (the *Sun*), a 'vile fishwife' (*Daily Mirror*) and a 'foulmouthed ex-shoplifter' (*Daily Mail*), until the public joined in the japes by standing outside the house waving 'Kill the Pig' placards, thereby turning the whole delightful episode into a clever pastiche of *Lord of the Flies*.

They were wrong incidentally. Jade isn't a pig. From some angles she looks a bit like Martin Clunes, aged five, peering through a porthole. But not a pig.

Anyway, the gods of *Wife Swap* decree that Jade must move in with Charles for a week in the Ingrams' Wiltshire home (floral prints, Le Creuset cookware, faint air of jovial fascism), while Diana takes up residence alongside Jeff in an Essex flat (widescreen telly, laundry draped over radiators, meals eaten from the lap).

Of course, what happens next is genuinely very funny indeed, and while it may lack the demented bellowing matches of recent *Wife Swaps*, there's plenty of painful moments to wallow in.

Wince! As Jade walks into the Ingrams' home yelping, 'It's the cheat's house!' Gasp! As Jeff repeatedly refers to Diana's age ('Firty nine – that's me mum's age') and takes her for a night out in Romford. Vomit! As Charles Ingram says he'll miss having sex with his wife and confesses to having enjoyed 'a top-up' the night before the swap. Wonder! Why anyone involved agreed to take part in the first place. Feel! Vaguely! Superior! To absolutely everyone on screen!

Or alternatively, give your sneering muscles a rest, with something classily classless: *Walking with Sea Monsters* (BBC1), in which wildlife expert Nigel Marven travels to the Jurassic era to swim alongside great big wobbly seabeasts. The whole thing's so spectacular and convincing, any children watching will come away permanently confused as to what's real and what isn't – which added to my enjoyment no end.

Great fun – although I did feel a brief shudder during a sequence starring an ugly blank-eyed sea monster whose jaws are locked in a permanent sneer. Just for a moment I thought I was watching a mirror.

You *Are* Her Majesty the Queen! [29 November]

You are all scum. Common, cap-doffing, bottom-of-the-food-chain scum. Don't argue. Compared to our glorious royal family, you're just another dark streak on humanity's toilet pan.

But don't despair. The *Mirror*'s recent undercover scoopery uncovered invaluable details regarding their personal habits, making it a doddle to simulate the royal lifestyle in the comfort of your own hovel. Simply use these easy-to-follow instructions, and hey-presto – you'll believe you *are* Her Majesty the Queen!

Here's what you'll need: a partner willing to dress up as a footman, a television set, a remote control, a tray, and some dinner. For the sake of accuracy, the dinner should consist of something suitably hoity-toity, like chargrilled swan's brains in a fox-blood jus, and the footman should stand in the corner, repeatedly tugging his forelock so hard that he keeps bashing his forehead against the ground. Oh, and you should probably pull a face like the Queen as well: try to capture her effortless charisma by locking your features into a permanent half-hearted grimace, as though you're trying to excrete a tinfoil pine cone without anyone noticing.

As the clock strikes eight, sit back as your subservient footman brings you your dinner (trying not to slosh fox blood down your lap as he does so), then pick up the remote control that he should have placed carefully to the left side of your plate and plunge head-first into Her Majesty's favourite TV programmes. And realise what a flat-out bozo we've got on the throne.

Yes, because first up on the Queen's viewing schedule it's *East-Enders* (BBC1). This is progress in action, folks. The late Queen Mum got to know London's cockernee rabble by personally touring the East End in the wake of the Blitz, and was rewarded with years of mindless gratitude from tedious Pearly Kings (whose glittery costumes doubtless attracted the attention of low-flying Luftwaffe pilots in the first place). Queen Elizabeth II doesn't need to be quite so pro-active, since the BBC helpfully brings all the grit of East London kicking and screaming into her living quarters four times a week (with an omnibus on Sundays).

Since the Queen lives inside an impenetrable bubble of pomp and horseshit, she doubtless thinks *EastEnders* is a hard-hitting documentary. Think about it: she has more contact with the plebs in Albert Square than the plebs outside her own front gate. Right now, she probably believes the East End is teeming with unconvincing gangsters and resurrected publicans. None of whom ever swear, spit, or sound off on controversial topics. Even Michael Jackson has a firmer grasp on reality than that.

Worse is to come, because next up, Her Gloriousness likes to watch *The Bill* (ITV1/UK Gold). Or rather, she doesn't. According to the bogus footman, she said, 'I don't like *The Bill*, but I can't help watching it.'

Funny that. I feel exactly the same – but only because it's always fucking on. ITV show it 89 times a week, and it's heavily rotated on satellite. They say you're only ever three metres from a rat in London – I say you're only ever three seconds from the opening credits of *The Bill*. And if *EastEnders* is supplying Her Superiorness with a warped view of Londoners, *The Bill* must convince her that her own constabulary spend more time shagging than, say, tracking down would-be royal assassins. Which explains why she looks so nervous whenever she's in public.

So much for the soaps. For a dose of cold hard realism in the royal household, it falls to the Queen's final favourite – *Kirsty's Home Videos* (Sky One): impossibly, a down-market version of *You've Been Framed*. Terrifyingly, this supplies the only unguarded, unsanitised look at everyday citizens the Queen will experience in her entire life. And what does she see us doing? Mooning, gurning, and tumbling like idiots, accompanied by comedy sound effects.

No wonder she looks like she hates us.

'Can you tell what it is yet?' [6 December]

The singer Gabrielle once claimed 'dreams can come true'. She was lying. Dreams don't come true. If they did, the nation's offices would be full of people who'd accidentally turned up for work with no clothes on. And I'd have slept with Madonna when I was 13.

Besides, if they *did* come true, they wouldn't be 'dreams'; they'd be 'premonitions'. Of course, Gabrielle already knows this – but hey, 'premonitions' would've been harder to scan.

Anyway, to recap: *Dreams do not come true.*

Nightmares, however, come true on a daily basis – and usually on television.

I'm currently working on a theory that much modern TV is actually derived from the collective nightmares of our national subconscious. It works like this: machines have become self-aware, Terminator-style, and have decided to punish mankind for years of abuse by slurping our darkest fears from the ether and relaying them back to us via our beloved TV screens in the hope that we'll all go mad. I call this the Freddy Krueger Manoeuvre, and it explains, among other things, the peculiar chill you feel each time you see Linda Barker miming a scissor motion at the end of those Curry's adverts. For another prime example of this, look no further than *Rolf Harris at the Royal Albert Hall* (BBC1). Rolf's famous for asking, 'Can you tell what it is yet?', but despite having wracked my brains for several hours, my answer is, 'No, I don't actually know what this is.' On the one hand, it's a tribute to Rolf's fifty years in showbiz. But it's also a charity concert in aid of the Prince's Trust. Which aspect is least important? I don't know.

Rolf himself is centre stage throughout: does that make him a tiresome egomaniac or a born entertainer? I don't know. Why does Jon Culshaw turn up halfway through, wearing two false legs, doing an impression of Russell Crowe as a four-legged gladiator? *I don't know*.

There's no doubt that Rolf is – as Prince Charles himself puts it in a VT mini-tribute – a 'much-loved institution'. He's certainly stuck his thumb into a wide variety of pies: art, cartoons, music, consumer electronics (well, the Stylophone anyway), silly sound effects and dying household pets. I'm referring to *Animal Hospital* there, incidentally. *In no way* am I suggesting Rolf has *ever* stuck his thumb into a dying household pet. Although that's just about the only thing he hasn't done in the name of entertainment.

Look up the word 'wacky' in a dictionary, and you'll find a picture of Rolf. Chances are he put it there himself. He's not shy. In fact, he spends this entire show – a tribute to himself, don't forget – wearing a shirt whose pattern consists of the words 'ROLF HARRIS' repeated over and over in block capitals. In the real world, that kind of egomania would be unforgivable, but since this is Rolf – zany uncle to several generations of British telly viewers – it's somehow completely acceptable.

See, it's hard not to love Rolf. No, really – and it's just as well, because he tests the goodwill of a nation to breaking point here. Among the surreal highlights: Rolf performing an excruciating rap with Big Brovaz (you can actually *see* their credibility imploding on stage); Rolf playing the Stylophone with John Humphrys and Sally Gunnell; Rolf performing a cover version of 'Roll with It' (renamed

'Rolf with It') alongside Jon Culshaw (who's impersonating Rolf and Liam Gallagher *at the same time*); Rolf doing an eerie song about a dying sailor, accompanied by a tiny, dancing, wooden doll. Beloved entertainer? Maybe . . . but can you imagine being stuck in a lift for six months with this man? You'd end up dashing your own brains across the floor just to make it stop.

At least that's how you'll feel until halfway through the show, when Rolf pulls off a flawless, engaging performance of 'Jake the Peg', and suddenly you'd forgive him anything.

Why? *I don't know*. But it *must* be a nightmare. Because dreams don't come true.

The Pudge-Faced Sea Monkey   [13 December]

You can hunt high, you can hunt low, you can sift through the gene pool . . . but I defy you to unearth a more instantly objectionable little berk than Sam Nixon, the pudge-faced sea monkey currently tipped to win *Pop Idol* (ITV1).

Aside from a briefly dipped toe at the start of the season, I'd managed to completely avoid Cowell and company this time round. Or so I thought, until last week, when I unexpectedly stumbled across it in much the same way you might unexpectedly step barefoot on a dog turd.

Once I'd got over the shock of discovering *it's still bloody going* (the current series seems to have been running since 1913), I found myself reeling at the remaining four popettes: a 12-year-old advertising executive (Chris), a male Stepford Wife (Mark), Sonia from *EastEnders* scowling at a funhouse mirror (Michelle) and, most disturbing of all, one of the puppets from the 1970s children's TV series *Cloppa Castle* (Sam). Of the four, Mark was worst, but at the end of the show it was Chris – the only one with a sense of humour – who got hoofed out, leaving a one-horse race in his wake. With only Alison Moyet junior and a piece of singing cardboard for competition, Sam simply cannot fail. And that's a tragedy. Because he's a tit.

It's wrong to judge people by appearance alone but in this case I'll make an exception. Sam is a gnome. A troll. A claymation

Photofit of Mo Mowlam. And he sports a semi-ironic mullet explosion on his head, like the bastard offspring of Limahl and Pat Sharp. That's not a haircut – that's a cast-iron guarantee of mediocrity.

Well, look here, ITV. It's getting cold, Christmas is coming, everyone's stressed out and to be honest we could do without Sam's hypnotically punchable mug soiling our screens, papers and record-shop windows for the next two years. Which is why I implore everyone reading to tune in tonight and turf him out. Oh, and if you're out shopping this afternoon and you see someone buying the *Pop Idol* Christmas single – a soul-bummingly dreadful cover version of 'Happy Xmas (War is Over)' – kick them to death on the spot.

Speaking of rubbish, have you SEEN *You've Been Framed* (ITV1) lately? It's never been sophisticated – as entertainment, it's always been on a par with sharing a tent with someone who thinks performance farting is hilarious – but now the bottom of the barrel has been scraped clean away and the programme is frenziedly digging its way toward the earth's core.

First, they've replaced Lisa Riley with Jonathan Wilkes, which is a bit like substituting a lump of sick for a lump of snot: equally bad yet somehow worse. Wilkes has hair like a brown wave of effluence and a dimple that makes him look like he's been leaning chin-first on a pool cue for the last six days.

Worse still, there's a new string of palpably desperate 'format points' which help them repeat their dwindling selection of footage again and again. There's a segment in which kids introduce their 'favourite' classic clips (i.e. whatever the production team has shown them that morning), a bit where Wilkes exposes a suspected 'fake' clip by rewinding it and showing it several times in a row (despite having cheerfully introduced countless obvious fakes moments earlier) and, most shameless of all, a finale in which he invites us to enjoy several of that episode's highlights again (which in the case of the 'fake' clip was actually the *third* time we'd seen it).

In summary then: both *Pop Idol* and *New You've Been Framed* are rubbish, particularly compared to this week's low-profile, low-budget edition of *The Art Show* – something called *How to Watch Television* (C4), which was written and narrated by me and is therefore great. Don't miss it!

Fight for a ticket!

Look at Me!   [20 December]

Once upon a time, if you wanted to be famous, all you had to do was get your face on television – and bingo, that was that. There were only a handful of channels; no websites or Xboxes vying for the audience's attention. It was just you and several million viewers at home. Getting on the box was like sticking your head through every window in the country simultaneously, grinning like crazy and shouting 'Look at me!' – yes, just like that, except it didn't terrify the occupants. Instead they grew to love you as a 'famous person'. They'd harass you in supermarkets; bug you for autographs at motorway service stations. Kiss you at the urinal. All you'd done was appear on their screens, but to them you were magic incarnate. Not any more. There are 15 billion channels out there. You'll need to do more than smile and wave if you want to get noticed. In fact, in 2003, the only sure-fire way to command attention was to risk your own life, live, on camera.

First came *David Blaine: Above the Below*, a sort of one-man *Big Brother* with a smaller catering bill. The moment Blaine's perspex door slammed shut, the nation was divided. Was it a trick? Was it art? Was it a man doing tit-all in a box for ages? Whatever it was, lucky and/or demented Sky viewers could sit watching it 29 hours a day (OK, 24 hours – it just felt longer). Those without satellite dishes had to make do with popping along in person to hurl abuse and tomatoes.

While the drawling, soporific Blaine committed slow-motion suicide over a 44-day period, the altogether twitchier *Derren Brown* threatened to achieve similar results in a nanosecond, by blasting his head apart on live television. Of course, had Brown's stunt actually culminated in an onscreen bonce-burst, C4's broadcasting licence would've been revoked before the first skull fragment hit the floor, and consequently the outcome was never in doubt. Nonetheless, the finale made supremely creepy viewing, largely because Brown himself is one of the canniest showmen to have emerged in years: the sight of him gulping, sweating and holding a gun to his head was the year's third most frightening image.

In second place: Linda Barker's 'snip snip' mime from the Curry's commercials, narrowly pipped to first place by 'The All-New Shock and Awe Show', available round the clock on most channels throughout March and April.

Never one to turn a blind eye to suffering, particularly when it's accompanied by eye-popping explosions, Sky News welcomed the war with open arms, rapidly mutating into an exact copy of the fascist TV news network from *Starship Troopers*, replete with spinning 3D graphics (rippling flags, advancing tank columns, soaring jets; if they'd thrown a 200-foot flame-throwing penis into the mix no one would've batted an eyelid), white-knuckle shakycam reports from the field and a ticker tape filled with 'breaking news' cunningly disguised as hysterical conjecture.

The BBC, meanwhile, found itself a sex symbol in the form of Rageh Omaar, dormouse of doom. ITN had to make do with John Suchet shouting over an endless procession of blurry green JPegs that apparently constituted 'live footage'.

Despite the surfeit of cameras, very little blood was shown on screen. A fusty ignoramus might sneer that the TV coverage treated the war like a video game, whereas the reality is actually worse: the average modern video game is more realistic and even-handed than the average TV news bulletin.

Speaking of news, *Tonight with Trevor McDonald* secured the year's biggest TV scoop: Martin Bashir's remarkable interview with Michael Jackson, during which the unhinged superstar cheerfully confessed to sharing his bed with children. After some predictable mud-slinging, Jacko bounced back with a starring role in a Santa Monica police mugshot, in which his face looks disturbingly like a child's drawing: as though they asked a four-year-old to create a likeness in crayon.

With all this bizarre non-fiction pouring into our living rooms, it's not surprising common-or-garden reality TV finally began to falter, the lacklustre *Big Brother 4* a case in point: a household of identikit yoof-droids (eerily reminiscent of the hateful Doritos Friendchips gang) who consistently failed to screw, argue, or do anything of interest, and proved so wholly unmemorable that even Federico himself has forgotten who he is.

The follow-ups to *Pop Idol* and *Fame Academy* also failed to generate much interest – indeed, the only reality show to really make a mark was C4's *Wife Swap*, which brought middle-class milquetoasts and warty proles into direct contact, then invited us to enjoy the inevitable slanging match as though it were a sitcom; Penelope Keith and Kathy Bates playing neighbours at war. The formula spawned a surreal one-off 'celebrity' special featuring Jade from *Big Brother 3* and Charles 'Coughing Major' Ingram – a programme so hazardously post-modern it was in danger of creating a wormhole into an alternate universe filled with dense ironic matter.

Jade also featured briefly in an episode of *Boys and Girls*, a shameful, insulting, unwatchable bum-spill of a programme, and the most embarrassing mistake Channel 4 have made since the broadcast of *Mini Pops*. Still, every cloud has a silver lining – the show's microscopic viewing figures finally proved once and for all that Chris Evans really isn't the genius he assumed he was throughout the late 1990s.

If *Boys and Girls* was the year's worst programme, what was the best? It's a toss-up between reliable, ongoing imports such as *The Sopranos*, *Six Feet Under*, *CSI*, etc., and the newcomers: *State of Play*, *Buried*, *Curb Your Enthusiasm* and *Little Britain*. The programme that kept me most firmly glued to the screen was *24*, although on the evidence of the few episodes I've seen, the third series (airing here next year) is a crashing disappointment. And thank God for that, because I was starting to turn into one of those frightening 'series disciples' – the sort of person who walks around *Buffy* conventions with a cape and a hard-on, taking it all far too seriously.

So that's 2003 over, then. Coming next year: 'Shock and Awe II: The Shockening', on Sky's all-new 3D news channel. Probably.

He Who Safeguards Who [27 December]

Knock, knock. Who's there? Yes, he is. He's there on your screens this week in *The Story of Doctor Who* (BBC1), a blob of festive nostalgia serving twin purposes: to celebrate the fortieth anniversary of the Doctor's first outing, and to whet viewers' appetites for the forthcoming remake.

Thankfully, this is the first retrospective clip show in years that doesn't consist of the most obvious archive footage interspersed with Paul Ross and company firing crap out of their mouths. Instead, it takes the daring step of actually interviewing the people involved, from the toppermost star to the bummermost Dalek-operator. As a result, you might actually learn new things about the Doctor, as opposed to being told how Kate Thornton used to watch from behind the sofa while Vernon Kay hums the theme tune over and over again until you feel like machine-gunning everyone in the world to death.

For instance, we learn that many of the monsters were played by PC Tony Stamp from *The Bill* (aka actor Graham Cole), who admits that he got so into it he used to pull scary faces from inside the costume. We also learn that Jon Pertwee was so tickled by the line 'I reversed the polarity of the neutron flow' in one script, the writers subsequently included it at every opportunity (henceforth, whenever Dr Pertwee had to fix anything, he claimed to be 'reversing the polarity of the neutron flow' (a handy phrase I once heard a plumber use shortly before charging me £300). We learn about the preposterous 'Whomobile' – a risible 'flying car' complete with British licence plate (introduced at Pertwee's suggestion) and the most terrifying monster in the show's history (a toy troll that silently strangled people).

In fact, just about the only thing we *don't* learn about is the God-awful 1996 TV movie in which the Doctor, played by Paul McGann, was shown racing through the streets of LA on a motorbike and snogging his assistant. That seems to have been airbrushed from history completely, and quite right too – although it's a shame we can't go back and pretend Peter Davison, Colin Baker, and Sylvester

McCoy never happened either (because the one thing Doctor Who should never be is a fey wuss). Which brings us to the burning question of who's Who next. Whoever's in charge – he who safe-guards Who – must choose an actor who can do Who justice.

They've already made one great decision by bringing in Russell T. Davies to write the scripts; here's hoping they don't louse it all up by hiring Alan Davies to play the Doctor (as has been rumoured and, given the brainless casting on display in most mainstream BBC dramas, not entirely unlikely). The sight of that curly-haired, mumbling, joy-strangler shuffling his way around the galaxy would cause an epidemic of outraged vomiting among all but the most mentally stunted viewers. Result: a ratings malfunction, which no amount of polarity-reversing could save. They might as well cast Sylvester McCoy again and have done with it.

In fact, I can only think of seven people who'd be worse than Alan Davies. And they are: Ross Kemp, Paul McCartney, Jamie Oliver, Neil Morrissey, Julian Lloyd Webber, Paul Simon and Peter Sutcliffe.

The bookie's second favourite is Richard E. Grant, and they could do far worse than him: he's suitably British, he's tall, unhinged-looking and Americans would recognise him. He's also played the Doctor a couple of times on the radio. Yes, he'd be better. Basically, what I'm saying is: *anyone but Alan Davies*. Or Ralf Little. Or Vernon Kay. Or anyone from *EastEnders*, *Holby City* or *Merseybeat* (unless you're also casting Leslie Ash as a Sea Devil). And no comedians either, apart from Jerry Sadowitz. Oh, and if you're looking for someone to play Davros, would it be cruel and childish to suggest Glenda Jackson? Ah. Right. Thought so. Sorry.

PART FIVE 2004

In which Peter André achieves erection, Friends cease to be there for you, and television get s a village idiot of its very own.

'Everyone drove drunk back then' [17 January]

Booze used to be the Brit's greatest ally. Take Churchill: he practically sweated whisky. A taxi driver once described 1950s London to me in terms of everyone being permanently sodden – 'everyone drove drunk back then – if you had a crash in the middle of the afternoon, chances were the bloke you ran into was drunk, the copper who nicked you was drunk, the witnesses, the ambulance driver, the doctor that patched you up – all of 'em drunk' – and it all sounded rather jolly. In reality the capital's pavements probably just stank even more of urine and sick then than they do now.

But our relationship with alcohol has cooled over the years. Alcohol isn't our friend any more, which is why any soap featuring a scene in which anyone so much as sniffs the cork from a wine bottle has to run a liver cirrhosis helpline number in the end credits. It's also why we have programmes like *Drunk and Dangerous* (BBC1), a tut-tutting look at the havoc wrought by the nation's glugging habits, and why booze ads have started urging you to 'drink responsibly' (thereby annihilating the whole point of drinking in the first place).

The social stabilisers are firmly on, in other words – which is why it's refreshing to run into shows like *Shameless* (C4) and *Toughest Pubs in Britain* (Sky One), both of which openly celebrate the joys of drinking, swearing, spitting and getting your head kicked in. One's fact, the other's fiction, and each is as cartoon-like as the other.

Shameless revolves around the Gallagher family, a bunch of hand-to-mouth Mancunians living on the sort of housing estate that slowly knocks itself down from within, thereby saving the council the bother of sending in bulldozers in a few years' time. They're teenage scallywags with obligatory hearts of gold, tumbling around their oblivious, boozy dad Frank (played by David Threlfall as a clownish, Ghost-of-Christmas-Future version of Liam Gallagher). Each night, Frank ends up sparked out on the living-room floor, languidly vomiting his way through an alcohol-induced coma. It's hard not to admire the man.

Reading some of the pre-transmission hype for *Shameless* you could be forgiven for expecting the finest drama serial ever made. This happened for two reasons: 1) it's from Paul Abbott, who wrote *State of Play*, most journalists' favourite show of 2003, and 2) it's jam-packed with earthy, poverty-stricken northerners who swear a lot, with funny accents and everything, and there's nothing us professional southern sissies love more than that.

None of which is to say *Shameless* isn't really, really good – because it is – but if you approach it expecting something akin to a council estate version of *Teachers*, as opposed to a work of life-altering resonance, you've less chance of walking away disappointed.

You've less chance of walking away *at all* if you venture into one of the *Toughest Pubs in Britain* (Sky One), a cheerful pop-doc hailing a selection of downright terrifying establishments which put the 'hole' into 'watering hole'.

Cue uplifting stories of East End hard men crapping in pint glasses, and a man walking into a Sheffield pub wielding a machete because he'd misplaced his hat there the previous night. Windowless scum-pits, sawdust-and-blood-spattered guzzle houses . . . you name it, it's here, discussed with a disarming frankness: one landlord describes his clientele as 'losers . . . you know – going-nowhere people'.

The highlight has to be the Wyndham Arms in Merthyr, which bristles with toothless, white-haired Welsh psychopaths, every single one of whom would fight you to the death, if only on the grounds that they're so near death anyway it makes little difference to them.

The star of the Wyndham Arms is the decrepit Bob (looks-wise, imagine Bill Oddie getting his teeth kicked out in a thunderstorm), a man whose personal mantra is 'Fuck everybody else'. Bob once set his own hair on fire in order to intimidate a pair of French tourists who walked into the pub by mistake – proof that old-fashioned knockabout comedy isn't dead, even if Bob himself isn't far off.

But that's booze for you. Cheers!

I Love Powderkeg Britain   [24 January]

Is it just me, or are the 1990s turning into the 1980s, and the 1980s into the 1970s? Tonight on Channel 4 there's a superb documentary called *Strike: When Britain Went to War* (C4), and it's full of clips from 1984 that appear to have been shot in 1974 – a wash of dull colours, fag smoke, manky teeth and grey skies.

Quaint period location aside, the other thing that makes *Strike* feel so exotic is the startling level of rage it contains. The footage from Orgreave, where flying pickets and policemen clashed in huge numbers, plays like a contemporary bulletin from a civil war in an eastern European state that can't afford basic weaponry, let alone modern clothing: a civil war fought with fists, sticks and plastic shields, but a full-blown war nonetheless, complete with all the savagery and passion that accompanies it.

I'd quite forgotten just how divisive the miners' strike actually was. In fact, to a 13-year-old middle-class southerner, the biggest news story of 1984 was the release of 'Jet Set Willy' on the ZX Spectrum. It's quite shocking to watch crowds of miners and policemen going at it like the opposing forces in *Return of the King*, and contemplate just how oblivious I was at the time. Thankfully today I can combine my need for video-game escapism with a basic grounding in current affairs simply by playing 'Osama bin Laden's Top-Up-Fee Snowboarding' on the Xbox. Now that's progress. Anyway, back to 1984 – and specifically, the neat way Margaret Thatcher handed a gift to populist historical documentary-makers everywhere by compelling the police force to dress and behave like a gang of futuristic oppressors in a neo-fascist state, in the very same year that loads of adverts, TV shows and films were playing riffs on Orwell's *1984*. She even had the decency to personally survive a bomb blast, thereby appearing indestructible – just like *The Terminator* (also released in 1984). As such, although they don't actually use any clips of *The Terminator* for Thatcher-intercutting purposes (the cowards), this is one of the most visually arresting way-back-when nostalgia shows you could wish for. Admittedly, the opening sequence, in which talking-head interviews are juxtaposed with clips of Torvill and Dean, might initially panic you into thinking you've stumbled into the seventeenth repeat of *I Love 1984* (although 'I Love Powderkeg Britain' would be a more fitting title), but stick with it, since the meat of the programme consists of fascinating anecdotes from active participants, the best of which – and given the nature of civil war, the most paradoxical – concern groups of strangers brought together by the strike (an unlikely alliance between Welsh miners and Sikh community leaders being a case in point).

Today, most pits are closed, of course. Shame. If we held the miners' strike now, it'd be far slicker. It's easier to organise mass demonstrations now that everyone's got a mobile – and you can simply text the word 'SCAB' to passing strike-breakers, instead of shouting it at them. If only they'd held off until the technology was available.

Speaking of things that should be closed down, avoid *Luvvies: The Awards the Stars Don't Want to Win* (ITV1), the 'wacky awards' show with hilarious categories like Worst Dressed Star, which last year tried to make Les Dennis look like a bad sport for refusing a Loser of the Year prize for having a failed marriage. In other words, it was indefensibly bad TV, constructed by scum for the entertainment of idiots. As in last year's show, 'some of the winners have taken it on the chin and will be in the studio' (thus disproving the show's title), while 'others have been tracked down and forced to accept their awards'. What, at gunpoint?

Perhaps they'll dish one out to injured Daniel Bedingfield's parents (another Loser of the Year, or perhaps an Avid Merrion Lookalike Award for his ginger mop and neck brace) at his hospital bedside. Or maybe they'll find someone whose partner's just died, and give them a Loneliest Star Award. Either way, hilarious.

'This is a slam-dunk' [31 January]

Say what you like about the misery of human suffering, but it's a barrel of laughs when you're not directly involved.

The proof? *Crisis Command – Could You Run the Country?*

(BBC2), a fun little game show about massive loss of life, in which three civilians are handed (hypothetical) control of the emergency services and the military during a (hypothetical) disaster. I think it's meant to be serious, but naaaah. This is a black-comic master-piece if ever I saw one. If the producers had taken the light-hearted route – called it 'Never Mind the Body Count'and asked Avid Mer-rion to present – it wouldn't have turned out half as funny.

Our host for this hour-long chucklefest is BBC news correspon-dent Gavin Hewitt, who reported on 9/11 and the Bali bombing, and recently made a guest appearance in the Hutton enquiry. Gavin isn't exactly a bundle of laughs – in fact he's incredibly, unbe-lievably serious; throughout childhood, all the ice-cream vans in his home town played the theme from *Panorama*. Physically, he looks a bit like a New Labour version of the Grim Reaper, nicely complementing the show's tone.

Following an opening sequence in which phrases like 'terrorist attack' and 'massive outbreak' float gaily around the screen, Gavin steps from the shadows and immediately starts shouting at us.

'Each day our papers and news bulletins are full of stories of catastrophes that one day could hit Britain,' he booms. 'If only one of them were to occur, the results could be catastrophic.' Call me a doomed pedant, Gav, but isn't that what you'd expect from a catas-trophe? Gav? Gav?

Ah, Gav isn't listening: instead he's welcoming three contestants to his command bunker, one of whom is Simon Woodroffe, founder of Yo Sushi and the sort of man who can use macho-suit phrases like 'This is a slam-dunk' with no trace of irony. With him running the country, disaster seems assured.

And sure enough, it is: within the first two minutes Waterloo sta-tion puts 1,000 commuters out of their misery by suddenly explod-ing, and things only get grimmer from thereon in, as rogue airliners approach the capital, mysterious power cuts hamper res-cue attempts, and thousands of terrified Londoners trapped in the Underground start wondering whether they'll ever get a mobile signal again.

Just to make it all as chillingly convincing as possible, the scenario unfolds via mock news bulletins from the BBC, Sky and ITN – with real newsreaders reading them out and everything! Yes! This is your chance to see Peter Sissons describing a disaster in which you and your loved ones may soon perish!

The three contestants quibble and argue over what to do – with military advisors and spin doctors on hand to offer advice and grim statistics – as things go from bad to worse. Still, it's not all doom and gloom: at one point Simon makes a decision that causes thousands of people to die, and his face is an absolute picture.

Fun, fun, fun – and it should make a change from the compulsory spectacle of *I'm a Celebrity* . . . (ITV1), the reality show you love to hate to love. For all the pre-talk about John Lydon having knifed his own credibility in the throat by agreeing to appear, I can't help thinking it's the best thing he's done in years. I prefer the new Johnny: acting the arse in the jungle, as opposed to sneering condescendingly on chat shows, like Kenneth Williams without the jokes.

Peter André with an erection [7 February]

Peter André with an erection. That'll be my overriding memory from this year's *I'm a Celebrity – Get Me Out of Here* (ITV1) – the Six-pack Midget climbing from Jordan's bed with a visible salute in his pants, right there on the telly. Like all horrifying spectacles, it's now permanently imprinted on my subconscious, and I feel somehow violated. Changed. Not that the preening twonk should be allowed to achieve full arousal in the first place. He might breed. The government should step in; clap his sac between two breeze blocks and end the André lineage here and now. We owe it to future generations. Besides, it'd make a great Bushtucker Trial.

And there are enough Z-grade ding-dongs in the world already. For proof, tune into *I'm a Celebrity Get Me Out of Here: Live* (ITV2): a live stream of outback coverage and much, much less. Viewers are encouraged to share their opinions via text message, and their subsequent witterings are superimposed over the live footage in a seemingly endless spool. As a snapshot of the mental condition of twenty-first-century Britain, the results ain't encouraging. The average texter has the IQ of a small puddle. They can't even spell the contestants' names properly, even when they're printed right there onscreen. 'I LIKE JORDEN SHE IS FIT.' 'KERRY U R SOOO BRAVE!!!' 'BROKKET DONE A GUFF.'

Seriously, who sends this stuff? Reading the endless dribble, it's hard not to picture a nation of hairless, boneless, *Matrix*-style pod-people soaking in Petri dishes, jabbing outsized thumbs at their phone keypads, barking like seals each time their messages done go get on the telly box. Then there are the creepily poignant messages: 'RAZOR 2 WIN!!! ALSO LUCY WILL U MARRY ME? SIMON.' 'PETER IS ACE FROM JULIE. PS SCOTT I MISS U.' Swear to God, it's an unforgiving glimpse into one barren existence after another. This isn't a TV programme, more a coin-operated sounding board for the nation's vegetables. In fact it's easy to forget the celebrities pootling about in the background; without John Lydon, there'd be nothing worth watching.

Away from the jungle now, and the BBC's woes continue, as a new series of *24* starts on Sky One. First Dyke quits: now Jack Bauer's jumped ship. Fortunately for the BBC, on the evidence of the first few episodes it ain't much cop third time round. Such is the pile-up of unlikely developments, it might as well open with an animated sequence in which Kiefer Sutherland literally jumps over a shark to piss in the viewer's face.

For starters, Kim is now working at CTU. Not only is this unlikely (in the last series she was an au pair; now she's a fully qualified computer-security expert?), it's also asking for trouble. Give it two weeks and she'll be helplessly entangled in Ethernet cables while the office goes up in flames. Next, they've given her a love interest: he's called Chase and he chases terrorists for a living. He's also Jack's sidekick. Naturally, Jack doesn't know Chase is dicking his daughter. Wonder if he'll find out? Jack, meanwhile, has problems of his own – and here comes a minor *spoiler* so look away if you're sensitive – he's addicted to heroin.

Yes, heroin. He's become Smack Bauer. It seems he went under-cover and had to impress some drug dealers by going all *Train-spotting*.

And guess what? On the very same day he decides to kick the habit – cold-turkey style – yet another terrorist plot threatens LA. This time it's a bag of cocaine containing a virus that could kill millions . . . within just 24 hours! Fancy! Oh, and President Palmer, last seen dying following a bioterrorist assassination attempt? Total recovery. But guess what. It's re-election time and he's got an important vote to get through today and blah blah blah. *24* was always implausible; now it's just a dumb cartoon. Having a new leading bad guy who looks like Rowland Rivron doesn't help either. Come in Jack Bauer . . . your time is up. Shame.

Watching Tron through a Kaleidoscope [14 February]

What in God's name has happened to the revamped ITV News (ITV1)? Have you seen this mess? The phrase 'graphical overkill' doesn't come close. It's like watching Tron through a kaleidoscope.

Really, you've got to pity Trevor McDonald. A life of tireless dedication to broadcast news, and what's he got to show for it? A nightly gig barking tabloid-style headlines from within Stakker's 1988 'Humanoid' video. Because surely this daft relaunch is aimed at thirty-something ex-ravers with a soft spot for dated cyberdelia . . . and almost no one else. Get Altern 8 to remix the theme tune, hand Sir Trevor a pair of Orbital-style torchlight specs and bingo: the illusion's complete.

Perhaps I'm wrong, but there's something odd going on here. Witness the way Trevor sometimes swivels round to introduce a previously unseen sports reporter standing on a far-off gangway, swatting graphics around like she's Tom Cruise in *Minority Report*. Trev turns back to camera for a second and poof! The lady vanishes. Why do the background graphics seem to speed up throughout the second half of the programme? Why are the shorter stories interspersed with computer-generated stings showing a glass planet exploding? Why are there no doors and windows for Trevor to leave through? Is he really there? Is any of this news actually happening? I can't tell any more.

And what's with the mysterious runic symbol covering the floor of the set? Go on, have a good look at it this Monday . . . Is it some kind of sign, like a crop circle? Or maybe an ancient Egyptian ankh? Or perhaps it's a first taste of the emblem we'll all have tattooed on our foreheads when the new world order finally seizes control? Only time will tell – but don't be surprised if this time next year a policeman turns up at your front door sporting the symbol on his uniform, shortly before ushering you and your neighbours into a fleet of silent, windowless vans.

On Wednesdays, *Director's Commentary*, a comedy series often described as 'original' and 'hilarious', usually follows the news, which is annoying for two reasons. Firstly, a videotape containing precisely the same idea, but performed by Adam Buxton, was boot-legged and circulated over a year ago. Secondly, while Buxton's tape focused on a more deserving (and, at the time, contemporary) tar-get – The Priory, starring Jamie Theakston and Zoë Ball – *Director's Commentary* consists largely of a torrent of screen-kickingly pre-dictable dribble spoiling footage of antiquated programmes no one remembers.

The solitary joke seems to be 'Ha ha – listen to this man taking these shit old shows seriously', but since we can't judge the pro-grammes in question on their own merit (hardly any dialogue is audible), and since the majority of ITV's present output is easily 20,000 times worse than any number of cheap 1970s drama serials, the whole thing is redundant. It's a sad state of affairs when one-joke series like this and *Monkey Dust* get hailed as 'comic genius' simply on account of feeling vaguely 'new' (as opposed to, y'know, 'funny').

Still, don't despair. A genuinely interesting comedy series starts this very week: Vic and Bob in *Catterick* (BBC3), the new comedy drama from Reeves and Mortimer – a sort of manic cross between 24 and Christ knows what. After a slightly shaky start in which it seems in danger of turning into *League of Gentlemen* meets *Little Britain* (it shares cast members with both), *Catterick* settles into an agreeably malformed groove, and contains some of the funniest lines I've heard in ages. Being more 'daft' than 'dark' (good news for anyone who enjoys laughing at jokes), containing admirably stupid performances and hilariously baffling visual asides, *Catterick* is the most promising new series so far this year. And it's less surreal than the ITV news. Fancy.

'You think you're hard? You ain't hard' [21 February]

A group of tattooed thugs are kicking and punching their way through a series of panelled doors while Steve McFadden commentates on the action in a voice so gruff it makes your ears itch: 'Michael, the ex-Para, is storming into first place. His legs are going like hydraulic battering rams, turning the doors into matchsticks.'

Yes! It can only be *Britain's Hardest* (Sky One), a modern, sociopathic take on *It's a Knockout* that has to be seen – and seen at least twice – to be believed. The format is simple. Each week, five self-styled 'hard men' take part in a string of bleak and disturbing activities. One man is eliminated after each round; the winner goes on to the semi-finals. At the end of the series, someone gets crowned Britain's Hardest Man – and hopefully tear-gassed, bound and slung in a cell situated at least 10,000 miles away from me.

Everything about *Britain's Hardest* is designed to ooze menace. The ringmaster is Extreme Fighting champion Ian 'The Machine' Freeman, an intimidating Geordie who looks like the kind of man who'd drive a wooden tent spike through your face if you accidentally broke wind in front of his kids. He spends most of the show standing in the centre of a barbed-wire cage situated inside an abandoned warehouse; the contestants (muscle-bound dunces to a man) are led in with sacks over their heads and ordered to sit down and listen to him.

Then there's the events themselves: aside from the aforementioned door-smashing, our frowning brutes have to smash blocks of concrete with sledgehammers, withstand being chained up and dunked headfirst into ice-cold water until they almost drown, and finally fight man-on-man atop an elevated concrete plinth. If I were in charge of the BBC, I'd pinch these rounds and liven up *Call My Bluff*.

Between events, the competing tough nuts are forced to indulge in some painfully artificial WWF-style 'trash talk' for the cameras. Since most of them can barely string a vowel together, let alone a sentence, this is the funniest part of the show, as they face each other off with soaringly imaginative exchanges like this:

THUG #1: You think you're hard? You ain't hard.

THUG #2: I'm harder than you. You ain't hard at all.

THUG #1: You're dreaming, mate. I'm the hardest.

THUG #2: No, you're dreaming. And having a laugh. I am hard and you are soft (etc., etc.).

Steve McFadden's links, growled from a patch of urban waste ground, provide further hoots. He doesn't look hard, just unhealthy, rasping and wheezing like some lardy, red-faced flabbo who's just carried a beer keg up the stairs and urgently needs a sit-down before his arteries rupture. Apocalyptic though it is, *Britain's Hardest* doesn't spark quite the same Oh-my-God-these-really-are-the-end-times thrill as *Back to Reality* (C5), TV's latest experiment in auto-cannibalisation, and perhaps the most queasily unreal reality programme yet. I think it's the location that does it: a full-scale house, complete with garden, constructed inside a cavernous TV studio. As the inmates sit yapping round the 'outdoor' picnic table, their voices reverberate off the studio walls, leaving the whole thing feeling like it's happening 'backstage' somehow. It's oddly watchable, but only in the way that watching a chute-less skydiver taking photographs of his own backside as he plunged to his death would be watchable. Because that's what this is: the latest example of TV's continued descent into babbling, solipsistic oblivion.

Back to Reality represents nothing less than a gossamer-thin barrier separating the real everyday world from a swirling dimension of as-yet-unfathomable sewage and nonsense. We don't know what we're messing with here, but it sure ain't natural.

Just like *There's Something About Miriam* (Sky One), the dating show with a twist, which also starts this week. Ha ha ha! They kissed a chick with a dick! Ha ha ha! Ha ha! Ha! Genius! Ha! Ha! HA HA HA! Urgent request to God: please end world five seconds prior to broadcast.

Thank you. Over and out.

I've Made a Right Wilkes of This   [6 March]

Who – or what – is new dating horror *Love on a Saturday Night* (ITV1) aimed at? OK, so the average ITV viewer has a caper-sized IQ – but seriously, can anyone sit through rubbish of this magnitude without feeling sickened and cheap? Play the tape to half a rat's brain floating in a saucer full of brine and it would feel it was being talked down to.

I'm a bitter, alienated misanthrope who can't sit on public transport without wanting to machine-gun everyone in sight – but clearly I've got nothing on the ITV network, because to broadcast this nationwide you'd have to seriously despise mankind.

So what's wrong with it?

Problem 1: It's a mess. It doesn't know what it is. It's like twenty-eight different also-ran dating shows mixed together and spat in the viewer's face. One interminable segment after another, spilling onto your carpet like a tossed deck of cards. And every single one of those cards has the word 'DURRR' printed on it in squat black print, because the manufacturers hate you for being so stupid.

Problem 2: Those masks. Part of the show revolves around a member of the public picking a potential date from three wannabe suitors, each of whom has their face obscured by a brightly coloured mask. The effect is eerie, with contestants left looking like balaclava-clad rapists (men) or recovering burns victims (women). Or Mexican wrestlers. Or gimps. And there's something a bit *Eyes Wide Shut* about the whole thing. They should rename this section 'Vague Sado-Masochistic Undertones on a Saturday Night'.

Problem 3: Davina McCall. Why can't this nasal, squawking witch of Eastwick just go away and leave us alone? Ever peered into her eyes? Go on, tune in tonight and take a big fat look. See them? Those onyx little beads in the middle of her head? They're dark and cloudy and dead. Like a shark's. And you know what that means? It means she knows it's a terrible show. She's lost in this wasteland and she can't escape. Well listen here, McCall, we'll forgive you eventually. But get off while the going is good – jump ship! JUMP OFF THE SINKING SHIP, DAVINA! Then take a break of, oooh, eight years or so. And then – and only then – will we consider allowing you back on our screens.

Problem 4: Jonathan Wilkes. Fresh from his triumph on *You've Been Framed* (where he effortlessly achieved the impossible by being twice as grating as Lisa Riley), Mr J. Wilkes Esq. returns to our screens again, like a turd you can't flush away. He's the Cheggers to Davina's Noel, out in the field with live reports and pointless grinning.

Last week, a member of the public said 'fuck' as Wilkes pounced (thereby turning the show into 'Fuck on a Saturday Night') so there'll probably be a delay in place tonight. Fuck's quite a rude word, but if he encountered me live on air I'd turn the air so blue he'd have to swim home. Besides, as far as I'm concerned, the word 'Wilkes' is a swear word in its own right. I've started using it in everyday parlance, as in: 'Jesus, I've made a right Wilkes of this,' or, 'Ergh! It stinks of Wilkes in here!' Try it out. Pass it on.

Problem 5: It's ten years long. OK, so actually it's just an hour, but somehow *Love on a Saturday Night* feels time-stretched way beyond that; it actually redefines all previous notions of time, which flies when you're having fun and drags when you're not, but actually stops and goes into reverse whenever Davina or Wilkes are onscreen. Watching this programme from beginning to end is like working all day in a job you can't stand.

Problem 6: It's beneath us all. And that's its biggest flaw. This isn't light entertainment. It's an insult, aimed at a notional plebeian mass that largely exists in the low-wattage brains of the show's creators.

Love on a Saturday Night? More like 'Contempt on a Sickening Scale'.

Young People are Idiots   [20 March]

This week, BBC2 shows us what might happen *If . . . The Generations Fall Out*: a bleak and frankly implausible vision of the year 2024 in which the nation's youth rise up to terrorise the pampered, ageing generation by, er, vandalising their cars and smashing a few things up. Trouble is, the generations always fall out. They've been doing so for years. And it happens for a simple reason: adults are pompous and young people are idiots. We deserve each other.

Still, once you're an adult, few things in life are quite as enjoyable as watching someone younger throwing an epic tantrum and being flatly ignored, which is why *Brat Camp* (C4) is such good fun. The pitch: take six 'problem teenagers', ship them off to a new age 'short sharp shock' punishment/treatment camp in Utah where they're forced to hike for miles in the desert every day and essentially live the life of medieval serfs – then sit back and watch as they sulk, moan, burst into tears and generally throw toys from prams non-stop for months.

The twist: their parents have signed custody of the kids over to the camp, so there really is no escape – no matter how big a tantrum they throw (and these are Olympian tantrummers), the only way home is to break down and conform.

Result: funniest show on Channel 4 so far this year. The 'camp' isn't really a camp at all – it's an unremitting wilderness in which they have to build their own shelters to survive. They're not given so much as a Kendal Mint Cake to liven things up; in fact they don't even have eating utensils, and have to eat breakfast using a stick, like monkeys. The scheme is called RedCliff Ascent, and it's run by a group of Rambo hippies taking inspiration from ancient Native American life. They use names like Stone Bear and Rising Wolf: their regime is a curious blend of new age patience and hard-nosed fascism. Fancy haircuts and body piercings are banned (hard luck for Rachel, who arrived sporting so much metal you could've sharpened her head and made an iron railing of her) and anyone who utters a swear word has to pick up a rock and carry it round for hours: yet if you disobey the rules, instead of being shouted at and forced to do squat-thrusts until your knees bleed, you're subjected to hours of calm insistence that it really would be easier for everyone if you just got on with it. It's a set-up that would drive almost anyone insane. But the kids deserve everything they get. Some (notably Charlie and Dan) show early promise, but most are in dire need of a good, hard breaking, particularly James and

Fran. James, the poshest in the camp and therefore the most instantly punchable, is already a towering monument to sour Little Lord Fauntleroy prickery – an arrogant, belligerent little turd who not only thinks the world revolves around him, but that the way it revolves just isn't good enough. He's clearly destined to grow up into a steel-hearted Chelsea estate agent unless RedCliff Ascent can knock some soul into him. Fran, meanwhile, is the ultimate example of a spoilt only child, displaying hitherto-unimaginable levels of self-pity – shrieking in the world's face one minute, blubbering that no one likes her the next. Her entire vocabulary consists of whining sounds and petulant insults, and if the Utah desert doesn't sort her out, I'd recommend tying her to a gigantic arse-kicking machine for the next 200 years.

Halfway into the series, all of them are already showing signs of positive change, and I wish them well in their transformation. Furthermore, I can't help thinking we could do with a RedCliff Ascent of our own in Britain, particularly if we want to avoid the nightmare vision of the future unveiled by BBC2's *If*. Ideally, it would accept children as young as four and force them to walk 200 miles a day in the rain until they shut up and realise it's never a good idea to run around pub gardens shrieking, dribbling and irritating people like me. Because so help me God I will hit them.

'It just isn't fair' [27 March]

Fran hasn't improved much, then. And I suspect that for fellow followers of *Brat Camp* (C4) this is good news, because the inherent flaw in the programme is that as the kids' behaviour improves, so the entertainment value of their antics diminishes. The situation was becoming so dire even Charlie, the breeze-block-headed thug who mere weeks ago seemed hell-bent on systematically punching the entire population of the world in the face, found himself penalised for being too helpful.

So praise be for Fran and her incessant, self-centred whingeing. Never have I seen anyone so tirelessly dedicated to making their own life difficult and unpleasant. To label Fran 'her own worst enemy' would be an almighty understatement. She's her own arch-nemesis. The commandant in her own death camp. Seeing her in action is like watching someone pissing on their own cornflakes, then bursting into tears because they taste funny.

For God's sake Channel 4, give her her own show once *Brat Camp* finishes. Put her on the news. She'd be the greatest war reporter in history: 'I'm here in Kabul – someone's just been shot, and OW, they've landed on my foot and IT JUST ISN'T FAIR.'

Fran's lack of progress seems hopelessly magnified because all the other brats have undergone seismic personality changes since arriving in the Utah wilderness. Take Dan, who's blossomed from a brooding, nihilistic rain cloud of skunk-infused misery into some-one who actually smiles now and then. OK, so he still looks like Mick Jones circa *Big Audio Dynamite*, but RedCliff Ascent can't cure everything.

Then there's Tom, aka Mike Skinner from the Streets, who spent his first few weeks pretending to be mad before realising he wasn't fooling anyone. Now he's a transformed man, funny and likeable, as is the aforementioned Charlie.

This week marks the final instalment of *Brat Camp*: here's hop-ing the now-inevitable 'catch-up' Christmas special finds Fran fully cured of her self-flagellating mindset. If she can channel that ener-gy into something useful, she could be the next female prime min-ister. Or she could just sit around crying in the desert. Time will tell.

Speaking of female prime ministers, this week's edition of the increasingly ludicrous *If . . .* (BBC2) tackles the thorny problem of what might happen if women ruled the world. Well, nearly: actual-ly, in this nightmare vision of the year 2020, men still rule parlia-ment but the chicks have everything else sewn up. The majority of businesses are owned and run by women, the American President is a bitch, and Walkers have announced a new range of oestrogen-flavoured crisps.

Men are increasingly redundant – not just in the workplace, but the bedroom too, since scientific advances have rendered our testi-cles superfluous to requirement (so you might as well slam them in a car door for a laugh – go on, it'll be funny). Most terrifying of all, Ronnie Barker and Ronnie Corbett are forced to wear dresses and escape the attention of Diana Dors' sexy leather-clad death squad. Yes: this is just like The Worm That Turned, but with bigger, unintentional laughs.

We men must fight back now before this nightmare comes to pass, so thank God shows like *Zero to Hero* (C4) are here to show us how to make sense of masculinity in the twenty-first century. Essentially *Scrapheap Challenge* meets *Batman*, it's a show in which 'comic-book fans' construct ridiculous gadgets against the clock in order to complete a 'superheroic' task. This week they have to scale an eight-metre wall of metal. Contestant one decides to use magnets, while number two knocks up a wall-clinging suction device from a pair of old vacuum cleaners.

Throughout their ascent, both are forced to wear humiliating 'superhero' costumes while a masked woman in a pink leotard dangles from a wire firing silver balls at them. *X-Men* it ain't. But brothers, at least it's a start.

'Come drink from my brimming tankard of despair' [3 April]

'I saw six men kicking and punching the mother-in-law. My neighbour said, "Are you going to help?" I said, "No, six should be enough."'

'I went to my doctor and asked for something for persistent wind. He gave me a kite.'

'Come drink from my brimming tankard of despair.'

Three quotes from beloved entertainer Les Dawson there. And in case you're looking for the joke in the last one: forget it. It's taken from *Les Dawson's Lost Diaries* (C4), a surprisingly moving portrait of a fantastic comedian and Britain's finest bad pianist. Raised in a Manchester slum, he initially tried his hand at boxing, despite being a frustrated author at heart: he later visited Paris and tried to write a novel, before returning home to embark on his comedy career in grim northern working men's clubs (which, according to programmes like this, were all subterranean ogres' caverns with real ale dripping from the stalactites, populated by ruthless, grunting, brown-toothed bigots). Instead of being 'toughened' by these no-nonsense audiences, Dawson went down like a lead balloon night after night, never tasting success until he appeared on TV's glitzy *Opportunity Knocks*, from which point on his career skyrocketed, while gnawing self-doubt festered in the background.

Still, forget 'tears of a clown': Dawson was a professional miserablist, and it was this grim, permanently disappointed persona that made him so popular. That and the face. He had an amazing face, like Shrek opening a court summons; a toad with a stomach ulcer; a semi-inflated warthog on 60 Rothmans a day.

This all makes for a diverting programme, my main bone of contention being the presence of Air's latest album on the soundtrack. It's only been out a few months and already it's becoming a cliché – if I hear 'Alone in Kyoto' accompanying one more montage sequence I'll puke. This is supposed to be a TV show, not an advertising creative's dinner party. Isn't there an EU Air limit that we can apply?

Speaking of limits, *If . . . We Don't Stop Eating* (BBC2) this week examines what might happen if, well, if we don't stop eating. Drawing on painstaking research, predictive theory and expert opinion, the programme soon uncovers the startling truth: we'll get fat. By 2020, it seems, the average backside will be the size of a cottage, the inner cities will consist of 'fat ghettoes', and the obese will be forced to sit inside gleaming white pods by research scientists working on special pie-thwarting technology. Imagine *Gattaca* starring Giant Haystacks and you're halfway there.

But hang on – according to last week's show, by 2020 women will be in charge, so it's all their fault. Oh, and according to the editions before that, this'll be taking place during an inter-generational war, while a black prime minister oversees the carnage. Except he can't, because we've run out of electricity and the lights have gone out. That's the problem with following the extrapolation highway: it leads directly to Nonsense Avenue. *If . . .* has provided reasonable entertainment and a fair few unintentional laughs, but perhaps instead of trying to scare us they should've examined even more arbitrary hypothetical scenarios – such as 'If . . . They Don't Ban Ringtones', or 'If . . . It Starts Raining Hammers', or 'If . . . Dogs Could Play the Guitar', or 'If . . . We All Suddenly Turned into Hairless Egg-Like Blobs and Made a Sort of Humming Sound Whenever We Went to the Toilet'.

After all, given the current state of the world, with the news closely resembling a terrifying hi-tech 're-imagining' of the Old Testament, it's hard to get that worked up over a 'nightmare scenario' in which everyone looks a bit Johnny Vegas thanks to the doughnut industry. Anyway, by 2020 you'll probably be able to lose weight by simply e-mailing all your excess fat to an undernourished Cambodian baby. That's what I'm banking on anyway.

Now shut up and pass the lardy cake.

Sliced, Mashed, Carved and Sewn   [10 April]

It's pretty-boy week on Channel 4, what with *The Truth About Take That* and *Battle of the Boy Bands*, so let's celebrate with a friend-of-a-friend story someone once told me, about a bloke who worked on CD:UK who complained the worst thing about it was the smell.

Once the lights go on, a TV studio becomes a hot, dank cavern, so you can imagine how bad it gets when you're also dealing with an audience of several hundred pubescent girls getting physically aroused each time Charlie from Busted raises one of his massive eyebrows. Sweat pours down the walls and the air's so thick with musk if you jumped in the air it'd take you half an hour to sink back down to the floor. What, exactly, are they getting so worked up about? Not the music, but the faces, the pretty boy-band faces – bland, non-threatening, impish little fizzogs, grinning and pouting and oohhing and aahhing their way through one safety-scissor melody after another. And as I accelerate into my 30s, the boy-band faces grow more youthful with each passing month. Take McFly. To my weary eyes, they look like a troupe of cub scouts trying for their Pop Proficiency badge. They should be advertising Wall's Balls, not standing astride the Top 40. And the audiences are even younger. The other week T4 showed a Blue concert, and I swear the front row consisted entirely of squealing foetuses.

These aren't musicians. They're not even pop stars. Let's be honest. Let's call them what they are: children's entertainers. In fact, let's tattoo that phrase on their foreheads. And if they protest, let's ship them off to Balamory and burn them to death inside a gigantic wicker Fimble.

Naturally, I'm just jealous because they're pretty and I'm not. In fact, look up the word 'pretty' in the dictionary, and you'll find a picture of my face – listed under 'antonyms'. But at least I'm not as desperate as Mike and Matt Schlepp (I swear that's their real surname), twin subjects of MTV's new plastic-surgery horror show *I Want a Famous Face* (MTV).

At the start of the show, Mike and Matt are ugly. Very ugly. Greasy hair, beak-like noses, and dense constellations of pus peppering their faces. Squeeze their cheeks you'd get enough lemon curd to fill a bathtub. Naturally, the local girls shun them, but Mike and Matt have a plan: to undergo extensive plastic surgery that will leave them both looking like Brad Pitt. Holding up a pair of DVD covers, Mike explains he's going for the *Meet Joe Black* look, while Matt favours *Legends of the Fall*. And then they're off, under the knife: having their faces sawn open, sliced, mashed, carved and sewn.

In case the gruesome surgical footage isn't enough to put impressionable viewers off, while Mike and Matt recover, the programme finds time for a sob story aside. A young man, aspiring to become an actor after seeing *I Know What You Did Last Summer*, who underwent surgery and ended up with a crooked nose that makes a squishing sound whenever he pinches it. 'I think it's full of blood or something,' he moans.

Then it's back to Mike and Matt, and some hilarious footage of them sitting around in bandages, clutching bags of frozen peas to their swollen faces and wondering aloud whether they look like Brad Pitt yet. When the bandages finally come off, we see the truth: no, they don't. They look like slightly blander versions of themselves. The local bimbos now embrace them: good news for

Mike and Matt, bad news for anyone who respects basic human values.

It's great that Mike and Matt can afford $10,000 worth of surgery each in order to gain the respect of their peers, but I do wish they'd simply carried out a Columbine-style massacre instead. It would've been cheaper. And funnier. And somehow less depressing.

Unhinged, Cackling Carnival Clowns [17 April]

Saturday . . . Saturday . . . Saturday is *Tiswas* day. And in most people's heads, it always will be. The gleefully anarchic weekend kid's show lobbed its last custard pie way back in 1982, yet despite the number of paunchy media-industry blokes banging on endlessly about how fantastic *Tiswas* ('Today is Saturday, Watch and Smile') used to be, nothing's surpassed it in the twenty-two years since the last edition.

Until now. *Dick and Dom in da Bungalow*, which has just finished its run on BBC1, has single-handedly atoned for the BBC's unbroken quarter-century run of turgid, anaemic Saturday-morning fare, which started with *Swap Shop* and continued with dull children's tea parties like *Saturday Superstore*, *Going Live*, and the desperately-titled *The Saturday Show* (which sadly returns today, replacing *Dick and Dom* until September). So what's so good about *Da Bungalow*? It's simple really: Dick and Dom spend most of their screen time sloshing gloop around, smashing things, cracking toilet gags and pulling goonish faces – and they do it with total conviction and obvious relish. There's also – and this is important – there's also a vague sense of menace surrounding it: a faint whiff of unhinged, cackling carnival clowns that makes the show feel genuinely subversive, genuinely alive.

The nation's children should be forced to watch this show, preferably with their heads clamped in position so they can't turn away. Because what's the alternative? Answer: crap like *Ministry of Mayhem* (ITV1), ITV's embarrassing answer to *Dick and Dom*. The title is fitting, because this feels like government-approved 'mayhem': anarchy with the jagged corners smoothed away. It's a show that says, 'Hey kids! Let's have a wild, chaotic time! Within a set of closely monitored parameters, obviously!' The hosts try hard, but there's no disguising the black glint of death in their eyes. It's half-hearted fun conducted at gunpoint. The most telling difference between this and *Da Bungalow* is the attitude toward celebrities.

Ministry of Mayhem makes the mistake of thinking every kid on the planet wants to see shiny, hairless presenters shoving their tongues so far up the arses of the boys from Busted they could lick their ribcages clean from the inside (actually, there *is* a sizeable audience, but it's older, gayer, and frankly unlikely to be up so early on a Saturday morning). And of course, this being ITV, there's a commercial break every three seconds, meaning the freewheelin', devil-may-care, let-it-all-hang-out wackiness is regularly interrupted by high-pressure sales pitches designed to turn your child into a grasping, selfish idiot. It's been ages since I last saw the Saturday morning kiddie ads, so naturally the products on offer horrify me. It's all 'Little Baby Bluetooth' and 'My First GM StrangleBot'. Most disturbing of all, Action Man has undergone a radical makeover: back in the 1970s he looked like the kind of man who'd knife you in the throat if you stepped on his toe, now he's a cookie-cutter pretty boy who resembles Keanu Reeves on steroids and rides a gay 'combat surfboard' into action. Christ, what a loser. The choice is clear: if you want your offspring to become cretinous, sycophantic, fashion-obsessed pod people, let them watch *Ministry of Mayhem*. If you want to expose them to something that will make their brains skip around with glee, tune in to *Dick and Dom*.

Except sod it, you can't until they return in September. Ah, well. Until then, fill the kids with sugar and sit them in front of 'Tom Clancy's Splinter Cell' on the Xbox. The graphics are great, it contains precisely no Girls Aloud videos, and best of all it'll teach them how to kill a blameless security guard by lurking in the shadows for half an hour before sneaking up behind him and snapping his neck like a fucking breadstick.

Scoff all you like, but it might come in handy some day.

A Bum-Kissing Contest   [8 May]

All things must pass. Everything that has a beginning has an end. Death comes to us all. The lights are going out all over Europe. The final edition of *Parkinson* (BBC1) goes out tonight and the world wipes a tear from its eye. It's the end of an era. In fact it's more than that. It's the end of an era as viewed from the deck of an epoch crashing bow-first into the iceberg of time. A sign of the times, and a moment to pause for sober reflection. Let's join hands, bow heads, and hold a fortnight's silence to mourn its passing.

Actually no. Let's not. Parkinson was off our screens for sixteen years from 1982 to 1998 and the world never once stopped turning on its axis, so why the forthcoming transition from BBC1 to ITV1 is being discussed as though it holds any significance whatsoever is beyond me. It's a chat show. Who gives a toss? Besides, since its 1998 return, the Parkinson show's been a nauseating load of old celebfellating claptrap anyway. Watching Robbie Williams burping on and pointlessly on about his struggle with the bottle and his own irrepressible brilliance is no compensation for a glaring lack of Muhammad Ali or Rod Hull and Emu.

By and large, present-day Parkinson guests fall into two camps: glassy-eyed Hollywood stars who treat the whole thing like just another junket, and smaller home-grown names so thrilled to be considered 'big' enough to grace the chat icon's line-up they practically grin themselves to death right there onstage.

Then there's 'Parky' himself, who seems to spend half his time revelling in his image as a curmudgeonly professional Yorkshireman unafraid to call a spade a spade, and the other half fawning over his guests like an obsequious peasant granted an audience with a minor royal. When I watch Parkinson, I don't see amiable rapport, fearless questioning, or stunning revelations: I see a bum-kissing contest between an inexplicably revered silver-haired tortoise and an entourage of chummy, twinkle-eyed chancers. The air's so thick with bumptious self-celebration it makes your gut churn.

And the stars aren't that big anyway. Take tonight's line-up: Bruce

Forsyth, Boris Becker and Patrick Kielty. I wouldn't cross the street to watch them piss in a teacup. There's also musical support from two perfect examples of the sort of painfully unchallenging pap-merchants routinely lauded as 'proper music' by idiots: the Corrs and Jamie Cullum.

Cullum deserves special mention, because he's particularly odious – an oily, sickening worm-boy, presumably grown in a Petri dish specifically for appearances on middle-of-the-road chat shows like this. Swear to God, if I have to see this gurning little maggot clicking into faux reverie mode ever again – rising from his seat to jazz-slap the top of his piano wearing a fake-groove expression on his puggish little face – if I have to witness that *one more time*, I'm going to rise up myself and kill absolutely everybody in the world. Starting with him and ending with me. Cullum should be sealed inside a barrel and kicked into the ocean, not hailed as a genius on Saturday-night TV. I hope they spend more time with Patrick Kielty than they do with him, which is saying something, because he's a man who exudes likeability like a rock exudes blood.

So I won't miss Parkinson. In fact for me, the sole note of remorse accompanying his evacuation to ITV is the reason behind it: he's flounced out because the BBC wants to broadcast highlights from the Premiership in his prized 10 o'clock slot. As far as I'm concerned, that's a disaster, since watching football is one of the very few things on earth I enjoy even less than watching Jamie Cullum slap his bloody piano. And, knowing my luck, he'll be hosting it.

Give-Away Buffoonerisms   [15 May]

You should always judge people by their actions, not their words. Obvious, really. You wouldn't believe Peter Kurten, the 'monster of Düsseldorf', who murdered nine Germans in 1929, had your best interests at heart just because he told you he did. Especially if he was sticking a bread knife in your eye at the time.

'Actions, not words' is the mantra of *Body Talk* (C4), an absorbing two-parter in which Dr Peter Collett examines the body language of the rich and famous in a bid to prove what tossers they are. And succeeds. Programme one deals with the language of power, and concentrates on politicians. Collett identifies the characteristic movements (known as 'tells') that Blair, Bush and co. make whenever they're feeling nervous, confident, aggressive, or sexually aroused. Actually, he doesn't cover arousal. Thank Christ.

Take Gordon Brown, who can't sit still when Blair is speaking. Collett observes him at a Labour Party conference, anxiously fidgeting his way through a well-received speech from Blair. On fast motion, he turns into Robert Lindsay in *GBH*.

Blair, meanwhile, has a habit of sliding his hands into his front pockets when he's feeling awkward. He thinks it makes him look relaxed: in reality, it makes him look like an embarrassed shop-window dummy with some sort of bum disorder. Perhaps unsurprisingly, he often affects this stance when he's required to pose alongside psychotic, lying drink-drivers. Called George Bush.

Bush is a body-language goldmine. He often looks more like a frightened boy than a president, albeit a frightened boy with 24-hour access to the most fearsome nuclear arsenal the world has ever seen. Whenever Bush feels scared and out of his depth, he chews the inside of his mouth. Alarmingly, he chews the inside of his mouth pretty much all the time. That's probably how he choked on that pretzel.

There are other examples of Bush's give-away buffoonerisms, including some fascinating games of physical one-upmanship between him and Bill Clinton. Ask the pair of them to walk side by side and it quickly degenerates into a hilarious dick-swinging contest, with each attempting to stride in a more commanding, statesmanlike manner than the other. The berks.

And this is just the stuff that's been caught on camera. I'd love to see Bush's private body language: the faces he pulls while trying to pass a particularly rigid stool for instance, or the delighted reeling jig he doubtless performs each time he bombs another town full of unarmed brown folk. Or when he was choking to death on that pretzel – I'd love to have seen the way his legs shook and popped around as he clawed at his throat, desperately gulping for air. Hoo, boy – if the White House has CCTV footage of that they should release it on DVD, backed with comic piano music and a voice-over track of Iraqi schoolkids laughing at his hateful, shuddering face.

Anyway. It's a good programme and you should watch it. The same applies to *I Am Not an Animal* (BBC2), the new comedymation (someone bread-knife me for inventing that phrase) about a group of recently liberated talking animals coming to terms with the outside world.

If, like me, you spent the first half of last week's episode bewildered by the sheer weirdness of the animation (which looks a bit like a colour supplement hallucinating into your eyes) and the number of characters, fear not. Consider that your learning curve: now it's taken care of, you can get your teeth into the rest, which is funny, clever, demented, and, perhaps most importantly, the only TV show you'll ever see in which a horse has to build himself a makeshift hand out of twigs in order to ring a doorbell. Well, until something called 'Horse Twig Doorbell Challenge' turns up on cable, that is. And according to Nostradamus that isn't due for another fifteen years – a full twelve after Bush finally blows us all up. Get your kicks in while you can.

'I'll be there for you' [22 May]

'I'll be there for you . . .' Not any more you won't. Wave goodbye to your *Friends* (C4) because they're about to vanish for ever. Apart from Joey, who's poised to enter the spin-off dimension, presumably in a show that consists entirely of him crying alone in an empty room.

In case you're a rabid fan who's spent the past fortnight trying to avoid finding out what happens in this final episode, don't worry – I won't blow any 'surprises' here, so relax. Breathe out. Unbutton yourself. Not that much.

Of course, you'd have to have poked your eyes out with a teaspoon to somehow dodge the finale-spoiling screengrabs and photos plastering the tabloids the day after its US broadcast, so you'll be enjoying the show in sound only – but you can't have everything.

(While we're on the subject, the single worst spoiler in history is the front cover to the VHS edition of the original *Planet of the Apes* movie, which is largely taken up by an artist's impression of Charlton Heston slumped disconsolately in front of a half-buried Statue of Liberty. What next? A collector's edition of *Seven* housed inside a full-scale replica of Gwyneth Paltrow's severed head?).

Anyway: *Friends*. Or more specifically, 'The One I Warmed to Against My Will'. When it started a full decade ago, I was virtually pre-programmed to despise it. That clean-cut, anodyne cast. Those newspaper articles about the wonderful haircuts. The whooping audience. That bloody theme tune.

Unfortunately, my steel-clad cynicism was permanently undermined when I accidentally caught an episode and found myself laughing. Afterwards, shuddering, I vowed to avoid it at all costs in case it shattered my cosy misanthropic worldview.

But recently, given its ubiquity in the Channel 4 schedule, I realised I'd become a fan by osmosis. I think it's the writing. No matter how many accusations you hurl at *Friends*, you can't deny it's funny. And engaging. And tightly plotted.

In fact, the way the plotting works is impressively shameless: most episodes open with a pre-credits sequence in which Character A bursts into Central Perk to nakedly deliver some crucial exposition – 'I've got a job interview tomorrow!', 'I just met this really hot guy!', 'I found a magic whistle!' and so on – to be met by a chorus of quickfire gags from Characters B to D that a) make you laugh and b) distract you from the sheer cheek of establishing the storyline in such an unabashed manner. What's not to admire?

Then there's the performances, which are absurdly cartoon-like, yet rarely seem quite irritating enough to make you want to kick the screen in and start machine-gunning the neighbours. Matt LeBlanc, in particular, is responsible for more violent mugging than all the crackheads in New York put together. It's appropriate that he's going on to star in a spin-off called simply *Joey*, because he spends most of his screen time pulling silly faces and going 'durrrrr', like the matinee-idol equivalent of a mid-1980s English schoolboy. They should shoot his new show through a horse collar and enter it into a gurning contest.

Still, Joey's the only cast member who hasn't become a wizened old twig, as evidenced by the title sequence, which cuts jarringly between contemporary snippets of our diet-ravaged chums and the ancient original opening credits in which they cavort in a fountain like bloated Cabbage Patch kids. It seems the NBC canteen serves nothing but soil and tiny pebbles to keep its million-dollar superstars in trim; compare this to *EastEnders*, where every cast member blobs out after three weeks in the Square and, in between takes, there's a guy shovelling battered pies down their necks in a desperate bid to ensure they're too fat to fit the narrow aperture of the Internet wank-cams in their dressing rooms.

What with this and *Frasier* evacuating our living rooms, it's hard to see how our American cousins can ever make us laugh again. Unless they re-elect Bush. But that'd be very hollow laughter indeed.

Fantasy DG [29 May]

So, then: the BBC appoints a new director-general, and once again I've been inexplicably overlooked. Cowards, the lot of 'em. Still, just in case the government goes mad again and decides to scapegoat Mark Thompson out of office, I might as well lay out my wares for the first time in public with a quick game of 'Fantasy DG'. Here, in no particular order, is a list of the changes I'd implement if I were suddenly placed in charge of the Beeb.

1 Remove all trace of football from the schedules
I firmly believe all sport should be tucked away on pay-to-view satellite channels, not smeared across the public-broadcast schedules like brown goo in a dirty protest. OK, this policy is founded on personal prejudice – *I hate sport* and football is the worst offender – but I'm in charge now, so we're getting rid of it. Actually, no – we'll still show it, but in a form that'll deliberately enrage the fans – by superimposing an obtuse East European cartoon over the footage, accompanied by the sound of loud, atonal trumpets. Consider it retribution for the years of tedium and bellowing I've had to

endure from the fans, every single one of whom is a despicable idiot.

2 Revamp *Casualty* and *Holby City*
The storylines are boring, the characters uninspired – so let's distract attention from that by upping the gore quotient 2,000 per cent. Patients aren't allowed in unless they've got an eye hanging out at the very least, and all operations will be carried out with crowbars and chainsaws. Charlie from *Casualty* will be put in charge of a new Anal Trauma wing for obese people with hideous gaping bum wounds, and it'll all go out in surround sound, daily, at teatime.

3 Poach Trisha from ITV and lock her in a windowless room full of clueless council-estate scumbags
And broadcast the results 24 hours a day on a dedicated digital channel. I defy anyone to think of anything more entertaining.

4 Ban *EastEnders* from attempting storylines involving gangsters
Unless said storyline culminates in a gang of twenty hardened cockney thugs thrashing Little Mo to death with broomsticks, I'm simply not interested.

5 Introduce late-night adult versions of tired stalwarts
Examples: 'Adult Countryfile' (rutting in haystacks), 'Nude Antiques Roadshow' (pensioners' unclothed bodies evaluated by experts), and 'Bergerac Hardcore' (repeats of *Bergerac* with brand new, digitally created pornographic interludes in which Charlie Hungerford ravishes the entire population of Jersey).

6 Put a playable version of 'Tetris' on Ceefax
Self-explanatory, that one.

7 Outdo ITV with new, ultra-cruel reality shows
Such as my oft-mentioned 'Heaven Can't Wait', in which people coming round from operations wake up to find actors dressed as angels standing by their bedside, who inform them they've died and gone to heaven, before reuniting them with deceased relatives (actually junior researchers wearing convincing latex masks). Or

perhaps 'Celebrity D-Day', in which the Omaha Beach landing is re-enacted by famous folk, using live ammunition. The list is endless; the only thing holding us back is basic human decency.

8 Televised hangings for licence-fee dodgers
Or stick their heads on poles and dot them about in the background of popular drama serials as a warning to others of their kind. In these difficult times, the BBC needs a DG who rules with an iron fist.

9 Let Paxman actually hit people
Another self-explanatory one, there.

10 Broadcast the four-minute warning on April Fools' Day
Then wait until all the fuss had died down, and questions had been asked in the House, and an angry population had demanded my immediate resignation – and then do it again, because it'd be even funnier the second time round.

So there you have it. Those are my initial suggestions – but why should I have all the fun? E-mail your own DG fantasy lists to me courtesy of the *Guide*, and I'll pick the best and run them in a future column. During a quiet week, naturally.

'Dis Negro's attractive' [5 June]

Yes, it's *Big Brother* time again and, as per tradition, I'm going to spend the remainder of the column slagging off the housemates and trying not to catch my own reflection in the monitor lest I gaze deeply into my own eyes and marvel at the sheer aching pointlessness of the task.

Anyway, here's a handy cut-out-and-lose guide to the twelve inmates – a cast of asylum seekers, bisexuals, transsexuals and left-wing anarchists apparently chosen specifically to infuriate Richard Littlejohn, who probably thinks he's watching a live feed from the Labour Party conference.

First up, Marco, a homosexual ghost-train skeleton so implausibly camp he makes Mr Humphries look like the Terminator.

Marco's a true multi-tasker: he distributes his time equally between squealing, squawking, shrieking, screaming, yelling, yelping and screeching. He's the human equivalent of fingernails down a blackboard, and is therefore the quintessential *Big Brother* resident.

Straight after Marco went in, Ahmed, a homophobic former asylum seeker, followed. The look of fake delight on his face as he first greeted Marco was a joy to behold. At 44, Ahmed simply doesn't fit in with anyone else in the house. Therefore, another quintessential *Big Brother* resident.

Then there's Jason, resident bozo. A former Mr Best Buttocks, South Lanarkshire who moisturises his butt-cheeks to keep them looking happy, Jason is a slight but buffoonish presence, floating round the house getting his bum out every eight seconds. He'd have been great in *The Poseidon Adventure*, where he could've undercut the serious tone every few minutes with some well-timed mooning but, in this context he's just, well, an arse.

Dan is the second gay housemate and, apart from a stupid haircut, seems fairly normal, so we'll bypass him – and dull pretty boy Stuart – and go straight on to Victor, an incredible prick and the worst black male role model since MC Hammer. Victor spouts self-aggrandising bullshit with the single-minded determination of an industrial self-aggrandising bullshit machine. With a straight face, he's claimed that 'My DNA stands for Dis Negro's attractive' and 'When it comes to ladies, right, you can call me "The Plumber" 'cos I like to lay pipe.' He's also bragged loudly about the girth of his penis. 'It's like major girff, man – I can hardly get it in.' Victor's currently the most likely candidate for an onscreen shag, possibly with a piece of furniture.

Next, Kitten, played by Jarvis Cocker, Tracey Thorn and Rick from *The Young Ones*. The kind of hardcore, hard-left lesbian who previously only existed in Littlejohn's imagination, Kitten's the most sensitive of the housemates, yet hamstrung by one fatal flaw: a tendency to drone about politics in an unbroken and largely inarticulate stream, until her voice becomes an omnipresent low-frequency burble, like the sound of a particularly boring corpse damply mumbling itself to sleep in a coffin.

Vanessa and Michelle are this year's glamour girls; the former a South African blonde, the latter a bisexual wannabe Page 3 girl from Newcastle-upon-Tyne. Neither has much to say, but that's all right, since their job is to wear bikinis and bend over a lot. Both will be coming soon to a downblouse/upskirt celebrity screengrab website near you, where thousands of lonely males can masturbate over them at leisure.

Who else? Ah, there's Shell, a posh horsey blonde who gets squiffy and also gets her bum out (this year's dominating theme), and Emma, this year's token thickie, who has the added bonus of sounding like every episode of *Creature Comforts* you've ever seen. And finally, Nadia, the Portuguese transsexual, who at the time of writing hasn't revealed her 'big secret' to the other inmates. I suspect that she's actually Pedro Almodóvar in a shiny fat suit.

So there you have 'em. Nigh on unwatchably hateful to the last. 'S what *Big Brother*'s all about, innit?

Sport Sport Bloody Bloody Sport   [12 June]

All change yet again in the *Big Brother* (C4/E4) house, which is proving tricky to chronicle. I write to a Tuesday morning deadline, which means by the time Saturday morning rolls around half my words are obsolete. This wasn't a problem last year, because nothing actually happened throughout the entire series ('Day 65 in the Big Brother house – Cameron is asleep. Jon is staring at a wall and thinking about quarks'), but *BB5*'s already brought us fights, rooftop protests, nudity, heavy petting and a bit where Marco spewed up on a merry-go-round. What's a guy to do?

The housemates keep shifting character too. Last week I dismissed Jason as a pointless bum-flasher; suddenly he's become so stern and serious he makes Peter Sissons look like Jim Carrey. Thank God for Victor, who continues to be an arsehole, as predicted.

Still, what's making this series so watchable is the 50/50 split between gurgling imbeciles and uptight tossers. With that in mind, and since it's Tuesday morning, let me predict the events for the rest of the week: on Wednesday, dim robo-seductress Michelle bared her breasts, then her bottom, then her breasts again, in exchange for a 10 pence IOU from Victor. On Thursday, Vanessa got upset when stretched-out-gay-idiot-baby Marco done a whoopsie on the carpet. And last night, Emma dribbled chocolate down her front for a full hour while Dan mopped her face clean and tutted a lot.

If, for some mad reason, watching the above for the next eight weeks doesn't appeal, never fear, because throughout this period the TV schedules are full of exciting, exhilarating SPORT! for you to watch whether you want to or not.

Don't worry if you lose the listings and don't know when it's on: helpful TV schedulers routinely make it easy for you to stay abreast of all the latest SPORT! by shifting everything else clean out of the way in order to accommodate it. Yes, for months on end, you too can look on in dismay as an unseen sports fan assumes command of the remote, bullishly forcing you to watch SPORT! instead of, say, the latest episode of a beloved drama serial halfway through its run.

This situation is nothing new of course, but it's gone on far too long, and in the age of digital sister channels and hard-disk recorders, there's simply no need for this madness to continue. I dream of the day a continuity announcer utters the words '. . . and if you want to keep watching the snooker, turn to BBC3 – meanwhile here on BBC2, we'll continue *as fucking scheduled.*'

SPORT! fans may moan that they can't get BBC3, and boo hoo that's not fair – tough, idiots. We non-SPORT! fans are becoming radicalised by years of abuse. Right now, with Euro 2004, you can't avoid football, even if you don't watch the so-called 'matches' themselves – it's omnipresent.

There it is, in the ad break – look, there's Jamie Oliver having a matey kickaround in his garden, followed by fifteen soccer-themed beer commercials, capped off with a multi-million-pound block-buster ad in which overpaid footballing megastars are deified on behalf of shoe companies whose products are sewn together by penniless Korean slaves getting amphetamines injected into their eyeballs every 10 minutes so they don't fall asleep during their 87-hour shift. Hooray for football!

Here's praying England lose, and lose quickly. May the 'beautiful game' be damned. And the same goes for Wimbledon, and cricket, and rugby, and snooker and darts, and any and all future sports not covered in this polemic. Even if someone invents nude moon volleyball, I'm not interested.

In fact, I'd actually rather watch Marco sicking up on the swings *every day for the rest of my life* than sit through yet another minute of SPORT SPORT BLOODY BLOODY SPORT.

In summary, then: bollocks to sport and bollocks to everyone who likes it. For ever and ever. Amen.

Get a Grip   [26 June]

Life would be unbearable if you didn't have your vices. They come in all shapes and sizes – cigarettes, alcohol, chocolate biscuits, going mental with a cricket bat at bus stops – and they all provide a brief respite from the trudging monotony of everyday existence. Is that so bad? Of course not. Bad habits are fun.

Yes, fun. Which is precisely why the world's killjoys are continually circling above your head, harping on at you to stop. Case in point: *You Are What You Eat* (C4), a new 'dietary makeover' show in which a nutrition expert rifles through the shopping basket of a self-confessed blobbo, then tuts and frowns and whines in their face for half an hour.

This week's victim is Michelle, a bloated office-bound manatee who spends most evenings shovelling cake into her face in a desperate bid to make life fun again. Her constant diet of crisps, biscuits and microwaveable hermit slop has turned her into a flatulent human waterbed, but fortunately healthy-eating guru Dr Gillian McKeith is on hand to help her mend her ways with a crash diet of organic brown rice, lentils, steamed carrots, tofu, twigs, bracken, soil and mulch.

Naturally, Michelle finds it hard to stomach at first, partly because anyone who says they actually like brown rice is a lying masochist, but mainly because Dr Gillian McKeith strikes her as a charmless, judgemental, hand-wringing harridan. Disgusting cake-wolfing glutton she may be, but in this respect at least, Michelle is absolutely right.

A quick look at Dr Gillian's official website reveals two interesting things. Firstly that she's incapable of smiling naturally on camera (the rictus grin in her official photo makes her look like she's trying to poo out a pine cone – which, given her diet, she probably is). And secondly that she has her own range of holier-than-thou Dr Gillian health-food snacks, including a 'Living Food Love Bar' which will 'nourish libido energy and feed love organs'. Yes, feed love organs. I'm not sure you're supposed to put it in your mouth.

The love bar's lip-smacking listed ingredients include potency-wood root, sprouted daikon seeds, ho shou wu leaves, wu wei zi berries and catuaba bark. And if that doesn't whet your appetite, perhaps Dr Gillian's accompanying 'message of love' will:

'My primary reason for developing this Love Bar is that it serves as a platform, like a stage, to garner your attention, and then to be able to communicate my message of unconditional love . . . love your partners in life, your neighbours, and especially your enemy. When you can finally love your foe or even the faceless stranger yonder, then and only then will you elevate your physiology and your soul.'

In other words, it's Snickers for arseholes.

Might I suggest a new makeover show called 'Get a Grip', in which I lock Dr Gillian in a windowless room for six weeks and shout at her to see sense? Because there's something inherently hateful about the growing ranks of nannyish smuggos in the world – gym-loving, anti-smoking, free-range solipsists who actually brag about how much water they drink, and shake their heads with pity if you crack open a packet of Monster Munch. So you'll live longer – so what? Look at the company you'll be keeping and weep.

Anyway, infuriatingly enough, after an initial bout of disobedience, Michelle follows Dr Gillian's instructions and emerges two stone lighter and far better-looking. I watched these scenes through a haze of tears, shovelling takeaway pork down my gullet. The day I inevitably join the squat-thrusting, vegetable-steaming replicants draws inexorably closer.

First piece of evidence: I've quit smoking – and voluntarily, unlike the inhabitants of *Big Brother*, whose violent bust-up occurred the day the fags ran out. If Channel 4 wants further fireworks, they should draft in Dr Gillian to cook the housemates' meals each night. There'd be heads on poles within hours, guaranteed.

Unnecessary Ordeals [3 July]

'Sallum walked three paces to where Landau lay sprawled across the sofa. He rammed the pistol into his open mouth, fired, and stood back. Brain tissue was now spattered across the cream fabric. Sallum dipped a finger into the gooey mess and lifted it to his nose. The smell of infidel decadence.'

That's a gripping extract from *Greed*, the best-selling paperback from Chris Ryan – author, *Ultimate Force* co-creator, SAS posterboy and frontman for *Pushed to the Limit: Britain's Toughest Family* (BBC1), the BBC's wholesome new reality show in which everyday families undergo a series of prolonged, gruelling and entirely unnecessary ordeals, partly to prove to themselves what good eggs they are, but mostly because they're idiots.

Yes, idiots. It's week one and they're up the mast of a tall sailing vessel, puking into a violent thunderstorm. Well, durrr. This is the twenty-first century, for Christ's sake. We've got beanbags and DVD players. There's no need to hang around outside in the cold and the rain, having the palms of your hands ripped raw by a length of wet rope. Eighteenth-century sailors used to do that, but they had no choice in the matter, and hated every second. Do it through choice and you're not being life-affirming, you're being an idiot.

Still, it's fun to watch them suffer. For about five minutes. Unfortunately, this programme's 55 minutes longer than that and it's riven with faults. For starters, there are just too many participants: ten whole families, plus Chris 'Infidel Decadence' Ryan and the ship's crew, leaving a grand total of forty-plus plucky dullards bobbing about and looking rather pleased with themselves. For an hour.

Furthermore, this being a BBC production, the families in question are largely middle-class types with a faint whiff of the hockey field about them. Ruddy of cheek, sturdy of build, and stupid of surname: they've all got bloody weird family monikers like the Durkins, the Crebers, or best of all, the Gecks. On paper, the Gecks sound like an exciting new Greenwich Village rock band. In reality, they're in charge of the tombola at your local village fête.

Things liven up a tad towards the end when the ship returns to port, and two mums with vertigo are cruelly forced to abseil from the largest council block in London, but you can't help thinking that Britain's *actual* toughest family wouldn't have time to appear on shows like this – they'd be far too busy earning a crust and dealing with life at the shit end of the wedge. And waking up every day inside the very tower block the mums are abseiling down.

Speaking of tough families, the Krays provide obvious inspiration for *The Long Firm* (BBC2), a new four-part mini-series based on Jake Arnott's crime thriller. As with *House of Cards*, it's a prime example of a televised adaptation substantially improving on its (overrated) source material. Because this is superior, solidly entertaining stuff, which on the evidence of episode one could well go on to become a long-running series in its own right. And yes, it's an East End gangster thriller, but one that somehow doesn't feel like it's treading over-familiar ground – thanks to assured direction, flashes of genuine wit (that's *genuine* wit, as opposed to the Guy Ritchie variety), and an excellent cast (Mark Strong single-handedly makes Harry Starks feel like an enduring televisual icon by the end of the first instalment).

In fact, the only thing wrong with it is that it's on BBC2 and not BBC1. Although come to think of it, at the same time on the same day, BBC1 is providing some formidable competition in the form of an all-new series of *Rail Cops*, the white-knuckle fly-on-the-wall documentary about the British Transport Police, in which, thrillingly, 'Jeff Nelson deals with missing luggage at Birmingham New Street.'

And they say there's a lack of drama on BBC1.

Boo Hoo Hoo, It's a Tragedy for Television   [31 July]

Oh boo hoo hoo, Saturday-night telly ain't what it used to be. Once upon a time every family in the nation would tune in en masse to watch Forsyth and Tarbuck and Edmonds and Smith (Mike): an entire population huddled round its screens like suckling piglets round a sow's tit. Now the Saturday-night schedules are the equivalent of a deserted alleyway full of bin bags and urine, and boo hoo hoo, it's a tragedy for television.

Well, yes, maybe, but it's a good thing for people as a whole. To the best of my knowledge, Saturday-night television has always been gaudy and more than a little bit shit: perhaps the plummeting figures reflect an evolving populace that just can't take it any more. Why should the average 12-year-old sit indoors watching rubbish with Granddad when they could spend the evening outdoors, knocking back alcopops, texting their friends and knifing each other instead?

Besides, you don't need to call in Poirot to solve the mystery of the falling ratings. Just look at what's on. Take *Johnny and Denise: Passport to Paradise* (BBC1), an absolute car-and-plane crash of formats, tinsel, and post-modern irony – a nightmare fusion of *Noel's House Party* and *TFI Friday*.

It opens with Johnny and Denise singing the theme song, which might be a neat idea if it wasn't for Johnny's glaring inability to carry a tune. He might sashay like a Vegas showman, but he sounds like a cow trying to moo the Lord's Prayer.

And it's downhill from there: the rest of the show is an aimless drizzle of apparently unconnected games and routines, interspersed with the duo's grating jabber: Denise has a touch of the call centre about her, while Johnny deals in ceaseless flip irony, over-*emphasising* words at *random*, and inserting camp *dramatic* pauses. Into every. Other *sentence*. It soon becomes infuriating – although it did give me an idea for an interesting televisual experiment in which *Newsnight* assigns Vaughan to report on Slobodan Milosevic's war crimes trial at The Hague, just to see how well his hip tongue-in-cheek facade performs under the conditions.

Over on ITV, Saturday-night telly means blaring crap like *Celebrities Under Pressure* (ITV1), which is now presented by Vernon Kay, TV's village idiot.

Kay is a one-man walking blight-on-our-culture, a dog-haired toby jug, a self-satisfied banality engine, a git, a twit, a twat and an oaf. He dribbles tedious, repeated references to down-home life back in Bolton, presumably to underline what a *Phoenix Nights*-style man of the people he is, although from where I'm sitting he looks and sounds more like an unjustly elevated simpleton than a likeable everyman. He shouldn't be on television – he should be sitting on a country stile wearing a peasant's smock and chewing on a hayseed, some time during the Dark Ages (and preferably at the height of the Black Death).

I'm not a fan.

Still, if you can withstand Kay, you might be able to stomach the programme itself, which is almost as shit as he is. The basic premise: a totally past-it or impossibly obscure 'famous person' must complete a task in order to win prizes for a not-particularly-likeable prole family unit. First, however, they have to live with said family for a week, producing a short video diary in which they wibble on about what a lovely welcome they've received from these simple scummy plebs, and how loveable their shitty, squawking, pointless kids are. If the task was to look down a lens and spit lies, they'd have won already.

Then, immediately following this bumcast, ITV insults the nation still further by broadcasting *Simply the Best* (ITV1), which is *It's a Knockout* without the funny costumes or Stuart Hall: the only two things that made it bearable in the first place.

So then: Saturday night telly lies dead on its arse. Boo hoo and hoo. Move along now people, move along. There's nothing to see here. Nothing to see.

Just Plain Shit [7 August]

Sick and tired of being talked down to? Of course you are, stupid. Everywhere you look, you're being patronised, you poor little thing.

You can't even smoke a fag and slug a coffee without being told CONTENTS OF CUP MAY BE HOT and reminded that SMOKING KILLS.

And what about computers? They're bloody patronising. Look at all those little folders with names like My Computer or My Documents, My this and My that. Well duhhhh – who else's stuff is it likely to be? Todd Carty's?

Obvious labels, everywhere you look. And that includes the TV listings: programme titles are getting increasingly insulting with each passing week.

Last week, ITV brought you a sex-swap documentary called *My Mum Is My Dad*; this week Channel 4 brings you *My Breasts Are Too Big* (C4), a heart-rending look at women whose breasts are too big. Who knows, it might be the most sympathetic documentary ever made, but that title reduces everyone in it to the level of a freak, clearly labelled for the benefit of passing masturbators.

If Channel 4 were being honest, of course, they wouldn't have bothered with the 'documentary' element, and instead simply paid some women to bare their chests in front of webcams, broadcast the results live on air, and called it 'My Breasts Are Too Big, Or Too Small, Or Just Right, Or Whatever – Who Cares, Just Watch 'Em Jiggle – LIVE!!!'

A name like that would hoover up even more idle perverts than *My Breasts Are Too Big*, and stands a better chance of providing the viewing figures they're patently, nakedly, embarrassingly chasing. Who cares if your audience consists of clueless masturbators, as long as there are millions of 'em, eh?

Speaking of honest titling, it's about time they came up with a new name for the equally patronising *Bo' Selecta* (C4) – something that better reflects the show's contents. Something like 'Witless Pipdribble', perhaps, or 'Astronomically Dismal', or just plain 'Shit'.

Earlier this year, I sat on the Bafta jury for Best Comedy Programme. *Bo' Selecta* didn't win, but it was one of the four final nominees. Why? Because the rules stipulated there had to be four nominees. No one really wanted *Bo' Selecta* to be there. That's how bad it is.

(For what it's worth, I wanted *Harry Hill's TV Burp* to get the recognition it deserves, but the rest of the panel considered it worse than *Bo' Selecta* – the philistines. They also outvoted me by nominating BBC2's *Double Take*, perhaps the most dismally pompous 'comedy' series I've ever seen.)

Anyway, what's wrong with *Bo' Selecta*? How long is a piece of string? It's just amazingly, hideously, unacceptably, reason-defyingly awful: a 45-minute vomit of mirthless swearing and canned laughter, aimed squarely at the kind of cow-brained retard who spends 98 per cent of their waking life wondering which ringtone to download next. We should be rounding these people up and chemically neutering them, not broadcasting shows in their honour.

Perhaps most frustrating of all, there are some *genuinely* funny ideas amidst all the crap. It was funny once (and precisely once) to see Craig David talking with an unlikely northern accent and caring for a pet kestrel. But that seems like a very long time ago, and now all we're left with is a worthless, offensively feeble show that purports to mercilessly skewer the cult of celebrity, but actually crawls along behind it on hands and knees, begging to kiss its bumhole clean.

Ooooh, pleeeease, Patsy Kensit – will you appear on our show? In a series of crashingly unfunny sketches? So you haven't got a comic bone in your body – so what? You're faaaamooousss, mmm, mmm, kissy kissy kiss kiss.

Christ, it's just plain *embarrassing*. If I worked on *Bo' Selecta*, and my parents asked me what I did for a living, I'd lie and say I sat in a dustbin giving blowjobs for pennies. Just to retain some dignity.

A Big Hand for the Letter 'X' [11 September]

Ladies and gentlemen, a big hand for the letter 'X'. It's the most versatile letter in the alphabet. A singular 'X' can denote a kiss, the location of buried treasure, or a mistake in a schoolboy essay. Bunched together in a trio, it can spare your blushes when confronted with a fxxxing rude word, or denote red-hot bum action on the wipe-clean cover of a Ben Dover DVD. It's easy to draw and it's worth about 500 points in Scrabble; it brought us the X-Files, the X-Men, American History X, and now, most exciting of all, *The X Factor* (ITV).

The 'X' in the title represents showbiz 'je ne sais quoi', although it might as well be a roman numeral since this feels like the tenth retread of ITV's tried-and-tested talent-show format. Not that this is precisely the same as Popstars and Pop Idol, oh no. There are several key differences.

Difference number one is the presence of Sharon 'The Osbournes' Osbourne on the judging panel. Crowbarred in between spud-faced Louis Walsh and fuck-faced Simon Cowell, she's already the star of the show; a benevolent empress hen. Whereas Cowell's trademark putdowns have become wearingly familiar (with every other hopeful being 'the worst singer I've heard in my life'), Mrs Ozzy retains an ounce of humanity, alternating her slaggings with sympathetic advice, at one point breaking into tears when faced with a pleading contestant. She's hard to dislike.

Difference number two: Kate Thornton takes the place of Davina McCall, which means the show is no longer hosted in the style of a shrieking Harvester barmaid buying a round of drinks on her hen night; instead it's overseen by the straight human equivalent of a scarcely detectable kitten's fart. No progress there, then.

Difference three: the producers have added a 'reaction booth' outside the audition room, in which rejected wannabes can (and do) sob their hearts out on camera – and judging by the level of nigh-on suicidal despair on display, it's only a matter of time until someone slashes a wrist and sprays blood at the lens. If you love watching people wailing in despair, the blub booth is a great idea; next year, let's give the entrants the option of leaving the audition room via a sixteenth-floor window. They could teeter on the ledge threatening to jump while a celebrity negotiator on the ground (Frankie Dettori, say) tries to talk them out of it using a loudhailer, winning £100 for charity each time he saves a life. Great human drama – and you could always show footage of the ones who jump regardless in some kind of X-Factor X-treme Uncut spin-off on

ITV2, their pavement splatterings edited together in a poignant slow-mo montage backed with some Coldplay or something.

The final difference between *X Factor* and *Popstars* is perhaps the most significant one: the addition of an entire category for anyone aged 25 and over. The 16–24s may be desperate, but at least they've got youth on their side: the elders are a morass of jowls, grey hair, sagging breasts and broken dreams, so theirs is the most disturbing group of all, consisting largely of feverish last-chancers, deluded 'eccentrics' (i.e. the mentally ill) and OAPs.

In a fair world, Cowell and co. would be harder on a tone-deaf grandmother than a talentless teenager, on the grounds that old folk can take it (having been alive long enough to come to terms with an unfair world). In reality, when faced with a well-meaning old biddy whose voice warbled unsurely from one note to the next like a drunken moose trying to navigate a maze in the dark, the judges told her she was lovely and put her through to the next round. Cowards.

Finally – quick, unrelated question: during *X Factor*, did I *really* see an advert for a sinister new kiddies' health drink called 'Munch Bunch Drinky Plus'?

By God, I think I did.

How Clean is Your Arse? [18 September]

I once had an idea for a conceptual art exhibit. The idea was simple: I'd cut out one of those adverts for chintz that appear in tabloid Sunday magazines (you know: a collection of miniature ceramic *Star Trek* kettles; hand-painted plates commemorating ten years of *A Touch of Frost* – that kind of thing). I'd send off for it – closely obeying the 'SEND NO MONEY NOW' in the process – then blow the advert up as big as possible, and fix it to the first wall of the gallery.

Once the goods arrived, I'd put them on a plinth in the centre of the room. And once I received a request for payment, I'd blow that up and hang it alongside the advert. But I wouldn't pay a thing. Each time a demand arrived, I'd blow it up and hang it on the wall of the gallery, until eventually I'd be hanging up court summonses and bailiff threats.

God knows what it would all 'mean' – I just thought it might be funny. But I never got round to doing it, on the grounds that it was a massive waste of time. And that's the only difference between me and the performance artists showcased in *The Art Show* (C4) – they haven't bothered making the distinction between worthwhile and time-wasting.

Take the man who spends hours dangling from a tree, like a piece of fruit. 'I think I'd do it whether it was art or not,' he explains – which is just as well, because it isn't. It's just a berk hanging off a tree. Nonetheless, it bemuses a few passers-by, which tickles our man no end.

'It's like being a witness to something,' he says, which is a poncey way of saying 'It's something you look at,' which in turn describes practically everything in the world. Watch a dog taking a shit in your garden and you're 'being a witness to something'. It also means the dog is a conceptual artist, and that's not a turd curling out of its bum, it's his latest work.

The main difference is that the dog is probably more likeable and less conceited. 'This is more important than Hollywood or politics,' screeches a prick dressed as a cyborg; a girl whose work consists of being chased by a black box on wheels offers the stunning revelation that 'in a way, what I'm doing is self-indulgent'.

Their get-out clause, of course, is that you're 'allowed' to find it laughable if you want – which is big of them. In fact, any reaction whatsoever validates their performance. Even suspecting they're a bunch of show-offs who can't act or perform comedy, and are using the 'artist' badge as a flimsy justification for wasting the world's time – even that's a valid reaction as far as these twats are concerned.

More time-wasting in *Too Posh to Wash* (C4), the follow-up to *How Clean is Your House?* And it really should be called 'How Clean is Your Arse?', because having run out of mentally ill householders to ridicule, Kim and Aggie are now training their sights on people with poor personal hygiene.

Their first victim is Barry, who smells. Barry rarely showers, does-n't wash his hair, and spends his evenings picking his feet then eating with his hands, ingesting athlete's foot fungus as he does so.

Kim and Aggie's advice ranges from the obvious ('Have a wash'), to the absurd ('Wash your hair with beer and vinegar'). Sadly Barry doesn't make it to the end of the show, abruptly withdrawing his support after a lab report proves he doesn't wash his hands properly after going to the bog.

Viz used to run an excellent comic strip called 'The Bottom Inspectors', in which a group of Gestapo-like officials pounced on unsuspecting civilians and scrutinised their backsides for signs of poor wiping technique. Kim and Aggie are a bum-hair away from making it a reality.

The performance artists are up their own arses. But at least they're not up other people's, like these two crotch-sniffing hags.

Damage Limitation   [24 September]

It's amazing how many bad things start with the letter 'D'. Death, doom, damnation, despair, destruction, disaster, Davros, Des'ree, Da Republican Party . . . and now *Dirty War* (BBC1), the spiritual heir to classic BBC scarefests like *The War Game* and *Threads* – two shows that could convince almost anyone to commit suicide by the time the end credits stopped rolling.

So how does it measure up? Could it give you nightmares? Does it leave you reeling with queasy, futile horror? Will it stink out your living room with a sense of looming cataclysm so overpowering you'll want to cry all the water out of your body and swim away to deadland?

Not really.

Simply put, the prospect of a dirty bomb going pop isn't quite as horrifying as the complete and utter destruction of the world, something *The War Game* and *Threads* had on their side. In fact, the body count is surprisingly low.

Having said that, the programme as a whole feels uncomfortably authentic, and should leave you feeling, oooh, 70 per cent less secure than you do right now. Depressingly, it also leaves you certain that a dirty bomb will *definitely*, *absolutely* and *unequivocally* go off at some point in the near future. That's a given. *Threads* urged the audience to reconsider the madness of nuclear proliferation; *Dirty War* simply asks the authorities to provide sufficient damage limitation.

And it's gripping. There's a fair amount of clunky dialogue in which officials quote statistics at one another, but the overall sense of clammy hysteria is both undeniable and frightening.

Still, it's not all bad news. For one thing, the need for immediate decontamination means that if a dirty bomb goes off near your office, you'll get to see all your workmates stripping off and showering, like, totally naked. Honestly, you'd see it all: bums, balls, boobs, fannies, willies – the lot.

I can't stress this highly enough – you will *definitely*, *absolutely* and *unequivocally* see your boss's bum.

Secondly, since a dirty bomb would leave a large section of the capital uninhabitable for decades, house prices would tumble – thereby allowing me to finally gain a foothold on the property ladder. Christ, I could probably buy Clarence House for 25p.

So there you go. Always a silver lining.

There's more death on offer in *Mediums: Talking to the Dead* (BBC2), a remarkable three-parter following some of the nation's leading corpse whisperers as they ply their trade.

From where I'm sitting, the vast majority of them are despicable liars – ghastly, bare-faced, ruthless, coin-eyed, opportunist, exploitative, nauseating lickpennies prepared to milk the grieving and bewildered for everything they've got, and I'd sincerely like to glue them face-first to a dining table and kick their arses purple with a pair of concrete boots.

That's how I usually feel about mediums.

Yet even I was flummoxed into silence by Gordon Smith, 'Britain's Most Accurate Medium'; who's either the most amazing trickster I've ever seen, or genuinely psychic, or genuinely conversing with the dead.

Not only is he the most humble medium involved in the show,

he's the only one who doesn't seem to rely solely on guesswork and fibbing. Smith's communications are spot on, first time, every time – right down to the full Christian and surnames of the deceased.

Every fibre of my being tells me it *must* be a trick, but I'm damned if I can see how it works. Mind you, I used to think that about Derren Brown, until his latest series seemed packed with obvious stooges and he rather lost his mystic sheen.

Speaking of Derren Brown, I recently noticed the publicity for his live shows contained a quote from this very column – 'Clearly the greatest dinner party guest in history . . . or the scariest man in Britain.'

Curiously, the full sentence originally read 'Clearly the greatest dinner party guest in history – he's either a balls-out con artist or the scariest man in Britain.'

He must've erased the con artist bit with some super-magic 'mind control', eh? Now that's magic!

Screen Burn FAQ

How can I go about getting a cushy job like yours?
God knows. Tim Lusher, editor of the *Guide*, asked me to submit a sample column and that was that. If you want to write for a magazine or newspaper, your best bet is to send them some relevant samples and hope they like them. If they turn you down, and you still believe in your own abilities despite the mounting evidence to the contrary, set up a website and write your own columns on there. Update it regularly, keep your writing short and to the point, and if you're any good and/or lucky you'll get a job offer eventually.

Why is it called 'Screen Burn'?
For a description of what 'screen burn' itself means, read the 'Live and Dangerous' article in the 'Pre-Screen' chapter. As for why I thought it made a good name for the column, I think it was a pitiful attempt to sound all cool and hard and that. Christ, I hate me.

Have you ever met anyone you've slagged off?
Yes. But they usually don't realise it's me, and I'm fucked if I'm going to draw their attention to it. Besides, I'd feel bad. Kate Thornton recently held a door open for me as I was entering a building, and as she did so, she smiled so sweetly I felt guilty for describing her as 'the human equivalent of a scarcely detectable kitten's fart' the previous Saturday. But that way madness lies.

A major advantage of not having a whopping great byline photo above each column is that you get to retain some anonymity. Another advantage is that people won't point at your photo and laugh a lot and say 'no wonder he's so bitter' for six thousand hours.

Do you choose what you're going to watch or does the Guide *choose it for you, or what?*
By and large, I look through the schedules in advance and choose

whatever I want. Then I phone up the broadcasters and get a pre-view tape biked over, assuming one's available.

If there's going to be a big feature in the *Guide* about a particular show, I'll generally avoid it, in order to reduce overkill. Also, Grace Dent writes a very funny column about soaps every month, so I can't cover those. Which is a pain when the deadline's drawing near and all you've got to go on is a few ropey old documentaries about archaeology, I can tell you.

Don't you ever actually like anything?
Of course. You couldn't do a job like this if you didn't essentially love television. But as I said in the introduction, reading about pro-grammes I've liked is far, far duller than reading about the stuff I didn't. It's worth pointing out, incidentally, that in 'real life' I'm nowhere near as angry as you might think. In fact I'm often polite to the point of being craven. Basically, I'm a pussy.

Index

ff

Dawn of the Dumb

'I don't get people. What's their appeal, precisely? They waddle around with their haircuts on, cluttering the pavement like gormless, farting skittles. They're awful.'

Polite, pensive, mature, reserved . . . Charlie Brooker is none of these things and less. Picking up where his hilarious *Screen Burn* left off, *Dawn of the Dumb* collects more of Brooker's best TV writing, together with uproarious spleen-venting diatribes on a range of non-televisual subjects – tackling everything from David Cameron to human hair.

Rude, unhinged, outrageous, and above all funny, *Dawn of the Dumb* is essential reading for anyone with a brain and a spinal cord. And hands for turning the pages.

ff

The Hell of it All

'Mankind clearly peaked about forty years ago. It's been downhill ever since. For all this talk of our dazzling modern age, the two biggest advances of the past decade are Wi-Fi and Nando's.'

The collapse of civilisation has never felt this funny (unless you're a sociopath, in which case it's been an uninterrupted laugh riot since the days of the Somme).

In his laugh-out-loud collection of misanthropic scribblings, hideous Q-list celebrity failure Charlie Brooker tackles everything from the misery of nightclubs to the death of Michael Jackson, making room for Sir Alan Sugar, potato crisps, global financial meltdown, conspiracy theories and Fearne Cotton along the way.

This book is guaranteed to brighten your life, put a spring in your step and lie to you on its back cover.